F.V.

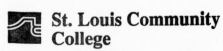

Springer Series: FOCUS ON WOMEN

Violet Franks, Ph.D., Series Editor
Confronting the major psychological, medical, and social issues of today and tomorrow.
Focus on Women provides a wide range of books on the changing concerns of women.

Colette V. Browne, Dr.PH, MSW, is Associate Professor of Social Work at the University of Hawai'i in Honolulu, Hawai'i and faculty affiliate with the University of Hawai'i's Center on Aging. As a social work educator and research, she also holds a doctorate in Public Health. Dr. Browne is the author of numerous articles and book chapters on feminist thought, gerontology, and ethnogerontology, as well as social work and public health practice. She is also coeditor, with Roberta Onzuka Anderson, of *Our Aging Parents: A Guide to Eldercare* published by the University of Hawai'i Press (1985).

Women, Feminism, and Aging

Colette V. Browne, DrPH

 Springer Publishing Company

Springer Publishing Company, Inc.
536 Broadway
New York, NY 10012-3955

Cover design by Margaret Dunin
Acquisitions Editor: Bill Tucker
Production Editor: Pamela Lankas

98 99 00 01 02 / 5 4 3 2 1

Library of Congress Cataloging-in-Publication Data

Browne, Collette V.
   Women, feminism, and aging
      p. cm.—(Springer series, focus on women)
   Includes bibliographical references and index.
   ISBN 0-8261-1200-5
      1. Aged women—United States—Social conditions 2. Aging—United States—Psychological aspects. 3. Feminist theory—United States. 4. Feminist psychology—United States. I. Title. II. Series.
  HQ1064.U5B765   1998
   305.26'0973—dc21   98-10304
                                                      CIP

Printed in the United States of America

*To the memory of my grandmothers
and to my daughters*

Contents

Preface

The day after I brought my new daughter home from the hospital following her birth, this manuscript came back from the publisher for revision. The connections between women's productive and reproductive responsibilities never before seemed so clear to me nor more profound. Checking a citation on the computer while nursing my daughter on my lap was not how I had envisioned finishing this project. But, my life, like so many other women's lives, is filled with such interruptions and joys. Somehow we learn to function with them, albeit with certain amounts of frustration, challenges, and a lot of frozen and take-out food.

I wrote this book because it was clear to me, and to a growing number of other writers and scholars, that most of the problems associated with aging—poverty, chronic health ailments, limited social roles, increasing dependencies, and caregiving—correlate more to women than men although men are far from immune to them. And yet there is little evidence to suggest that with advanced age women's lives will dramatically improve in the coming years.

Drawing from feminist theories' contributions and omissions, together with the writings of other gerontologists, social welfare analysts, and older women themselves, I wrote this book with a number of thoughts in mind. I wanted to challenge present paradigms built on society's devaluation of aging women, offer a critique of current and proposed social welfare strategies, and suggest personal and politically feasible directions that can benefit older women. I also hoped to begin the process of developing a new epistemology of women and age, building on ideas from older women's words and writing.

There are three features to this book that I hope can extend our thinking on behalf of older women. First, a feminist life-span perspective on aging is suggested as a tool to reconceptualize age issues from women's life experiences. This perspective acknowledges, among other themes, the interlocking of women's problems with each another and with each stage of the life cycle, the relationship between gender and power throughout women's lives, and the challenges associated with ageism. Women's inequalities are seen as intersecting with and being shaped by gender, race, class, other oppressions, and sociohistorical time. Second, this framework, together with others, leads to a feminist age analysis. Such an analysis critiques the underlying premises behind and the effectiveness of public and private policies in meeting the needs of aging women. And, finally, this book suggests some beginning thoughts toward an epistemology of women and age that documents women's strengths together with the problems and opportunities that present themselves as a result of age.

There are many acknowledgments I would like to make. First, I thank the many older women whom I have met and talked to who have guided me with this work. Throughout the last 10 years or so, a number of older women have been role models for me and have influenced my thoughts and writing. Sadly, some are no longer with us. The women I would especially like to thank include Bella Argintineau, Lillian Ito, Faith Lai, Laura Manis, Shimeji Kanazawa, Pauline Matsumura, Mabel McConnell, and Myrtle Schattenburg. I hope those I neglect to mention will forgive me. I thank gerontology for giving me a career I love. But it is feminism that has given me my wings to care about women, to respect women and myself, and to dream a larger vision about people and justice than I thought possible.

In many ways, a book such as this one is truly a collaborative effort. This is because there are so many individual people who must be thanked for their contributions. A number of colleagues from the University of Hawai'i were invaluable to me in providing support, encouragement, and the necessary critiques that make the ideas presented here, one hopes, sharper and more inclusive. These are Dr. Rowena Fong, Dr. Joyce Chinen, Dr. Betty Mulroy, and her mother, Mrs. Dorothy Mulroy, and Dr. Kathryn Braun. Dr. Meda Chesney Lind, Dr. Anthony Lenzer, Dr. Gene Kassebaum, Dr. Elizabeth Clark, and the late Dr. Larry Koseki, as members of my doctoral committee at the University of Hawai'i's School of Public Health, provided early assistance with formulating ideas about women and aging. A number of students at the University of Hawai'i were also helpful in helping me to galvanize my earlier thinking. Students enrolled in the course, Women and Aging, taught in the summer of 1994, were a wonderful source of inspiration and thinking, as are the students whom I have had the privilege to teach in graduate and undergraduate gerontology and policy courses at the University's School of Social Work. A number of graduate students also assisted in various stages of research and editing. These are thoughtful, capable women, and the book is stronger because of their commitment to women and aging. To May Harrington, Jamie Detwiler, Crystal Rowland—mahalo! (thank you!). I am indebted to my secretary, Louise Young, for her patience and skills in helping with this manuscript.

Numerous other colleagues provided additional critiques and ideas. Dr. Crystal Mills from Eastern Michigan State University and Dr. Amanda Barusch from University of Utah took time and effort to improve the ideas presented in these pages. A very warm and sincere appreciation is extended to these two women. Also, as a number of these chapters first appeared in earlier forms in numerous other journals, I wish to acknowledge the numerous anonymous reviewers for their insights. I am also deeply grateful to Dr. Nancy Hooyman of the University of Washington and Lorraine Gutierrez of the University of Michigan. As editors to a special edition of the *Journal of Applied Social Sciences* on feminism and social work, in which portions of chapters 1 and 7 come from, I extend a warm thank you for their helpful comments and direction for that earlier piece of work.

Susan Chandler not only offerred me her friendship but also her home on Cape Cod for a peaceful setting to write in. And also to Margot Quadros, Alicia Price, Susan Kent, and Susan Brennen—thank you for the support throughout the last 20 years.

Two women whom I consider sisters of the heart and spirit provided invaluable guidance throughout this entire project. Dr. Noreen Mokuau of the University of Hawai'i critiqued earlier chapters and gave the emotional encouragement to persevere that is so necessary in writing projects such as this one. And to Dr. Jeanette Takamura, my mentor, who has always been a friend par excellence—a very special thank you. Her abilities to strive for the highest ground have truly made this book possible. The many hours I have spent with both of these women has nurtured my soul at times when I doubted my abilities to complete this project.

To my parents Raymonde and Cliff, and sisters Linda and Maggie, and brother David—a great deal of appreciation goes your way for believing in me. To my grandmothers whom I knew, and to my great-grandmothers whom I did not know, you were with me throughout this process. Most important, my love goes out to my wonderful husband, Mac, and daughters Marisa Mireille and Taylor Melelani, our newest addition. They had to live with me throughout this project and still continued to offer me their love and encouragement. You are my joy, my life.

Finally, to the people of Springer Publishing, especially Bill Tucker, Managing Editor, who believed in this book before I did and Pam Lankas, Production Editor, who was skillful and patient throughout this process— thank you. Special appreciation is also sent to other colleagues at Springer for their encouraging words and assistance and for their support of publishing works in aging.

Feminism and Gerontology: A Feminist Life-Span Perspective on Aging

> All writing is confession.
> —Cherríe Moraga

Two years ago, Nana, my father's mother, died. She was 95. She had hoped to live to be 100 years old, but multiple health problems did not grant my grandmother her wish. Her life was both hauntingly familiar and dissimilar to many women today. For many years, she was a single mother after her first husband, my father's father, deserted her. She was forced to leave my father when he was young in the care of others while she toiled in a factory. But it was not only her gender and marital status that disadvantaged her in her life. Born in 1899, she was defined by the sociohistorical standards of the time as a "half-breed," the child of a Native American mother and an Irish father. Her parents died when she was young, and so she and her sister were raised in orphanages. At various times, she would be sent to foster homes, only to be returned when her foster parents learned of her ethnic heritage and race. She spent most of her life denying her ethnicity, and it was not until she was in the last decade of her life that she could speak of the many racist, hurtful acts directed against her as a child. The years did not erase the pain, for she would cry even at the age of 95 with such memories.

She married twice and had four more children after my father. But her second husband was abusive, and they divorced when she was in her forties. She helped the war effort with her factory job. Yet her meager retirement income reflected the fact that she was a working-class woman. In truth, her life was characterized by multiple oppressions. In some ways, her life actually improved when she retired, for she then had a small pension and Social Security income, and was able to receive a number of social welfare benefits. She derived satisfaction from her family and the many friends she had developed in her lifetime. She was one of the kindest women I ever knew.

Nana probably felt she had very little in common with my Grandmére, my mother's mother. Grandmére was born in Africa to French parents. In many ways, she was privileged from birth. Her parents ran a successful winery, and when Grandmére came of age she married a young man who would become a magistrate for the French colony of Tunisia, where they lived. She had a beautiful home and six children and had the assistance of others to help her with their care. Whether or not she reached her own dreams I do not know—her life outside of her family was not a subject about which there was any discussion.

Twice Grandmére experienced war, and twice she lost all of her material belongings—first during World War I, and then again during World War II. But she was lucky. She told us that when the Americans liberated Tunisia from the Germans, they found the beginnings of a crematorium. Because Grandmére was Jewish, she and her family knew that they had been rescued in time to escape cruel, fiery deaths.

The postwar peace Grandmére had hoped for was not to be. When Tunisia became an independent nation in the late 1950s, she and my grandfather once again lost all they had, as they were forced to migrate to France. Nonetheless, my grandparents were fortunate that several of their children eventually became very successful and provided them with financial help in their old age. Otherwise, their later years would have been poor ones. Grandmére died when she was in her early sixties. There was so little that doctors knew then about women's health, and even less about the health of older women.

Both my Nana and my Grandmére were remarkable women whose lives were influenced by many factors—gender, race, ethnicity, social class, age, personal biography, and the sociohistorical period in which they lived. They enjoyed variable advantages and suffered from numerous disadvantages at different times in their lives. Neither lived a life of safety and security. Although their lives, and those of so many other older women, are not recorded in history books, they contributed dearly—and at great personal cost—to the lives of their families and society. There is much I do not know about my grandmothers. But I cannot help but wonder: How precisely were their lives different from those of other older women today?

OLDER WOMEN AND FEMINISM

When asked, most younger women describe what they hope their later years will be like—a life where they are contributory, healthy, financially comfortable, and surrounded by loving family and friends. There are reasons for such expressed optimism. Over the past 30 years, women have made remarkable progress in politics, the arts, the labor force, athletics, and education. Women are beginning to dominate the work force. Growing numbers of politicians are keenly aware of the need to pay attention to women's needs and to avoid the "gender gap," at least prior to elections. More women are elected to office. Some are beginning to make their way to middle management, although executive levels still elude women in general. More often than not, advances in women's status have come about as a direct result of advocacy and legal action led by the feminist movement, which also gave rise to increased educational and work opportunities. All women hope that such advances will benefit their lives not only today, but well into their older years.

Although the results of such an affirmative picture are beginning to be seen in the lives of some older women, recent studies and census reports alert us to a vastly different picture for the majority of them, especially those who are single, over the age of 75 and widowed, and women of color. In part, this is because women, throughout their lives, face a number of problems that have not been prevented or in some cases acknowledged as legitimate issues and corrected or compensated by society: unequal pay, segregated employment opportunities, unmet health and social needs, continued sexual harassment and assault, and assignment to unpaid caregiving duties. Such gender inequalities only exacerbate women's problems as they age (Hess, 1990; Older Women's League, 1990). No-fault divorce laws, age discrimination, nonresearched health concerns, demeaned physical appearance, and bias in pensions and Social Security leave older women, the majority of the aged population, vulnerable and at risk (Allen & Pifer, 1993; Barusch, 1994; Browne, 1994; Garner & Mercer, 1989; Haug, Ford, & Sheafor, 1985; Hooyman & Kiyak, 1993; Stone, Cafferata, & Sangl, 1986; Verbrugge, 1989). And for most women, it is not only gender inequalities that they face. Unfortunately, it seems that the best is not necessarily to be. Projections suggest that the economic and health concerns of aging women (Hess, 1990; Ozawa, 1993), and particularly of older women of color (Allen & Pifer, 1993; Dressel, 1988), will increase in future years, in part due to extant policies that support the persistence of inequalities between the sexes and races. Indeed, as we will see, the consequences of many of the issues women face in their younger years become crystallized disadvantages with age.

In this book I discuss the interface of feminist theory, women, and aging, and in so doing attempt to outline a potential new vision for older women and for work with older women. I have a number of objectives in writing this book. I aim to identify and analyze some of feminist theory's contributions and apply its theoretical contributions, as well as its conceptual gaps, to reconceptualize what aging can mean to women. Each theory discussed offers themes that can promote a new view of aging and yet are not without problems. Even among those discussed in this book, differences abound. While classifying certain feminist authors in specific categories, I realize that allegiances, even among feminists, can be fluid and changeable. The point of discussing these feminist writings was not to emphasize some and leave out others—rather, it is my intent to pull out themes that can help us to develop alternatives to the present devaluation of older women by society. I hope to accomplish this by noting feminist theory's potential promises and omissions so that its ageism can be confronted and resolved; by developing a tentative analysis as background for what a feminist theory could look like that would make aging women's voices central to the analysis; and by helping to delineate the connections between the levels of differences that exist among women—race, class, age, sexual orientation, and others.

Thus, I seek to synthesize and extend the literature on feminism, particularly as it addresses and does not address the aging process and the needs of aging women; add to a number of frameworks that critique present paradigms and policies; and offer some beginning thoughts toward an epistemology on women and aging—that calls for a more respectful vision of women and women's issues in later life. Although I offer a critique of some feminist theories for their general exclusion of aging women from both their analyses and texts, I also believe that feminism is held to bear the most promise for improving older women's lives.

Feminism provides an appropriate theoretical framework for the study of women in society—their contributions as well as their tribulations (Abramowitz, 1992; Anderson, 1988; B. G. Collins, 1986; Freeman, 1990; hooks, 1984; Van Den Bergh, 1995; Van Den Bergh & Cooper, 1985). From its earlier focus on gender differences, gender roles, and the deleterious effects on women of social norms and expectations, feminist theory has more recently moved toward a perspective that acknowledges the salience of the issue of power—that which is oppressed and that which exists as strengths—in women's lives. I believe that feminist theory can offer a new understanding of the ways in which the lives of older women can be transformed by moving aging women to center stage and by reconceptualizing social welfare from a woman's point of view. Such a critique requires an analysis of the relationship between gender and power throughout the life cycle.

Many of the problems faced by older women are a direct result of a lifetime of multiple oppressions. Yet, until recently, the issues about older women were curiously absent from the feminist agenda. More than 20 years ago, gerontologists Myrna Lewis and Robert Butler sought to broaden the feminist perspective by asking: "Why is feminism ignoring older women?" (Lewis & Butler, 1972). The answers to this question still evade us, however, for writings on the interface between aging and feminism remain in a growing and still formative stage (Calasanti & Zajicek, 1993; Friedan, 1993; Gibson, 1996; Perkins, 1992; Reinharz, 1986; Russell, 1987).

The good news is that literature written by and about midlife and older women has increased dramatically in the past 15 years. Indeed, older women finally appear to have been "discovered" in much of gerontological literature. Although some of these writings have taken a feminist approach (Browne, 1994; Gibson & Allen, 1993), many do not. The increasing numbers of older women and their unique problems as they age provide feminists and gerontologists with added impetus to re-examine the relationships between gender, age, and power for the potential of these variables to affect a difference in the quality of women's lives.

To date, feminist theory, analysis, and study have focused primarily on issues relating to production and reproduction—issues that appear to lose much of their potency when considering later life (Gibson & Allen, 1993). One reason feminists have ignored older women issues was offered by Cherry Russell, an Australian feminist. She noted that many earlier works by feminists in the 1970s reflected the young age and social location of these feminists, since "after all, the personal is political" (1987, p. 130). Gibson and Allen (1993), while agreeing with Russell, add that social policies for the aged have been developed to "privilege and correspond with the interests, experiences, and preferences of men, advantaging them in relation to women" (p. 79). They further blame the "gerontophobic nature" of society that inclines feminist theory and others to resist the study of age. Feminists are, however, beginning to examine age theory because feminists are themselves aging, and because critical gerontology and postmodernism have promoted a greater awareness of feminist theory and methodology in gerontology and vice versa.

More recently, both feminism and aging have attracted fresh attention from scholarly circles and from the popular media, but not all of it has been positive. In part because women have been so equated with the family, many of the issues about women portrayed in the media are cloaked with concerns over family values and women's roles. Thus, what one often reads are articles that discuss the demise and disintegration of feminism. At best, such themes claim that feminism has outlived its purpose as its goals have all been met; at worse, feminism has harmed women and society. As a result of these writings, a number of feminists, such as Susan Faludi and Gloria Steinem, have warned of a backlash against the equity reforms that were accomplished during the feminist movement's second wave. Others have criticized the feminist movement for not doing enough. Still others, like Nadine Stosser, Camilla Paglia, and Christine Sommers, have taken feminist theory to task for its research methodology, its gynocentric (female-centered) world views, and its choices of strategies that have focused less on equity reforms and more on societal transformation. Feminism, like other social movements, has undertaken numerous strategies to reach its goals of a better life for women—ranging from the questioning of paradigms to political strategies that include integration, assimilation, segregation, and transformation. One ignored group has been aging women. I hope to continue the work of a number of feminist gerontologists in correcting this omission by providing factual data to support the claim that older women are a population-at-risk, but also a population of strength. It is in this disentangling of women from existing myths that we can begin, as Glenn (1987) argues, to "challenge basic paradigms and develop alternative conceptualizations" about women's lives (p. 349). This is an important aim because society's views of older women are too often based on untruths.

It is necessary to define how "feminism" and "feminist theory" will be used in this book. Feminism includes multiple theories on women, power, and inequality. According to legal theorist Catherine MacKinnon, feminism:

> sees women as a group and seeks to define and pursue women's interest. Feminists believe that women share a reality, and search for it, even as they criticize the leveling effects of the social enforcement of its commonalities. Women's commonalities include, they do not transcend, individual uniqueness, profound diversity (such as race and class), time, and place. Feminism's search for a ground is a search for the truth of all women's collectivity in the face of the enforced lie that all women are the same. (1989, p. 38)

Feminism, then, is about understanding women's lives in terms of advantages and disadvantages from their gender, race, class, age, and other sites of oppression, and about understanding the gendered position of power and domination in a collective as opposed to an individual sense. As such, it is an oppositionalist movement against modernity and patriarchy. Feminist theorist bell hooks voiced it in this way:

> To me feminism is not simply a struggle to end male chauvinism or a movement to ensure that women will have equal rights with men; it is a commitment to eradicating the ideology of domination that permeates Western culture on various levels—sex, race, and class to name a few—and a commitment to reorganizing U.S. society so that the self development of people can take precedence over imperialism, economic expansion, and material desire. (1981, p. 194)

I draw from MacKinnon's and hooks's definitions of feminism for a number of reasons that will be explained in greater detail throughout these chapters. A theory is feminist, according to MacKinnon (1989) when it is critical of gender as a determinant of life chances of women and society's unjust treatment of women. There are numerous feminist theories that will be examined in this book that attempt to disect the gender, age, and power relationship. Thus, I will not argue for one specific form of feminist theory over another—I believe all have value. Instead, I will emphasize that feminism is about ensuring equality for women while also seeking a transformative society—a society that recognizes women's problem as inequality (MacKinnon, 1989). Feminist theory is also about developing interventions to stop all oppressions. It looks to a new vision of society that conceptualizes and promotes not only gender justice, but justice for all peoples. As feminist economists Teresa Amott and Julie Matthaei (1991) argue, "Gender oppression cannot meaningfully be split off from other kinds of oppression. . . . Only through such awareness can we construct a political practice that is truly liberatory" (p. 353). And, as hooks (1984) adds, feminism has the potential to be transformative if it can counter its racism. I suggest, together with other scholars, that age issues and oppression by ageism must be confronted in what Patricia Hill Collins (1991, p. 225) has referred to as the "matrix of domination" in order for solidarity to occur.

In the last 15 years, the number of books on feminism and on aging women has risen dramatically, an encouraging trend. Many have greatly enriched the study of the epistemology of gender from a feminist perspective or the study of aging women; few have attempted to explicate the relationships between the two. The ideas presented in this book are thus a compilation of growing and changing ideas that look, either directly or indirectly, at the relationships between feminist theory and aging women. To reiterate, a number of different perspectives on feminist theory are examined in this book, and the potential of both feminism and gerontology to improve women's lives is analyzed. The writings of many of the authors I discuss describe the sociohistorical, psychological, sexual, racial, and biographical life experiences of women, and discuss how feminist theory is a source of knowledge, power, frustration, and disappointment to many women. This frustration and disappointment, along with knowledge and power, must be understood if we are serious about extending feminist theory to include the empowerment of aging women.

OLDER WOMEN AND THE STUDY OF GERONTOLOGY

The nation's fastest growing population consists of older adults, the majority of whom are women. This "graying of America" has not escaped the country's attention, and has been reflected in increased coverage of aging issues in both scholarly circles and in the popular media. Aging is a biological phenomenon, influenced by genetics and date of birth. Like gender, it is influenced by and in turn influences society in numerous ways.

Among researchers, the interdisciplinary study of the psychological, social, and biological processes of aging is known as gerontology. Specifically, changes in intelligence, memory, personality, and motivation with age are viewed as psychological changes, while social changes focus more on changing roles and relationships over the life course. Biological changes, on the other hand, refer to the normal physical changes attributed to advanced years. These processes are interrelated with one another and do not develop in isolation. As we will see, such changes impact on society's treatment of the aged as well as on the aged's treatment of and interactions within society.

Gerontologists, especially social gerontologists, study ageism and the impact of processes associated with age on both older adults and society. They advocate for an examination of aging in a more positive and yet balanced fashion, as opposed to necessarily equating age with disease and infirmities. Their strategies have been to combat age discrimination and to advocate for increased research dollars to prevent and treat disease while promoting health behaviors and evaluating health treatments. They have also championed increased and equitable funding for policies for frail and other vulnerable populations. Their views, however, have been primarily White and male, despite the fact that ageism hits women earlier than it does men, and despite how intriguing the inconsistencies of the data on gender differences should be to both women and men. Women's stories—especially women of color, lesbian women, and the never-married—were left untold and unrecorded throughout this debate. Indeed, women have only recently become the focus of study.

Whereas gerontology associates aging with growth and development, much of the recent media attention has framed it as a problem borne by the individual, his or her family, and society at large. Concerns appear to concentrate on the economic costs of aging, with special consequences to social welfare. Indeed, a number of books and news magazines blame Social Security for the federal deficit (Peterson & Howe, 1988) and argue for "The Case for Killing Social Security" (Church & Lacayo, 1995). In an article in the *New York Times* magazine (May 19, 1996) entitled "The Birth of a Revolutionary Class," Thurow (1996) ascribes the poverty of children and the nation's debt to the burgeoning older adult population and their need for Social Security and other programs. Articles such as these routinely describe in catastrophic terms America's federal deficit and freely place the blame for the rising national debt on the shoulders of the nation's elders. Although data on the social and economic consequences of an aging population are contradictory, it is worth reminding ourselves that most of us will grow old, and that every generation both contributes to and receives from those who came before and after it. As the majority of the aged are women, we should be raising questions about who will be hurt most if society is convinced to turn its back on older adults.

INTERLOCKING FORCES OF SEXISM AND AGEISM

Notwithstanding diverse points of views in contemporary feminist thinking, there remains a level of common ground that ties most feminists to one another. Most feminists acknowledge that some differences exist between men and women, but that these differences are transformed into inequalities that disadvantage women throughout the life cycle. Feminists also agree that women are placed at a social and cultural disadvantage, and that gender is a phenomenon that reflects a social and sexual division of labor. Moreover, there is agreement that society has rarely allowed women the same opportunities compared to men, and that differential treatment is accorded to women depending on their race, ethnicity, culture, class, and sexual orientation. Subsequently, there is a growing understanding that not all women's lives are the same. As I discussed at the outset of this introduction, however, issues that impact more readily on aging women's lives are rarely discussed in feminist theories. For example, the lack of research on older women's lives, their diminishing social status, the consequences of their years of nonpaid caregiving, and their increasing impoverishment with advanced years leads far too many to a difficult old age.

"Sexism" refers to negative attitudes toward and public and private practices directed against women. Feminist strategies have been aimed at stopping bigotry and all discriminatory practices based on gender. Specifically, feminist study focuses on analyzing the epistemology of gender and the potential impact of new knowledge on women and social structures. Feminist theory aims to enrich the lives of women by ending their oppression. What has been missing is an acknowledgment of older women and a sensitivity to their concerns. This is in part because most feminists have not been gerontologists, although a number of feminists have addressed aging from a conceptual and theoretical perspective (see de Beauvoir, 1972; Friedan, 1993; Greer, 1991; Olson, 1982; Sontag, 1972). In this book I suggest a number of reasons for this lacuna and discuss the need to include aging women in feminist theory. I aim in this book, then, to critique feminist theories so that the contributions of older women can be acknowledged and celebrated, while also fostering a new heightened awareness toward the lives of aging women. Borrowing ideas from Black feminist theory, I look for the "both/ands"—the connections between feminist theory and aging—as opposed to examining such ideas dualistically, hierarchically, or unilaterally. Notwithstanding the recent expanded literature on menopause and books written by feminists who themselves are growing older, it is quite clear that there is still a great deal that contemporary feminist theory can contribute on behalf of aging women.

Although most feminists are not gerontologists, neither are most gerontologists feminists. This is so even though most of the problems associated with aging—poverty, chronic ailments, abuse, and caregiving—are correlated more so to women than men throughout the life cycle. While a growing number of gerontologists have integrated gerontology and feminist thinking, in general gerontologists have not made women's issues within a feminist perspective central to the study of aging.

More than 25 years ago, Dr. Robert Butler, a leading geriatric psychiatrist, coined the term "ageism" to refer to negative attitudes toward the aged and the aging process within a cultural group, that mask a society's fear of both the aging process and the aged. According to Butler (1975), ageism:

> can be seen as a process of systematic stereotyping of and discrimination against older people because they are old, just as racism and sexism accomplish this with skin colour and gender. Old people are categorized as senile, rigid in thought and manner, old fashioned in morality and skills. . . . Age-

ism allows the younger generation to see old people as different from themselves, thus they subtly cease to identify with their elders as human beings. (p. 12)

We now know with some embarrassment and anger that it was not until 1978 that the National Institute on Aging's Baltimore longitudinal study included women in its sample in the study of normative aging, and only in 1981 did the White House Conference on Aging have a special committee on women's issues. This was so even though women were and are the majority of the aging population.

Thus, feminists and gerontologists share a number of commonalities in addition to their neglect of aging women. Both begin with the understanding that sex and age are phenomena that are more shaped by social structure than by biology. Sex and age are also viewed as processes that are defined, shaped, and influenced by social and power relations. These power relations involve a hierarchical structure of both opportunity and oppression. Not all women suffer from patriarchy, but there is no evidence to suggest that women thrive in it. Similarly, not all elders are poor and disadvantaged, but a growing number, most of whom are women, live at or near the poverty line. The acknowledgment of power relations and the inequalities that result in power dynamics makes advocacy and activism a necessary component of both feminism and gerontology.

More recently, a number of theorists have begun to explore the relationships between feminism and gerontology (see Blieszner, 1993; Gibson, 1996; Hooyman & Gonyea, 1995; Laws, 1995; Ray, 1996; Reinharz, 1986). According to feminist theorist Shulamit Reinharz (1986), feminists and social gerontologists share a desire to "create a consciousness, a social theory, and a social policy which will improve the life chances of a special group" (p. 87). Feminists and gerontologists also acknowledge that age and sex are shaped by differences imposed by class, ethnicity and culture, sexual orientation, and other variables that often determine one's life chances. Moreover, women and older adults are two populations that are shaped by society's myths and ideas that more often than not limit their opportunities and abilities. Feminists and gerontologists seek to "deconstruct" and "reconstruct" misleading myths and misconceptions about women and older adults via research, education, and political struggle. Furthermore, both emphasize that the study of women and older adults must be conducted by integrating literature on cohort influences and the life course, including ones's social location and personal biography (Gonyea, 1994; Hess & Waring, 1983; Stoller & Gibson, 1994).

Hagen and Davis (1992), for example, identify a number of women's issues that clearly run across the life span. Among these are employment issues—women as worker and caregiver; health issues—reproductive health and long-term care; and poverty, among young women as well as the aged. Indeed, I also argue, along with a small but growing number of feminists and gerontologists, that the study of older women requires a feminist and a life-span perspective on aging for women. In essence, such a perspective acknowledges that many older women's issues carry over from a lifetime of reduced opportunity and oppression. Far from being victimized, women have developed their own paths of resistance out of a lifetime of discontinuity, change, wisdom, and accomplishment. We look to aging women, then, to provide us with new images of age.

Another concept receiving more attention from both gerontologists and feminists is diversity—diversity between elders and among women. Contemporary theories in feminism and gerontology are intent on examining the various iterations of diversity among women and the aged and the relationships of diversity in all of its forms to political and social structures—such as social welfare institutions. This is clearly a difficult task that is made more complex by the stereotypes and untruths that exist about women, older adults, and people of color. A point that I will discuss throughout this book is that ageism hits women harder than men, leaving them with their financial, health, caregiving, and social status seriously impacted. A feminist age analysis is employed in this book to explore women's oppression, diversities, and strengths, and to examine the canons, policies, and programs that attempt to promote well-being in later life.

While mental health by itself, and its relationship to aging, is a critical issue for all older adults, the reader who wishes to delve into such issues should look elsewhere. This book is not about the psychological issues that influence women's lives across the life span. Instead, what I focus on in this book is the relationship between feminism, aging women, and the role of social welfare and social work in women's lives. Social welfare refers to those institutions of both the public and private sectors that strive to improve people's lives. Numerous professions work in the field of social welfare. Social work, among other professions, seeks to address the nation's societal needs with a focus on social justice for all citizens. An examination of social welfare policies and programs shows us that many of the values, as well as the stereotypes, that society holds for and about women and the aged have been encoded in our policies and programs. Many social welfare programs, organized under the auspices of federal, state, and local governments, are built around an "explicit vision" of the welfare state, defined by Skocpol (1995) as benefits and services which "ensure a national minimum of protection for all citizens against old age, disability and poor health, unemployment, and other causes of insufficient income" (p. 12). Nationally, the most obvious examples of social welfare programs that critically impact aging women's lives are Social Security, Medicare, and Supplemental Security Income. Given that women end their years poorer and with more chronic ailments than men, one cannot say with any integrity that either the state or social welfare has adequately protected the needs of women.

DO WE NEED A FEMINIST LIFE-SPAN PERSPECTIVE ON AGING?

It is my view that feminism holds the greatest potential for making a real difference in women's lives. To be sure, a number of orientations, frameworks, and strategies have been developed over the past 10 years to improve the lives of older adults and, therefore, older women (see Cox & Parsons, 1994; Estes, Gerard, Zones, & Swan, 1984; Greene, 1986). Abramowitz (1992) and Miller (1990) offer feminist critiques of social welfare in general, and the more recent book by Hooyman and Gonyea, *Feminist Perspectives on Family Care: Polices for Gender Justice* (1995) provides an excellent analysis of caregiving across the life span using a feminist framework. Although a number of the tenets of such frameworks may seem similar to the one I introduce in this book, most do not begin where a feminist age analysis does—with the lives, needs, expectations, challenges, and triumphs of aging women. Nor do these frameworks have as their primary focus strategies to promote the well-being of older women.

A feminist life-span perspective on aging, as a suggested mode of analysis built on the work of feminist theorists and gerontological and social work scholars, is offered as a tool to reconceptualize issues around women and age. It focuses on redefining old age from a woman's perspective, and suggests a number of alternate strategies to improve the lives of older women. This perspective acknowledges the interlocking of women's problems with one another and with each stage in the life cycle. Drawing ideas from postmodernism, a feminist analysis also explores, deconstructs, and reconstructs what is considered knowledge about the gender–age relationship in linguistics, power relations, social structures, and social welfare. Women's inequalities are recognized as following them throughout their lives and as intersecting with and being shaped by gender, race, class, other oppressions, and sociohistorical time. A discussion of the effects of the additional force of ageism on women's lives and an analysis of feminist theory itself is also offered.

It is my belief that the feminist theories discussed in these chapters provide a vantage point for advancing the needs of older women. As a theory in the making (hooks, 1984) feminism has the potential for a more inclusive politic. In the absence of a life-span perspective to the study of women, however, the issues most often discussed in contemporary feminist writings—antipornography, abortion rights, sexual harassment, affirmative action, family violence, child day care, all critically important issues— often do not appear to directly extend to the needs of older women. However, these concerns are rooted in the sexual division of labor and do not end with advanced age. In addition to the foregoing issues, there are numerous others that feminist writings should include in their discourse—rising poverty rates among women in later life, assignment to unpaid caregiving duties, and increasing divorce rates, to name only a few.

To uncover the relationships between aging and feminism, a feminist age framework must examine other forms of domination and exploitation for their connections with feminism and ageism. This includes the exploitation that exists between younger and older women. Younger women do exploit older women, or at least are complicit in society's social devaluation of older women by denigrating their physical appearance, exploiting their caregiving, being financially dependent, and ignoring or undervaluing their life experiences and wisdom. But younger women also care about older women—they are their daughters, their granddaughters, their friends, and their low-paid or nonpaid caregivers. Exploitation is also not a one-way street, nor it is evident only in person-to-person relationships. As will be discussed in later chapters, present social policies that attempt to respond to the needs of the frail aged have been predicated on what feminist scholars Gibson and Allen (1993) have referred to as a "parasitic relationship" on the low-paid or unpaid work of women. Older women can also exploit younger women emotionally and financially. Thus, there is a tension among women that is not congruent with the notion of sisterhood and the strategy of solidarity.

A feminist theory and accompanying analysis argues for social, economic, and political equality between men and women (Turner, 1984). A feminist age analysis, using ideas from a feminist life-span perspective on age, critiques the underlying premises and public and private policies in conceptualizing and responding to the needs of aging women. What a feminist age analysis offers, then, is a view that is more inclusive and complex compared to liberal and gerontological theories, and which promises a more integrated sense of feminism's importance to older women and men. I focus, then, not only on ageism but on feminist theory and practice around domination with a focus on older women. We should not shy away from asking: Is feminism ageist? We can explore this question by examining if the lives of older women have voices in feminist literature, and if not, have we noticed? Have we heard their silences as well as their words? Are their needs on the feminist agenda, and if so are they promoted? As was noted earlier, feminists have begun to use their own experience of aging to expand our thinking. On one level, this can be applauded; on another level, it leads to suspicions—if White feminists grew more colorful with age rather than more wrinkled, would they have "discovered" racism?

Although a critique of feminist theory in its treatment of aging women is helpful, I do not blame feminists for ageism. Ageism is not a problem because feminists have not made it central to their discussions. Rather, it is a product of a society that exploits workers and sees little economic or social gain from the increasing numbers of the aged. As citizens in an ageist society, it should not surprise us that feminists can be ageists. Nonetheless, it is disappointing. Moreover, it again points out how much work is required to show the connections among all forms of oppression. If one believes that all forms of domination are interrelated, then ageism is a problem and an opportunity for feminists around which to build solidarity for women's well-being throughout their lives. Thus, a feminist life-span perspective on aging adopts a life-span approach to the study of women's oppression. Pulling ideas from feminist, gerontology, and social work theories and frameworks, it applies this perspective to the particular and specific life experiences of aging women.

Elements within a feminist life-span perspective on aging allow us to see the connections between feminism and gerontology and the contributions each can make to the other. Feminists have offered gerontologists a number of methods by which to "deconstruct" gender and other categories. They have also offered strategies for activism. In turn, gerontologists have made available to feminists some riveting information, namely, that women live a great deal longer than men and concomitantly become more numerous and more in need of support, financial security, and social welfare services. Gerontologists have also pointed out the potential for increased power bases. Together, gerontologists and feminists must examine how to make these later years of life worthwhile and successful for today's and tomorrow's older women. Finally, there is an important role for middle-aged and older women. They must insist that their voices be heard and respected, not only by feminists and gerontologists but by society at large.

ORGANIZATION OF THIS BOOK

What I hope to do is to document and support the work of feminist theorists as they move society to one that is more respectful of women and all people. Thus, I have three voices in writing this book—as gerontologist, feminist, and social worker. As a gerontologist and social worker, my interest has been and is with older women. It is often a difficult subject about which to maintain a discourse because of society's treatment of aging women. Most younger women grow old to become tomorrow's older woman—so how can we be concerned with young and middle aged women and not address the needs of older women? Likewise, as a feminist-gerontologist, I find it is difficult to understand how one can be concerned with older adults as a gender-neutral term and yet not see or be concerned about women, the majority of the elderly population, as they grow older.

I must note that I have written this book as both observer and participant. As a social scientist, I have been trained to be an observer and to document in objective, scientific fashion my observations and analysis of aging women. As a woman growing older, as a woman with older family members—a mother, aunts, sister—I am also a participant. I thank multicultural feminists for their emphasis on "both/and" for helping me reconcile these various parts of myself, and for hopefully making this book coherent and consistent in its themes and writing.

This book is divided into four sections and ten chapters written over a 7-year period. A number first appeared in earlier forms in other publications and have been presented at numerous professional conferences. Earlier portions of chapters 1 and 7, including the feminist life-span perspective on aging, were originally presented at the 1993 Annual Program Meetings of the Council on Social Work Education in New York City and the American Society in Aging in Chicago, and were later published in *Feminist Practice in the 21st Century*, edited by Nan Van Den Bergh (Browne, 1995b). However, the earlier version of this framework neglected to place a proper focus on ageism as a force that impacts on the life of aging women, and this has been corrected. Earlier portions of chapters 2, 3, and 10 were originally published as "Feminist Theory and Social Work: A Vision for Practice with Older Women" in *The Journal of Applied Social Science*, *18*(1), 5–16 (Browne, 1994). This material was also presented at the 1994 Annual Program Meeting of the American Society in Aging held in San Diego. And, an earlier version of chapter 8, "Empowerment in Social Work Practice with Older Women," was first presented at the 1990 Annual Program Meeting of the American Society on Aging in San Francisco and later published in *Social Work*, *40*, 358–364 (Browne, 1995a). Each of these chapters, then, have greatly benefitted from comments by editors, conference participants, and reviewers. In writing this book, I have made every attempt to find gerontology content in feminist writings, and I have been consistently disappointed when I could not do so. Perhaps it exists where I did not look, and if this is so,

I apologize to those authors and take all responsibility for any such omissions.

Part One and chapter 1 provide background data on aging women. The chapter begins with a systematic examination of aging women issues using census data and relevant research, as well as readings from the words of older women themselves. Chapter 1 thus provides a profile of older women in America today, and also discusses the political and social realities of women as they age in a society which is on the verge of a new millennium. I have felt that this was important because so many of the myths about older women on which public policies are built are so demonstrably untrue; for example, myths about the wealthy older widow traveling around the world on cruise ships on the life-insurance money from her deceased husband. I began this Introduction by noting that many of older women's needs are also the problems of younger women, and that many older women's problems are exacerbated with age as a result of ageism. Contrary pictures—that portray all older women as wealthy widows—have been used as an argument, albeit a tacit one, to decrease social welfare benefits for the aged. After all, if the elderly are well off, why should social welfare support them? What is left out of this discussion is the fact that the aged are primarily women, and that, as a whole, they desperately need their social welfare benefits to survive. Such a discussion does not negate the fact that some older women are financially comfortable, and that all older women have strengths. Still, aging is a challenge to most women, one made more difficult if they are in poor economic standing and physical health. Some of the problems associated with aging impact on both men and women. In this chapter and in later ones, I focus on how they affect women due to their greater vulnerability from work and family histories, societal norms, and expectations, and for many the added effects of racism, classism, and heterosexism.

Part Two presents information on various contemporary feminist theories and the ways in which they have and have not addressed the needs of aging women. Specifically, chapters 2, 3, and 4 identify themes from feminist literature that encourage new conceptualizations about women and aging. These are loosely categorized as liberal and cultural feminisms, multicultural and postmodern feminisms, and radical and socialist feminisms. A number of theorists and writers are discussed, including Simone de Beauvoir, Barbara Macdonald, Audre Lorde, Carol Gilligan, Patricia Hill Collins, Gloria Anzaldua, Nancie Caraway, Catherine MacKinnon, bell hooks, and others. There are two points important to note here. One is that, given the wealth of feminist writings, these themes are not understood to be inclusive of all feminist thought. The writings are primarily contemporary and Western, and therefore have their limitations. Second, this grouping of various feminist schools of thought could have clearly been organized differently. A major disagreement in feminist theories today is whether or not women are seen as "different from men." Two distinct schools of feminist thought, cultural and socialist feminisms, recognize and applaud women's difference from men. In contrast, liberal, postmodern, and radical feminisms generally believe that this focus on difference is not only misplaced but harmful to women in the long run, although some radical and cultural feminists agree that women need to foster a separate culture from men. Regardless of how these chapters are organized, my point here is that themes from these writings offer us ideas that challenge the ways in which gender and age are conceptualized and lived. Such divisions are not meant to mask the potential for feminism to be transformative; rather, these categories are for definition only. Neither do their differences mask the commonalities they share in understanding women's place in a male-dominated society. Regardless of how feminist theories were or could have been grouped, what remains true is that the need to extend feminist theories to the life situations of older women is in its beginning stages.

Following the identification of feminist themes, we then move to Part Three. This section examines various strategies for change and their implications for aging women. Chapter 5 discusses present public and private policies and social welfare interventions that address the life situations of women. Included here are the conservative "New Right's" agenda as well as liberal strategies. In contrast to content presented in the previous chapter, Chapter 6 presents a feminist life-span perspective on aging, building on previous knowledge and frameworks developed by gerontologists, feminists, and social workers, that moves us toward the formulation of some new thinking and strategies for change. Chapter 7 uses this perspective, or framework, to critique what is effective as well as problematic with present political and social welfare strategies; this is a feminist age analysis. One concept often discussed in feminist literature is empowerment. Thus, chapter 8 examines present conceptualizations of empowerment and suggests a new reconceptualization of the term with and on behalf of older women. Part Four concludes with a section on aging women and a new feminist aging theory. Thoughts toward an epistemology on women and aging are tentatively presented in chapter 9. The concluding chapter calls for new strategies for change and for a new vision for feminism and feminist theory and practice with older women. Drawing from feminist theory's contributions and omissions, together with the writings and words of older women themselves and the works of other gerontologists who may or may not be feminists, this book illustrates the connections possible between feminism and gerontology, offers a critique of current and proposed social welfare strategies, suggests politically feasible directions applicable to social welfare that can benefit aging women, and looks to aging women to develop a new epistemology on women and age.

CHALLENGES AND DILEMMAS IN MY WRITING

I have felt a number of dilemmas in writing this book and I acknowledge the writings of feminist sociologist Patricia Hill Collins for making the dilemmas and the strategy clear to me. In the Preface to her thoughtful book *Black Feminist Thought: Knowledge, Consciousness, and the Politics of Empowerment* (1991), Collins discussed wanting to use an epistemological framework in the preparation of her book that would "be used . . . to assess existing Black feminist thought and to clarify some of the underlying assumptions that impede the development of Black feminist thought" (p. 17). One of her strategies was to have her discourse be inclusive of many women and not just academic theorists, while at the same time retaining rigorous and scholarly integrity. I wanted this book to be a scholarly examination of feminist theory and gerontological studies as they apply to aging women. But I wanted this book to be accessible to many women and relatively free from academic jargon. Because aging concerns all of us, I especially wanted midlife and older women to read this book and to share their comments with me. Making the book approachable to a wide range of audiences had me puzzled over my writing style. Readers will no doubt see this reflected in these chapters. I alternately use the pronouns "we" and "our" as well as "they" and "their." I have tried to make this book both scholarly and popular, theoretical and applied. Moreover, and to support the legitimacy of women's voices, I have purposefully sought out and chosen to use their own words, as opposed to my interpretations of their writings. Thus, this book includes the voices of many women—thinkers, theorists, activists, and everyday older women—rather than just my own. I understand that this runs the risk of making the book seem less scientific and less rigorous. If it results in a more accessible book, however, then I will have met one of my major objectives.

A second dilemma for me was the question of how to emphasize the heterogeneity that exists among older women. I have sought to bring the diversity among aging women into the mainstream of these chapters without having race and class appear to be tacked onto the discussion. I am doubtful that I have been successful. Nonetheless, I am indebted to the writings of numerous feminists who have guided and enriched my thinking—bell hooks, Nancie Caraway, May Sarton, Patricia Hill Collins, and many, many others. Differences among women abound. Nonetheless, there is a good chance that a meeting of any group of women would focus on their hopes for their daughters, sons, lovers, and friends to be free from harm, free to pursue opportunity, and free to make their own life choices. We need a more dynamic view of feminism that remains accountable to its past and inclusive in its future.

A third caveat left me hesitant to write this book. It is my belief that one should never write where one does not live. Although my 13-year-old daughter sees me as quite old, others will not, and may question my authority to write such a book. I have pondered this myself. Taking a life-cycle approach to aging, one that allows me to see age as a part of life's continuum as opposed to "younger versus older," has diminished this concern for me. I am sure that my perspectives will change over time. For now, I am thankful to the many women of all ages, but especially those older than I am, who have helped me with this book, and who continuously enlarge my thinking and vision.

Finally, I have been hesitant to write this book because I do not consider myself an expert in feminist theory. Rather, I am a gerontologist and a social worker who is also a feminist. The contribution I hope to make is to draw from feminist theory so that the needs of older women can better be met on both personal and political levels.

TOWARD AN EPISTEMOLOGY ON WOMEN AND AGE

Feminism, unlike other frameworks, has accomplished social and political reform by offering a number of different analyses and critiques of the sources of women's oppression and by outlining and demanding strategies to end it. The celebration of who women are is also characteristic of many feminist writings. Expanding on ideas and themes from feminist theories and from older women themselves, I take a beginning step toward a new epistemology of women and age.

Epistemology is the study of knowledge, but it also questions how knowledge is developed and shared. Thoughts toward a new epistemology of gender and age must begin by acknowledging the multiple determinants of women's oppressions throughout their lives, the relationship between gender and power through the life cycle, and the role of social structures in shaping and maintaining such oppressions. Moreover, a new epistemology of gender and age critiques the lack of research on older women and seeks to remedy this problem. It also highlights and illuminates the inconsistencies in social welfare's treatment of aging women and of our own complicity in their mistreatment. At the same time, it seeks to respect older women and document their strengths in numerous forms, and their own power sources. By refusing to fall into dualistic thinking, a new epistemology of gender and age rejects the artificial choice between equity reform and societal transformation and instead, sees the value in these and other strategies. Feminists and gerontologists have begun to focus more attention on the lives of aging women, but they need to do more. Feminists need to demand from gerontologists that they make all women central to their study including aging women, women of color, and others. In turn, gerontologists must press for aging women's representation in feminist theory. I do believe that it is through such critiques and analyses that the potential for exposing and expanding feminist and gerontology theory in new and exciting ways can be born. In sum, a feminist life-span perspective on aging is presented to explore women's oppression, diversities, and strengths, and to provide a mode of analysis that is based on a definition of old age from women's lived experiences. Using this framework, a feminist age analysis examines and critiques the underlying premises behind paradigms, policies, and programs that impact older women's lives, suggests a number of strategies to improve the lives of older women, and, ultimately, looks to a new epistemology of women and age for a more respectful vision for women—and men—in the later years.

I hope that this book offers something of value to aging women as well as men and women who work with aging women, who are concerned about their well-being in later life, and who are committed to issues of equality and fairness. Perhaps those worried about their mothers, aunts, sisters, lovers, and friends will have reason to pause and ask what feminism can offer to ensure a better life—a more equitable life, a less violent life, a more inclusive life—for the women they know and love. I would like to think that this book—with its insistence on diversities between women and on linking theory and practice, connecting the public and private spheres, and connecting the young with the old—will be of special interest to those who work with older women. It is my hope that an exchange of thinking will occur among midlife and older women, gerontologists, feminists, and others.

I also hope that this book will be viewed for what it is—an invitation for a new and ongoing discourse on feminist theory and gerontology—rather than a discussion on the merits of various specific feminisms. Just as we need multiple theories on aging, we also need numerous frameworks to understand women growing older. Women's complex and textured realities require this. So, I look forward to reading the work of others in this area. In this book, I argue that feminist theory is a critical and yet still incomplete discourse for developing a new epistemology on women and aging. It remains my hope that this book may open the doors to a new look at feminism as it relates to women growing older.

This book seeks an answer to the question: Can feminism advance the well-being of older women? Should it? How can it? How should such strategies be formulated and implemented? Feminists and gerontologists need to continue to address these questions by identifying and understanding those critical variables that determine the status of older women. According to Collins, "Self-conscious struggle is needed in order to reject patriarchal perceptions of women and to value women's ideas and actions" (1991, p. 27). Therefore, an examination of the literature on feminism and aging can itself be a strategy for promoting solidarity between ages. It can uncover, empower, and listen to the voices of women as they ponder their own and society's aging. An epistemology of women and age would seek new answers and ask new questions; and both its questions and answers would strive to be rich and multilayered, encouraging new thoughts toward what a fresh perspective can offer a society committed to justice. What is critically important is that we begin to ask the questions that must be raised: Why are so many older women poor? Why are Black older women the poorest of the poor? Why are so many poor older women without pensions and adequate housing? Who really benefits when women spend their years taking care of others? After a lifetime of contributions, why do women earn so little of society's respect and care? How can we incorporate what older women have to say about their lives as older women? And, finally, once we understand the answers to some of these questions, what can be done to formulate a new vision of aging women, recognizing their strengths and paths of resistance? What options and strategies do we follow to ensure change and make a difference? I hope that in some modest way continued discourse on the interaction of feminism and gerontology will be stimulated so that we arrive at a more respectful vision of older women than we have today, and, in the process, we create a society that is more just in its treatment of all people.

PART ONE

Women and Aging

Women's Status in Later Life

> Mr. President, I am not a young lady. I've lived a long life. I'm an old lady.
>
> Comment by Maggie Kuhn, founder of the Gray Panthers, to President Gerald Ford, who introduced her as a "young lady."
>
> —Doress-Worters and Siegel

Like other industrialized nations, America is an aging society. In 1995 there were 33.5 million elderly Americans (aged 65 or older), composing one eighth of the total population (American Association of Retired Persons [AARP], 1996a). Since the 1980s, we have seen a 22% increase in the number of older adults, and projections estimate that this population will double in size to reach nearly 66 million by 2025 (Taeuber, 1993).

A critical variable in the study of human development is gender (Bohan, 1993). This is especially true among older adults, for whom the majority are female. In 1995 there were 19.8 million older women and 13.7 million older men, or a ratio of 145 women for every 100 men (AARP, 1996a). The gender ratio favoring women increases with age, so that by the time adults are in their mid-eighties, there are nearly 100 women to every 42 men (U.S. Bureau of the Census, 1993c). Four in five centenarians are women (U.S. Bureau of the Census, 1996). By 2010, nearly half of all adult women will be at least 50 years of age (Allen, 1993b). And, in a recent issue of *Aging Today* (American Society on Aging, 1996a), Cynthia Taeuber and Paul Siegel of the U.S. Census Bureau predict that "if the average yearly rates of death for people at older ages continues to decrease, the average life expectancy will rise to 100 by the year 2050" (p. 14).

Despite these unprecedented demographic developments and the fact that the needs of the aged are often the needs of women (Forman, 1985; Hess, 1985; Markson, 1983), feminists and gerontologists have been slow to address the concerns of older women (K. H. Gould, 1989; A. Hartman, 1990; Lewis & Butler, 1972; Perkins, 1992; Reinharz, 1986; Rodeheaver, 1987; Russell, 1987). More recently, important contributions by feminist (Friedan, 1993; Greer, 1991; Steinem, 1992) and gerontological scholars (Allen & Pifer, 1993; Arendell & Estes, 1987; England, 1990; Gonyea, 1994; Hess, 1990; Hess & Waring, 1983; Hooyman & Gonyea, 1995; Lopata, 1987; Quadagno & Meyer, 1990; Turner & Troll, 1994) have broadened society's perspective on gender issues significantly with an increased focus on the needs, opportunities, and challenges faced by midlife and older women in the United States. However, it can be argued that feminist contributions to gerontological literature, and conversely gerontological contributions to feminist literature, remain in a state of infancy, despite their great potential for improving women's lives.

The subject of women's oppression has been the topic of serious debate among feminist scholars for more than 30 years. Feminists define gender as a sociocultural construct shaped by social structure and public policy (Hess, 1990). Gender inequality throughout the life cycle often results in women entering old age with far fewer resources than men. Feminists have focused much of their critique on understanding the relationships among gender, power, and privilege. More recently, feminists have turned their attention to how the experiences of ethnic, lesbian, never-married, and other marginalized women make them both similar and dissimilar to one another, and to diversity's subsequent challenge to feminist solidarity (Anzaldua, 1981; Caraway, 1991; P.H. Collins, 1991; hooks, 1981, 1984; Lorde, 1984). Gender, like race and class, is a hierarchic system constructed by society. Not all women face the same challenges due to the influences of race and class and other forms of oppression.

Research on women and aging has documented women's greater longevity compared with men and their problems with long term, disabling conditions (Verbrugge, 1989). Studies also document the fact that women generally end their years with stronger social supports and friendships than do men (Lewittes, 1989; Reinhardt & Fisher, 1989). However, as described by a number of authors, women face a number of problems throughout their lives that have profound consequences with each advancing year: the dual labor market; unmet social, economic, and health needs; targeting for assault; and assignment to unpaid caregiving duties (Abramowitz, 1992; Browne, 1994; Hooyman & Kiyak, 1993; Kingson & O'Grady-LeShane, 1993). For too many women, age discrimination, bias in pensions, demeaned physical appearance, the paucity of research data on health conditions, and other gender inequalities exacerbate women's problems as they age, leaving them vulnerable and financially, physically, and socially at risk (Crawley, 1994; Davis, Grant, & Rowland, 1990;

Hess, 1985, 1990; Minkler & Stone, 1985; Older Women's League, 1990; Ozawa, 1995; Rix, 1984). Projections into the 21st century suggest that the economic and health concerns of aging women (Hess, 1990; O'Grady-LeShane, 1990; Ozawa, 1993), and particularly older women of color (Axinn, 1989; Dressel, 1988; Jackson, 1985; Taeuber & Allen, 1993), will only increase, in part due to present policies that continue to neglect the life-cycle needs, choices, and realities of women's experiences.

I begin this chapter with a description of the current and projected status of older women in America. The consequences for women of a lifetime of inequalities between the sexes are presented, with a focus on their financial status, caregiving roles, health condition, and social lives. Such an analysis requires not only growth of the female aging population, but also that its diversity be made central to this discussion. It acknowledges the extent to which the interlocking of women's problems with one another and with each stage in the life cycle are enmeshed (Anderson & Collins, 1992; O'Rand, 1996) and the specific problems which are results of age discrimination. Aging is thus viewed as a cumulative experience with women's inequalities and opportunities, their disadvantages and advantages, following them as they age, and as an experience shaped by ageism as well as other sites of oppression.

FINANCIAL STATUS

Women's retirement income is generally determined by wages earned through their own past and present employment or that of their spouse. This income reflects numerous gender-based experiences and challenges women face throughout their lives, such as job discrimination and work segregation; limited earnings, entitlements and other supports in home and work life; inconsistent work patterns; the absence of Social Security or private pension credit for unpaid child and elder caregiving responsibilities; increasing years of singlehood; and age discrimination in employment, all of which lead to inadequate Social Security benefits (Davis et al., 1990; Moon, 1990). Mimi Abramowitz, author of *Regulating the Lives of Women: Social Welfare Policy from Colonial Times to the Present* (1992), attributes women's financial insecurity to what she refers to as "the family ethic":

> In brief, the family ethic, which locked women into a subordinate family role also rationalized women's exploitation on the job. By devaluing women's position in each sphere, the ideology of women's work and family roles

satisfied capital's need for a supply of readily available, cheap, female labor. By creating the conditions for continued male control of women at home and on the job, the economic devaluation and marginalization of women also muted the challenge that increased employment by women posed to patriarchal norms. . . . Targeted to and largely reflecting the experience of white, middle class women who marry and stay home, the family ethic denied poor and immigrant women and women of color the "rights of womanhood" and the opportunity to embrace the dominant definition of "good wife" and mother because they did not confine their labor to the home. (p. 39)

A number of scholars have noted that it is not just poor young women who grow into poor older women. Middle-aged women are also at risk of poverty in later life as a result of divorce, job segregation and discrimination, and years of unpaid caregiving duties (Quadagno & Meyer, 1990). Although some women have benefitted from their dependent role, and some older women are financially secure, the overall picture of older women's economic status is disheartening. Women are disproportionately represented among the poor and near-poor, and older women of color are among the most severely impacted.

OLDER WOMEN, POVERTY, AND SOCIAL WELFARE ASSISTANCE

In *Poverty in the United States, 1992* (U.S. Bureau of the Census, 1993a), the official definition of the poverty threshold was identified as an amount set by the federal government and adjusted annually to account for inflation. Those who live below this threshold are considered poor, and near-poverty has a threshold 25% higher than the poverty threshold. Approximately 3.7 million older adults live below the poverty line, and another 2.3 million are near poverty (AARP, 1996a). The poverty threshold in 1992 for a single, elderly individual (age 65 and over) was $6,729 in earned income; the near-poverty threshold was $8,411 (U.S. Bureau of the Census, 1993a).

Simply put, older women are poorer than older men. The poverty rate for all elderly people is 14%—nearly double that of the under-65 adult population. Although women constitute 58% of older adults, they account for 74% of the poor (Taeuber & Allen, 1993). Elderly women (16%) are more apt to be poor than older men (9%) (U.S. Bureau of the Census, 1996). Looked at another way, whereas 13% of older adults age 65 and older are poor, nearly 75% of this group are women (Taeuber & Allen, 1993). Moreover, nearly one third of all older women have incomes within 150% of the poverty line (Malveaux, 1993), and 74% of the beneficiaries for old age assistance under the Supplemental Security (SSI) program are women (Taeuber & Allen, 1993). Even when government transfers are considered, women's poverty rates are 30% higher than men's (Burkhauser, Duncan, & Hauser, 1994). It is an undeniable reality: Women are at high risk for poverty in later life.

Women are poor for a number of interconnected reasons. Marital status is a great determinant of poverty for women because it often is the main eligibility criteria for Social Security and pension benefits. In 1990, most older men were married and most older women were not. Nearly half of all widowed and divorced women 65 or older had an income below $7500 (U.S. Bureau of the Census, 1991). Among those 65 years of age and over, nearly four times more widows live in poverty than do married older women. More than half of the widows who are poor were not poor before the death of their husbands (U.S. House Select Committee on Aging, 1992c). Moreover, among divorced older women, the poverty rate is 24% (Meyer, 1990).

Unfortunately, widowed and divorced older women are often "lumped together" in census and other reports, masking important differences in income status between the two populations. For one, divorced older women are generally younger than widowed older women. According to a report of the Congressional Symposium on Women and Retirement, House Select Committee on Aging, William Crown and colleagues (Crown, Mutschler, & Schultz, 1992) reported that half of divorced and separated women over the age of 45 are under 55 years of age, compared to one-third of single women or one-sixth of the widows. And, while more than 75% of widowed women are 65 years of age and over, less than 25% of divorced and 25% of separated women are in this age group.

Second, poverty rates among divorced women are the same or higher than that of widowed women. What is alarming is that the economic status of a small but growing number of divorced older women appears to be worsening. There are primarily three reasons for this dilemma. These are: (1) the increase in marital instability, single parenting, and rising divorce rates; (2) the shift in women's increased responsibilities for their own financial independence; and (3) the growing importance of employer-sponsored pensions for ensuring an adequate retirement income that are often unavailable or difficult for women to earn due to present retirement policies. Contrary to popular myth, alimony payments are received by only 4% of older divorcees (Crown et al., 1992).

Like marital status, living arrangements are also related to income and poverty status. Among elderly people who live alone, 77% are women, usually widows (U.S. House Select Committee on Aging, 1989), who are six times more likely to be poor than their male counterparts (Taeuber & Allen, 1993).

Another predictor of poverty is increased age. Forecasts for the 21st century predict that, compared with men and married couples, unmarried women, primarily the oldest widows, will continue to be at financial risk. Of unmarried women who receive pensions, half will receive less than $1,200 annually, compared with $4,000 annually for men (Ozawa, 1993).

Race is yet another determinant of poverty among older women. Throughout their lives, women of color tend to be poorer than White women. Their poverty is persistent, the result of being placed at cumulative disadvantage. The multiple influences of race, class, gender, and age are inextricably linked in American society and leave their mark on women's potential for economic survival in later life (Dressel, 1988; K. H. Gould, 1989; Taeuber & Allen, 1993). Malveaux (1993), for example, notes that among Black women, unlike White women, a history of low earnings appears to be more a function of poverty than marital status. And, although Black women constitute 5% of the elderly population, they account for 16% of the poor elderly (U.S. Bureau of the Census, 1991). Alarmingly, among Black elderly women living alone, 63% of those age 75 and older are poor (AARP, 1993). The poverty rates for Hispanic women are double that of White females (Malveaux, 1993), and Asian and Pacific Island older women over the age of 75 years have poverty rates as high as 40% (Kim, 1983). Particularly vulnerable are the most recent immigrant Asian groups—Vietnamese, Hmomg, and Laotian—and Pacific Islander populations—Samoan and Tongan (U.S. Bureau of the Census, 1993b, 1993d). Furthermore, census data tell us that divorced older women (who are most at risk for poverty) are also more apt to be members of a minority population in contrast to single, married, or widowed women (Crown et al., 1992).

Most older women rely on Social Security, an entitlement program that is the nation's primary social insurance program, as their main or only source of retirement income. By definition, entitlement programs are those whose benefits are determined by set eligibility requirements and benefit levels, as opposed to federal appropriations. Examples, other than Social Security, include Medicare, Medicaid, and military pensions. Another critical public assistance program that many poor and near poor older women turn to is the federal Supplemental Security Income (SSI) program. SSI, established in 1974, is a means-tested program that aims to provide a minimum guaranteed income to low-income aged adults and the disabled. Nearly two thirds of its beneficiaries are women, and of those who receive benefits on the basis of age, three-fourths are women (U.S. House Select Committee on Aging, 1990a, 1990c). It has been estimated that nearly half of those who may be eligible for SSI do not even apply to the program, however. Zedlewski and Meyer (1987) suggest that some of the reasons for nonparticipation include the lack of transportation to and from the application office, the difficulty with the application process itself, shame and negative connotations of "welfare," and feelings of an invasion of privacy. Among those who do receive its benefits, the dollar amount is not sufficient to remove beneficiaries from the poverty or near-poverty threshold. Those who do apply and receive its benefits find that they still live on or near a subsistence level of income. The U.S. House Select Committee on Aging found that this is "because the federal cash assistance provided is less than the federal poverty level, especially in states that do not adequately supplement the federal benefit level" (1990a, p. 73).

In general, the poorer one is, the more vulnerable one is to housing difficulties. Housing assistance, while not a form of direct income assistance, includes a number of federally and state-supported programs to promote independent and financially affordable housing options. Housing is an especially critical issue for older women as increased longevity, along with widowhood, leaves the majority of older women living alone. According to the U.S. Senate (1988), older adults comprise over 45% of those receiving public housing benefits and 48% of those receiving rent-subsidized units. Beginning with the Reagan era in the 1980s, however, federal funding for public housing has been diminished by nearly 70% (Mulroy, 1995). As a consequence, it is harder for older women to "age in place" in the setting of their choice.

The three major government housing programs include public housing, Section 202 of the Housing Act of 1959, and Section 8 of the Housing and Community Development Act. Although specific eligibility requirements differ, all are means-tested programs. In other words, their target populations are low-income adults and families. Public housing provides housing to older adults, the poor, and those who have physical and/or mental disabilities. Some housing projects are segregated by age, some are not. Several researchers have argued the benefits of segregated housing for older adults, stating that elderly beneficiaries tend to feel safer and less lonely in such settings (Burby & Rohe, 1990). In contrast to public housing, Section 202 attempts to meet the needs of older adults whose income is somewhat greater than that allowed by public housing eligibility criteria, but who can not pay independently for their own housing. Funds from Section 202 provide low-interest construction loans to nonprofit organizations or sponsors and many, in conjunction with Section 8 rent subsidies, offer housing rents at substantial savings to older adults. Finally, rent subsidies are provided via Section 8 to low-income adults and families.

However, this program, like the other housing programs, is not an entitle-ment program. Its funds are extremely limited, with small percentages of eligible older adults able to receive services. Hence, senior housing units often have 3–5-year wait lists. Since the early 1990s, nearly 26% of public housing units have been set aside for older persons, an allotment which may provide some additional relief (U.S. Department of Commerce, 1992).

OLDER WOMEN, WORK, AND RETIREMENT INCOME

The median income from all sources of older persons in 1995 was $16,484 for men and $9,355 for women (AARP, 1996a). The major source of income for older adults is Social Security. In contrast, only a small percent-age of older adults—16% of men and 9% of women—remain in the workforce (Taeuber & Allen, 1993). Most older women are retired or are spouses of those retired. Among older women who work, the majority are divorced and separated. Whereas women's participation in the paid labor force has increased, their occupational profile continues to reflect job segregation and discrimination. Despite guarantees of the Fourteenth Amendment of the Constitution, Title VII of the Federal Civil Rights Act of 1964, and the Equal Pay Act of 1963, women still face inequality in earnings, hiring, and promotions. Among women age 50 years or older, 58% are employed in the sales, clerical, and retail business, usually with poor earnings and limited benefits (U.S. Department of Labor, 1990). Women earn less than men throughout their lives, which continues in retirement due to wage-based public and private pensions. The additional dilemma of age discrimination is faced by midlife and aging women who enter the job market late, only to find that their limited marketability and education leaves them markedly disadvantaged. Middle-aged and older women of color are most at risk of being disadvantaged (Taeuber & Allen, 1993). The following sections examine the nation's public and private policies to ensure an adequate retirement income for older women.

Social Security

The Social Security Act of 1935, together with its subsequent amendments, provides Old Age Survivors, Disability, Health Insurance (OASDHI), commonly referred to as Social Security, for eligible workers and their families. Enacted under the presidency of Franklin Delano Roosevelt following the nation's worst economic depression, the Act was intended to provide the American family with income protection when wages were lost to retirement, disability, or death. It is a mandatory universal social and health insurance program. As noted by the U.S. House Select Committee on Aging (1992a), this entitlement program tends to "protect a family that consists of a lifelong paid worker (typically a husband), a lifelong homemaker (typically a wife), and dependent children" (p. 9). Nearly 95% of older adults receive Social Security benefits (Alaska, 1994).

There are five contemporary issues that effect Social Security benefits for women: (a) dual entitlement, (b) caregivers years, (c) marital status, (d) windfall reduction provision, and (e) government pension offset (U.S. House Select Committee on Aging, 1992b). *How Well Do Women Fare under the Nation's Retirement Policies?*, a report from the U.S. House Select Committee on Aging (1992b), provides the following critical information with respect to these issues.

1. *Dual Entitlement.* The social security provision that a person who is entitled to both a worker's benefits and a benefit as a dependent (spouse) or survivor's benefit must choose whichever is the greater rather than getting both benefits. Due to the wage gap between men and women, as well as the tendency for women to enter and exit the paid labor force more frequently than men, women often earn benefits that are lower than the spousal benefit to which they are entitled on their husband's earnings record. Since 1960, the number of women dually entitled on both their record and that of their husbands increased from 5 percent to 22 percent, but for these women, their dependent benefit based on their husband's record is greater. In effect, under dual entitlement, many working women pay Social Security taxes for no additional benefit. Even though most dually entitled women rarely collect on their own worker benefit, the family's disposable income is reduced by her contribution to FICA. A two-earner couple may contribute more to the system but actually receive less in benefits than a one-earner couple making the same income.

2. *Caregivers Years.* Caregiving is not credited in the Social Security benefit calculations. According to the same Congressional report, "a worker's individual benefit is based upon earnings during their computation period. Benefits are calculated based on a 40 year work history, with five years of lowest income removed. A zero is thus entered into a worker's earnings record for each year he or she is not working. On average, men spend about one year out of the work force compared to women who spend 11.5 years due to caregiving responsibilities."

3. *Marital Status.* As previously noted, marital status is a key predictor of aging women's poverty risk. The most at-risk aged women are those who are divorced or never married.

4. *Windfall Reduction Provision.* Many women are not familiar with this term. It refers to a reduction in Social Security as a result of one's pension based on employment that is not covered by Social Security (certain

state and local pensions). Typically, this lesser known provision results in a lesser benefit to the worker or spouse.

5. *Government Pension Offset.* A retired government worker's Social Security benefit, as a spouse or widow, is reduced by two-thirds of the value of the government pension. If, for example, a woman received $600.00 per month in civil service retirement based on her work history, and she is entitled to a $400.00 per month Social Security widow's benefit, her widow's benefit will be zero because two-thirds of the $600.00 completely eliminates the Social Security benefit. (pp. 11–17)

Most feminist scholars believe that there are additional causes of women's financial insecurity in old age. These include women's assigned roles, societal expectations, and resultant choices; discrimination; the dual labor market; inequities in pay for both full-time and part-time employment; and work policies that are neither family-responsive or family-friendly. As a result of some or all of these factors, most men receive Social Security benefits as a worker and most women, especially White women, receive Social Security benefits as a dependent. However, recent figures reveal that the number of women age 62 years and older who receive dependent benefits has declined from 57% in 1960 to 39% in 1993 (U.S. Office of Social Security Administration, 1993). In 1992, the average Social Security monthly benefit amount for retired workers averaged $735 for men and $562 for retired women. In contrast, in the same year a retired worker, usually a male, received $735 and the benefit for the nonworking spouse was $338 (U.S. Office of Social Security Administration, 1993). Given women's traditionally low wages, the rising divorce rate, and the fact that survivor's benefits for widows often have traditionally been higher than retirement benefits based on a woman's own work history (Ozawa, 1993), this trend will not result in improvements to most women's future financial status.

Nonetheless, Social Security has done a vital job in keeping older women above the poverty line and providing essential protection to widows. The poverty rate for older widows who are beneficiaries of Social Security, although high, would be even higher without the benefits of Social Security. A number of women's organizations are calling for specific changes to Social Security which would improve women's lives. Those, which will be discussed in chapter 7, and that reflect a feminist age analysis include the re-evaluation of the dual entitlement clause, women's work patterns, and caregiving penalties that exist in Social Security and private pension policies. A controversial issue surrounding Social Security has been posed: While it may not have caused women's poverty, should it not nonetheless cure it?

Private Pensions

Social Security paired with a private pension provides a more adequate retirement income than Social Security alone. Unfortunately, private pensions are rarely accessible to women, due to their predominance in noncovered employment sites and because pension policies are modeled after male work patterns. Women tend to have shorter work histories and consequently have difficulty in meeting vesting requirements. Women can have pensions based on their marital status, but pensions based on another's work history are precarious at best (Abramowitz, 1992). Only half of men and one fourth of women receive pensions. Furthermore, pension coverage is the least accessible among low and low-to-moderate income workers (U. S. House Select Committee on Aging, 1992a, 1992b).

The passage of the Retirement Equity Act of 1984 (REACT) and the Employees Retirement Income Security Act (ERISA), together with vesting changes in the Tax Reform Act of 1986 (TRA), will result one hopes in improvements in women's financial security in their later years. As will be discussed in chapter 7, pension accessibility and regulation remain critical issues for older women. When women receive a pension, their benefits tend to be less than men's. In 1990, the combined mean monthly Social Security and pension income for male retirees was $1,160, 45% higher than the mean for women, which was $800 (Taeuber & Allen, 1993). Far too few couples planned with joint-survivor plans for older women outliving their husbands. Widows are actually at greater risk of being poor than when they were married. Even among widows who had not been poor when married, the death of their husbands leave many close to poverty or living in it. A report by the Subcommittee on Retirement Income and Employment of the House Select Committee on Aging (1992b) echoed a similar comment:

> Social Security and private pension plans are not designed to deliberately discriminate against working women, but the bottom line result of our policies is that women are still far more likely than men to spend their retirement years in poverty, with one of the most significant predictors of income security being their marital status. (p. 1)

Other Government Income Programs

In addition to having a job that provides pension coverage, there are a number of other issues that affect working women's ability in their earlier years to plan for their later ones. These include pay equity, antidiscrimination measures, child care, and family medical leave. The Equal Pay Act of 1963 mandates that employers pay the same wages to male and female employees in the same job. It took an act of Congress to specify this. The following year, Title VII of the Civil Rights Act was passed, prohibiting wage discrimination on the basis of race, sex, religion, or national origin. Sadly, evidence persists of the intractability of gender discrimination in employment.

The federal government has been slower to address the need for child care for working parents. Most federal assistance prior to the 1980s was directed at low-income families receiving Head Start subsidies or assistance through the Social Services Block Grant programs. More recently, the establishment of Flexible Spending Accounts (FSA) under the Economic Recovery Act of 1981 has provided some help. In short, the Act allows employees to pay for their child care expenses using "pre-tax dollars." Employees may project their child care costs for that year (up to $5,000) and then have this amount withheld from their gross salary and refunded with proof of childcare expenses. And, while changes in the 1996 Welfare Reform legislation intended to provide some day care expenses to women working as an incentive to stay off welfare, every state's benefits differ in allocation and eligibility.

Probably the most recent policy that has the potential to positively affect women's incomes throughout their work and retirement years was the passage of the 1993 Family and Medical Leave Act (FMLA). It essentially provides for limited family leave for a sick child or an ailing elder family member. It is one of the nation's most progressive policies acknowledging the public's responsibility in the provision of care to dependent persons, and the difficult choice between work and family that must be made because of the absence of employment family leave policies. Importantly, it acknowledged women's role in caring for the young and the old in stating that

> due to the nature of roles of men and women in our society, the primary responsibility for family caretaking often falls on women, and such responsibility affects the working lives of women more than it affects the working lives of men; and that employment standards that apply to one gender only have serious potential for encouraging employers to discriminate against employees and applicants who are that gender. (Public Law 103-3, 107 Stat. 6-7)

Few would argue against the merits of the policy as a first step in recognizing that women comprise a growing segment of the nation's workforce and that the absence of family leave policies poses a severe hardship on women. However, for reasons that will be discussed further in chapter 7, the policy falls short for many women, especially single parents, women of color, older women, and gay and lesbian women. So, while some progress has been made in this area, women's life patterns have not been fully addressed.

WOMEN AND CAREGIVING

Caregiving is a critical issue for Americans today, especially for women, who compose approximately 75% of the nation's caregivers (Stone et al., 1986). The care that women provide to their families, friends, and lovers is known as family care, whereas the care that is more specifically provided to elder family members is often referred to as caregiving and eldercare. Pearlin and his colleagues (1990, 1992) define caregiving work to include activities and experiences involved in assisting relatives or friends who are unable to provide for themselves. Such care can include helping an aged father balance his checkbook to the more inclusive and labor-intensive custodial care when parents become frail and bedbound. Some scholars have noted that caregiving in America is frequently invisible, usually devalued, generally assigned to women, and not necessarily restricted to care provided in one's own home (Baines, Evans, & Neysmith, 1992). As Naomi Gerstel and Sally Gallagher (1994) have found, women care for family members in their home and do most of the kin-keeping, or caring for those outside their household, as well.

Four divergent trends will affect how caregiving will be defined and practiced in American society in the 21st century: (1) the increasing number of older adults, especially the oldest-old; (2) the changing patterns of American family life; (3) the increasing number of women in the paid work force; and (4) the devolution of government. As England (1990) correctly warned, expectations that women can do it all "are on a collision course" with the increasing number of dependent persons and the declining numbers of caregivers (p. 9).

EFFECTS AND CHALLENGES OF CAREGIVING

Social and demographic changes have resulted in both the public and private sectors asking who will take care of frail elders (Rivlin & Wiener, 1988; State of Hawaii, Executive Office on Aging, 1993; Takamura & Seely, 1994). As Hooyman and Gonyea (1995) comment in their well-researched book, *Feminist Perspectives on Family Care: Polices for Gen-*

der Justice, what is undergirding these policies (and lack of policies) "basic assumptions about the nature and structure of family life; the role of the family and the state; and the relative values of privacy, independence, and interdependence" (p. 12). The availability and accessibility of long term care—services provided to frail elders and other functionally impaired persons over a sustained period of time—is a critical issue for aging women, because they are both the chief consumers of these services and the primary caregivers of frail elders. In fact, there is no way to discuss long term care without discussing the issues surrounding caregiving. As we will see in later chapters, present policies place high demands on caregivers—primarily middle-aged and older women—to care for the frail with little or no assistance. Caregiving may have its joys, but studies also document the startling consequences of caregiving on the emotional and physical well-being of the caregiver (George & Gwyther, 1986; Zarit, Reever, & Bach-Peterson, 1980). Because such work is considered by government and society at large to be "nonwork," there are also enormous economic consequences to women who are caregivers. In essence, the years of caregiving without public or private pension credits and the conceptualization of caregiving as the woman's domain, together with present retirement and health care policies, make caregiving a financially risky activity for women (Abramowitz, 1992; Baines et al., 1992; Browne, 1994; England, 1990), especially for those in low-paying jobs (Kingson & O'Grady-LeShane, 1993).

The number of years spent caregiving and out of the paid work force has an inverse relationship to the amount of benefits earned in Social Security in one's own name. In the present Social Security system, benefits are computed based on the average earnings a woman or man makes over a period of 35 years. Few caregivers have any understanding of the concept of "zero years" that are attached to their records for every year of "nonwork" and the consequences of such calculations on their retirement income. In 1990, Chairman William Hughes of the Subcommittee on Retirement Income and Employment, House Select Committee on Aging (1990b), gave this opening statement in a hearing to discuss the relationships among women, poverty, and caregiving:

> While women often assume the majority of caregiving responsibilities, spending on average, eleven and a half years out of the workforce caring for children or elderly parents (compared to 1.3 years for men), the Social Security program does not recognize these caregiving years. Rather, it penalizes them by averaging a zero into their benefit computation, thereby reducing their monthly benefit. . . . Although very few realize the impact of Social Security zero years, or are aware of the dual entitlement provision

until it is too late, many women reach retirement or face widowhood with diminished incomes because the years they spent caregiving have significantly decreased their Social Security benefit. . . . These assumed caregiving duties bear directly on women's lower wages, lower pension benefits, and lower Social Security benefits. (pp. 3–4)

Few consider, as Arendell and Estes (1991) have accurately pointed out, that demanding such "free" work from women has huge benefits for both the government and public sector, as it relieves them from having to pay for the entire costs of long term care. Caregiving also can hide the real cost of such "free" work. How much longer such benign neglect can be ignored is simply a matter of time. According to the U.S. Congressional Budget Office (1988), the number of older women living alone will jump from 6.4 million to 17.7 million—a 179% increase—from 1983 to 2030. Often, older women living alone have fewer resources, so who will be their caregivers? The shifting of the costs of long term care to the family, that is, to women, will continue into the 21st century if public policies continue to promote traditional gender-role duties, negate the value of the aged to society, neglect the protection of older women who live alone, define caregiving as nonwork, penalize women in the Social Security system who provide caregiving, ignore the needs of employees who are caregivers, and ignore the need for a noncategorical long term care program with adequate funding.

Caregiving of the frail, especially among paid caregivers, has other potentially dangerous consequences. As we have stated, most paid caregivers are women, who serve as nurses, nurses aides, and other home care assistants. Few are aware of the hazards of such occupations. A recent report from the Bureau of Labor Statistics (1994), for example, provided this information:

A sizeable proportion of the victims of nonfatal violence were caregivers in nursing homes and hospitals. Ironically, some of these workers were injured by intransigent patients, who resisted their assistance; others were assaulted by patients prone to violence. Most of these caregivers were female nurses and their aides. And typically they required about three to five days away from work to recuperate from their injuries.

In addition to the lack of information on the potential risk for violence directed against caregivers, the literature on caregiving also fails to include the consideration of race and class influences. Discussions on the dichotomies between paid and unpaid work, and between the public and private spheres, generally ignore the lives of lower-class and economically disadvantaged ethnic minority women. These women, contrary to most White middle-class women, have always been expected to provide both paid and unpaid work, and to work in both the public and private (domestic) spheres for minimal salaries. Furthermore, working-class and ethnic minority men often end up leaving work or retiring early due to poor health, with the resultant need for caregiving from their spouses. The recent cutbacks in some services affects these families the most, as private home care is not within their economic reach.

There is some evidence that caregiving patterns differ by ethnicity, and a number of different explanations have been offered. One states that cultural traditions may result in a family member choosing to provide care at home as opposed to using professional institutional or community-based services (Mui & Burnette, 1985). In contrast, other researchers suggest that lower service utilization and higher rates of in-home caregiving by minority families is a result of discriminatory admission and service policies by the dominant society and its institutions (Falcone & Broyles, 1994).

There is also a growing awareness of the type of caregiving many older women provide to their grandchildren when their own children can not fulfill their parental responsibilities. Studies by Minkler and colleagues (1993) detail the increasing prevalence of such care and the difficulties facing older women who provide it with little or no financial assistance from public or private sources. Today, 3.4 million children are cared for by their grandparents, and many think this number is a conservative one. The fact that child care, like long term care, is privatized in this country has growing implications for older women. This is because women are often expected to provide "free" care throughout their lives to both the young and the old without compensation or retirement credits and benefits.

Several more just policy options have been proposed as alternatives to present policies related to caregiving. Among these are dropping all years of nonpaid work when providing caregiving from penalization in the Social Security system, and reducing the age for widow's benefits from age 60 to 55 years. These and other policy recommendations will be discussed in chapter 7.

HEALTH ISSUES

Old age is not synonymous with poor health. As Lois Verbrugge (1989) points out, however, physical health problems do increase with age. Good health requires an active and willing partnership between the individual and those whom former Director of the National Institute on Health, Dr.

Bernadette Healy (1991), referred to as "the agents of information"—individuals and places that provide the requisite knowledge which allows informed choices to be made about health, health practices, and lifestyle. Of all the concerns over growing older, the potential loss of ones health and functioning is the most alarming to both men and women. Nearly 50 years ago, the World Health Organization defined health as a state of complete physical, social, and mental well-being. Such a definition embraces a holistic perspective for health and ability, recognizing the interaction of physical health with other factors such as spirituality, the environment, psychological factors, economic status, and the availability of social supports. In contrast to health, "health functioning" refers to one's ability to perform certain tasks to remain independent, such as bathing, eating, grooming, and toileting, as well as activities that focus on home management. Preserving health and health functioning are two primary concerns, particularly among older adults, since the ability to maintain an independent lifestyle is influenced by both.

Although age and frailty are not entirely synonymous terms, we know that the longer one lives, the greater the risk for increased vulnerability and its subsequent need for assistance. Nearly 5.2 million persons 65 years of age and over now need assistance in order to remain in the setting of their choice (U.S. Senate Special Committee on Aging, 1988). In general, Blacks, women, and the poor have higher rates of functional disabilities compared to Whites (Taeuber, 1993).

In addition to the distinction between health and health functioning, any discussion of the health of older adults must differentiate between acute and chronic illnesses. This distinction is especially important for older women, who end their years with more chronic ailments than men. Acute illnesses are usually temporary conditions, such as injuries from car accidents and infections. While the incidence of acute illnesses usually decreases with age, they are more debilitating and require more care among older adults than in the case of younger populations. Chronic ailments, on the other hand, are more long term, have no known cure, and more often than not leave the person progressively debilitated. Older adults are more apt to develop chronic than acute ailments and to suffer limitations in their physical functioning from both acute and chronic ailments. The National Center for Health Statistics (1990) has reported that more than 80% of older adults have at least one chronic ailment, and that more than half have at least two. Most commonly diagnosed chronic ailments among those 65 years of age and over are hearing impairments, heart diseases, arthritis, and hypertension (Taeuber, 1993). The health of older adults is more often characterized, then, by more long term illnesses, resulting in serious implications to themselves personally, their families, and for the financing and delivery of health care. We can expect more adults to live to advanced years with functional impairments as a result of chronic diseases as we continue to benefit from medical technology and improved health practices.

The good news is that older adults in general report being healthier than we once stereotyped them to be. Using data from the Census Bureau and other government studies, Taeuber (1993) found that three out of four noninstitutionalized older adults between the ages of 65 and 74 years listed their health as good, very good, or excellent, and that at any one time nearly 95% live in the community, not institutions. Whether such reported good health is a result of improved health practices or is due to policy effects (e.g., the reimbursement trend against institutionalization) is unclear.

OLDER WOMEN'S HEALTH ISSUES

Historically, women have generally been neglected as subjects of large-scale research studies. Thus, far less is known about the health of aging women than aging men. In a 1990 hearing before the Subcommittee on Housing and Consumer Interests of the Select Committee on Aging (1990c), U.S. House of Representatives, House Select Committee on Aging Chair Maky Lloyd noted:

> Poor policies, policies biased against women, and policies that are improperly implemented, cause real life tragedies. Older women consumers of health care and their families pay tremendous physical, emotional, and fiscal costs because we do not have adequately funded research to examine diseases that primarily affect them, and because the research for diseases that affect everyone often utilize only men in clinical trials. (pp. 1–2)

For example, research on certain mental health diseases that tend to affect women more so than men (i.e., bulimia, depression, and panic attacks) have been poorly funded (U.S. House Select Committee on Aging, 1990c). Recent studies, however, have documented sex differences in physical health status among older adults and have begun to focus on gender-specific and gender-related issues such as breast cancer and osteoporosis. Lest we think that women's health is receiving equal consideration, we need only to look at funding levels allocated for AIDS, and by comparison, breast cancer. Although $1.6 billion was provided for AIDS research in 1990, worthwhile in itself, only $19 million was allocated for basic breast cancer research (U.S. House Select Committee on Aging, 1990c).

An interesting paradox in the United States is the gender longevity gap—the fact that women, on average, report more illness and health care utilization and yet live 7 years longer than men. At present, a woman's life expectancy in this country is 79 years; for men it is 72 years. Women who live to age 65 can expect to live an additional 19 years, about 4 years longer than men (U.S. Department of Health and Human Services, 1991). Within these expectancies, race differences abound. Native Americans and Blacks have shorter life expectancies, for example, while Japanese-and Chinese-Americans have longer life expectancies compared to White Americans. Throughout the life cycle, men's death rates are higher than are women's (Taeuber, 1993).

The gender differences in health status, morbidity, and mortality rates have led researchers to investigate possible antecedents, although none have been conclusive (Verbrugge, 1989; Waldron, 1976; Wingard, 1982). Studies suggest that mortality rates for both men and women have continued to decline, attributing such increases in longevity to improvements to medical technology, wider access to medical care, improved public health measures, and the adoption of more positive lifestyle behaviors (Verbrugge, 1989). Although men have made greater gains recently than women have in lengthening their life span (Sempos, Cooper, Kovar, & McMillen, 1988), women continue to live longer, and will make up the majority of the elderly population in the 21st century, with White women living longer than Black and Hispanic women. So, while older women are "individuals who have incorporated a whole constellation of roles, characteristics, and experiences into their self concepts, gender and race [continue to be] . . . master statuses channeling . . . women into certain roles and impinging on their lives at every turn" (J. Freeman, 1996, p. 600).

What mortality rates show us is that older men and women die from the same major problems, even though their death rates differ. In other words, while men and women develop similar chronic diseases with advancing years, men develop their chronic diseases earlier, and they are more life-threatening; women's chronic ailments, on the other hand, are less often fatal and more long term in nature (Taeuber, 1993; Verbrugge, 1984, 1989). Heart disease, cancer, and cerebrovascular disease account for 75% of deaths in older males and females (National Center for Health Statistics, 1990; Verbrugge, 1984). At older ages, however, women's mortality rate for heart disease rises much more swiftly than men's past age 65, and a larger proportion of women than men die from diabetes and atherosclerosis (Verbrugge, 1989). High blood pressure, anemia, and orthopedic, digestive, and urinary problems are also more common among older women (Verbrugge, 1989). Individually and together, these problems impact on one's ability to live independently. The following sections provide more recent data on the health status of aging women.

Heart Disease and Stroke

Cardiovascular diseases (CVD) and specifically coronary heart disease (CHD) are the leading causes of death for those 65 years of age and over (Corti et al., 1995). Commonly referred to as "heart disease," CVD has remained the major cause of death in America for the past 30 years. Heart diseases and cancer have been equally prevalent as causes of death among the aged. Death from heart diseases, however, rise in the later years, and account for more than 44% of deaths that occur among older adults (Taueber, 1993). In sharp contrast to prior knowledge and assumptions, we now know that heart disease also affects women. More women die from heart disease than from breast and other forms of cancer combined (Notelovitz & Tonnessen, 1996). Annually, more than 500,000 women die from cardiovascular diseases. It is also one of the major causes of disability in older women (Corti et al., 1995). Furthermore, more than half of all women over the age of 55 years have high blood pressure, placing them at high risk for stroke. Women over age 65 who have heart attacks are twice as likely to die as their male counterparts (U.S. House Select Committee on Aging, 1991). The typical warning signals for heart attack are shortness of breath and pain from underneath the breastbone, in the neck, and in the arm. Older adults may or may not have such symptoms. Recent research suggests that a symptom of heart attack among older women may be back pain, as opposed to the more expected and thus more easily diagnosed pains in the neck, breastbone, and arm. It is not difficult to see how this lack of information could lead to more cases of undiagnosed heart disease.

In addition to symptom differentiation by gender, certain diseases and conditions of the heart are more prevalent among women. For example, women have been found to have mitral valve prolapse (MVP) eight times as often as men. According to a recent issue of the *Harvard Women's Health Watch* (1996), the mitral valve "is one of several gates within the heart that keep blood flowing on its proper course and regulates the flow of oxygen rich blood between the left atrium and the left ventricle" (p. 4). The condition known as MVP refers to a backwash of blood or mitral regurgitation that, as a result of a valve abnormality, flows backward into the upper chamber rather than away each time the ventricle contracts. While not life-threatening by itself, MVP may lead to heart arrhythmias (disturbances in heart rhythms) and increased risk for stroke and heart failure. Why this condition is more common among women than men is not clear.

Recent studies provide some good news about coronary heart disease (CHD), although not necessarily good news for women. Coronary heart, or artery disease, refers to the buildup of heart plaques on the walls of the coronary arteries which supply oxygen and other nutrients to the heart muscle. There have been declines in death from CHD over the past 30 years, but men appear to have benefitted more than women from such death rate declines (Sempos et al., 1988). Additionally, women appear to do worse than men with less invasive procedures for the treatment of artery-narrowing plaques, such as angioplasty (the use of a miniature balloon attached to a catheter to open clogged arteries). Moreover, greater numbers of women compared to men die while undergoing coronary bypass surgery to restore blood flow to heart muscle (Notelovitz & Tonnessen, 1996).

But there may be some good news for women. Results from two recent surveys indicate that the long term outcome for women undergoing angioplasty may be as good as for men. Data from patients in the National Institute on Health's (NIH) National Heart, Lung and Blood Institute's PTCA registry (people who underwent angioplasty) found that men and women had shorter days of hospitalization and similar long term survival rates (Detre et al., 1995). The second study from the Mayo Clinic also documented similar rates of long term survival for men and women, although men did undergo more coronary artery bypass surgeries thereafter (Bell, Berger, et al., 1995; Bell, Gill, et al., 1995). Still, the lack of research on women has led to a number of theories as to why women may not do as well with certain interventions. Notelovitz and Tonnessen (1996) offer several explanations for why women fare so poorly. They suggest, as reasons, women's "smaller size, their more advanced age, the existence of other illnesses when they are diagnosed with heart disease, or because women receive less than adequate or delayed medical care" (p. 7).

Unfortunately, data that suggest that women's health is improving from such interventions do not point to all women benefitting equally. Black women age 65–74 die from cerebrovascular disease at twice the rate of White women (Manton, Patrick, & Johnson, 1987). Although the majority of older women are not disabled, White women suffer more from chronic illness and debilitating diseases than White men, and Black women have more disability days compared with White women (Fahs, 1993). And, in a recent study of nursing home residents in Texas, a team of researchers found that Mexican American nursing home residents were more functionally disabled than non-Hispanic White residents, a result of more acute and chronic illnesses compared to White residents (Mulrow, Chiodo, &

Gerety, 1996). It has been suggested that a decline in deaths from heart disease would result in the most dramatic increase in the nation's life expectancy.

After age 45, women are more likely to experience elevated blood pressure that can led to stroke. More than half of all women over age 65 have high blood pressure. As the nation's third largest cause of death, high blood pressure follows only heart disease and cancer as a threat to individual health. High blood pressure and blood clots can result in stroke. A stroke occurs when blood to the artery in the brain or neck is decreased or stopped, resulting in serious disability or death. Although stroke is more common among men, more women than men die from it, and it remains the chief cause of disability for both sexes (Notelovitz & Tonnesen, 1996). Disability from stroke may be temporary or permanent, depending on what part of the brain has been damaged. In either case, the need for sustained long term care services becomes critical in maintaining well-being and independence.

Osteoporosis

Osteoporosis is another disease that has serious consequences for women. Characterized by bone loss, it is the result of an interference with the process whereby bone is broken down, or resorbed, or replaced with new bone. With age, bones become thin and porous and can no longer bear the weight of the body. After menopause, the rate of resorption exceeds that of rebuilding, and bone loss occurs. The disease occurs slowly and affects more than 24 million Americans, 90% of whom are elderly women (Gambrell, 1987). Women actually beginning losing bone loss in their mid-30's, but are not aware of it because the disease has no easily recognized symptoms. But, by the age of 65, there is a 35% reduction in their bone mineral content, and a 50% reduction by age 75. This increases the risk of bone fracture, resulting in accidents, hip fractures, fear of falling, and loss of independence. Many hip fractures are associated with postmenopausal osteoporosis, and it has been estimated that up to 35% of these patients die within 6 months from postoperative complications (Gambrell, 1987). The fear of hip fractures is a real concern for women, as one of every six White women will have a hip fracture during her lifetime (Cummings et al., 1995).

Estrogen Replacement Therapy (ERT) has been recommended as a treatment to increase bone density. While possibly protecting some women from osteoporosis, there are increased risks for uterine and breast cancers associated with long term use of estrogen. Hormonal Replacement Therapy

(HRT), or estrogen with progestin, is now recommended by many doctors to reduce these cancer risks. Although the estrogen dose is smaller today than 20 years ago when it was first prescribed, ERT and HRT remain controversial treatments. Both treatments are discussed more fully later in this chapter.

A woman's lack of estrogen may also affect her risk of heart disease. This is because LDL cholesterol rises an average of 25 points after menopause, which contributes, researchers believe, to the increased risk of heart disease among postmenopausal women. The National Institute of Health's (NIH) Women's Health Initiative, the largest clinical and observational research study ever conducted on women, will examine the major causes of death and disability in postmenopausal women: heart disease, colon and breast cancer, and osteoporosis. Currently being studied are interventions to investigate the long term use and risks of HRT; low-fat diets to prevent breast and colon cancers and heart disease; and calcium-Vitamin D supplementation to prevent colon cancer and osteoporosis. Results will not be available for at least another 10 years, however.

Because of uncertainties regarding hormonal therapies, some physicians are now recommending to their menopausal and postmenopausal patients the use of nonpharmaceutical procedures—such as maintaining body weight, limiting caffeine intake, stopping smoking, keeping HDL and LDL cholesterol within the normal range through careful diets or special medications, control of hypertension and diabetes, eating a low-fat diet rich in antioxidants, and participating in regular aerobic exercise like brisk walking (Cummings et al., 1995; *Harvard Women's Health Watch, 1994*).

GENDER HEALTH

In addition to heart disease and osteoporosis, women face numerous sex-specific issues in health as well as changes in their health due to the result of risk factors, class status, genetics, health practices, and age. Among these are problems associated with menopause and incontinence, as well as more serious health problems such as lung, breast, uterine, and cervical cancers and Alzheimer's Disease.

Menopause

Menopause, the cessation of the menses, is a natural phase and major transition in a woman's life cycle. It marks the end of a woman's capacity for childbearing. Contrary to what is often found in the medical literature, menopause is not a disease. During this time, a woman's ovaries stop producing ova, or eggs, resulting in a decrease in estrogen and progesterone levels in the body. The average age for menopause in this country is 50 years, but menopause can occur 10 years earlier or later. Menopausal symptoms and accompanying characteristics typically include physiological changes, psychological conditions, a changing social status, and the combined effects of all these changes. Some women expect to experience discomfort, loss of sexual desire, sexual attractiveness, depression, hot flashes, vaginal changes, and headaches. Others experience few or no symptoms. Some report an increased interest in sex, since birth control is no longer a worry. For those who experience sexual concerns, it is not clear whether such concerns are a result of hormonal deficiencies or of society's expectations about the inappropriateness of sex for older women.

When viewed as a disease, the primary medical response to treating symptoms such as hot flashes has been to replace the "lost" estrogen with Estrogen Replacement Therapy (ERT). Estrogen is now the leading prescriptive medication in the nation. Both ERT and Hormonal Replacement Therapy (HRT) are being promoted as miracle treatments that may prevent heart disease and, as previously discussed, osteoporosis in postmenopausal women. HRT can effectively alleviate many of the short-term uncomfortable symptoms of menopause, such as headaches and hot flashes. Research is now investigating the possible long term benefits of hormone treatment. However, questions persist about the effects and consequences of these treatments due to the lack of data from randomized, controlled trials and the increased risks of breast and endometrial cancers.

Data so far appear contradictory. Results from a population-based investigation using cross-sectional data on nearly 5000 women found that estrogen, with or without progestin, significantly raised the level of high-density lipoprotein, or HDL (the "good" cholesterol) believed to offer protection against heart disease. While sounding promising, it may also increase the risk for endometrial hyperplasia, an overgrowth of cells that indicates a potential precancerous condition (Nabulsi et al., 1993). Progestin was added to prevent endometrial cancer. Whether or not its addition negated the potential protective effect of ERT against heart disease is not at all clear. Data from this study do not determine whether heart disease rates actually decreased or whether breast cancer rates increased from ERT use.

More potentially sobering news was recently reported in the Nurses's Health Study. Data from this study suggest that breast cancer risk increased by 40% in women over ages 50–64 and 70% in women ages 65–69 who were on Hormonal Replacement Therapy. Some good news was that the risk for breast cancer did not increase if HRT was taken for less than

5 years, and excessive risk ceased when treatment stopped (Colditz et al., 1995).

In contrast to the "deficiency model" of menopause to which Hooyman and Kiyak (1993) refer, they see that menopause should be viewed instead as a normal life transition, with normally lower estrogen levels among postmenopausal women. Indeed, in societies such as some in Asia, women rarely report negative symptoms from menopause. Many women have begun using nonmedical approaches to respect their aging and minimize uncomfortable menopausal symptoms. Such approaches include rituals to celebrate one's aging, increased levels of exercise, use of support groups and herbal remedies, and a low-fat diet. Alternatives such as these are especially important for women who can not take hormone therapy— women who have had breast cancer (although some physicians may prescribe hormone treatment if the woman is "cancer-free" for 5 years), severe migraine headaches, a history of thrombophlebitis, and hypertension. The truth for many menopausal and postmenopausal women is that serious decisions are being made about their health with very little data about the consequences to their short-term or long term health.

Women's desire to learn more about their own health and also to make informed decisions has spawned a whole new area for publishers. There are an increasing number of books written about menopause that are very good. Among some of these are: *A Woman's Guide to Menopause* by Dr. Lois Jovanovic with Suzanne Levert (1993), *The Menopause Self-Help Book* by Dr. Susan Lark (1994), and *Natural Menopause* by Susan Perry and Dr. Katherine O'Hanlan (1992).

Lung, Breast, Uterine, and Cervical Cancers

More women die from lung than from other types of cancer, and lung cancer is correlated to cigarette smoking. Women are twice as likely to be not treated for lung cancer than men (Council on Ethical and Judicial Affairs of the AMA, 1990). Breast cancer, another serious health risk for women, remains the most common cancer in women, with its incidence increasing with age. While breast cancer is accountable for more than 32% of all cancers in women (U.S. House Select Committee on Aging, 1991), over one third of breast cancer patients still do not receive appropriate treatment. This is despite recent advances in diagnosis and treatment. A number of etiological factors have been identified in relation to breast cancer, but none are conclusive at this time. Age is one factor, as approximately 80% of women with breast cancer are over the age of 50 (U.S. House Select Committee on Aging, 1991). A recent study found that elderly women account for 44% of all newly diagnosed cases of breast cancer, and 93% of them are diagnosed before the disease has metasticized. Also found was that elderly women with breast cancer sought help with larger tumors, were less likely to have breast surgery, and were less likely to undergo chemotherapy following surgery. In effect, they were treated less aggressively the older they became. This difference in treatment was not attributable to other medical problems caused by advancing age (Hillner et al., 1996; Newschaffer et al., 1996).

There also appear to be differences between pre-and postmenopausal breast cancer victims, with different prognoses and tumor cell characteristics. According to Hooyman and Kiyak (1993), the chances of a woman developing breast cancer have risen from one in sixteen to one in nine just in the past two decades, while information on prevention, diagnosis, and treatment has fallen behind.

This may be changing. According to a report released by the U.S. Department of Health and Human Services (USDHHS *News*, 1995), the death rate for breast cancer declined by 4.7% between 1989 and 1992, which was the largest drop since 1950. However, these figures are misleading, for they ignore women's ethnic differences. When diversities are examined, we see that while rates have dropped by 5.5% for White women, they rose by 2.6% for women of color. Older women of color, due to their economic status and discriminatory services, are often less likely to receive mammograms and to have less access to quality health care.

A recent Medicare policy change has attempted to improve this situation. In January 1, 1991, Medicare began reimbursing for mammogram screenings as a biannual benefit for women over 50 years of age. However, a recent study found that even after this policy change, mammographies were substantially below recommended levels. Economics played into this, with women lacking supplemental health insurance at highest risk for failing to undergo mammograms. Requiring copayments was another obstacle (Blustein, 1995). In another vein, the rates for cervical and uterine cancers have also increased dramatically, and yet women over the age of 60 have been found to be least likely to request annual Pap smears from their physicians (Older Women's League, 1987).

Incontinence

Another potential health concern for women, especially women over the age of 60, is incontinence, or the involuntary loss of urine. While not an inevitable aspect of aging, it remains an embarrassing and socially isolating problem when untreated. The good news is that it can often be controlled and treated with exercise, medication, diet changes, surgery, and even a simple technique such as "crossing one's legs" (*Harvard Women's Health Letter*, February, 1995). Kegel exercises are one form of exercise that involve performing movements to strengthen the pelvic floor muscles (the muscles around the vagina) and can produce positive results in 6 to 12 weeks. If incontinence can not be treated, there are a number of products on the market that can help with its management.

Alzheimer's Disease

It is estimated that 4 million Americans are diagnosed with Alzheimer's Disease, a progressive neurological disease resulting in serious mental impairment and eventual death (Hooyman & Kiyak, 1993). Most prevalent among older persons—especially those over the age of 70 years—it has recently received more attention because former President Ronald Reagan is one of its victims.

Alzheimer's Disease has important gender implications for two reasons. First, a number of studies suggest that the disease is more prevalent among women. Women are more likely to live in a nursing home than men—46% compared to 28%—and Alzheimer's Disease is a major reason why women live in such facilities (Kemper & Murtaugh, 1991). Second, as women are the primary caregivers of the frail, the increasing numbers of elders with this disease pose escalating demands on women for long term custodial care.

WOMEN, DISABILITY, AND HEALTH CARE

After the age of 75, gender differences in patterns of illness and disability become more striking. Disability is a major concern among the aged. As was previously mentioned, a chief cause of disability is heart disease, but there are other causes as well. Soldo and Manton (1985), for example, have estimated that more than half of women over the age of 75 are seriously disabled by heart disease. Other diseases and impairments that can result in varying degrees of disability include stroke, osteoporosis, and arthritis. Some of the major effects of such diseases are decreased ability in mobility, such as walking and climbing stairs (Fried et al., 1994). Other activities affected are the abilities to independently perform toileting, get in and out of bed, eat, dress, and bathe. The resultant increase in dependency has implications for one's overall physical, emotional, and financial health. The greater the dependency, the more likely one may end up in a nursing home or other resident care facility.

Seventy-five percent of nursing home residents are female, the majority of whom depend on Medicaid payment for care. Their dependency is generally a result of three reasons: (1) older men are likely to be married and their wives care for them in their own homes; (2) women older than 75 years have outlived their spouses and have few available resources for home-based care; and (3) women cannot afford private long term care services. In her review of caregiving patterns among older married couples in Australia, Gibson (1996) suggests another reason: that men are often less willing than their wives to provide the hands-on care associated with caregiving when their spouse becomes frail.

While longevity has its benefits, it is also true that the longer one lives, the greater the chance that one will be become frail and need long term care services. Women's involvement in the issues around long term care is not only as consumer. Women should also consider that 90% of paid aides to older adults, regardless of whether the care provided is offered in the home or institution, is provided by women, primarily women of color. And the wage and benefit packages of such employment are rarely able to lift them from poverty or near-poverty status (Minkler & Estes, 1991).

Discussions about health care that neglect the economics of health care and the issue of long term care would be sadly incomplete. Recent figures from the National Center for Health Statistics are nothing but alarming. Personal health expenditures in the United States more than tripled from 1980 to 1993, and now total over $782 billion in 1993. Hospital care expenditures accounted for $327 billion or 42% of the total, while physician services cost $171 billion (22% of the total). Nursing home costs totaled nearly $70 billion, or 9% of the total (National Center for Health Statistics, 1995). In recent data collected by the Roberts Wood Johnson Foundation on costs of chronic disease, direct medical costs for treating such conditions was at $425 billion in 1990, or 61% of the United States' health budget (Ingram, 1996). It is no wonder that paying for health care is a major worry among older adults.

The organization of the present health care system with its emphasis on acute care results in older adults spending 15% of their income on health care costs (U.S. Senate Special Committee on Aging, 1992). Due to their poor economic status, many older women rely on government assistance to pay for their health care. Job interruptions, part-time status, and the concentration of women in cottage industries and small businesses often results in women having no employment-based health care coverage throughout their lives. Those who do have health coverage through a spouse can have this coverage end by divorce or separation or with the death of the spouse. For many mid-life and older women, especially women of color, it is not financially feasible to buy private health insurance, even if they are eligible to purchase it. Many are forced to rely on Medicare and Medicaid.

Medicare and Medicaid: Paying for Health Care

Two entitlement programs that provide health benefits for older Americans are Medicare and Medicaid. Medicare, or Title 18 of the Social Security Act, is a health insurance program that covers those 65 years of age and over, the blind, and those with permanent disabilities. Part A, hospital services, is funded through an employee/employer tax. Part B, physician and outpatient services, is funded by beneficiaries. In addition to Medicare, nearly 75% of persons 65–84 years of age have some supplemental private health care coverage. Due to the high cost of such care, Whites are more apt to buy such coverage.

Medicaid, or Title 19 of the Social Security Act, is a public assistance program which covers health care costs for the financially needy. As a public assistance program, Medicaid requires that prospective beneficiaries prove their low-income status through a "means" test which is usually administered by state public welfare departments. Not a test at all, it is actually a set of eligibility criteria that demands proof of indigency. Sixty percent of Medicaid beneficiaries are low-income women (Davis & Rowland, 1991). Unfortunately, because of the program's income-eligibility requirement, the aged who receive Medicaid are often stigmatized. However, the lack of any affordable funding mechanism to pay for the expense of long term care services, whether in the community or in institutions, results in low-income and middle-class older adults having no recourse but to seek assistance from Medicaid. In part because of this, the federal government has increased its scrutiny of Medicaid. While older adults make up 12% of the nation's population and 13% of all Medicaid beneficiaries, they receive nearly one-third of the total Medicaid budget. This is primarily a result of the high cost of institutional care, that is, primarily nursing home care (National Center for Health Statistics, 1990). Older adults can also receive some in-home support services through the federally funded Older Americans Act, and through Title 20 of the Social Security Act, the latter of which is usually administered by state welfare departments. Both programs have seen decreases in their federal expenditures over the years. It is not expected that funding levels will be able to respond to the escalating care needs of the disabled and the frail.

It has already been noted that family and work histories play a large role in whether or not one even receives Medicaid. Race has also been found to be a significant predictor of Medicaid use. Using data from the National Long Term Care Survey (NLTCS) on the distribution of Medicaid benefits to frail older persons, Madonna Harrington Meyer (1994) found that women, Blacks, and Hispanics had the greatest need for long term care, but had access to the least resources with which they could respond to those needs. Because women tend to be poorer than men, and women of color tend to be poorest of all, every dollar spent on health care represents a greater percentage of their income. While women's health needs differ from men's, it is long term care that is most critically needed by them, but is least funded by any government insurance programs.

In part due to their greater longevity, women have longer periods of chronic health problems than men. The present health care system provides limited reimbursements for chronic care, whether it is provided in acute, nonacute, or home settings. Older women's diseases are less frequently fatal and more frequently chronic than men's. Thus, the kinds of care they most often need are the nonacute services, such as personal care and respite care. It is these types of services that are not covered under Medicare and most health care plans. The end result is that their special needs are not addressed adequately by the health care system.

Health Care Treatment and Research Bias

As if the lack of data, contradictory data findings, and inadequate health insurance were not enough, aging women appear to face prejudicial treatment from the health care system in breast and other types of cancer treatments. In a special address to members of the American Society on Aging at their annual program meeting, author and health analyst Emily Friedman (1996) had this to say:

> We have a health care system that discriminates too much against certain kinds of patients. The older you are the less likely you are to have a Pap smear, and the less likely you are to get a mammogram. This type of discrimination within the health care system is simply unacceptable, and it is very rarely talked about. (p. 1)

Negative physician attitudes present significant barriers to women accessing quality health care. Studies have documented that doctors treating older women take less time with them, give them less complete examinations, and prescribe more drugs than they do for men (Armitage, 1979; Leonard, 1991). For example, women over 80 years of age are two to three times less likely to receive two-step surgery and postmastectomy rehabilitation than are younger women (Hynes, 1994). Dr. Denise Hynes of the MidWest Center for Health Service Research and Policy analyzed data from the National Cancer Institute's Care Community Evaluation on inpatient and outpatient care of 4,000 women across the country with local or regional stage breast cancer. Dr. Hynes found that younger women were more apt to receive two-step treatment compared to older women. Step one is when a biopsy to determine tumor cell type, stage, and status is conducted followed by step two, or surgical removal of the tumor. According to Hynes, these findings suggest an age bias in health care diagnosis and treatment. Moreover, women over 60 are the least likely to have annual Pap smears (Older Women's League, 1987), a serious omission since aging women have high rates of cervical cancers.

The lack of data on women's health should be improved now that Congress has mandated that women and minorities be included in all federally funded research studies and that policies to include women in studies be developed, implemented, and enforced (U.S. House Select Committee on Aging, 1990c). Furthermore, the previously mentioned Women's Health Initiative of the National Institute on Health, funded by Congress in 1991, seeks to address many of women's critical health issues that were ignored in past studies. Using more than 40 sites nationwide, this longitudinal study will examine many of the critical issues facing pre-and postmenopausal women, such as the risks and potential benefits of HRT; the role of diet in breast cancer; and vitamin use in prevention of osteoporosis.

WOMEN'S SOCIAL LIVES

In addition to financial health, caregiving roles, and health status, the social lives of women are shaped and influenced by a lifetime of messages that have serious consequences with each advancing year. Canadian feminist author Leah Cohen, in her book *Small Expectations: Society's Betrayal of Older Women* (1984), describes the problem this way:

> While poverty is a substantial part of the problem, it is by no means the total issue. All women, regardless of their income level or educational attainment, experience aging as a social judgment. Older women lack

the freedom to exercise control over their own lives. As we age, we are progressively infantilized by doctors, gerontologists, drug companies, the media, and volunteers. The power of each of these groups is reinforced by older women's traditional socialized passivity. Often older women find that they have little or no power to define their own goals in life. This realization has a profoundly negative effect on their self-esteem and leads irrevocably to a diminished sense of dignity. (p. 242)

In preparing for her own research on the lives of vibrant older women in their 70's and 80's, Celia Hurwich (1982) found that studies on older women too often characterized their lives by life stages, patterns, expectations, and choices associated with their stereotypical roles in the family—motherhood, caregiver, empty nester, and widowhood. In doing so, such studies have actually reinforced these lifestage stereotypes and have ended up ignoring those women whose lives do not fit well into such classical stages. Older women who are divorced, never married, lesbian, or who have had professional lives are rarely discussed.

To best understand older women's life situations, then, one must expose and dissect the myths that all women have come to accept as true when they become old (which, in conventional language, means anyone past 40 years of age). As social work scholar Ann Weick (1994) articulated so well:

The dynamics of oppression rest on the sands of delusion and myth. To create oppressive human relations, there must be a myth about people's fundamental inadequacy and the corresponding myth that someone else (some individual, some class of people, some institution) has the power to save them. There must also be social processes which insure that the message of inadequacy is reinforced in multiple, daily ways so that the myth itself will not be challenged nor the challengers go unpunished. In this way, the myth persists, even when its basic assumption about human beings is so flagrantly wounding. (p. 220)

The societal messages that aging women receive differ from those given to men—mainly, that the family is their main responsibility and obligation; that with age they become less attractive and less sexual, more so than their male counterparts; and that their overall worth decreases concomitantly with their capabilities. The messages are so ingrained that few consider debating or contradicting them. One message that they are not given is that their years of caring for their children, other's children, and the ill and the aged will have serious ramifications for their financial security in later life. As noted by the late activists and cofounders of the Older Women's League, Tish Sommers and Laurie Shields, authors of

Women Take Care: The Consequences of Caregiving in Today's Society (1987), a woman can expect to spend more years caring for an aging relative than for her own children. While motherhood has many blessings and joys, the responsibilities of caring for the young and the frail are consistently devalued and rarely compensated in the marketplace, whether in salaries or retirement credit via private pensions or Social Security. And, as Sommers (1975) also commented: "Motherhood and apple pie may be sacred, but neither guarantee economic security in old age" (p. 11). It is in large part due to such family responsibilities, together with the lack of responsive policies, that motherhood and caregiving are economically risky behaviors for women. And yet motherhood can be and often is a joyful and satisfying experience, and appears to have some benefits for aging women, as it provides the possibility of being on the receiving end of the caregiving relationship.

THE EMPTY NESTER OR BLOSSOMING WOMAN?

Depression among postmenopausal women has been considered the domain of either the medical community, due to women's physiological changes, or the psychology community, due to mental health status secondary to women's changing roles and relationships. As researchers like Glick and others noted more than 40 years ago, the "empty nest syndrome"—when children leave home to lead their own lives and parents are left pondering what to do with theirs—can be experienced by both men and women (Glick, 1955; Glick & Park, 1965). However, women were felt to be perhaps more susceptible to this life stage, primarily because men died so much younger than their wives. In fact, and for many years, psychologists and gerontologists argued that women's risk for depression rose following the emptying of the nest. Such findings probably made sense at the time to researchers, who were overwhelmingly male. Researchers saw middle-aged women as losing both their sexual appeal and their children at the same time and concluded "What else could there be for women to live for?"

Such research findings began to be disputed with the work of scholars like Bernice Neugarten and her colleagues, who studied women entering into this and other developmental stages. What she and her associates found contradicted the earlier hypotheses—rather, that this time of life is actually associated with somewhat higher levels of life satisfaction (Neugarten, Wood, Kraines, & Loomis, 1968); that old age for aging women is a time of great possibilities and excitement (Neugarten, 1968,

1975); and that women's greatest productivity often came in the later years (Neugarten & Datan, 1974).

Additional recent studies continue to contradict the earlier negative findings and interpretations. The so-called empty nest was found to be, after an initial adjustment period, a time of new freedom and opportunities for many women, and a time of higher satisfaction than previous years (Baruch, Barnette, & Rivers, 1983). Husbands and wives could rediscover their primary relationship. Their marital bond was often strengthened. For others, an empty marriage ended, since it no longer had to be sustained for the "sake of the children." A more positive interpretation regarding women's changing roles is that such changes actually may provide them with the building blocks for dealing with stress and discontinuities (Riley & Riley, 1986, 1989). As Betty Friedan (1993) notes, women's roles continually change over time as opposed to a male trajectory, and may well result in women developing skills and strengths for coping and adapting to loss and change.

An earlier, often-cited longitudinal study that investigated the differences in well-being and health with lifestyle and social-role characteristics is the Maas and Kuypers' Forty to Seventy Study (Maas & Kuyper, 1974). The researchers examined continuity and change in the lives of 142 aging adults (47 males and 95 females) who had participated in the 1920s in two earlier studies: the Berkeley Guidance Study and the Berkeley Growth Study. Researchers identified autonomous women who were "person-oriented" as having better health and less physical disability than women who centered their lives around marriage, children, and home. Work-centered mothers were profiled as the healthiest and most satisfied with life.

The Maas-Kuyper sample was White, educated, and middle class. Hence, their findings may not be necessarily applicable to working-class women employed at two jobs as the sole income earners for their families. Still, a number of researchers predict that future cohorts of women will be better equipped to cope with a changing society and changing roles, as they are developing coping mechanisms from their multiple roles as wife, mother, worker, friend, and caregiver (Riley & Riley, 1986). The ability to develop and sustain relationships and friendships and the role of advocacy in many older women's lives are examples of adaptive strategies and strengths achieved through discontinuities and change.

Celia Hurwich's (1982) work, mentioned earlier, is one of the more interesting and groundbreaking studies on the lives of older women. Dissatisfied with how contemporary research and literature described older women, Hurwich set out to study vital women in their 70s and 80s who contradicted the pervasive negative views of older women as doddering, incompetent, and burdens to themselves, their families, and society at large. Using the in-depth interviews of oral history techniques, she studied 10 older women in her quest to identify factors that have contributed toward their reaching a vital old age. Hurwich believed that, if such factors could be identified, then surely the rest of the aging and future aging population would want to model their own lives around those who have aged successfully.

At the onset of her study, Hurwich thought that older women who were aging successfully would attribute such well-being to a good diet and a steady exercise program. Instead, attitude was the single most important factor for these women's well-being: an optimistic perspective as demonstrated by a sense of aliveness and adaptability to external events and situations. This quality was evident in each of the 10 women she interviewed, even though these women's lives were quite different from each other's. Thus, successful aging appears to be related to one's attitude toward life and life's experiences. In contrast to previous studies, Hurwich found that traditional life-cycle roles neither completely nor adequately described the lives of these women. Even those who were married and who had children did not describe themselves in relation to their husbands or their children. In contrast to a picture of older women as depressed and lonely following the empty nest, Hurwich found 10 older women who were vibrant, contributory, and who were thoroughly enjoying their lives. Nine of the 10 stated that their old years were their best time. All maintained close relationships with people of all ages; each trusted in themselves and in humanity; all had health problems, but were hardly withdrawn from life; and, among those who had enjoyed their roles as mothers, none felt that their children were the most fulfilling or defining part of a woman's life.

Of course, women or men can and do miss their children when they leave home. It would be odd to not do so after having spent 20 or so years together. However, what emerges from the Hurwich study and others is a more balanced and liberating picture of women, their potential for growth across the lifespan, and the advantages and rewards of growing older. What successfully aging women tell us is that they develop their own strategies to cope and to cope well with changing life phases. They are, at once, both empty nesters and blossoming women.

Just how common the empty-nest life stage will be in the near future is itself disputed. At least one sociologist, Peter Uhlenberg (1996), suggests that growing numbers of women may never experience an extended "empty nest" phase of life, due to reasons that include late life marriage and childrearing; societal acceptance of childlessness; and increasing divorce rates. It may well be that role differentiation is becoming more complex that was originally discussed.

WIDOWHOOD AND DIVORCE

A combination of factors results in women spending one-third of their adult lives as single women. One factor is the prevalence of widowhood among older women, and consequently the greater likelihood that they will live alone than their male counterparts. While more than half of those 65 years of age and over are married and live with a spouse in an independent household, 74% of men, compared to only 40% of women, are married (U.S. Bureau of the Census, 1991). In contrast, women over the age of 65 are nearly five times more likely to be widowed than are men of the same age group (AARP, 1996a). Furthermore, widowed men usually don't stay single, but are seven times more likely to remarry than are widows (Longino, Soldo, & Manton, 1990).

Another factor for women is living alone and the growing divorce rates. Divorce rates for older women, while lower than for those younger than 65 (AARP, 1996a), are increasing, generating painful realities. Divorced women earn less and are at greater economic risk than widows. Whereas a widow can receive 100% of her late husband's social security pension, a divorced woman must have been married at least 10 years in order to be eligible for a social security pension based on 50% of her ex-husband's benefit. Interestingly enough, once he dies, the ex-spouse can collect 100% of the husband's pension. Black and Hispanic older women are widowed earlier than their White counterparts, facing the dilemmas and challenges of widowhood sooner.

As discussed in the previous section on economic status, widows are more at risk of poverty than their married counterparts, with subsequent implications for health accessibility and affordability, decent housing, and adequate nutrition. For many such women, their life choices, responsibilities, and the effects of racism and classism leave them financially dependent on a husband or on a low-paying job. Some older women find themselves ill-equipped to be independent adults at a time when they must plan to survive throughout the rest of their later years. Societal expectations that men will be the bread winners has relegated many older women to feeling helpless and unprepared when their husband dies—unable to balance checkbooks, deal with household repairs, and manage their everyday affairs. Ironically, this effect is not as pronounced among many minority and poor older women, who have often been compelled by harsh realities to be financial partners with their husbands, or been the family's financial mainstay throughout their lives.

Earlier studies have noted that widowhood can bring loneliness (Lopata, 1969, 1979) but more contemporary research does not support the "lonely, sad widow" portrayal. A study conducted by the University of Hawai'i found that older widows of various ethnicities were more apt to describe their widowed years as more joyous than were their male counterparts (Browne & Braun, 1995). This is not to say that loneliness is not a problem for widowed women, but it may be that widows rebound more quickly with the help of friends and family than do widowers.

FRIENDS AND LOVERS

Friendships are valued resources, regardless of age. There is increasing documentation of the value of friendship for women throughout the life cycle. The feminist author Germaine Greer, writing in *The Change: Women, Aging, and the Menopause* (1991) states that despite all of the challenges of later life, friendships, along with liberty and spirituality, provide women with some of the peculiar satisfactions of being older. Whether it is friends or family members who offer older women the most comfort and companionship is not clear (Hess & Waring, 1983). Nonetheless, the need for friends appears to increase as women outlive their husbands, as children lead their own lives, as women retire from jobs and lose contact with co-workers, and as friends die. As a group, women may be at greater economic risk, but there is much evidence that they have stronger social supports than do men (Lewittes, 1989; O'Rand, 1983) and that women's later life friendships are characterized by mutual emotional support and caring. Many social service interventions for women have recognized their need for emotional and interpersonal connections with others in the development of support groups, friendly visitor networks, and other programs.

The need for intimacy does not end with age. Many older women, like younger women, find value in having lovers. Betty Friedan, in *The Fountain of Age* (1993), describes the ways in which older adults can reaffirm and review "those life-enriching bonds of intimacy in old age" with not only sexual partners, but with children, parents, and friends. She says:

> We need new social groups if the old ones lock us into stereotypes, or lock us out because of them. We must continually beware of our own tendency to try to repeat—or defend against—ways of loving that sustained or betrayed us in youth, retreating behind self-erected walls of isolation or frantic

public activity to avoid rejection, humiliation, instead of risking, risking, risking the reality of intense, shared, intimate experience. Intimacy in old age, maybe more than in youth, has to involve pain, mistakes, uncertainties. But we are free enough now and strong enough to embrace it all in ways we were afraid to before. . . . The crucial challenge in age (in and beyond marriage) is to continually make the occasions to deepen the touching and shared disclosure that is the true glue of intimacy—with friend, neighbor, or colleague, son or daughter; parent or grandchild; any lover. (p. 290)

Society in general, however, continues to have a difficult time seeing older women as sexual. Paul Newman can be a heartthrob in his 70s and star opposite a forty-something Melanie Griffith, but what about the roles for women in their 70s? With age, older women can have the same needs for companionship and sexual response as younger women can. However, for many heterosexual older women there are decreased opportunities for sexual expression, due to societal messages, myths, and norms about aging women's sexuality. One such norm has allowed, perhaps even encouraged, men to be with younger women, but has not allowed women the same choice. As husbands die or leave, the older woman finds fewer men her age available. This leaves older women with few real options, as there remains a stigma against older women who choose to be with younger men. A number of researchers have described normative sexual changes with age. Interestingly enough, most find that men and women can and do remain sexually active well into old age, and often rate their sex lives as either the same or better than when they were young (Starr & Weiner, 1981). Furthermore, social location and historical time affect a woman's sexuality. Masturbation had great stigma attached to it when the present cohort of older women were younger. Many were raised to believe that intercourse was functional primarily for procreation purposes. An older woman may wonder if she should be sexual, and if so, who is supposed to be an appropriate sexual partner for her.

Not all older women are or were married, have children, or are heterosexual. The literature on these older women is clearly limited. Many lesbians, for example, have had to cope with a lifetime of discrimination and stigma that can affect their well-being. Some studies have found that middle-aged and older lesbians, compared to heterosexual older women, are healthier, more career-conscious, better educated, and closer to families and friends (Braito & Anderson, 1983). Older lesbians, however, do not benefit from policies that continue to define family and marriage in the patriarchal norm. Lesbian couples are less likely to be entitled to economic support, and to have access to each other's health benefits or survivor benefits in either private pensions or Social Security. Furthermore, many of the issues facing older women are the same whether one is lesbian, heterosexual, or never-married—chronic ailments, sex-and-race segregated employment, and the responsibilities as caregivers to family members (Gottleib, 1989). On the other hand, there is some research that suggests that a lifetime of stressors may result in older lesbians adjusting better to the aging process than heterosexuals, due to learned coping strategies developed during their younger years (Friend, 1991; Quam & Whitford, 1992).

PHYSICAL APPEARANCE AND SEXUALITY

One effect of patriarchal society, together with its socialization of females, is that women throughout their lives are defined by their physical appearance and sexuality. In writing about women of age, wisdom, and power, author Barbara Walker (1985) observes:

> In real life also, signs of old womanhood are not supposed to be seen. Women are socially and professionally handicapped by wrinkles and gray hair in a way that men are not. A multi-billion-dollar "beauty" industry exploits women's well-founded fear of looking old. This industry spends megafortunes to advertise elaborately packaged, but mostly useless products, by convincing women that their natural skins are unfit to be seen in public. Every female face must be resurfaced by a staggering variety of colored putties, powders, and pastes. Instead of aging normally through their full life cycle, women are constrained to create an illusion that their growth process stops in the first decade or two of adulthood. There is an enormous gulf between a society like this and earlier patriarchal societies where elder women were founts of wisdom, law, healing skills, and moral leadership. Their wrinkles would have been badges of honor, not shame. (p. 31)

A somewhat similar point of view was expressed by social work scholar Naomi Gottleib (1980), who believed that society's emphasis on youth and beauty has negative implications for women's changing physical appearance and sexuality. Rather than physical changes being viewed as signs of character and distinction, a woman's aging appearance marks the end of her worth as defined by her sexuality and her ability to reproduce. Many women have received privilege and some power from being defined by their beauty in their earlier years, and so it is not surprising that many try desperately to retain such traits that had brought them so much approval and even financial gain. But, while every person should look the way she or he wants, to try to always look younger than one's chronological age is eventually self-defeating. We all grow old. In the *Beauty Myth* (1991), author Naomi Wolf elaborated on this bias against older women when she observed that women's magazines "ignore older women and pretend they don't exist. Magazines try to avoid photographs of older women, and whey they feature celebrities who are over 40, "retouching artists" conspire to "help" beautiful women look more beautiful, i.e., less their age. To airbrush age off a woman's face is to erase [her] identity, power and history" (pp. 82–83).

To find out just how older women are portrayed in the media, researchers from Eastern Illinois University examined the image of middle-aged and older women in magazine advertisements (Bailey, Harrell, & Anderson, 1993). They found that older women were rarely depicted in such magazines as *Good Housekeeping* and *Time*. In contrast, the *Journal of the American Medical Association* (JAMA) published numerous advertisements that showed older women. However, such advertisements—targeted toward selling to those who care for aging women—showed women in a somewhat less positive light than in the other magazines. On a more positive note, the researchers noted that JAMA advertisements on older women depicted them more positively than they had in 1987. Other studies have found similar results. In other words, older women are rarely represented in the media, and when they are, such depictions ignore racial diversity and reinforce negative, fearful images of aging for women (AARP, 1996b; Vasil & Wass, 1993).

The concern to look young with the aid of expensive creams and intrusive and expensive surgeries is obviously more of a concern to those who can afford it. Feminist author Shevy Healey (1986) described her own feelings about the cremes and dyes women use to hide their aging, equating it with footbinding in Ancient China or other methods used to torture women to make them more acceptable to men:

> We can feel horror at what centuries of Chinese women had to endure. Do we feel the same horror at the process which determines that gray hair, wrinkled skin, fleshier bodies are not beautiful, and therefore ought to be disguised, pounded, starved to meet an equally unrealistic (and bizarre) standard set by patriarchy? The desperation with which women work to remove signs of aging attests only to the value they place upon themselves as desirable and worthwhile, in being primarily an object pleasing to men . . . the old have done what all oppressed do; they have internalized the self-hatred embodied in the ageist stereotyping. First, they try to pass, at least in their own minds if not in the minds of others. They separate themselves from the "others," the old people. (p. 60)

In addition to a changing physical appearance, women find that they are no longer viewed as sexual beings, in sharp contrast to their younger years when they were clearly defined and valued for their sexuality. Women, according to Susan Sontag (1972): "become sexually ineligible much earlier than men do. A man, even an ugly man, can remain eligible well into old age. He is an acceptable mate for a young, attractive woman. Women, even good-looking women, become ineligible (except as partners of very old men) at a much younger age. Thus, for most women, aging means a 'humiliating process of gradual sexual disqualification' " (pp. 31, 32). Women are told to hide the signs of their aging, and yet, as Barbara Macdonald (1983) and Cynthia Rich argue, surely a process so well hidden must have power. And while women should refuse to let society define their social lives and worth on such superficial criteria, it is difficult not to become demoralized when one is bombarded by such negative images and messages. As Simone de Beauvoir (1949) has stated, we are both subject and object. At a time in women's lives when they finally begin to become increasingly visible to themselves, they become invisible to others. This battle to ward off the aging process is futile even if one works at it full time. Germaine Greer (1991) adds: "Unless she consents to enter into the expensive time consuming and utterly futile business of denying that she has passed her sell-date time, she has sooner or later to register the fact that she has been junked by consumer culture" (p. 373).

And it is a battle, at least as far as the advertising world is concerned. One has only to look at the language used to sell such lotions and creams: "Buy (such a product)—the first defense against aging!" Another advertisement for Oil of Olay exclaimed: "Aging, I intend to fight it every step of the way!" But lately, we are beginning to see an increased sensitivity to aging (and diversity) among some advertisers and companies marketing beauty products. Advertisements today are more apt to show us middle-aged women who are telling us to enjoy our age, and, after all, what does age have to do with well-being? Such advertising balances health and looking good at any age, and reflects a more positive and accepting view of aging. If advertising is a fact of life, then we at least need more of it to be nonageist and nonsexist.

Research, in fact, provides some contradictory information about how older women are judged by their appearance. Mary Harris' (1994) study of the relationship between age concealment and gender among nearly 300 adults is an example. On one hand, while aging signs were considered unappealing to both men and women, these signs were viewed as especially unappealing to women. The findings gave some support to Sontag's theory of the double standard of aging (1972). Respondents indicated that aging appears to hit women earlier due to societal norms and women's appearance, but, far from just being a matter of vanity, a woman's "attractiveness" had implications for her job security. Subsequently, and perhaps because of the fear of ageism on the job, female study participants did not rate other women negatively who used concealment products. In fact, evidence suggests that these women were trying to protect their jobs, and so age concealment products may well be a pragmatic response to ensure financial security.

But do men and women really view women's aging more negatively than men's? In an earlier study, Dr. Berman and her associates at Florida State University (Berman, O'Nan, & Floyd, 1981) sought to investigate the double standard of aging by social situation. In other words, are middle-aged women judged more or less attractive than men, and do the responses differ by who is asked and in whose company one is asked? This study asked women in private (alone), women in a same-sex group, men in private (i.e., alone), men in a same-sex group, and a mixed-sex group to assess the appearances of pictures of average-looking men and women in their middle years. Two hundred male and female undergraduates were provided pictures and rated them for their emotional appeal.

The results were quite intriguing. While middle-aged men were judged more attractive by both men and women in groups, both male and female participants privately judged middle-aged women as more attractive than middle-aged men. These findings could be interpreted to speak to social conditions and social pressure—that of the expected response of their group, reflecting social denigration of aging women. It is interesting to note that, on an individual level, participants did not judge women's aging as harshly as they did men's.

The idea that women are somehow no longer attractive (notwithstanding the qualities of achievement, caring, warmth, and social skills) may have financial implications for them in two ways. The woman who never planned for the day when she could not trade her worth on her looks finds herself becoming increasingly vulnerable with each year. She may fear that her husband, if she is married, will leave her for the proverbial younger woman. What will happen to her financially? In the job market, regardless of her marital status or sexual orientation, she may find herself neither listened to nor paid better or even comparably to the younger men and women with whom she works. The older lesbian may face discriminatory and ageist practices if she "comes out," and can run the real risk of jeopardizing her financial security. We need to question the paradigm that limits women's sexual options, and we need to rethink the criteria in which people are found to be desirable and contributory by outward appearances that are judged by how one retains a youthful look. As Greer (1991) expounds: "A grown woman should not have to masquerade as a young girl in order to remain in the land of the living" (p. 4).

Women, of course, have numerous social roles. Many of their roles share a number of commonalities—for example, the need for connections with something greater than themselves. Unfortunately, the negative consequences of many of these roles lie in the fact that such roles are usually nonrenumerated—for example, the grandmother, activist, or volunteer. Grandmotherhood is a potentially satisfying role, one that emphasizes love and the reciprocity between the generations. And, yet, as we have discussed, there is increasing evidence that grandmothers are being asked or relegated to care for their grandchildren when their own children can not cope with the financial or emotional responsibilities. They do so with little access to social services and financial assistance (Minkler, Roe, & Price, 1993). Women are also activists in numerous organizations, and volunteer to help in all sectors and settings. But such positions are rarely paid, offer no benefits, and usually provide little privilege, prestige, or power. Although the roles of grandmother and volunteer can be potentially empowering to the women themselves and to others, older women's worth must be recognized and reimbursed and their financial health protected.

ALIVENESS, ADAPTABILITY, CREATIVITY, AND GROWTH

In contrast to the negative images of older women, opposing portrayals describe older women's lives as being characterized by aliveness, adaptability, creativity, and growth. Not surprisingly, most of such writings are authored by aging and older women themselves. Celia Hurwich (1982) presents the lives of older women in her study realistically—with both the challenges and opportunities shaped by many factors, including age. Alice Day's (1991) study of "remarkable survivors"—older women who have aged successfully—describes "success" in this way. Old women stated that they wanted to be content with what they have and to have warm remembrances of earlier times; to be self-reliant and independent in their own homes for as long as possible without having to depend on children or welfare; and to have a dependable spouse. What we also learn from other venues and from authors such as May Sarton, Ruth Harriet Jacobs, women of the Hen Co-op, and others is the indominability of the human spirit in the face of death, their love of life, their commitment to their community, their ability to balance their present experiences, and their desire for self-growth through a variety of different experiences.

CONCLUSIONS

What is observed from the limited, albeit increasing, research on older women's economic, health, and social status presents an interesting paradox. As Turner points out, female superiority in longevity is a mixed blessing (1984). Great diversity exists among women, and yet some common themes emerge. Women live on the average 7 years longer than men, and often end their years with stronger family and social supports. Nonetheless, women come to retirement poorer than men because of a different work history, shaped by the gender and race division of labor that relegates women to unpaid work in the home and poorly paid jobs in the work force. Women also face the subsequent inaccessibility, inequality, and inadequacy of public and private pensions; the social role expectations and choices in caregiving; and the political decisions that have promoted or failed to correct the effects of age, race, and gender discrimination. Whereas women were often neglected in research, more recent work documents their different health patterns and their diverse health, long term care, and social welfare needs. Finally, women experience different societal norms and, while they are perhaps advantaged in their social relations, they live in a society that values their contributions and worth less than those of older men. What we see is the growing number of aging women who are refusing to accept society's negative images of themselves. What we also see from the data in this chapter, then, are numerous commonalities among women in their later years. Nonetheless, there are also multiple determinants that distinguish women from one another—their historical, racial/ethnic, and cultural backgrounds and socioeconomic status—as well as women's varying abilities to provide for their needs and to access their own, their families, and society's resources.

Contemporary Feminist Theories and Aging

Liberal Feminist and Cultural Feminist Theories and Aging

> We have to tell each other the way it really is, growing older, and help each other name the possibilities we hardly recognize or dare to put a name to when we sense them in ourselves.
>
> —Betty Friedan

Feminist literature contains a number of theoretical and methodological themes which are used to study gender. I believe that they hold numerous implications for women as they age. Feminist theories can thus be used as a basis for understanding and critiquing society's views and values on aging, especially how aging impacts upon women. This chapter and the following two draw their ideas from a number of feminist scholars and theorists. I will focus on those themes that move us toward a new epistemology of women and aging.

A number of feminist theorists (Humm, 1992; Marks & de Courtivron, 1980) have referred to feminist theory as "feminisms" because of their multiple orientations and perspectives about women, from their diverse lives and experiences to the varying sociohistorical periods in which they have lived. This chapter will draw from themes most often associated with liberal and cultural feminisms. Chapter 3 examines feminist theories that make women's diversity central in their discussions and postmodernism's contributions to feminist thought. Chapter 4 focuses on radical and socialist feminisms. This discussion of various schools of feminist thought is not used to deny the commonalities that exist among them, nor the disagreements within them. Neither does this discussion seek to negate the contributions of other feminisms not discussed in these pages. After the identification of such themes, subsequent chapters will propose a new vision for transforming gender and social/political realities to benefit women throughout their lives, specifically in later life.

LIBERAL THEORY AND LIBERAL FEMINIST THEORY

Liberal political theory assumes that people can make meaningful life choices regardless of their gender, race, class, sexual orientation, or age. Liberal feminism, based on liberal political theory, has as its primary emphasis attention to individual liberties, autonomy, and equal rights and equal opportunities. It holds the expectation that the state has the will and the power to promote equality and social justice. Liberal thought was developed during the Age of Enlightenment. Most Women's Studies students are quite familiar with a number of the 18th-century theorists and thinkers who followed and were influenced by this so-called age of reason: Mary Wollstonecraft, Sarah Grimké, and later Elizabeth Cady Stanton, Sojourner Truth, Harriet Taylor, and others.

Liberal feminism believes that it is the denial of equality to women and their differential treatment on the basis of sex without regard to race, individual desires, interests, or merits that interferes with women's abilities to participate fully in the economic and social order (Abramowitz, 1992). Consequently, this social treatment of women violates liberalism's guarantee of liberty and justice for all. Among liberal feminists, gender is understood to be a socially constructed phenomenon. The main difference between liberal thought and feminist liberal thought, according to Abramowitz, is that "liberal feminism accepts liberal political theory but argues that its practice excludes women" (p. 21). It believes that men and women hold the same potential for achievement in life and blames women's "difference" or lack of achievement on blocked access to education and well-paid careers. While liberal theorists believe that some inequality is natural in life, it is when it is based on gender that it becomes problematic to liberal feminists. Therefore, many liberal feminists argue that sex should be irrelevant to life's opportunities, except when sex is relevant to a woman's safety or ability to perform a specific task. Liberal feminists also argue that the state, conceptualized as a neutral body, should be the only legitimate force to guarantee women's rights in both the market and the home.

Following this line of thought, liberal feminism advocates for self-determination and freedom of choice. Communal responsibility, while important, often takes a back door to individual freedoms. Liberal feminists recognize that women's work, regardless of the setting, has been and continues to be devalued. Concerned with issues such as equal pay in the public sphere, they often accept the public/private dichotomy. Their strategies usually count on "reasoned arguments and legislative change," relying heavily on the state to either incorporate women into the mainstream or to compensate them for the functions that they provide society

(Abramowitz, 1992). In this sense, they are more reformist than revolutionary. Therefore, the liberal feminist agenda includes laws that prohibit discrimination against women in wages, hiring, and promotions, and promotes laws which allow for full access to social welfare programs. Liberal feminists argue that what they desire is to break down male-defined categories to "expand the possibilities for female life experiences by freeing women from the limitations of the male constructed woman" (Cain, 1993, p. 238).

There are numerous benefits, as well as problems, with feminist liberal thought. It is easy to agree that woman should not—must not—be defined by men or be limited by them. However, other tenets of liberal feminist theory are not so agreeable to many women. For example, the liberal feminist reliance on the state for ensuring women's rights is problematic, in that it assumes the state is not biased against women and that state interventions will not undercut individual freedoms and rights (Abramowitz, 1992). Furthermore, even though the women's rights movement had some of its origins in the antislavery movement (A. Davis, 1981), it has also retained a history of racism within feminism (hooks, 1981, 1984). For the most part, second-wave liberal feminists have not corrected this problem, and have continued to neglect and negate the voices of marginalized women. Consequently, the fact that the social welfare system often replicates the racist, sexist, and homophobic society for which it works is often ignored. More recent legal feminist scholarship is attempting to correct this omission. Nevertheless, the liberal feminist school has added to the empowerment of women in its advocacy efforts toward improved access to better jobs and education for women.

Liberal feminism is most associated with two schools of thought that will be discussed in the following sections: (1) Women and Inequality, or Women as the Marginalized "Other"; and (2) Women as Equal to Men. Also discussed in this chapter is Cultural Feminism, or Women as Different from Men (also referred to as "difference feminism" and "essentialism"). Recent scholarship in cultural feminism conflicts with many of the ideas of traditional feminist liberal theories. The "Women as Equal to Men" camp, for example, deplores an emphasis on difference. This focus on difference at times has resulted in a call for gender separatism as a political strategy among women in order to support women's "culture." Still, while there are points of disagreement among these schools of thought, there is a primary reason for their grouping together in this chapter. As noted by MacKinnon (1989), regardless of whether the argument is for or against women's difference to men, the male standard remains the referent point for both. The debate among these schools continues to be both lively and intense. In this chapter, each of these schools of thought will be discussed regarding their focus on older women, or themes, applicable to women growing older.

WOMEN AND INEQUALITY—WOMEN AS THE MARGINALIZED "OTHER"

Women's inequality to men is a major theme in feminist literature. Simone de Beauvoir, first-wave feminist thinker and existentialist philosopher, wrote of the dual challenge of being a woman and being old in two critically acclaimed books. The first is her provocative essay on women's position in society, *The Second Sex* (1949). No biological determinist, she believed that one is not born a woman but is socialized into becoming one. De Beauvoir was the first to write of woman as the "other," a secondary citizen excluded by men from the center, the mainstream, of power. In contrast to woman as "other," man was "subject," with the result that the distribution of society's resources such as better pay and more prestige are directed to him. In order to legitimize this paradigm, de Beauvoir believed that women's inferiority had to be proved. She recognized that women had difficulty fighting such an inferior status and living authentically because they had no power due to their hidden past and history, no religion of their own, and no solidarity with other women. Furthermore, de Beauvoir believed that women needed to make their rational side stronger. She argued that in order to accomplish this, women must be freed from the tyranny of reproduction.

More contemporary feminist authors have picked up on the theme of women as the "other." In *Sister Outsider* (1984), for example, Audre Lorde extended the idea of the "other" to all marginalized persons in patriarchal society—women, the poor, ethnic and racial populations, gays and lesbians, and the aged.

De Beauvoir has been criticized for her lack of awareness of ethnic and race issues, for being nonpolitical in her orientation, and for her focus on women's self-determination as opposed to materiality—women's economic and moral solidarity. Her later years, however, were more concerned with the need for societal change. At the age of 60, de Beauvoir wrote *The Coming of Age* (1972), wherein she detailed society's mistreatment and devaluation of its elder citizens. Using historical accounts and personal biographies, she exposed the negative treatment of the aged and their own apprehension and dread of growing old. The book was criticized for its focus on the well-educated and the famous rather than the life of the average person. Many gerontologists, especially in the United States, sharply criticized the book for its negative depiction of aging. But, as an existentialist, de Beauvoir was not sentimental about aging and older people, and did not hesitate to describe the frailties of age. She strongly believed that one's personhood, even with increased frailty, was created by one's actions, and that it was through productivity that self-identity developed. De Beauvoir argued that age, like gender, should not be shaped by biology, but by that which people produce in their lives. Indeed, de Beauvoir's definition of successful aging was one of independent productivity that leads to a balanced and fulfilled life. In *The Coming of Age*, she devoted little time to women's issues other than a focus on women's changing physical appearance, and yet she was quite aware that the study of aging in her time neglected women. She criticized researchers for their neglect of old women, noting that: "as a personal experience, old age is as much a woman's concern as a man's—even more so, indeed, since women live longer. But when there is speculation upon the subject, it is considered primarily in terms of men" (1972, p. 89).

According to de Beauvoir, it is difficult for older adults to experience true aging, because it is unrealizable in its present state. Aging has been defined by society, and it is this outsider's point of view that has resulted in old age being unrealizable. She criticized society's limits on older adults. For example, she described forced retirement in this way:

> We are told that retirement is the time of freedom and leisure: poets have sung "the delights of reaching port". These are shameless lies. Society inflicts so wretched a standard of living upon the vast majority of old people that it is almost tautological to say "old and poor": again, most exceedingly poor people are old. Leisure does not open up new possibilities for the retired man; just when he is at last set free from compulsion and restraint, the means of making use of his liberty are taken from him. He is condemned to stagnate in boredom and loneliness, a mere throw-out. (1972, p. 6)

However, far from seeing such rejection as only negative, de Beauvoir sees its opportunity:

> Many old people, rejected by society, find that the rejection works in their favour, since they no longer have to trouble about pleasing. In them we see that indifference to public opinion which Aristotle called "shame-lessness" and which is the beginning of freedom. It means they no longer have to practise hypocrisy. . . . They no longer defined themselves by their social function: They felt themselves to be individuals, with the power to decide upon their conduct not according to accepted ideas but according to their own wishes. (1972, p. 488)

What upsets older adults, according to de Beauvoir, is society's mistreatment of the aged and the finality of death. In examining society's treatment of the aged, little escaped her scathing eye. She shared her thoughts with her readers after watching a television program on old age whereby a hidden camera recorded interviews between old women and social service assistants who were attempting to provide quality care. De Beauvoir observed:

> It was extremely painful to see the old women getting lost among their papers, vainly searching their memories, making desperate attempts at understanding their position. Even more painful was their humility, their crushed, beseeching attitude. The old people have the feeling that they are begging, and many cannot bring themselves to it. (1972, p. 241)

She argued in her later years that feminists and society at large should be more concerned with societal change in its treatment of the aged. To de Beauvoir, society's old-age policies were "scandalous." She exclaims:

> Society cares about the individual only in so far as he is profitable. . . . Once we have understood what the state of the aged really is, we can not satisfy ourselves with calling for a more generous old "age policy", higher pensions, decent housing, and organized leisure. It is the whole system that is at issue and our claim cannot be otherwise than radical—change life itself. (1972, p. 543)

She envisioned a utopian society in which the negative concepts of older age would all but vanish because each individual would participate in communal life and be a contributory citizen—a world where age would not matter. Notwithstanding the criticisms of her work, de Beauvoir brilliantly articulated women's inequality to men, sought social change to promote the well-being of the aged, and extended conceptualizations of sexual hierarchy to include age, seeking both to question and dissolve the tension between young and old.

WOMEN AS EQUAL TO MEN

Liberal feminist thinkers of the second wave advocate for the ending of women's oppression through the gaining of legal, political, and social rights for women within the existing social and political structures. The groundbreaking and earlier works of Betty Friedan in the *Feminine Mystique* (1963) and Zillah Eisenstein's *The Radical Future of Liberal Feminism* (1981), and the more contemporary works of Naomi Wolf (1991,

1994) in particular focus on the social meaning of gender. In the liberal school, women are seen as the same as, or equal to, men. Any differences that exist are due to the social construction of gender that has defined women as inferior; the impact of women's reproductive responsibilities on abilities in production (or vice versa); and barriers to equality.

The earlier writings of Betty Friedan and other liberal feminist writers focus on reform directed at society's meritrocratic structures (education, health, economics, polity) in which rewards are allocated and that have led to gender inequality. A criticism of liberal theory, however, is that it has too often sought common ground at the expense of marginalized women and neglected a critique of patriarchy and capitalism. Other feminists became dissatisfied with liberal feminism's reformist nature. Eisenstein (1981), for example, became disenchanted with liberal legal reform in later years, and advocated instead for more radical changes. She criticized liberal feminist thought for its neglect of patriarchy and sex-gender segregation.

More recently, writers like Naomi Wolf in *Fight Fire with Fire* (1994) extend this liberal, individualistic criticism of society to a criticism of women themselves. Taking an ahistorical stance, Wolf is critical of women who have come, in her view, to adopt the victim role. Victim feminism, according to Wolf, is when a woman seeks power through an ideology of powerlessness. In contrast, she defines "power feminism" as when a woman is tolerant of assertiveness and lays claim to her full participation and rights as a human being. All women need, according to Wolf, is their voices and enough financial backing to change their lives. Hence, women will be taken seriously when they take themselves seriously. Her focus on women's abilities and strengths is a needed and welcome addition to feminist writing.

Older women's voices, too, must be heard. One criticism of Wolf's perspective is that it seems close to "blaming the victim" by ignoring the role of oppression throughout women's lives. It is not just women's careers that can be shut down. Voices can be shut down as well due to experiences early in life from sexism, racism, cohort influences, classism, homophobia, and historical forces that discount one's worth. The sociologist Patricia Hill Collins writes of her experiences with racism, classism, and sexism that nearly left her without a voice as a child:

> I saw nothing wrong with being who I was, but apparently many others did. My world grew larger but I felt I was growing smaller. I tried to disappear into myself in order to deflect the painful daily assaults designed to teach me that being an African American, working class woman made me less than those who were not. And as I felt small, I became quiet and eventually was silenced. (1991, xi)

Wolf's perspective appears to ignore the influences of personal biography and sociopolitical influences so well reflected in Collins' writing. Wolf also neglects the reality of ageism. The older woman who was taught to serve her husband and to do so quietly may find it difficult to act differently or to assert her own desires. People can and do change, and yet it is difficult to do so within a pattern of lifetime learned attitudes and behaviors. Moreover, it is more than the ability to speak that can be lost—more importantly, it is the possibility of a different life. MacKinnon (1987) notes that when one is silenced and powerless, one is "deprived of a life out of which articulation might come" (p. 31). Many older women can not admit to feelings of anger and resentment over their lives because it is considered so inappropriate among certain populations and classes. To criticize older women for not being able to express their anger, no matter how justified, and for having led the life that they have lived ignores the role of history, development, and other forces of the social order that shape behavior and limit opportunity. Ageism can also lead older women to feel devalued, ignored, and patronized.

Even among contemporary so-called liberal feminists, there are a range of opinions regarding ideology, dogma, and political strategy. Camille Paglia, in her scholarly and controversial book *Sexual Personae: Art and Decadence from Nefertiti to Emily Dickinson* (1991) argues that sexual stereotypes have some biological basis in the context of human (gender) relations; that, regardless of what some contemporary feminists argue, women and women are gloriously and naturally different. The reasons that women end up being exploited when their behaviors reflect such sexual stereotypes are not fully discussed.

Another recent and controversial book that offers a different view of feminism is Christina Sommers' *Who Stole Feminism? How Women Have Betrayed Women* (1994). Sommers argues that gender feminists, so-named because of their emphasis on transformative ideas and ideologies, have stolen feminism from the traditional liberal feminists, whom she refers to as "equity feminists." The former, according to Sommers, are found in the leaders of the American women's movement and academia. They believe in a male patriarchal world in which men conspire to keep women down and advocate nothing short of gender war.

In contrast, Sommers advocates for feminism to work within the system to make the changes necessary to improve the lives of women. A self-admitted feminist scholar and philosopher academic who has benefitted from gender-specific laws and policies, she generally ignores the plight of women not like herself—working-class women, women of color, and old women. She further argues that gender feminists have used faulty research methods to tantalize the general public into thinking that women are oppressed. Sommers believes that women have experienced great success, and that women only have to keep fighting within the system to earn more benefits. She criticizes gender feminists for their strategies that have alienated and silenced both women and men. Working women who struggle on minimum wage, women who work in domestic and caregiving jobs, and women of color appear to be of little interest to her. Neither is there any attention given to the extraordinary levels of poverty among older women, and the reasons behind this national disgrace.

In contrast to Sommers, a small but growing number of feminists are beginning to write about aging, perhaps in part because they are experiencing aging themselves. As one author notes, the feminist cry that the "the personal is political" resonates with a stronger timbre the older one becomes (Russell, 1987). Two well-known and well-respected feminist authors who have tackled women's aging have been at the vanguard of second wave feminism—Betty Friedan and Germaine Greer. Feminists and women in general owe a clear debt to Friedan and Greer for their various works on women and society. Both have written impressive books that detail different aspects of women and aging. What I hope to do in the following sections is to expand the discourse on women's possibilities and responsibilities with age through critical readings of two of their most recent books.

In *The Fountain of Age* (1993), Friedan articulately and passionately describes the potential, the possibilities, and the creative realities of aging. Extending themes from de Beauvoir's *The Second Sex*, Friedan too rejects biological determinism and women's inferior status to men, instead advocating for older adults' equality. In other ways, however, Friedan's work is strikingly different from de Beauvoir's *The Coming of Age*. While noting challenges of age, Friedan's focus is one of growth, not decline. Using a mix of personal interviews, research findings, and observations, she examines a number of issues of importance to older women; for example, health care; ageist research studies with faulty methodologies; and the critical importance for women to forge their own self-definitions. Friedan also discusses the common developmental stages of women in their later years—menopause, empty nest, caregiving, divorce, widowhood—all of which are framed as challenges, and not problems, of aging. In Friedan's view, whatever problems exist are actually challenges, adventures, and new ways to think and be—indeed, the adage of crisis and opportunity, or what the late psychologist Erik Erikson (1963, 1982) described as the last stage of psychosocial development, integrity versus despair. With its positive view of aging, especially for women, the book is enjoyable to read. Many gerontologists will end up agreeing with Friedan's themes—to a point. Gerontologists were spending inordinate amounts of time on aging as a problem; Friedan was right to want to offer evidence to reverse the trend.

And yet, on some levels, her perspective is a limited one. The women she interviewed were for the most part educated, and many were famous. The exceptions to this were rare. Many of the women were middle-class, or had been middle-class prior to widowhood or divorce. Yet even these women prospered with age. There was scant mention of working-class women, or women of diverse cultures and backgrounds. Friedan's quest was to look at the successes of aging, but surely examples of successful aging exist among those not White and middle class. Limited attention is spent on any analysis of the interlocking effects of racism and sexism on social policy and the need for changes in societal structures if all women are to gain gender justice. Nonetheless, Friedan's feminist background is valuable in its emphasis on the value of connections and the correlation of aging with generativity, empowerment, and potential. Building on her previous work on the analysis of power and gender, Friedan turns her analysis to one of power and age, and gives needed attention to women and aging within a broader societal perspective.

One of the areas Friedan discusses that clearly should be the concern of women of all ages is the medicalization of the menopause. Friedan intimates that the overriding cause of the medical profession's "menopause mania" is the sheer size of the market, and not a concern for women's health (1993, p. 403). She sharply criticizes the sample and surveillance bias in studies that investigate the benefits of estrogen treatment for postmenopausal women, and looks suspiciously at studies that tell women that its use will lengthen their lives. To Friedan, such attention to the medical aspects of menopause is alarming, for it seems to eradicate the benefits to women of the women's movement that refused to define women by reproductive functions or the lack of them. She instead advocates for a view of menopause as a natural phase of life rather than as a disease. Friedan calls for science to look more holistically at women, and to be more concerned with the personhood of the individual rather than if they or are not menstrual (p. 484). She also turns this feminist analysis on the "right-to-die" movement, asking important questions—whose personhood is important (and to whom), who defines it, and who decides one's right to self-determination?

She is more hopeful about entering a new era in society's treatment of women because of the Women's Health Initiative of the National Institute of Health and its investigation of the long term effects of diet, exercise, and other nonpharmaceutical measures of the health of older women. Friedan notes that Dr. Bernadette Healy, former head of the National Institute of Health (NIH) and its first woman director, had advised medical research to direct its attention to women whose lives have been harmed by the lack of research on their gender. Ironically, for this Healy was accused of making NIH political. However, because politics in the platonic spirit is nothing more than the collective life shaped together by people's deliberations, one can certainly argue that NIH's policy of excluding women has always been political—in its consequences, if not in its intent.

While this is not a focus of this book, Friedan discusses one of the more critical quality-of-life issues for women of all ages—caregiving. She relates that a friend wanted to live his life fully during the last stages of his terminal illness, and was able to do so because his wife quit her job to care for him. Friedan asks a critical question—"Could Joe have had this good death without his wife making her care her career?" (p. 548). It is not clear what happened to this woman after Joe died. What were the financial consequences of her caregiving to her own financial independence, and did she return to work? And Friedan does not emphasize what is needed on the political front to make the necessary changes to support family elder care.

A number of insightful themes are picked up in Friedan's work—notably, the relationships between age and authenticity, generativity, and the need for a new language for age. "Authenticity" is defined as the need for aging women to define themselves in their own words. According to a commonly held White male narrative, the aging woman should be either out of sight, or a servant—primarily, a doting grandmother. In a more positive vein, Friedan asserts that women need to define themselves, and that women-to-women connections and the hearing of lost voices can help to accomplish this end as women reconstruct their stories. She notes the challenge she faced herself in her desire to be authentic when her pursuit of youth blinded her to the possibility of aging. Friedan adds: "Somewhere in my search through unchartered territory, I began to realize that, whether we move or stay, we can and must find or make a new place for ourselves in age" (p. 381). Rather than worrying about this last age of life, the only thing women must do is to make self-defined changes in their own lives to give a life meaning. A challenge, then, is to find clues to a longer and higher-quality life; to make new roles for women (as defined by women); and to move beyond a view of women as victims. Friedan echoes de Beauvoir's view that society has made aging nearly unrealizeable. To counter this, women must break through the barriers of society to see what aging can look like.

Friedan also speaks of the challenge of aging as "generativity," or growth in the later years, based on the desire to pass on to future generations the benefits of one's years. The need and desire for connections—with other people and with life in general—may be a clue in understanding why women do so well with so little. Indeed, there is a growing body of literature that supports the value of friendships and intimacy to women's well-being throughout the life cycle.

In attempting to analyze why women live longer than men, Friedan posits the following from her observations of friends and women she has interviewed:

> In age, what seemed most important to the many vital women I have interviewed, and others studied, was not marriage and children or questions of body and beauty—the traditional female concerns—but "quests" that sometimes intersected with "male" careers but had not developed more deviously, randomly, serendipitously, into self-chosen purpose and structure. What also seemed important were new forms of intimacy—with men, even their own husbands; with other women; with their own grandchildren—across traditional lines of sex and age. (p. 164)

Friedan discusses feminist women and friends who gather in groups for rituals to affirm their age, their uniqueness, and their commitment to compassion and care for those they love, and notes that such rituals to honor aging women are growing in popularity (see Carol Harrison, n.d.; Kathleen Fischer, 1995). Celebrations such as these acknowledge the contributions and strengths of aging women, make their contributions more visible to society, and recognize the need for connection to not only the living, but to our foremothers. Friedan also helps us to see the importance of naming our possibilities. Somewhat similar to words from the French feminist Luce Irigaray (1980, 1981), Friedan argues that we need a new language that honors, not denigrates, aging women. Friedan notes that the terms for older women are hardly complementary—crone; geezer; granny. She suggests we either appropriate such labels, or change them.

One area neglected in this book is the diversity in the lives of aging women. By ignoring such differences, Friedan fails to highlight the higher financial and other risks among women who are marginalized, and the intersection of racism and sexism on women throughout their lives. Friedan rarely focuses on financial security for any group of women. Wealth is not necessarily the only key to sound well-being in later life, but its existence makes well-being more possible. But money doesn't appear to be much of a problem to the women she interviewed, although she does acknowledge women's risk of economic insecurity after divorce and widowhood. Friedan still romanticizes work. A more balanced view would see that work is not always fulfilling, and that for some, the best that can be hoped for is that it pays the bills. She also neglects to address many of the issues that impact on aging, such as emotional losses and increasing dependencies. An alternative view is to integrate these aspects of aging together rather than viewing them as polarities. In truth, aging brings a continuum of feelings and avenues that range from joy and tragedy, to losses and new experiences, and decreasing abilities and creative rebirths.

Another caveat to her work is more political. Friedan sees the need for a new political movement among older adults, but neglects the need for fundamental social and political structural alterations to truly change society's treatment of the aged. While she states that "Since the personal is political, I think part of the answer has to be a political movement that will effect the changes necessary for society to use productively the wisdom and generativity of age," she also says that "Acceptance, however, must first come from ourselves" (p. 621). The best strategy for our vital aging, according to Friedan, is: "to make the changes we need to make in our own lives to give them meaning to the very end. That is the best insurance for our vital aging, and for dying with life" (p. 548).

Among those older adults whom Friedan would describe as vital, most are involved in focusing their energies and wisdom on solving both old and new problems of society. She elaborates on some of the work of Elderhostel, the University of the Third Age started at Cambridge, England, The Institute for Learning in Retirement at Harvard, and the Chautauqua Institute. Age for many can be, as Friedan exclaims, an adventure. And yet any gerontologist would note a caveat here. While this is perhaps neither her sentiment nor her intent, Friedan appears to discount the importance of social status and political change for older women. The majority of older women could neither afford such attendance at these programs and institutes, nor feel comfortable in such surroundings.

Although Friedan can be thanked for giving us another vision of aging, her positive view of aging and of older women may be appropriated in ways she would not support—mainly, by policymakers who see older women as not needing programs to support their economic security as they are already secure. Friedan is gifted in seeking a broader view of aging—one that refuses to see age as only pathology—and one that refuses to see aging women as only victims or burdens. She urges those who study aging as a problem to instead expose the possibilities in the biological and social sciences and in feminist thought. It is in her emphasis on connections to younger women—and women's poverty as a life-cycle issue—that she makes beginning important contributions. Continued work on integrating life's dualisms in the end will forge stronger connections among the generations and make older men and older women more visible and heard.

Germaine Greer's *The Change: Women, Aging, and Menopause* (1991) is another contemporary and thought-provoking book on women and aging. Using historical accounts, biographies, poetry, and her own biting wit and intelligence, Greer discusses aging and women in her own voice. This is not a book for any woman who believes that she must, to quote an Oil of Olay commercial, "fight aging all the way." "Embrace aging" is Greer's message. She believes that the later years are a time to be authentic in a society that has defined woman in an exploitative manner. According to Greer, aging is a time for women to seek serenity, rebirth, spiritual growth, and power. She relates the story of Baroness Blixen, who, while in her 40s and dealing with mental and physical infirmities and longing for her adopted home in Africa, was reborn as the author Isak Dinesen.

We see themes in Greer's work that are part of the template for liberal feminist thought. Aging may be societally influenced and defined, but it is still a personal experience that one must come to terms with via individual freedoms and interpretations. Aging moves women from the active state to a more passive one, a reflective period that can bring great joy. It is in this movement toward self that the aging woman learns the value of authenticity. In order to have a reflective and serene old age, Greer argues that women must let go of an old image defined by others, for it is in this letting go that she will finally discover her lost potency. According to Greer, the aging woman is detached from society, but not disengaged. This disengagement is not defined in the usual dualistic Western way as the opposite of connection. In fact, Greer believes that women's greatest joys in age are liberty, friendship, and spirituality. She describes the power found in old women as emanating from their lack of emotional attachment and wasted energy battling with women's sexual and reproductive destiny. Instead, aging is more of a time of calm and freedom. Greer acknowledges that not all feminists agree with this view that women become more tranquil and peaceful with age (see de Beauvoir, 1972). Rather, any view of older woman as tranquil is, according to de Beauvoir, guilty of the worst gender-role stereotypes and also guilty of devaluing older adults.

Greer argues that women not only become more tranquil with age, but become more free. She believes that aging women can experience freedom for the very first time in their later years. In part, this is because "women are pushed to the margin with each advancing year and in this process begin to realize that everything is not about them, and that is the beginning of freedom" (1991, p. 372).

Similar to de Beauvoir and Friedan, and echoing "difference" feminists like Irigaray, Greer disapproves of the present language used to describe older women and finds such terms—babbling aunts, angry old maids, unstable and comical grandmothers—linguistically disabling. She also notes society's disdain for the physical signs of aging. But Greer sees time wasted in women's attempts to negate such a natural and empowering process. It would be better, she suggests, for women to understand that no matter what magic and expensive creams or lotions are bought and used, they will eventually be tossed out by a youthful consumer culture. For women, according to Greer, there is justice in the end to those willing to embrace aging. One strategy women can use to combat such devaluation and seek freedom, peace, and joy in later life is the practice of solitude and reflective thought. However, she neglects to discuss other possibilities that can also bring great satisfaction, that is, the joy that comes from other involvements, especially among those who see life's injustices and aim to move toward praxis rather than reflection. True to her liberal background, Greer generally ignores the issues of race and class among women. One can not help but wonder, then, if it is easy to experience such a time of calm if one has neither money nor supports. It is questionable if all marginalized people feel so free as they struggle for survival. Can age be a reflective, serene, and freeing time if one lives in a crime-ridden neighborhood because it is all one can afford? If one has aches and pains but can not afford to go to a doctor, or receives inadequate treatment when one does seek help? Is aging truly the "greatest adventure of all"? Although one cannot argue with the nobility of the thought, is this true for all women? Greer briefly acknowledges that working-class women may have a harder time when she says: "Some of the evidence seems to show that women who have been shortchanged by our education system, so that their minds are undeveloped and their imaginations unstimulated, never manage this transition (this new desirable state of invisibility) but remain blind and embittered" (p. 378).

Her comments come close to laying the blame on older women's personal biography, rather than on a social/historical/economic structure that limits women's access to education. Like Friedan, Greer does not address women's poverty per se, other than to note that most women do not have sufficient resources to pour money into denying their age via cosmetic purchases. Here she suggests that, rather than fight the inevitable, women have other resources to turn to that can be sources of great joy, such as spirituality. The increased awareness of mortality, according to Greer, can actually result in one enjoying every moment of life.

Her broader perspective on women's aging leads her to yearn for a new epistemology for women and aging, one that emphasizes connections with the greater good in mind rather than benefitting oneself. In speaking to a new vision, Greer is at her best. She notes:

The lifting up of the heart is a strenuous business and we must work our way into it gradually. This is not a joy that comes from lack of awareness or refusal to contemplate the pain of the world. It comes from the recognition of the bitterness of the struggle, not just for ourselves, but for everyone, and the importance of survival. (p. 377)

Greer's perspective, while not political in a traditional sense, is broad enough to include the terrain of connection as an empowering activity. Greer urges women to explore one aspect of authenticity in greater detail, arguing that they should feel no embarrassment about looking for relationships that do not follow the accepted paradigm (p. 383). Greer states: "The climacteric . . . marks the end of apologizing. The chrysalis of conditioning has once and for all to break and the female woman finally to emerge" (p. 387). She speaks passionately about women finally being free to chose the relationships they want, unencumbered by society's pressures.

Greer provides a clear view of aging as change, growth, spirituality, and as a challenge from within. However, her view is primarily apolitical. In Greer's comments, the main work here for aging women is internal, not structural. The work may be challenging, joyous, and fulfilling. Nevertheless, society is clearly let off the hook. According to Greer, one only has to let go of the negative image society has of the old woman to have a reflective and serene old age. While Greer suggests new conceptualizations of personal empowerment, any discussion of the effects of sexism and racism on public policies and their impact on women's lives throughout their life cycle is left for another book.

CELEBRATING DIFFERENCE: CULTURAL FEMINISM

Cultural feminism is the third school of feminist thought discussed in this chapter. While earlier writings associated cultural feminism with liberalism, in recent years it has taken a more radical approach, believing that women form a separate cultural group with distinct values and practices (Donovan, 1996). One of the major contributions of the second wave of feminism is to celebrate, rather than negate, these gender differences. Historically, feminism has fought against the systematic social stereotyping of sexual difference, generally arguing with Firestone (1970) that gender difference is an elaborate system of male domination. In contrast, cultural feminists, also known as essentialists and difference feminists, honor rather than negate differences between women and men, and among women. The search here is for universal truths among women that are different rather than inferior to those of men. While liberal theories scream for "sameness" with men, essentialism in contrast recognizes difference with men and claims the difference as positive. Essentialism, according to Van Den Bergh (1995), "underpins the bifurcation of gender-associated traits that are at the etiology of assumptions concerning what is masculine, as diametrically opposite (and superior) to what is feminine" (p. xiv). Thus, while essentialism attacks universalism between men and women, it celebrates universalism among women. In other words, essentialists acknowledge the sexualization of gender, but not its hierarchization.

A number of feminist theorists have written about women as different from men in language, psychology, and in the arts (see Cixous, 1976; Gilligan, 1982; Irigaray, 1980, 1981). A well-known theorist who has focused on gender differences in gender identity is Carol Gilligan (1982).

In her thought-provoking work, *In A Different Voice* (1982), Gilligan explores gender differences in morality, and finds that women have a different sense of moral development compared to men. Her study suggests that women have a morality of responsibility and value connections, in contrast to men's morality based on rights and their value of individuality. Women, according to Gilligan, define themselves in terms of their ability to care. Her more recent works aim to study the effect of such differences on the marital relationship and work, and the effects of the social order on young girl's development. According to essentialists, the primary problems faced by women are due to women's values not being affirmed in a male-centered society. Thus, they desire to change the social and political terrain to credit woman's superior moral voice and ability to nurture. This belief has important ramifications for older women, as we will elaborate further in chapter 7.

Essentialists also conceptualize differences in language, women's autonomy, and in the arts. Hélène Cixous and Luce Irigaray are two French feminists who focus on sexual differences in language. Cixous, for example, believes that gender differences in thought are structural. In *The Laugh of the Medusa* (1976), she discusses the importance of women's writing as essential for developing and nurturing authenticity. Women should not accept a domain that is the margin; rather, women should put themselves in the text. Discussing the importance of female connections with other women, Cixous believes that this celebration of difference is what makes women authentic. Detailing the wonder and beauty of women's eroticism, she praises the radical therapies of women's sexuality.

Irigaray, another French feminist theorist, states that women are born authentic, but that it is the social structure evident in the political spheres and the family that imprison women. Like Mary Daly, another feminist author, Irigaray believes that women must self-define. For this task, women must invent a new language that is woman-centered. And Julia Kristeva (1981), in her proactive essay, "Women's Time," questions society's definition of identity based on gender, instead calling for a new "generation or signifying space" that refuses to accept a dualistic conception of being based on whether one is male or female. Her work, while not directly addressing age per se, challenges us to rethink the use of chronological age as a source of meaning and identity.

Kate Millett, Shulamith Firestone, Patricia Cain, and Barbara Macdonald, on the other hand, see women as different from men in their sexuality. These and other authors critique feminist theory for the way that it has universalized the female experience from a heterosexual world view. Noting the lack of lesbian women's issues in feminist legal theory, legal scholar Patricia Cain (1991) discusses the bias of writings most often authored by heterosexual women that have made absent lesbian women's lives. In contrast, Cain suggests we examine the opportunity and education that gay and lesbian women offer heterosexual women in the experience of their reality of nonsubordination (to men). Such an understanding could potentially offer "the lesbian possibility as a solution" to women's second-class status (p. 274).

Another example of criticisms of liberal feminism and cultural feminism is *Look Me in the Eye: Old Women, Aging, and Ageism* (1983) coauthored by Barbara Macdonald with her younger partner Cynthia Rich. The primary voice in the book, however, is Macdonald's. She articulates with controlled passion and anger her experience with growing old in an ageist society, and the enmeshed and complex nature of sexism, racism, heterosexism, and ageism. As an aging woman, her poignant discussions gave a voice to those lesbian women whose difference was negated or ignored by feminists. She turns her critical thoughts toward the women's movement itself:

> I am still angry at the ageism in the women's movement. I am angry at what it does to me and at what it must be doing to many other women of my age. It also makes me distrustful of the movement itself, as it seems to me that such ageism, entrenched in the mind of the women of this second wave, must be some indication of the degree to which we all have internalized male values. (pp. 35–36)

Some of the more vocal criticisms of essentialism have come from the multicultural feminists (A. Davis, 1971, 1981; Trask, 1996) and postmodern feminists (Laws, 1995; Ray, 1996), to be discussed in greater detail in the following chapter. Angela Davis (1971), for example, is critical of any liberal feminist thought whose views are that society historically "offered protection to women," thus ignoring the fact that it was White middle-class women who received such "protection," and any thought whose desire to find commonality among women is always expressed in White women's views. The denial and neglect of Black women's work in both the public and private spheres has denied them their history. Davis says: "[The Black woman] was not sheltered or protected, she would not remain oblivious to the desperate struggle for existence outside the 'home.' She was also there in the fields, alongside with men, to be under the lash from sun up to sun down" (p. 7). Postmodernist feminists also reject this emphasis on women as a group, and criticize essentialism for generalizing and erasing "specificity, particularity, and history" (Caraway, 1991). Nancie Caraway, a feminist political theorist, and paraphrasing feminist scholar Sandra Harding, notes that the problem with the essentialist standpoint strategy "derives from its tendency not to challenge both the modernist intimacies between knowledge and power and the assumption of a single feminist story of reality" (p. 63). According to some postmodern feminists, political struggles are complex, and unity based on gender alone is nearly impossible. Postmodern feminists criticize difference feminists for their quest for universal truths, for in this quest marginalized women are ignored. The focus on difference is also attacked. Catherine MacKinnon, a leading radical feminist legal scholar (1989), argues that difference is the result, not the cause, of women's oppression. She agrees that differences between the genders exist, since "elevating half of the population while denigrating the other could not possibly result in sameness" (p. 224). MacKinnon argues, however, that the problem is not that "differences are not valued, the problem is that they are defined by power . . . whether [these differences are] affirmed or denied" (p. 219).

Many of these criticisms of difference feminism resonate especially for older women. With or without intent, essentialism supports the status quo by reinforcing the use of traditional gender-role stereotypes. In doing so, it deproblematizes the separation of the public and private spheres. For example, its analyses do not look to the relationships between women's work patterns and caregiving. Caregiving, as seen by essentialists, is not a problem if it is in the natural order of things, as opposed to a gender division of labor for women across the lifespan. Cultural feminism fails to understand how this division of labor affects women's quest for equality and does not consider, as did Zillah Eisenstein (1981), that women would start the race at a disadvantage because of such [caregiving] responsibilities.

Thus, cultural feminism fails to see the relationships between issues— caregiving and poor retirement income, caregiving and inconsistent work histories, caregiving and gender and race discrimination at work, and caregiving and domestic labor—and how race and class critically intersect with each of these issues. One result of such thinking is the justification of policies that promote the maintenance of traditional gender-role duties, and the shifting of more of the costs of long term care to the informal sector (women) under the Reagan and Bush years.

Nonetheless, cultural feminism's strength and contribution lies in its documentation of women's history and the influence of gender and power in the shaping and structure of language and thought. Essentialists find value in the study of women apart from men. This theme is especially important in understanding the differences between men and women who reach their later years with dissimilar family, health, social and work histories. According to Gilligan, "women not only reach mid-life with a psychological history different from men's and face at that time a different social reality having different possibilities for love and for work, but they also make a different sense of experience, based on their knowledge of human relationships" (p. 172).

More recently, cultural feminists, similar to radical and multicultural feminists, have adopted a theme more directed to social reform, believing that women's culture and political ethics can help envision a new and better world for all oppressed peoples. Contemporary cultural feminists are also more aware that gender alone does not guarantee women's perspectives and needs will be accurately and fairly represented by women in power as they enter the political arena. Instead, women must "remain faithful" to feminist values and ideas if society is to change to a more caring one (Donovan, 1996).

DIFFERENCE AND COMMON GROUND

This chapter has briefly examined specific examples of contemporary liberal feminist theory and cultural feminism as they relate directly or indirectly to aging women. A number of themes become evident in the works of liberal theorists de Beauvoir, Friedan, Greer, Wolf, and Eisenstein: women's inequality to men; the importance of self-definition; the textured relationships between women and power; the varied and multiple relationships between women's reproductive and productive responsibilities across the life span; the value of connections and intimacy in all its forms; age seen as generativity, rather than decline; and the need for a new language about aging and older women. We also see, however, the continued lack of attention to differences among women, especially those women who are more marginalized than others due to their race, ethnicity, age, or sexual orientation. In the end, liberal feminists generally pay less attention to patriarchy and capitalism, and instead view women's issues as those involving correctable inequalities, not oppression.

Additional themes evident in the writings of cultural feminists can help to guide us toward a new epistemology of women and aging. Similar to the "equality" liberal feminists, essentialists emphasize the value of connections, see the need for a new language by women to describe women, and hold a view of women as primarily a homogeneous group. How they contrast with traditional liberal feminists is in their celebration, rather than negation, of gender differences. Essentialism helps to establish a base for women's voices, and yet rarely questions gender stereotypes or age issues and consistently neglects marginalized women's needs and lives. Both liberal and cultural feminist theories have been criticized among multicultural, postmodern, and other feminists for being individualistic and ethnocentric, especially in their focus on White middle-class women (Caraway, 1991; hooks, 1981; Lewis & Butler, 1972; Trask, 1993). By ignoring women of color, aging women, and other marginalized women, they neglect diverse ways of knowing and can not hope to uncover marginalized truths. Perhaps because of this, many liberal and "equity" feminist theorists do not challenge the creation of knowledge as a form of male power, and so rarely deconstruct it. Consciousness-raising in the 1970s may have been one strategy aimed at helping women speak to their oppression, but it rarely understood that knowledge must be deconstructed, nor did it always end with political activism.

The liberal feminist emphasis on individualistic approaches and its reliance on the state to correct inequalities is also problematic, because it ignores the patriarchal nature of society. Furthermore, increasing access to work opportunities without acknowledging the intersection of racism, classism, and sexism neglects the deleterious effects of a lifetime of discriminatory practices on poor women and women of color. For example, the previous chapter outlined how the work patterns of Black women most resemble those of White men (Abramowitz, 1992), and yet they remain the poorest of the poor in later life—a direct result of low wages, not unemployment (AARP, 1992; Dressel, 1988).

CONCLUSIONS

As MacKinnon (1987) notes, feminism is not liberalism applied to women, since feminism is less concerned about gender sameness than about gender hierarchy and power. However, most women agree that improving access to education, work opportunities, and career advancement is essential in enabling younger women to plan their retirement years more independently and wisely than many of the present cohort of older women had the opportunity to do. But liberal feminism's focus on the state as a corrective remains problematic, and cultural feminism's homogenization and normalization of women's "cultural traits" leaves women in prime positions to be exploited. Nonetheless, the acknowledgment of a "culture" of women holds out the potential for aging older women to live their lives authentically and distinct from a male-defined experience.

Multicultural and Postmodern Feminist Theories and Aging

> To look for the place of gender in everything [should not] reduce everything to gender.
>
> —Catherine MacKinnon

Historically, feminists have called for the rejection of binary thinking—the separation of the world into dichotomous and hierarchical terms. Nonetheless, the conceptualization of difference remained a binary one, male/female. This focus on gender in binary terms, and its subsequent lack of attention to history, race, ethnicity, culture, and class resulted in oppositional and zero-sum relationships. Multicultural and postmodern feminists seek to sharpen feminist analysis to include the multiple layers of difference and specificity among women. This chapter explores feminist theories that extend the analysis of gender and power to issues that potentially divide and connect women to one another: those of race and ethnicity. A number of feminists have illustrated what is problematic when race is separated from gender (A. Davis, 1981, 1990; Dressel, 1988; Gutierrez, 1990; Harris, 1991; Morris, 1993) and when multiple differences are not examined (hooks, 1981, 1984; Lorde, 1984). As we will see, however, age continues to be a neglected variable, with the literature on older women of color nearly nonexistent (Mokuau & Browne, 1994; Ozawa, 1995). This chapter also seeks to pull out those themes most often voiced in multicultural and postmodern feminist theories that have the potential for adding to a new discourse on women and aging.

STANDPOINT THEORIES

In the 1970s feminists began to address the issues of racism and racism in feminism. These writings were simultaneously exciting, painful, and long overdue, and helped White feminists to recognize racism, like sexism, as a site of injustice, domination, and resistance. Feminists brought to the analysis of racism a critical understanding of how race, gender, and other oppressions interact with one another. In their examination of diversity, some began to question the underlying themes and utility around the quest for gender unity. Subsequently, a growing number of feminists concluded that the shattering of theories that homogenize women held out the best future for feminism to be both inclusive and accountable.

An increasing awareness of difference and diversity brought forth renewed interest in the Marxian idea of standpoints. According to Swigonski (1994), a standpoint is a position in society "involving a level of awareness about an individual's social location, from which certain features of reality come into prominence and from which others are obscured" (p. 390). People view the world from the place in which they are situated socioculturally (Van Den Bergh, 1995). Therefore, reality, like gender, is a social and political construction (L. V. Davis, 1994b; Hess, 1990). In America, that reality has been historically shaped by European male narratives, resulting in the dominant American vision of reality as White and male-centered. Standpoint feminists, in contrast, believe that all realities and grand narratives are grounded by one's place in society. Consequently, standpoint feminists understand that not all women are alike, nor do they share the same life experiences and struggles. Feminist scholar and author bell hooks (1984), for one, believes that struggle and marginality has provided Black women with a special vantage point and that it is this world view, so different from the world view of those with privilege, that assists Black women to "criticize the dominant racist, classist, sexist hegemony as well as to envision and create a counter hegemony" (p. 15). Swigonski (1994) adds that standpoint theory begins with the idea that the less powerful members of society experience a different reality as a result of their oppression. One result of living "on the margin" is the ability to see both perspectives and world views—that of the dominant society, and their own.

There is a political nature to standpoints. As articulated by Patricia Hill Collins (1991), there is a relationship between the standpoint of any oppressed group to its paths of resistance against such acts of oppressors. This is why standpoints, as Collins suggests, are suppressed, and why thought is related to action. One becomes empowered when exposed to a history of resistance to oppression and historical accounts of resistance and pride. Likewise, the silencing of history robs one of pride and leaves one disconnected to self and others.

Although multiple versions of reality exist, it is the vision of reality held by those in power that becomes legitimized and acted out in theory, law, practice, and policy. The effect of one group's being able to conceptualize reality is that people forget this is just a story or narrative constructed by those in power (L. V. Davis, 1994b). Women and members of other marginalized groups are often marked as flawed, with their deficiencies then used to justify their being barred from power. To counter this, multicultural and postmodern feminists stress the importance of hearing the situated voices—and silences—in all women's stories. The task for women, then, is to actively participate in conceptualizing reality from the lives they live. As such, multicultural and postmodern feminist thinkers have borrowed the use of standpoints from the analytic work of Marxist theory to focus on issues of diversity. In recognizing women's marginalization, these perspectives also understand that not all women are marginalized in the same way. While these schools share some common ground, this chapter will discuss multicultural and postmodern feminisms in terms of their specificity and their questioning of universal truths.

MULTICULTURAL FEMINISM

Some of the more exciting work in feminist theory today can be heard in the voices of feminist women of color, identified by some as "multicultural" or diversity feminists (Caraway, 1991; Humm, 1992). The name is somewhat problematic in its simplicity, as race itself is not the only defining character of a woman. Clearly, there are Black feminists who are Marxist, as there are multicultural feminists who define themselves as liberal feminists. Some, like Susan Stanford Friedman (1995), are critical of the term "multicultural," arguing that it "operates as a code signifying non-White races and ethnicity thus covertly reinstating the White/other binary" (p. 22). Nonetheless, the term will be used in this book for want of a better one.

Multicultural feminism has been described as theory that makes race and ethnic difference among women central to the analysis of women's oppression. A "theory in the making" (hooks, 1984), it advocates for the value of specificity and the importance of women's history as a first step in ending oppression for women of color (Caraway, 1991). It is political in its nature by seeking coalitions, rather than unity, for specific purposes and for real problems. Multicultural or diversity feminism endorses a politics that envisions and celebrates women's diversity and specificity while also teaching the lesson that "fragmented agents which don't congeal into wholes at certain strategic barricades likely will get vaporized" (p. 4). It offers a potentially important implication for older women, as the most financially at-risk population among older women are Blacks, Hispanics, and Pacific Islanders, especially those who are unmarried. It is this poor and frail female elderly population that relies most, according to social work professor Martha Ozawa (1993), on public assistance and Social Security, and who will be most hurt by cuts in social welfare.

Not all women of color are feminists. One of the difficulties for women of color has been the belief that one must choose either racism or feminism as one's overriding focus. In *Having Our Say: The Delany Sisters' First 100 Years* (1993), Bessie Delany describes her support of the civil rights movement, and her dilemma in choosing between it and the women's movement:

> I would have given life or limb to the cause. I wanted justice for my people, or at least a better life, a better shake! Sometimes colored women were not welcome in the movement, though. You got the message that some of the colored men thought the colored women should not be involved. Too bad, I was there whether they liked it or not. You couldn't keep me at home . . . I was torn between two issues—colored and womens' rights. But it seemed to me that no matter how much I had to put up with as a woman, the bigger problem was being colored. People looked at me and the first thing they saw was Negro, not woman. So racial equality, as a cause, won in my heart. . . . But one of the happiest days of my life was back in 1990, when women got the right to vote. (p. 202)

Haunani Kay Trask (1993), Hawaiian Sovereignty Movement activist and scholar, argues that White feminists, liberals, and Marxists share the same problem:

> Few members of these groups are willing to question their presence on our lands, or to learn our history, especially the periods that involve the illegal and immoral action of the American government. . . . Armed with their ignorance, Marxists see class, not culture; white feminists see women, not people; and liberals see only individuals and individualism. (p. 273)

It is White feminist ignorance, according to Trask, that leads them to not understand the "causal connection between our life conditions and our status as colonized people" (p. 266). Bell hooks (1984) also adds to this discussion, an important one, with her discussion of racism within the feminist movement—another barrier to solidarity among women. One potential strategy for a more inclusive feminism is for all feminists to read, integrate and cite the writings and words of women of color in feminist theory. While such work is necessary and desirable, such strategies will not make racism in feminist theory invisible, nor is this the only strategy available. Political action is another; so is friendship.

By countering the hegemony of White feminist theory, multicultural feminism exposes the flawed ideology of liberalism, with its emphasis on equality and the homogenization of women into a White middle-class model. For example, the examination of White, Black, and Hispanic women's economic status illuminates the problems of homogenization, with its real implications for older women. The favored condition of White women compared to women of color is inarguable upon analysis of older women's occupation, incidence of poverty, employment rates, and earnings history. Unlike most White middle-class older women, ethnic minority women and working-class women most often performed in both the home and in the marketplace. As Angela Davis (1981) writes:

> While [Black women] have seldom been "just housewives," they have always done their housework. They have carried the double burden of wage labor and housework, a double burden which always demands that Black women possess the persevering power of Sisyphus. . . . Like their men, Black women have worked until they could work no more. (p. 231)

The link between labor inequalities, life experience, and economic well-being in later life has been well documented (Hill & Tigges, 1995; Ozawa, 1995). As a result of these historical and economic influences and gender-role assignments, most White women in the present cohort of older women receive their retirement income as a dependent, usually attached to that of a White man. Consequently, because Whites have more power than people of color, White women usually receive a higher retirement income compared to minority women. Social Security, while never intended to guarantee older adults an adequate minimum income, does little to promote the economic well-being of lower- and middle-class older women and men. Therefore, it can be argued that the current Social Security system, by ignoring racial and gender inequalities in the labor market, has limitations in providing adequately for women, especially Black and Hispanic women (Meyer, 1990).

BLACK FEMINISM: A THEORY IN THE MAKING

According to P. H. Collins (1991), "Black feminist thought encompasses theoretical interpretations of Black women's reality by those who live it" (p. 22). A rich body of literature has emerged from Black feminists such as Collins, Angela Davis, Patricia Williams, Audre Lorde, bell hooks, Kimberlee Crenshaw, Paula Giddings, Angela Harris, and others. One of the more prolific and exemplary writers in this genre is bell hooks. Hooks writes movingly and eloquently of her experience as a Black woman in a dominant White society. She uses historical, cultural, and political analyses that focus on her relationships with other women and with men, and of the structural roots of all oppressions. Hooks also speaks to issues of racism in feminist theory (1981, 1984). She argues that it is the "individual opportunism in feminist theory that has undermined appeals for collective struggle" (1984, p. 7), making liberal theory an ideology for the bourgeois. Despite individual accomplishments, does a woman or a Black woman ever escape sexism or racism, or the experience of both? As Audre Lorde (1984) once asked, "What woman is so enamored of her own oppression that she cannot see her heel print upon another woman's face"? (p. 23).

According to hooks (1984), it is the privilege of most White women—so often not acknowledged by White feminists themselves—that results in feminist theory lacking wholeness, and leaves it unable to analyze the lives of women different from White feminists. Hooks admits that it may be easier to focus on gender when one has not experienced race oppression. In the Preface to her book, *Feminist Theory: From Margin to Center* (1984), hooks refers to Black women as living on the margin, "part of the whole" but "outside of the main body." Because minorities understand the margin and the center, it is this outsider/insider perspective that Black women have to share with other feminists in the "making of feminist theory" (p. 15). Hooks sharply criticizes feminist theory for not being grounded in history and politics, and yet frames this criticism in her desire to make feminist theory more accountable and inclusive. Black women have a critical role to play in the making of feminist theory, in part because much of feminist theory has suppressed differences by race and class. Nonetheless, hooks believes that sexist oppression is of primary importance, not because it is the basis of all other oppressions, but because it is the practice of domination most people experience, either as exploiter or exploited. Thus, challenging sexism is critical in the struggle to end all oppressions.

In contrast to a unitary theory on women, multicultural feminists emphasize particularity and specificity. They also offer a creative methodology, one that, similar to that espoused by the French feminists, notes the importance of language in controlling epistemology. Lorde (1984), for example, cautioned that the masculinist empirical model, which she describes as the "master's tools," can never be used successfully to end the oppression of women (p. 112). Moreover, multicultural feminism adopts a number of genres: oral histories, poetry, artistic symbols from culture, and autobiographies (P. H. Collins, 1989; hooks, 1984; Lorde, 1984). This new methodology encourages feminists to study gender, race, sexuality, and age in a way that can create connection from the tension (Lorde, 1984) by taking away the threat if one does not fit (Anzaldua, 1981).

Similar to Lorde and hooks, Patricia Hill Collins (1991) sees feminist theory as racist, but also discusses its relevance to Black women. She gives a voice to Black women's history and documents society's continued devaluation of Black women. She voices a number of core themes in her writing: the interdependence of experience and consciousness (the interaction of what one does and how one thinks); consciousness and the struggle for a self-defined standpoint (the struggle for an Afrocentric world view and a feminist sensibility); and the interdependence of thought and action (changes in thinking that may stimulate changes in behavior, and vice versa) (pp. 24–33). Black feminist theory, then, is about real people living in real-world situations.

A number of themes have emerged from the writings of these and other Black feminists: issues of male power and violence; the importance of the cultural history of African Americans; the relationship between thought and action; the critical importance of self-definition; the many layers of being a Black female; the acceptance that differences are always relational, rather than inherent; the need for feminism to be more inclusive; the tensions between alliances based on gender and race; the need for coalition-building; the understanding that wholeness and commonality are acts of will and creativity instead of passive discovery; and the recognition of strengths from women's struggles (P. H. Collins, 1989, 1991; A. Harris, 1991; hooks, 1981; Reagon, 1983; Smith, 1983; P. Williams, 1988). For such themes to emerge, Black women's voices and silences must be heard. The process, according to P. H. Collins (1989), is one of "rearticulating a preexisting black women's standpoint and recentering the language of existing academic discourse to accommodate these knowledge claims" (p. 747). While it seeks a more inclusive feminism, themes on Black aging women remain, for the most part, unarticulated.

THE MANY VOICES OF WOMEN OF COLOR

Multicultural feminists speak from many tongues and perspectives. Feminist theory, and especially the writings from multicultural feminists, acknowledges that the experiences of women have been suppressed. This has led to the use of alternate sites of knowledge—in music, the arts, and in the poems, short stories, narratives, critical essays, and memoirs of literature. By recognizing women as sources of knowledge, multicultural feminist theory articulates, authenticates, and validates women's knowledge.

In the past 20 years, a number of anthologies have been published that give voice to our community's history in all of its shades. These books detail cultural, social, and political conflicts, hopes for freedom, and strategies for nurturance, resistance, and struggle among women of color. In one of the earlier and most cited works by women of color, *This Bridge Called My Back: Writings by Radical Women of Color* (1983), its editors Cherríe Moraga and Gloria Anzaldua, together with their contributors, sought new horizons for women of color while emphasizing their heritage, their struggles with dominant society, and with each other. They discuss a theory in the flesh as one strategy whereby women can understand and frame issues surrounding feminists of many colors:

> A theory in the flesh means one where the physical realities of our lives—our skin color, the land or concrete we grew up on, our sexual longings—all fuse to create a politic born out of necessity. Here, we attempt to bridge the contradictions in our experience: We are the colored in a White feminist movement. We are the feminists among the people of our culture. We are often the lesbians among the straight. We do this bridging by naming ourselves and by telling our stories in our own words. (p. 23)

Aging is not a focus of this book, although Moraga, in the Foreword to the second edition, acknowledged that age will affect ideas as "We are all getting older, as is our movement." Instead, the book highlights the contributions of women of color to the birth of a more inclusive feminism: a focus on relationships between women, often with their mothers; and the multiple and complex differences that exist among women of color who have unique histories and perceptions about their lives.

Another strong contribution by women of color is *Making Waves: An Anthology of Writings by and About Asian American Women* edited by Asian Women United of California (1989). This anthology is authored by women and men who trace their roots to Asia and South Asia. Like the other anthologies discussed here, this book uses multiple methodologies as it seeks to give Asian women a site for their voices. One of the authors, Mitsuye Yamada, seeks her own authenticity by listening to the stories of her mother's life: "I . . . have come to know who I am through under-standing the nature of my mother's experience" (p. 74). These authors also seek to define themselves and their histories in their own words as opposed to an "identity [that is] built on the lore of the dominant commu-nity and not by their own history and stories" (Mazumdar, 1989).

Another more recent and yet just as exciting a contribution is *Our Feet Walk the Sky: Women of the South Asian Diaspora* (1993). This book is edited by the Women of South Asian Descent Collective, students from

Berkeley who are South Asian and South Asian immigrant women from Nepal, India, and other South Asian countries who now reside in North America. As in other anthologies, the writings appear in numerous forms, including poetry, critical essays, oral histories, film reviews, and short stories. Each of these creative contributions describe these women's social location within their community, with the wider interethnic community, and with dominant society. Contributions reflect the sociohistorical, cultural, and cohort influences on the lives of the authors. Among them are the desire to safeguard and record women's genuine traditions passed down through their mothers and their grandmothers; the need to record conflicts with parents and the educational system; and the willingness to share some of their problems and challenges over issues of acculturation, diaspora, and new affiliations. These issues suggest a reason as to why the contributors' own aging experiences are missing from the text. Instead of age, the authors emphasize the critical importance of race in their self-definitions.

Their thoughts about their mothers and grandmothers are beautifully told in poignant poems and short stories. Amita Vasudeva's "To My Grandmother" is a wonderful example. Vasudeva speaks of her connection with her grandmother and the meaning of her grandmother's death. She speaks: "I long to know how you think/I long to exchange ideas with you" (p. 64), as she sadly realizes the depth of her loss and separation. An attempt to bridge the gap between generations is found in the poetry of mother and daughter Sushila and Sumeeta Gawande. Another interesting intergenerational contribution is the article by a mother-daughter feminist-activist duo, Sayantani and Shamita Dasgupta, "Journeys: Reclaiming South Asian Feminism" which critiques White feminism while delineating the process, content, and methodology of diasporic feminists. The authors share their empowered thoughts and their journey toward political activism.

Like a number of Black feminists, many of the South Asian authors criticize feminist theory for its homogenization of women and its neglect of race and class issues, and offer their own interpretations as to why feminism has so often excluded women of color. Inderpal Grewal (1993) reprimands feminist theory's focus on upper- and middle-class issues and its definition of difference as one "reduced to curry, one than is consumed by the dominant classes" (p. 233). The problem with liberal and multicultural feminism is in its monolothic representations of women. Sayantani Dasgupta sees many lost opportunities of feminism, laments on raising a feminist daughter as an immigrant, and is critical of feminism that stereotypes South Asian women as passive. The importance of connecting to other ethnic women is stressed, especially those women who also occupy a place between and among cultures. By speaking in their own voices they refuse to not be heard—and their voices are theirs alone.

One of the more interesting anthologies recently published is *Food for our Grandmothers: Writings by Arab American and Arab Canadian Feminists* edited by Joanna Kadi (1994). This is an important contribution in part because it is written by women of different generations and classes. The authors, using articles, poems, and stories, talk about their struggle to find a name not defined by others, and the gifts from their grandmothers, great-aunts, and other important women in their lives whose contributions to family and country are often not mentioned. L. J. Mahoul (1994) writes touchingly about the lost voice of her grandmother. She speaks:

> Not too long ago, though, I glimpsed the other side of the coin: the silence regarding my grandmother's life. Why do we know so little about her life or even what she thought about her memorable experience—especially those from her childhood and early adult years? The silence does not reflect lack of interest, but lack of an appreciation of history and a preoccupation with current events in the family. . . . Much of the silence must no doubt be attributed to the fear of confronting the past and challenging comfortable myths about our histories. (p. 29)

One group rarely spoken or written about are Pacific Islander women, whose home or ancestors come from the Pacific Islands—Hawaiians, Chamorros, Samoans, Tahitians, Tongans, and Fijiians. A few Hawaiian scholars have written about feminism (Chai & DeCambra, 1989; Trask, 1993, 1996) and its potential as well as its problems for Hawaiian women. In speaking of feminist thought, Hawaiian scholar Noreen Mokuau sees the need for connection, one that is directed toward a greater source. She explains in this way:

> Central to my cosmographic perspective is the belief that my identify is linked to my ancestral past. Ancestors of Hawaiian, Chinese, Japanese, German, English, and Scottish descent continue to influence, through genetics and spiritual power, my evolution as a woman. With a constancy of her spiritual presence, great-great-grandmother Nana Harbottle, a woman who died before I was born, inspires a reverence in me of the natural world, and a strength within me to seek a balance in life. (Mokuau, August 15, 1996)

Finally, Beth Brant's edited work *A Gathering of Spirit: A Collection of North American Indian Women* (1988), is another powerful contribution to multicultural feminism. Its authors, Native American woman whose ages range from 25 to 65, also use creative methodologies, but unlike other books, *A Gathering* discusses the pride and heartache of being a colonized people. Again, aging is not a critical issue as a process. And yet, as in the case of the other anthologies, the richness in these women's words are evident in their poems and stories that detail their connections with their mothers, grandmothers, and elder women of their tribe. The writings are intelligent, tragic, and inspiring. Older women are viewed as not only their link to their past, but as repositories of spirituality and wisdom. Marilou Awiakta (1988) speaks of the advice and words of solace given to her by the grandmother:

> Putting my arms around the Grandmother, I lay my head on her shoulder. Through touch we exchange sorrow, despair that anything really changes. I'm ashamed that I've shown so little courage. She is sympathetic. But from the pressure of her arms I also feel the stern, beautiful power that flows from all the Grandmothers, as it flows from the mountains themselves. It says: Dry your tears. Get up. Do for yourself or do without. Work for the day to come. Be joyful. (p. 127)

Or perhaps this beautiful poem about missing one's link to a past through a grandmother: "I'm Making You Up" by Chrystos:

> Grandma we all need   partially deaf & busy with weaving   listens
>   through a thick blanket of years & sore feet
>   nods
> I cry about everything they did to me how horrible & can't
>   stand another while brown wrinkled you smile at me like sun coming up
> I stand next to you, pass wool absently you lay aside the wrong colors
>   without comment
>   I'm simply
>   Grandchild
>   babbling your sympathy warm & comforting as dust
> I sit in your lap your loom pushed aside
>   you feed me fry bread with too much maple syrup
> I pull your braids you cradle me deeper in your legs
>   folder to make a basket for me
> Grandma who died long before I was born
>   Come back
>   Come back (p. 153)[1]

A number of themes are articulated in these anthologies. Each, in their own way, educates White women to their similarities and dissimilarities

---

[1]From I'm Making You Up (p. 153), by Chrystos, 1988, in *A Gathering of Spirit* (B. Brant, Ed.), Ithaca, NY: Firebrand Copyright 1988 by Chrystos. Reprinted with permision.

with women of color in this nation. They accomplish this well, probably because White women are neither the referent point for these books nor the reasons for their publication. More important, the authors' purpose is to tell their stories in their own right—to reclaim their voices. These books help to clarify that it is not feminism per se that "will free" women but their own agenda based on the forging of a balance of "adaptation, marginalization, and between progressive politics and cultural preservation" (Dasgupta & Dasgupta, 1993, p. 123). Each of these books adds to our picture and flavor of the heterogeneity among women and women of color. The lives of immigrant women, "forced to flee" women, colonized women, and captured women spoken in their own words provide a warm, sad, and empowering picture. These writings give all women a clearer understanding as to why race can at times be more important than gender issues; why the intersection of race and gender is critical in understanding the past and present lives of women; about the importance of discrimination in providing both advantages and disadvantages across the life span; about the racism in feminism and feminist theory; about the need for connections with mothers and grandmothers; and about the high costs of being a person of color in this nation. Many of these authors neglect it as an individual and personal process although honor age as a link to their past. The importance of gender and race on women's lives, and the lives of their mothers and grandmothers, takes precedence in thoughts and actions for survival over issues of age.

Multiple Differences

Not all multicultural feminists are people of color. In Caraway's *Segregated Sisterhood: Racism and the Politics of American Feminism* (1991), the author does an exciting and commendable job in writing about racism in feminist theory and practice, as well as her hopes for a multicultural feminist society. White racism, defined by Caraway, is "the unseen signifier which tells us why and how it is that American feminism, in theory and in practice, is a project which has segregated black and White feminists and silenced the former" (p. 3). She centers her theory-building on Black feminist thought, and ends up asking difficult questions: How complicit are White women in denigrating women of color? How have they benefitted from oppressing their "sisters"? She seeks the "space to begin again" (p. 4) to move toward a true sisterhood, while accepting the consequences of White racism. Caraway contributes to a dialogue on multicultural feminism and demonstrates the dynamic capacity of feminist critique. But Caraway's goal, as a White feminist, is not to dwell in shame or denial; rather, she seeks to move toward a "coalition-friendly process driven theory of crossover multicultural feminism" (p. 3). By this, she refers to "multicultural coalitions without domination in which persons live together in relations of mediation among feminists with whom they are not in sisterhood but solidarity" (p. 201).

The recognition of multiple differences also speaks to the oppressions based on compulsory heterosexuality, and affirms the values of lesbian experiences (Lorde, 1984; Rich, 1976). The influence of class on women's oppression is another layer of difference (Bookman & Morgen, 1988) and is discussed further in chapter 4. Other feminists extend the critique of class developed by Marx and Engels to a study of the gender and race division of labor and the connections between race and gender to the economic subordination of women. As hooks (1984) notes, "Class struggle is inextricably bound to the struggle to end racism" (p. 3).

Multicultural feminists document a history of political activism and individual, multiple, and collective acts of resistance. There are reasons why political action is especially important among multicultural feminists. There is a myth that when people are educated about the plight of oppressed populations, especially women, a subsequent increased awareness will be reflected in the policies and practices that benefit women and acknowledge their oppression. But multicultural feminists understand that this is not so. The problem with women of color sharing their narratives is not that they are not shared. It is that they are so foreign to White society that they are not believed. Rather, they do not resonate with the view or experiences of the privileged. Consequently, political action and patterns of resistance take on a critical function among multicultural feminists— one cannot wait for the dominant society to sympathize and understand to advocate for change. Women of color know that they must continue their struggles of resistance first initiated by their grandmothers.

Political action by women on behalf of all women requires an understanding of the damage done to women of color and the willingness by White women (and men) to accept responsibility to change it via struggle and resistance (hooks, 1984). This is what hooks refers to as "the transformative potential of feminism" (p. 70). The goal here is not to replace one group in power with another. Nor is to, as Lorde (1984) described, develop a hierarchy of the oppressed. Rather, it is to make feminism more inclusive via accountability, a more accurate historic reconstruction of racism in feminist theory, and the need for political strategies.

Racial and Moral Reasoning

Feminist thinking benefits from Cornell West's (1992) discussion of the need to reconsider the thinking and framework of racial reasoning in support of a prophetic framework built on moral reasoning. Racial reasoning refers to the discourse that Blacks, or other marginalized persons, must close ranks and support other Blacks, regardless of the issue at hand, because of the hostile and racist national context in which they live. But, as Paula Giddings (1992) points out, "racial solidarity is not always the same as racial loyalty" (p. 441). Because race is a political and ethical construct, appeals to Black authenticity ignore both who is left out, and broader discussions that are needed around injustice and oppression. Leading to a limited dialogue, racial reasoning must be dismantled in favor of moral reasoning—a moral examination of the varied perspectives and situations of Black persons based on "ethical principles and wise politics" (West, 1992, p. 393).

Gender, like race, is also a social, political, and ethical construct. Previously discussed were a number of feminist themes that use the language of equality (women as the same as men); of difference (women as different from men); and of homogeneity (White, young, and middle-class). However, limited attention has been directed at revealing differences among women. Neither has much dialogue focused on the ways in which the process of socialization and injustice pits one group against another, with the result that each assigns the blame of their oppression on another group. This type of thinking leads to gender reasoning—the idea that "women" should support other women regardless of the issue at hand. But here again, who is left out of the definition of "woman"? Similarities among women can not trivialize or ignore their diversities. And, while different standpoints may well exist, difference is not necessarily better, nor is "sameness" a guarantee that one is sympathetic to a cause. If the Black feminist is ageist, if the White feminist is racist, if the older feminist is homophobic, who has benefitted in the end? No paradigmatic shift has been completed as long as feminists use the same conceptual apparatus of the dominant society in marginalizing some members of society while providing privilege to others. Moral reasoning does not rule out the possibility of solidarity among women, among races, between groups of women, and between young and old. Indeed, moral reasoning can be learned when people are exposed to the harmful effects of racism, sexism, homophobism, classism, ageism, and other forms of injustice. In clarifying the connections between such "isms," moral reasoning can expose the roots of oppression's base.

Feminist theory, then, can not only be a struggle to end sexist oppression (hooks, 1981, 1984; Stansell, 1992). Rather, it must search for the structural determinants of all oppressions; in particular, gender, race, class, and sexual orientation. While it pays close attention to women's issues, it is not only about women's issues. In speaking of Black Americans, West suggests that potential strategies to move from racial to moral reasoning include accepting a mature Black identity, the critical role of coalition-building for justice, and the promotion of cultural democracy. Likewise, the move to moral reasoning among women must include accepting and including the varied responses and life situations of older women in a new epistemology of women and age, and coalition and solidarity efforts within and outside traditional women's issues.

The writings of Black feminists and other women of color have, according to Caraway, "deconstructed the images, identifiers, presumptions, and methodology of hegemonic theory not only of androcentric world views but those of White feminism as well" (p. 5). The use of multiple multicultural narratives of women of color has demystified the "we" in women and brought new understandings around issues in history, accountability, and honesty. Hooks (1984) adds that Black feminist theory affords the kind of knowledge critical to our being to sort out the differences that make a difference. In so doing, the strength of multicultural feminism lies in its search and attention to difference and specificity, while avoiding a homogenization of women of color as it points out and redefines historical, cohort, and other differences. Arguing for difference does not discount the potential for solidarity among women. Indeed, a number of multicultural feminists suggest that solidarity is possible and perhaps even desirable if community can be found (Lorde, 1984; Trask, 1996). Audre Lorde (1984) adds this: "It is learning how to stand alone, unpopular and sometimes reviled, and how to make common cause with those others identified as outside the structure in order to define and seek a world in which we can all flourish. It is learning how to take our differences and make them strengths" (p. 112).

AGEISM IN MULTICULTURAL FEMINISM

While it is empowering to so many, multicultural feminism is not without problems. For all it adds to theory-building about women, multicultural feminism is as disappointing as liberal feminist theory in its neglect of age and aging women. It is disappointing because Black feminist and multicultural feminist theory understand better than liberal feminist theory what is problematic with universal truths and categories. Just as racism can help to expose the differences between illusion and reality in this country, an understanding of age issues can help feminists see the failure of liberal and multicultural feminist theories to truly understand domination. Merle Woo (1983, p. 143) is correct to ask: "How many white women have taken on the responsibility to educate themselves about third world people—their history? their culture"? We, in turn, can ask: How many younger women have taken the time to know women older than themselves—their history and their culture?

Without a transformative liberating theory, feminist theory remains ageist because it uses the "master's tools" (Lorde, 1984) in pitting young against the old, White women against women of color, and women against men. Many multicultural feminist writers write movingly of the contributions and strengths of their grandmothers, and in doing so reclaim not only their own voices but those of grandmothers, mothers, aunts, and other family members. But, one hopes that the family role is not the only way in which older women are perceived. What is disheartening is that the awareness of one's oppression does not extend to the oppression of others. Cherríe Moraga (1983) states it in this way:

> And yet, oppressed groups are forgetting all the time. There are instances of this in the rising Black middle class, and certainly an obvious trend of such unconsciousness among White gay men. Because to remember may mean giving up whatever privileges we have managed to squeeze out of this society by virtue to our gender, race, class, or sexuality. (p. 30)

Hooks (1984) asserts that people learn oppression from their awareness of their own lived experience, or what Caraway (1991) calls the contextualized meaning of their lives. Yes, there is racism and classism in feminism. This should not surprise us since feminists, like the rest of the nation's citizens, have been socialized by the dominant society that continues to negate the worth of many of the nation's peoples. But the fact that so few feminists have exposed the ageism in texts and in their own works is nonetheless disappointing. The voice of feminism from a privileged vantage point has excluded many voices and negated the relationships between race and class. Somewhere, age got lost as an issue, and with it the loss of bonding on shared strengths and patterns of resistance, and the potential power of solidarity.

Lorde (1984) was one of the few feminist thinkers to acknowledge the connection of all "isms" with one another. She saw that within this society, those who have been made to feel surplus and not worthy are made up of Black and Third World people, working–class people, older people, and women. She acknowledged that there exist differences among these groups, but adds that what is problematic is not the differences, but the refusal to recognize and deal with these differences creatively. She spoke concretely of ageism:

> As we move toward creating a society within which we can each flourish, ageism is another distortion of relationship which interferes without vision. By ignoring the past, we are encouraged to repeat its mistakes. The "generation gap" is an important social tool for any repressive society. If the younger members of a community view the older members as contemptible or suspect or excess, they will never be able to join hands and examine the living memories of the community, nor ask the all important question: "Why?" This gives rise to historical amnesia that keeps us working to invent the wheel every time we have to go to the store for bread. (pp. 116–117)

Hooks (1984) further argues that until we combat racism and classism and develop policies committed to end injustice, we will continue to see divisions in feminist theory instead of unity or solidarity. Lorde was also one of the few feminists who added ageism as a potential contributor to solidarity. Surely, the lives of older women, the documentation of the accumulation of endured inequalities throughout their lives and the multiple layers of their oppressions, provide ample evidence that affirms their life struggles and resistance.

Ageism, then, provides an unspoken opportunity for solidarity with other women and oppressed peoples. This may be because, an early death notwithstanding, aging is and will be a shared experience in the end for all. As all oppressions are related to those who dominate, ageism presents both a problem and an opportunity for feminism to build solidarity around women's and people's well-being. The neglect of the older woman in feminist writings is the problem, easily corrected. The opportunity lies in seeing how the process of aging and understanding society's treatment of the aged can help even those formerly privileged understand oppression from a broader experience. Among those oppressed, not all have an equal voice; some are more privileged than others. Ageism helps us to understand that a sole focus on racism, classism, or sexism will not transform society. Rather, feminist theory and praxis should examine domination in all its forms.

POSTMODERNISM AND FEMINIST THEORY

A somewhat related and yet different theoretical framework, postmodernism, offers new insights and themes that have potential in seeking a new vision for older women. A cultural and intellectual phenomenon, postmodernism is a philosophical orientation that questions the existence of established knowledge and universal truths. Postmodernists distrust the sincerity of grand theories that "are generalized to others; rather, they believe that each person constructs her own reality given her place in society and socio-historical period" (Giroux, 1991, p. 74). As an ideology and a philosophy, it stresses plurality, difference, and multinarratives. Postmodernism argues that history's grand narratives have come from 17th-century European males and that these narratives masquerade as truth and reason. In contrast, postmodernists believe that what is considered truth is only interpretation—the effects of the strengths of a particular form of power. Social reality depends on one's definitions and conceptualization.

Similar to multicultural feminist theorists, postmodernists can be considered anti-essentialists. They look to reread the texts and extend their search for knowledge to various forms of knowledge—poems, movies, novels, and philosophical treatises. Postmodern thought hears not only multiple voices, but understands that the voice of silence, as dissent, is critical for knowledge creation. It argues that the self is defined through both self-narratives that explain individual life experiences and through narratives that others construct about the self (Laird, 1994). Postmodernism differs from multicultural feminism in that gender and cultural identity are considered unstable concepts.

MODERNITY AND POSTMODERNISM

Modernity is postmodernism's opposing epistemological framework. While modernity stresses certainty, foundationalism, and epistemological essentialism, postmodernism claims uncertainty, specificity, diversity, and subjugated knowledge. With its emphasis on logical, rational, and empirical processes, modernity emphasizes the positivist tradition and created the scientific method. Postmodern feminist research, in contrast, works to uncover and analyze how social structures contribute to people's problems, especially those who have been marginalized (Van Den Bergh, 1995). According to Caraway (1991), postmodernism

> perceives the edifices of Western thought as increasingly fraught with uncertainty and ambivalence: transitions in geopolitical alliances, Third World resistance to Western political and intellectual hegemony; the horrendous environmental repercussions of "progress" in a nuclear age, and the continuation of structures of sexism, racism, and other imperializing prejudices of Western xenophobia. (p. 55)

Modernity, according to Giroux, is more than "patriarchy parading as universal reason, the increasing intensification of human domination over nature in the name of historical development, of the imperiousness of grand narratives that stress control and mastery" (1991, p. 2). Instead, Giroux suggests that the real strength in modernity may be as a "point of reference for advancing certain and crucial elements of democratic thought and revolution, the limits of its own historical tradition and for developing a political standpoint in which the breadth and specificity of democratic struggles can be expanded through the modernist ideals of freedom, justice, and equality" (p. 2).

POSTMODERN FEMINIST THEORY

Jane Flax (1987) notes the growing confusion over the grounding and methods presently used for explaining human behavior. Taking a postmodern stance, she suggests that feminists must "deconstruct our notions of reason and the state to reveal the effect of the gender arrangements that lay beneath their 'neutral' and universal facades" (pp. 620–621). Feminist theory has benefitted from a number of postmodern thoughts. For one, it provides a site of analysis for feminists not only to question the hegemony of European knowledge claims, but to question the claims of feminist theory itself. A key strategy for postmodernists is to hear the narratives of the "other" groups, so that forms and content of grand narratives can be challenged as well as new forms of knowledge produced.

Critical of the grounding of present methods to explicate women's experiences, postmodern feminist theory "challenges accepted ideas about race, gender, and class, along with personal rights, equality and difference" (Sands & Nuccio, 1993, p. 490). The categories of gender, race, and class by themselves are considered too simplistic and restrictive. Instead, multiple differences and layers of diversity, along with dissenting voices, are central to feminist analysis. Women cannot be spoken in the collective sense, that is, there is no "woman's point of view." Consequently, the categories of older women, minority women, and older minority woman are naive and problematic. The use of categories of women may actually be counterproductive if data on women is co-opted by the dominant society for purposes other than its original intent (Van Den Bergh, 1995). Therefore, there are no universal declarations; all categories of women should be deconstructed. One message found in postmodern feminist theories, also echoed in Black feminist theories, is the importance of reconstructing the missing voices of women, especially women of color, through their own stories and words. No perspective is better than any other, and no one should be used as referent points for others. And yet what does this do to any focus on women?

In a somewhat similar vein, postmodernism sees culture as pliant and fluid. At first glance, this view appears to reject the notion of culture as something substantial, as culture it is yet another construct that has been societally and historically invented and created (Pardeck, Murphy, & Choi, 1994). But such a view does not result in a definition of culture as insignificant. Instead, according to Pardeck and his colleagues (1994), "Given the interpretative character of social existence, values, commitments, and expectations become valuable for substantiating reality" (p. 343). Therefore, it is "understanding the interpretative cement that sustains certain norms that holds the key to explaining behavior" (p. 343).

The roots of postmodern feminist theory emanate from social constructionism, deconstructionism or poststructuralism, French feminist theory, and postmodern philosophy. There are a number of themes evident in their work. In brief, postmodern feminists are critical of logocentrism, instead questioning the existence of any logical and rational order to the world or any essential meaning. According to Ruth Ray (1996), a postmodern feminist gerontologist, social constructionism "challenges knowledge making systems and their presumed neutrality, asserting that truth and reality are not discovered but socially constructed and perpetuated as forms of power" (p. 676). We influence what we see—reality is not fixed. Social constructionists also believe that difference should be viewed as alternatives rather than as dichotomous variables, and that the voices of "everyman and everywoman" should be analyzed and involved to uncover truths. Subjectivity is viewed as a multifaceted process, and polarized thinking is viewed as leading not only to difference, but to hierarchies.

Poststructuralists, or deconstructionists, see meaning as unstable and open to various interpretations and study (Foucault, 1980; Giroux, 1991; Kristeva, 1981). The process of deconstruction is to hear and rearticulate the voices of suppressed texts. According to Sands and Nuccio (1993), deconstruction "is a way of analyzing texts that is sensitive to contextual dimensions and marginalized voices" (p. 491). Ray (1996) adds that it "challenges traditional views of language and its relationship to thought and reality. Deconstruction selects, intensifies and exaggerates and distorts" (p. 676).

Feminist postmodernism, then, seeks to document women's exclusion from texts. As a method, feminist deconstructionists attempt to "deconstruct," or break down analytically, society's values, policies, and programs that affect women. But, as people speak in many tongues, even the subject is precarious—due to cohort, history, and sociocultural constructs.

French feminist theory, another root of postmodernism, is also deconstructionist and shares some common ground with poststructuralists as it sees the relationship between language, power, and knowledge. Finally, postmodern philosophy, the fourth root, questions the existence of universal truths and laws. Instead, philosophers see wholeness and value in "local meanings and that even gender, race, class, and age are too reductive and therefore too restrictive" (Sands & Nuccio, 1993, p. 492).

CRITIQUES OF POSTMODERNISM

Feminist scholars Sandra Harding (1988) and Donna Haraway (1985) applaud postmodernism for its attention to specificity and diversity, but also offer their critiques. Harding (1988), for example, challenges the assumption of a feminist standpoint of reality. Instead, she argues that postmodern thought provides a method for rethinking wholeness by offering a new way to critique and look at reality. For a number of reasons, she believes that postmodernism and postmodern feminist theory are not always a compatible match.

In truth, postmodernism provides a dilemma and opportunity for postmodern feminist theory. Postmodernists generally do not recognize the significance of gender, race, and class because these are diverse and complex categories. In contrast, postmodern feminist theories "highlight, foreground, emphasize, insist on differences" (Sands & Nuccio, 1993, p. 492). Critical of essentialism, postmodernism looks to "women" with a small "w," desiring specificity while acknowledging plurality. Postmodernism is critical of standpoints, but it is this insistence on diversity in understanding women that gives it some common ground with the multicultural feminists.

Postmodern feminist theories critique feminist theories in social welfare for wanting it both ways—for eliminating false dichotomies and categories, and yet desiring categories (Sands & Nuccio, 1993). Nonetheless, Van Den Bergh (1995) believes that postmodernism has caused reverberations in the foundations of knowledge in both social work and feminism. This is because, according to Van Den Bergh, "postmodernism questions the veracity of grand theory or propositions concerning reality that are to be generalized and ubiquitously applied" (p. xiii). A number of other authors believe that postmodern feminism is especially compatible with social welfare with its emphasis on difference and respect for a changing demographic America (Sands & Nuccio, 1993). That is because, according to Sands and Nuccio (1993), the use of deconstruction brings out into the open the needs of marginalized people in their own words. and the impact of context on people's life chances.

Others criticize postmodern feminist thought for lacking "soulness" and for seeing a provisional subjectivity; for being too fatalistic and too removed from everyday life; and for being too apolitical (Caraway, 1991; West, 1991). Bhaskaran (1993) suggests that, while postmodernism can be helpful in its deconstructive methodologies, it "leans toward the abandonment of a coherent and empowered 'subject' " (p. 198). More specifically, West (1991) points out that postmodern feminists ignore cultural values and issues of race; that it is ahistorical and politically apathetic. Others disagree, noting that postmodernism, as an epistemological framework or approach, offers a contrasting view and framework for political struggle, with its suspiciousness of categories of people and in its questioning of "truth" (Van Den Bergh, 1995). In this way, Laclau (1988) and others argue it is a political act. Sands and Nuccio (1993) agree, noting that postmodern feminists, like other feminists, have a political agenda to change the social order to improve the lives of women. As such, they believe in ongoing political activism. This is because postmodernism, more so than other feminisms, questions established knowledge, as it understands that it is usually the privileged who are in positions to create and legitimize knowledge. Since the knowledge base of the powerful is not seen as a standpoint but as reality, postmodernists understand that one must reconstruct truth and see who is excluded.

A FEMINIST AGING CRITIQUE OF POSTMODERNISM

A small but growing number of postmodernist thinkers have begun to articulate a relationship among postmodernism, feminism, and aging. Ray (1996), noting gerontology's limited discourse with postmodernism, suggests that the reason for this is in part because of "its use of conceptual frameworks of biomedicine" (p. 676). She contends, however, that postmodernism is compatible with aging studies, and points to a number of scholars that are adopting or integrating postmodern theory and methodologies into their work. One strategy proposed by Laws (1995), another postmodern feminist gerontologist, is for gerontologists to focus on specific sites of oppression to highlight the ways in which ageism operates in this society—in particular, the waged labor market, the household, popular culture, the state, and the built environment. Laws, like Ray, notes that numerous gerontologists with a postmodern flair are attacking concepts such as age scheduling, the relationship between human capital and chronological age, the lack of attention to diversity among the aged, the exploitation of grandmothers within the multigenerational family, stereotypical representations of the aged in popular culture, the present debates over generational equity, and segregated housing for the aged (Diamond, 1992; Hazan, 1994; Moody, 1988; Woodward, 1991). Critiques such as these are necessary and worthwhile in illuminating the ways in which the aging process varies among the aged in this postmodern world.

Ray extends this line of thinking and advocates for a new postmodern perspective on feminist gerontology whose focus would be "to increase both self awareness and self critique on the part of gerontology as a field" (p. 679). According to Ray, studies in aging have focused on social inequities that seek to change beliefs that construct older people's roles and positions in society. But she notes its wider implications in challenging "what counts as knowledge of aging, who makes this knowledge, and how it functions in the world" (p. 675). She writes that continued discussion, argument, and dialogue are positive acts, as opposed to complacent certainty about aging and older adults among gerontologists.

There are many appealing arguments in favor of gerontological postmodern thought, especially its emphasis on the political nature of the production and dissemination of knowledge; its dissection of critical concepts and issues facing society today; its deconstruction of assumptions about aging women in public and private texts, policies, and laws; and its use of multiple methods in research. Still, feminists feel some tension with postmodernism on a number of points.

For one thing, postmodernism's attention on difference can lead to the exclusion of solidarity, ignoring the need for coalitions that can pursue collective ends. Furthermore, while some claim a political nature for postmodern feminism, it is sometimes difficult to see it. Caraway (1991), for example, perceives postmodernism as having "negative deconstructive strategies while multicultural feminist theory engages in positive reconstruction projects" (p. 58). The end result of postmodernism's deconstructive work is not clear, while the purpose of multicultural feminist theory's efforts at deconstruction is the creation of a more just society. Caraway argues that is this uncovering of and analysis of the deep context of our lives that is essential for multicultural feminist theory to become accountable and truthful. Self-reflective intellectual and political activity is what provides feminist theory with the opportunity to confront betrayals, and begin to work to move toward inclusion.

Additionally, coalition-friendly interventions can be sound conceptually, but difficult to engage within a postmodern framework. If one cannot speak of women's oppressions and inequalities in any common sense, how can one work toward group efforts for change? But commonalities exist:

Millions of women today are concerned about jobs, working conditions, higher wages, and racist violence. They are concerned about plant closures, homelessness, and repressive immigration legislation. Women are concerned about homophobia, ageism, and discrimination against the physically challenged. . . . And we share our children's dream that tomorrow's world will be delivered from the threat of nuclear omnicide. These are some of the issues that should be integrated into the overall struggle for women's rights. (A. Davis, 1990, p. 6)

Unity may be a difficult strategy for half the world's population because of its diversity, and yet solidarity via a kaleidoscope of coalitions responding to distinct needs and overlapping can be a workable strategy. Moreover, the focus on "older woman," criticized by postmodernists for being too "essentialist," does not appear to be compatible with a postmodern ideas of situated voices. But without a common voice, efforts toward solidarity are difficult at best. Such ideas also make work in developing feminist age theory difficult at best. Legal scholar Patricia Cain (1993) elaborates: "Postmodern thought poses a certain dilemma. Any theory requires some degree of abstraction and generalization. Thus, if feminists embrace the particular situated realities of all individual women, plural, we will find it difficult to build a theory, singular, to combat oppression" (p. 243).

From a social welfare perspective, themes and categories are helpful in knowing one's constituencies. Without them, it is more difficult to develop, organize, and advocate for those in need, whether in one's community or at the legislative level. The postmodern feminist emphasis on multiple layers of difference finds categories of women such as the displaced homemakers contestable in their neglect of race, class, and other differences. L. V. Davis (1994b), for one, has noted that "in their commitment to hearing multiple voices, all categories, including that of women, become fictions, needing to be dismantled, deconstructed" (p. 19). But, those who work on behalf of older women and other oppressed peoples find such categories helpful in their work with populations that need both definition and intervention. It is true, as Bhaskaran (1993) has noted, that some "gender skepticism" is good, because not all women are oppressed in the same way. But it is these exact differences that must be documented, because they have not been.

The use of categories remains suspect for postmodernists, even though many social welfare advocates use them extensively. We do not live, after all, in a gender-neutral or race-blind world. A question, then, remains as to how diversity and specificity can be served simultaneously. Sands and Nuccio (1993) propose a solution to adopt on behalf of aging women;

namely, we can accept some common oppressions that older women face. At the same time, feminists must be vigilant in documenting the diversity of older women and their special needs among a population that spans a 40-year plus time frame in addition to its class, race, ethnicity, and other differences. Postmodernism can provide feminism and social welfare with a method to critique policies (Van Den Bergh, 1995). Van Den Bergh offers a number of postmodern assumptions about knowledge creation that have implications for feminists, gerontologists, social workers, and others in the development of future frameworks. These include the questioning of essential truths and the underlying situation; partnership rather than domination; local rather than universal truths; establishing community meanings; deconstructing and reconstructing knowledge; and the links between knowledge and power. Readers are encouraged to read Van Den Bergh's preface to *Feminist Practice in the 21st Century* (1995) for a complete understanding of her analysis.

In sum, postmodernism offers challenges and dilemmas for feminist theory in its quest to be more democratic and inclusive. More important, postmodern feminism, unlike liberal feminism, recognizes the false truth in a neutral democratic social welfare state. But, as is the case in other readings, issues about older women are rarely discussed.

DIFFERENCE AND COMMON GROUND

There are some differences, as well as some common ground, between multiculturalists and postmodern feminists that lead us closer to a new epistemology of women and age. Both these schools question hegemonic thought, seek out suppressed and subjugated voices and silences, and understand that "knowledge" is related to power and hierarchy. Black and multicultural feminist theories add to other streams of feminist knowledge on the multivariate voices of women, and what is needed to bring such voices from "margin to center." In contrast, postmodernism helps us to understand how lives are constructed. Both see how race and gender are socially constructed and emphasize a plurality of voices. Some see all feminists as postmodernists, since both have deconstructive elements (Flax, 1987).

What postmodern and multicultural feminists have to offer is a conceptual place that underscores the absence of universal truths. The challenge among women, then, is to create unity without denying specificity. Both multicultural feminism, with its view of marginalized people, and postmodern feminism, with its focus on subjugated knowledge and suspicion of categories and universal truths, help to question society's fictive portrayal of older women, society's treatment of all women but specifically aged women, and women's treatment of each other.

While multicultural and postmodern feminists are better at reading the demographic changes than other feminist theories, the former theory ignores age and the latter theory has come to it late and with a limited discourse. As with other feminist schools of thought, age remains a relatively neglected concept. The deconstruction of "woman," however, is incomplete without inserting age into the equation. Without it, age hierarchies and differences among aging women are unacknowledged and disguised. Multicultural and postmodern feminisms, with their attention to diversity and specificity, can correct this. The feminist scholar Margaret Morganroth Gullette (1995) describes it in this way: "Because age intersects unpredictably with other attributes like race and class, scholars needs to challenge themselves to reread texts, looking to ageism and connect it to others sites of oppression" (p. 247). The cross-fertilization of multicultural and postmodern feminisms, along with knowledge about and critique of aging content, brings us that much closer to a new epistemology of aging and women. Feminist age theory can help us to rediscover older women's voices, and to deconstruct the mythical images of older women presented in the professional literature and the popular media. In truth, when the intelligence and contributions of older women are ignored or negated, the opportunity is lost to see their strengths, patterns of resistance, and ageism as a site of injustice. Ultimately, the view of age as struggle in both a positive and negative sense is also lost. Postmodernism may be critical of the category of "age," but the lives of aging women can not and should not be trivialized and ignored. Older women are more than mothers and grandmothers—they are not only our past and future. What must be regained, then, is who older women are as defined by older women.

CONCLUSIONS

Multicultural and postmodern feminism question universal truths and allow us to see how individual and societal neglect has hurt all women, but especially marginalized women—women of color, gay and lesbian women, and older women. Multicultural feminism has broadened our view of women to a more inclusive one that refuses to make any one group of women the norm for others. Postmodern feminism has added to our understanding of subjugated knowledge and knowledge creation. Like other feminisms, neither philosophy has focused extensively on the needs of aging women. Ideas from multicultural and postmodern feminist theories lead toward new conceptualizations of age by uncovering older women's voices and their silences, refusing to accept "universal truths" about aging that portray older women in only a negative and a condescending light, by rereading texts, and in validating the life experiences of older women as struggle, contribution, independence, and resistance.

Radical and Socialist Feminist Theories and Aging

> Power lasts only as long as the contradictory voices remain silenced.
>
> —Angela P. Harris

Two early schools of feminist thought that emerged in the 1960s and 1970s were the radical and socialist feminisms. Radical feminist theory sees women's oppression emanating from patriarchy, or a system of male domination supported by law, social organizations and policies, culture, religion, and societal norms. Socialist feminism, taking many of its ideas from Marxist feminists, blames women's oppression more on capitalism than patriarchy. While beginning with distinct and differing understandings of women's oppression, they have in more recent years become somewhat closer in their ideological thinking. In this chapter, I summarize both radical and socialist feminisms and examine some basic themes in their writings. Radical feminist theories, and to a lesser extent, socialist feminist theories, have generally omitted aging women from their extensive analyses of gender and power. Nonetheless, I believe we can uncover ideas from both sets of theories to guide us in understanding how feminism can be applied to women as they age.

RADICAL FEMINIST THEORY

The "radical feminism" label is applied to a broad range of theories and insights into the experiences of women. The emergence of radical feminism in the late 1960s came as a break with both liberal feminism and traditional Marxism (Abramowitz, 1992). Women's oppression is a result of their domination by men, or patriarchy, and not of blocked opportunities, as professed by liberal feminists. Patriarchy stems from the psychological and biological needs of men to dominate and control women. The differential treatment of women pre- and postdates capitalism. Consequently, gender is the critical factor in determining women's life experiences, and patriarchy is viewed as the most important and divisive factor for women. Gender structures every aspect of human nature and socioeconomic life. The gender division of labor is patriarchy's tool to suppress and oppress women, and ends in legitimizing the devaluation of women in the workforce and deproblematizing women's mothering and caregiving functions. Patriarchy enforces women's financial dependence on men, male/female marriages, and heterosexuality. Women employed in the paid work force find that their work too often remains in segregated work sites, such as clerical, sales, and support services. This relegation of women's work in both the public and private spheres is thus political, and has real consequences to women's lives. It is the radical feminist understanding of women's oppression as based in patriarchy and the gender relations of male domination and female subordination that has forced a new conceptualization of the state (Abramowitz, 1992).

Probably two of the earlier and more well-known political classics on radical feminism are Shulamith Firestone's *The Dialectic of Sex* (1970) and Kate Millett's *Sexual Politics* (1970). These and other feminist authors examined women's roles in society and saw society as exploitive. Millett and Firestone wrote of the issues surrounding male dominance of women. Both authors examined how patriarchal society, using biological determinism and male ideology, constructed an unjust and sexist society through the oppressive uses of discrimination, poverty, and violence directed against women. Millett described the ways in which all women are abused in the personal realm of sexual intimacy, coining the term "sexual politics." In offering her book as a "manifesto for revolution," she wrote:

> When one group rules another, the relationship between the two is political. When such an arrangement is carried out over a long period of time it develops an ideology (feudalism, racism, etc.). All historical civilizations are patriarchies: their ideology is male supremacy. . . . Sexual politics obtains consent through the "socialization" of both sexes to patriarchal policies. (1970, p. 111)

Thus, it is primarily through male-dominated ideology and biology, rather than capitalism, that women are subjugated to second-class status by men. There remains disagreement among these and other authors over whether or not justice can be achieved via working within the system as the rightful road to equality and as an end to oppression.

In contrast to liberal and Marxist feminist theories, Miller (1990) views radical feminism as relatively new and as not adhering to a specific political theory. Formed in reaction against the macho and sexist climate evident in the male "New Left" of the 1960s, radical feminists emphasized a theory and practice that was nonsexist, democratic, and spoke from women's experiences (Donovan, 1996). Its roots were in the perspectives and perceptions of primarily White, middle-class, college-educated American women of this era. Because of this, radical feminist theory stems from the range of experiences and perspectives of the women themselves. Radical feminist theory is limited by this perspective, particularly in describing the experiences of working-class women and women of color, but radical feminists have more recently given increased fresh attention to class, ethnic, and national differences (Jaggar, 1988). Still, radical feminists believe that uncovering and eradicating the systematic or root causes of all women's oppression transcends class and race, and unites all women in the struggle for liberation. Rather than the liberal quest for increased access into a man's world, radical feminism seeks a world that is more woman-centered. The radical feminist belief that women and men are fundamentally different from each other led many to advocate for a separate society for women, one in which women's values could thrive. This strategy was shared in the 1980s by cultural feminists.

A unifying element among radical feminists is the belief that women's oppression is the primary, most widespread, and deepest form of human oppression (see Firestone, 1970; Morgan, 1970). As Jaggar and Rothenberg (1984) indicate, "What distinguishes radical feminism from all other feminist theories is its insistence that the oppression of women is fundamental . . . [and that] . . . women's oppression provides a conceptual model for understanding all other forms of oppression" (p. 6). Women are viewed as a sex-class that is equivalent to an economic class of persons. Ultimately, as noted by Donovan (1996) in her review of feminist theories,

> Radical feminists came to believe that all these issues were interrelated, that male supremacy and the subjugation of women was indeed the root and model oppression in society and that feminism had to be the basis for any true revolutionary change. . . . Other central theses of radical feminism . . . included the idea that the personal is political; that patriarchy, or male domination—not capitalism—is at the root of women's oppression; that women should identify themselves as a subjugated class or caste and put their primary energies in a movement with other women to combat their oppressors—men; that men and women are fundamentally different,

have different styles and cultures, and that the women's mode must be the basis of any future society. (p. 142)

Earlier radical feminist solutions focused on combating the psychological and/or biological root of women's oppression in their work for the defeat of patriarchy. The elimination of biological differences of the sexes through technological advances became, for some, a key political goal. But others, such as Ti-Grace Atkinson (1974) asked a different question that resonated more deeply with most radical feminists: "How did this biological classification [of gender] become a political classification?" (p. 52). More recently, a number of radical feminists have suggested that the issue is not whether differences exist between the sexes, but rather how such differences are formed, interpreted, and structurally enforced. What these and other authors have in common is the radical feminist quest to end gender hierarchy and destroy sexism. Jaggar (1988) states it this way: "The theoretical task of radical feminism is to understand that [the patriarchal] system, its political task is to end it" (p. 85). Moreover, for radical feminism, the focus for analysis is on the collective group known as women (MacKinnon, 1989).

Contemporary radical feminist strategies emphasize women-centered perspectives and focus special attention on pornography, assault and rape, family violence, forced heterosexuality, and homophobia. Radical feminists' valued dialogues and political activities have reconceptualized how these and other issues are viewed, and have in turn reshaped public policy. Although radical feminists are critical of the cultural feminists' focus on difference, they hold specific areas of agreement with the essentialist argument that advocate for theory and practice to emanate from women-centered and women-identified experiences.

Zillah Eisenstein, a liberal feminist in her earlier days, later moved closer to radical feminist theories in identifying patriarchy, not limitations on women's options, as the reason for women's oppression (1984). It is the linkages that exist between capitalism and patriarchy, according to Eisenstein, that give liberal feminism its radical potential. Unfortunately, the White woman's perspective was too often used as a referent or standard for other women. For example, Eisenstein believed that women's mass entry into the workplace in response to capitalist needs would finally end patriarchal ideology. As women do their double shifts and as they realize that they still earn less than men, pressure for equal rights will be exerted. But if we used working-class and women of color—women who have always worked in both the public and private spheres—as our standard or referent point, we would be sensitized to some of the problems in Eisenstein's hypothesis. Black women have work histories similar to men's in years of work, but not in salaries or benefits. But their presence in the work force, while nothing new, has not altered racial and gender power inequalities. An analysis of these women's lives sensitizes one to the fact that it is not only gender hierarchies that exist, but racial ones. Eisenstein was correct, however, in criticizing liberal feminist theory for seeing the state as a mediator between capitalism and patriarchy and for not understanding that the state reflects the views of the dominant culture. More recently, she has extended her critical eye to cultural feminists' focus on difference as opposed to oppression. She attributed some hope for women in establishing nonpatriarchal types of families.

Her arguments do not specifically address the life situation of older women, and yet new family types and nonpatriarchal forms of the family are clearly evident among the present cohort of older women. Indeed, the majority of older women today live in nonpatriarchal types of homes—they live alone or with other women, whether it is in the homes of their daughters, in senior housing, or in nursing homes. Alternative lifestyles may be more acceptable to older women. The radical feminist focus on reconceptualizing the world to be more woman-centered can expand its thinking by examining the lives of many older women whose situations do not reflect traditional definitions of family.

A reconceptualization of the state's response to women's lives could be broadened in the following ways and with the following questions. For example, if caregiving was shared, reimbursed, or at least not penalized in public and private retirement programs, how could such changes affect older women? If women could work more easily because child care was both affordable and accessible, if their wages were at least as good as [White] men's, think about how their present lives and future later years could flourish. Since most older women are no longer married to men, should their benefits be based on their former marital status? And, if social welfare reflected the lives and experiences of aging women, what would it offer to all citizens?

In short, radical feminists emphasize women's political, rather than personal, agenda, and the need for women to advocate for changes in societal structures. Accordingly, revolutionary change is not only needed, but necessary. Furthermore, as patriarchy is defined, legitimized and sanctioned by the state, feminists must rethink their political strategies. Legal and social welfare reform is a critical but only a first step in the feminist agenda.

DOMINANCE THEORY

Discussed in chapter 2 is the essentialist or cultural feminism's focus on women's differences compared to men's, together with their focus on women's "culture." In contrast, some radical feminist theorists argue that a better way to understand women's oppression is to examine the issue of domination, not difference. MacKinnon (1987) asks this question:

> How do you know when a group is on the bottom? It may be some indication that they can be assaulted, and authorities ignore them; physically abused, and people turn away or find it entertaining; economically deprived, and it is seen as all they are worth; made the object of jokes, and few ask what makes the jokes funny; imaged as animal-like; confined to a narrow range of tasks and functions, and told it is all harmless or inevitable and even for their benefit as well as the best they can expect, given what they are. These are all true for women. (p. 30)

MacKinnon (1987, 1989) critiques liberal and cultural feminism for their attention to the same/difference theory of sex equality, i.e., the theory that women are like men or women are different from men. There is a built-in tension, she explains, "that exists between this concept of equality, which presupposes sameness, and this concept of sex, which presupposes difference. Sex equality thus becomes a contradiction in terms" (1987, p. 33). According to MacKinnon, liberal feminist theories emphasize difference, but are obsessed with sex difference, rather than the effects of sexism. Both concepts, she says, are only examples of liberalism talking to itself (1987). A more efficient strategy, she suggests, is to recognize that difference comes later; inequality comes first. Of course men and women are different, she argues. When one group is elevated and the other demeaned, one can not expect them to be the same. But it is gender hierarchy, not gender differentiation, that defines sexual politics. MacKinnon acknowledges that some differences exist between the sexes, and that, while patronizing, such differences are necessary to note. But women's chances for productive, reasonably safe, and respected lives depend more on an analysis of domination than difference. The problems, then, with gender-neutral strategies are that they use "the male standard and special protection [uses] the female standard," but she adds, "do not be deceived—maleness is the reference for both" (1987, p. 82). Subsequently, radical feminism does not look to patriarchy for help without women-centered and women-defined issues and without women's political activism. An equally critical point, according to MacKinnon, is that women "do not seek sameness with men. We do not seek dominance over men. To us it is a male notion that power means someone must dominate. . . . Our issue is not gender difference but the difference gender makes" (1987, p. 23).

MacKinnon's work is not without criticism by other feminists, especially in the area of pornography and free speech. MacKinnon, according to legal theorist Patricia Cain (1993) uses the rhetoric of domination and sexual subordination instead of equality, [and] radical feminists in the MacKinnon camp argue for changes in laws that will end the inequality of power. Sex equality, in this view, affirmatively requires protecting women from such things as sexual harassment, rape, and battering by men. An extension of this theory, controversial even today among feminists, is used to justify a ban on pornography because pornography is thought to contribute to women's sexual subordination. (p. 240)

While acknowledging the power of domination theory, MacKinnon is criticized for being guilty of gender essentialism, universalizing all of women's voices into one (A. Harris, 1991). Still, her works are brilliant analyses of power differentials between the sexes, and her most recent contributions extend the analysis of gender hierarchy's relationships to knowledge and politics, and the politics of knowledge.

SOURCES OF WOMEN'S OPPRESSION

Radical feminists believe that patriarchal control is a universal feature of all social systems and subsequent systems of oppression, serving those who perpetuate it, namely men (Firestone, 1970; Morgan, 1970). Sex is viewed as an organized division of social power, a social principle insepa-rable from gender and enforced to women's detriment (MacKinnon, 1989). Sexism, then, must be destroyed.

The identification of men and patriarchy as the oppressor allowed for the ways in which women experience oppression to be addressed. As some radical feminists indicate, the oppression of women by men occurs in every facet of their lives, but the discussion here will be confined to radical feminism's focus on: (1) reproduction; (2) control of women's sexuality and sexual orientation; and (3) violence against women. All three domains are often argued as composing the foundation for the patriarchal oppression of women.

Reproduction

One of the earlier and most notorious radical feminist attempts to provide an explanation of reproduction and women's oppression was by Firestone, briefly discussed earlier in this chapter. In *The Dialectic of Sex* (1970), Firestone argued that women's oppression is rooted in female biology, and that it is women's role as reproducer that results in her subjugation. Firestone explains that human reproductive biology has created what she calls the "biological family." This social construct is the result of two universal factors: the mother's increased vulnerability and need for protection during pregnancy and while nursing her young, and the infant's dependency on adults for survival, and especially on mother's milk. Firestone stated that:

> a basic mother/child interdependency has existed in some form in every society, past or present, and thus has shaped the psychology of every mature female and every infant . . . the natural reproductive difference between the sexes led directly to the first division of labor. (1970, pp. 8–9)

Women's oppression is thus attributed to reproductive biology; therefore, the liberation of women requires a biological revolution in which women are freed from the consequences of their biology. In addition to contraception, Firestone proposes that birth become something artificial, in which infants could be produced in the laboratory. This could result in "the freeing of women from the tyranny of their reproductive biology . . . and the diffusion of the childbearing and child rearing role to the society as a whole, men as well as women" (p. 206).

Despite its power and originality, feminists did not adopt Firestone's suggestions in using technology to solve the "problem" of biology. Jaggar (1988) suggests that this may be due to the emphasis which places reproductive technology, historically used by men to control women and reinforce male dominance, as a prerequisite for women's liberation. Firestone's strategy for liberation did not stress the need to change male power; it is this which is really the source of oppression, and not pregnancy itself. Rather than encourage women to be childless, other feminists encouraged women to rear children with feminist values (Rich, 1976). Ultimately, Firestone's radical perspectives shook up society as they advocated for women to be more like men. Today, her perspective looks dated, as it negates women's diversities, rejects the fact that many women desire children, and ignores recent biological findings.

Reproduction can not be fully discussed without including thoughts on childrearing and caregiving issues associated with the family. Contrary to Firestone's characterization of female biology as problematic, feminists such as Adrienne Rich and Mary Daly have made reference to the "power inherent in female biology" (Rich, 1976) and "the native talent and superiority of women" (Daly, 1978). In celebrating female biology, some have identified male biology as what is problematic. As Jaggar (1988) states:

> For some radical feminists, the main problem with male biology is simply that it is not female. At its most obvious, this has meant that men lack the

special life-giving power that women possess in virtue of their biological capacity to become mothers. Except for a very privileged woman, however, being a mother has always involved caring for a child as well as giving birth to it; motherhood is associated conventionally not just with female reproductive biology, but with certain psychological qualities such as nurturance, warmth, emotional expressiveness, endurance, and practical common-sense. Most feminists have been at pains to argue that this association results simply from the social fact that mothers have always provided childcare. For some radical feminists, manifestations of these psychological qualities and their biological ability to become mothers is problematic. (p. 94)

Radical feminists understand more than other schools of feminist thought that theories which support women's "natural or biological talent" for childrearing play a significant role in placing women in caregiver roles, and in excluding men from such roles. This ultimately serves as a disadvantage for many women, and will be further addressed in the discussion of socialist feminism. This is because, whether or not women work in the paid labor force, caregiving is more often than not assigned to them. This "extra" duty of the employed woman in the paid workforce is rarely supported by maternity leave, child care, or elder care benefits and policies. Where radical feminists fall short is in the neglect of a life-span approach to women's lives. A life-span approach could aid radical feminists to view reproduction and childrearing as neverending responsibilities for most women, and consequently issues for aging women as well, whether as consumer or provider. I will return to this point later in this chapter.

Sexuality

In addition to male control of women's fertility, many radical feminists view women's sexuality as a crucial issue in feminism. In the words of Andrea Dworkin (1981), "Male domination of the female body is the basic material reality of women's lives and all struggle for dignity and self-determination is rooted in the struggle for actual control of one's body" (p. 205). There is a connection between sexuality and power:

Since the 1970s, feminists have uncovered a vast amount of sexual abuse of women by men. Rape, battery, sexual harassment, sexual abuse of children, prostitution, and pornography seen as the first time in their true scope and interconnectedness, from a distinctive pattern: the power of men over women in society. (MacKinnon, 1987, p. 5)

And Bryson (1992) provides this summary:

> Existing sexuality is a symptom of patriarchal society, the product of a world in which men have authority, women are economically dependent and male needs and desires set the agenda in all spheres. Far from being "natural," sexual behavior becomes bound up with the idea of ownership, domination, and submission, and is conditioned by a man-made culture in which pornography is all-pervasive, sexual violence is tolerated, and women are treated as sex-objects. (p. 212)

Apparent in both statements are two themes found throughout radical feminist literature on women's sexuality: that women are oppressed physically by men through violence, and that women are viewed as sexual objects. For some, women's objectification is a "prelude and condition of slavery" (Rich, 1980a, p. 320), denying women control over their bodies, a fundamental struggle for women.

Control over one's body means being free from the forced motherhood and sexual slavery imposed by patriarchy. Rejecting heterosexuality is therefore one way of ending this oppression, since the social inequality between men and women makes it impossible to women for take control of their bodies as long as they remain in intimate relationships with men (Jaggar, 1988). Rich (1980b) and Dworkin (1981) have attacked heterosexuality as oppressive, believing that it is a political institution, rather than a natural expression of sexual desire, and something that was imposed upon women for the domestic, emotional, and sexual benefit of men. This perspective leads some radical feminists to see lesbianism and separatism as ways for women to take immediate control of their bodies.

Somewhat surprisingly, the radical feminist focus on the critical importance of control over sexuality and one's body does not extend to issues facing aging women. Advanced age usually does not remove sexuality from women's lives unless it is by choice. Indeed, aging women are confronted with issues relating to sexuality and domination in both the home and the marketplace. Older women's control over their bodies during and after menopause, in their later years, if and when they become frail, and during the dying process are all critical topics that will benefit from a radical feminist analysis.

Violence Against Women

Directly related to sexuality is violence or the threat of violence, the third foundation used by patriarchy to oppress and control women. While "male biology" is responsible for women's oppression, radical feminists have more recently acknowledged the role of socially constructed assumptions of human nature which serve to socially sanction behavior. As indicated by some feminists, "aggression and the 'need' to dominate form a routine part of what is accepted as 'normal' male sexuality" (Coveney, Jackson, Jeffreys, & Mahoney, 1984, p. 9). As one radical feminist adds, "Every man has power and privilege over women, whether he uses it blatantly or subtly" (Deevey, 1974, p. 24). Whether or not men exercise violence, women are oppressed by the fear associated with potential assault and violence and perceived vulnerability (Brownmiller, 1975). This has a heavy impact on women's lives, for as Jaggar (1988) points out:

> Whether or not she is actually assaulted, the knowledge that assault is a permanent possibility influences the life of every woman. Women are afraid to hitchhike, to take walks in the moonlight, to travel at night by bus or on a subway, to frequent certain areas of the city or campus. This fear restricts women's areas of residence, their social and political activities, and of course, their study and work possibilities. (p. 94)

Radical feminists expand our critical awareness of violence in the family by "exploding the myth of the universal, emotionally satisfying nuclear family" (Jaggar, 1988, p. 124). Families can be loving, supportive, and kind, but they can also be sites of domination and oppression, and for some, danger and even death. As the primary source of male ideological indoctrination for both sexes, radical feminists recognize the powerful force the family plays in women's lives. The political activism that radical feminists bring to this area have been models for other feminists. Nonetheless, while many of the victims of rape and violence are under age 30, middle-aged and older women are not immune to violence, assault, and harassment. Their stories have not been added to the narrative. When they are, their voices will make clear that violence against women occurs in all ages, and that violence is misogyny.

Thus, there is potentially fruitful ground to be contributed by radical feminists who seek to heighten and broaden an understanding of aging. Suggested here are four areas for their analyses: (a) a view of reproduction and caregiving from a life-span perspective; (b) an increased awareness of older women's need for control over their sexuality, and for lifestyles that may reflect alternate sources for love and affection; (c) older women's desire to control their health issues and the dying process; and (d) the study of violence across the life cycle. As one example, a broader definition of lesbianism—as women loving women along a continuum of varied and changing relationships—certainly rings true for many older women today. But there is little written about aging lesbians. The contributions radical feminists can make in this area have yet to be written.

TOWARD A MORE INCLUSIVE RADICAL FEMINIST THEORY

Radical feminist theories are criticized for the ways in which they have universalized the status of women, making gender the primary organizing force for women (see Cain, 1993; Trask, 1996). Their earlier focus on reproduction and the private spheres of life ignores the growing numbers of women who work in both the public and private arenas. Single mothers, working-class women, and women of color, as well as growing numbers of White middle-class heterosexual women, realize all too well that women work in both spheres to survive. Also, many multicultural feminists, who share the burden of racism with their husbands, sons, and lovers, find some radical feminists' strategy of seeking a separatist culture for women to be unappealing. But radical feminists acknowledge a critical point that most liberal and other feminists do not; that the state, far from being politically gender-neutral, is patriarchal in its views and policies.

Radical feminists also oppose the false knowledge perpetuated by patriarchal ideology, instead acknowledging that women must move toward an authentic self, "away from an inauthentic false reality" (Donovan, 1996, p. 154). The importance of authenticity—women defining their own experiences in their own words—is essential for women if they are to live in a woman-valued society. In the absence of a life-span perspective on the study of women, an opportunity to include aging women was missed, however. A life-span approach can result in feminists extending their critiques of the consequences of the devaluation of women's work in the private sphere to middle-aged and aging women in their role as caregivers of the aged, as well as the study of the effects of such caregiving work on an adequate retirement income. A feminist age analysis can better document the strengths of older women who, regardless of their race and sexual orientation, are trivialized and ignored by patriarchal society. On the other hand, it could be that this negation of older women's worth results in increased freedom for authenticity and self-definition. Nonetheless, aging women are missing from radical feminists' theoretical and research agenda as they are from other schools of feminist thought.

Radical feminists critique ideologies and social policies in their nonsupport of women. Their contributions directed at the life experiences of older women will enrich the discourse on age and social organizations. If this is not clear, then think about how rape and sexual harassment were conceptualized by a male-dominated society prior to the work of radical feminists. Think about how work is conceptualized today—as if the employee has no child care, eldercare, or home responsibilities. Think about how retirement benefits and programs are built on the male standard, excluding the majority of older women; how research has used the male standard to define normative aging, with the result that women are either ignored or pathologized; about the increasing rates of poverty among women; the rising numbers of violent acts directed against women of all ages; and how youth remains the referent point for beauty for both men and women. Finally, think about the decreasing number of long term care services and programs with society's concomitant push for eldercare to be family care (i.e., woman-care) at a time when more and more women are working full-time and are divorced, single, or widowed, and living in poverty or near-poverty situations.

In sum, radical feminism attributes women's oppression to gender hierarchy, a product of patriarchy, and seeks an end to sexism. A key issue for radical feminists is gender hierarchy and the role of ideology and the state in its perpetuation. Another critique questions the male standard as it is applied to women. The critical importance of authenticity—self-definitions apart from patriarchy—is paramount for women. Moreover, radical feminists alert women to the realization that what happens in the home has political ramifications for women. That is because the family, while a place of potential support, is also a site of domination and struggle (Hartmann, 1981).

Equality will only come when the gender distribution of power is understood and when it ends. What radical feminists can offer a new epistemology of women and age, then, is the insistence that older women define themselves so their multiple truths can be told; an understanding of the political and sexualized nature of women's oppression and inequalities; and an expansion of the discourse on sources and consequences of women's oppression to include analyses of reproduction, sexuality, control over health issues, and violence from a life-span perspective.

SOCIALIST FEMINIST THEORY

Socialist feminism is similar to other streams of feminist thought in that it seeks to understand the source and nature of women's oppression and how that oppression can be stopped. It differs from radical feminism, however, in that it builds upon the revolutionary and existing theories of Marxist and radical feminism to develop a political theory "that will synthesize the vast insights of radical feminism and of the Marxist tradition that simultaneously will escape the problems associated with each" (Jaggar, 1988, p. 123). More recently, socialist feminism constitutes a more inclusive approach to diversity that can lead to a "broader understanding of human activity" (Calasanti & Zajicek, 1993, p. 127).

Socialist feminist ideas are firmly rooted in Marxist premises and ideology. But because Marxism was developed without a major focus on women, its use in contemporary feminism has been and continues to be debated (see Hartmann, 1981; Hartsock, 1985; MacKinnon, 1989). Such doubts were recently espoused by Donovan (1996), noting that since Marx concentrated "primarily on men and masculine circumstances . . . the legitimacy of such concepts applied to women may be seen as intrinsically suspect" (p. 65). Nonetheless, Donovan and other feminists believe that Marxism is important to contemporary feminist theory, even though its "fit" to feminism is uneven. A brief discussion of Marxism and the writings of its most famous theorists, Karl Marx and Frederick Engels, is beyond the scope of this book. Rather, some of its major ideas will be briefly summarized here, with greater attention to contemporary socialist feminism.

Similar to radical feminism, socialist feminism advocates for freedom from reproduction. But unlike radical feminists, socialist feminists see patriarchy as more rooted in economics than psychology and domination, defining it as "a set of social relations between men, which have a material base, and which, though hierarchical, establish or create interdependence and solidarity among men that enable them to dominate women" (Hartmann, 1981, p. 14). More recently, socialist feminism has centered its analyses on the multiple and complex layers of oppression and the ways in the "ways that the power relations of capitalism (class domination) and patriarchy (male domination) together structure ideology, the social relations of gender, class and race, and the overall organization of society" (Abramowitz, 1992, p. 24). Ideas found in socialist feminism recognize the interlocking nature of class, gender, and racial domination, while not ignoring other systems of oppression (Calasanti & Zajicek, 1993). Therefore, this perspective makes a commitment to understanding the life situations of women of color, working-class women, disabled women, poor women, lesbians, and old women—as well as White, financially privileged, heterosexual women (B. Smith, 1983). Subsequently, socialist feminists, unlike radical feminists, see no universal "woman."

While sharing the radical feminist critique of liberal theory as obscuring the class and power relations of the state, socialist feminism focuses more than radical feminism on the impact of patriarchy and capitalism, the gender division of labor, the dialectic between the spheres of reproduction and production, and the impact of these on poor women and women of color. As Abramowitz argues, together these have regulated the lives of women. Socialist feminism looks at the economic status of women and the economic relations between men and women. Consequently, the gender division of labor is as important as class divisions of labor.

Socialist feminism examines how women's domestic labor favors capitalism and patriarchy while reinforcing women's exploitation in the market. This benefits men more than women. But it also sees the contributions of such labor to both systems. With its focus on poor and minority women, socialist feminists understand that the distinction between public and private spheres is and always has been nonexistent for many women, especially the poor—a point lost on many liberal feminists. Recognizing the influence of reproduction on women's productive lives, socialist feminists define reproduction more broadly to include kinkeeping, and political, community, and ideological work. These feminists advocate, then, for changes in both ideologies and institutions that do not support women.

MARXISM AND WOMEN'S OPPRESSION

The following section, based on the writings of Donovan (1996) and Hartsock (1985) identifies the central insights of Marxism. Historical materialism, the basis for Marxist thought, asserts that culture and society are based in material or economic conditions. In other words, it is man's social being that leads to consciousness, and not his consciousness that leads to his being (Marx, 1967). Speaking in the words of class conflict and class consciousness, Marx argued that a class or group exists when it consciously sees itself as a class, usually in opposition to a ruling class. He developed sophisticated theories about capitalism and labor and the value of work, and blamed capitalism and industry for workers' feelings of alienation (Marx, 1967).

Capitalism, or the historical commodification of labor, began when workers were made to work for wages. With industrialization and capitalism, workers became things, or commodities. A growing alienation occurred, according to Marx, when the Eros, or joy, of work was removed, leaving workers unhappy and isolated from their production. Far from only affecting the worker (the man), this dissatisfaction spread like a disease to the worker's family and to society. One result of capitalism was the development of the separate spheres of production and reproduction.

Male ideology defines production as that which is created in the public sphere; in contrast, women's production, or reproduction, occurs in the private sphere of the home. Men found that many of the goals of their work in the public sphere were paired hand in hand with the capitalist market economy. In contrast, many women found that they were relegated to the private sector or to segregated employment by men and capitalism and devalued and exploited in both (Calasanti & Bailey, 1991).

A product of his gender, place, and time, Marx saw the gender division of labor as natural and based in biology. But he also understood that a wife and children, under capitalism, became private property owned by the husband. He envisioned a classless society, where men and women not only enjoyed work but saw work as an opportunity for creative activities.

It was up to Engels, however, to discuss the role of women in the revolution in his book, *The Origin of the Family, Private Property, and the State* (1884). He conceded with Marx that the sexualization of the division of labor was both normative and acceptable. However, he did not agree with the hierarchization of the division of labor. Instead, he argued that men and women should hold equal power, whether work was done in the home or in the market. He attributed the cause of women's oppression to the privatization and denigration of household labor. Furthermore, Engels hypothesized that it was men's control over women's reproduction that maintained women in their caregiving roles. Since the work done by women at home had no exchange value in the market, it was neither rewarded nor respected. Concurrently, with the increasing value of wealth, that is, men's work, the family became male-dominated, as men needed to ensure paternity to pass down their assets and wealth. Husbands became, according to Engels, the bourgeoisie, and wives the proletariat. The solution, according to Engels, was for women to embrace public life and for the single nuclear family to cease being the main economic unit of society.

CONTEMPORARY SOCIALIST FEMINISM

Contemporary socialist feminists, similar to radical feminists, assert that patriarchy and capitalism are at the root of women's subjugation. From a socialist feminist perspective, women's oppression is evident in male domination over women's labor in the home and at work (Hartmann, 1981). Male domination of these interrelated realities creates a patriarchal social order of which men are the ultimate beneficiaries. This social order also remains stable because those who dominate each realm—namely, males—benefit from such domination.

Building on Marxist feminist theory, which views women's oppression as the result of capitalism and class, and radical feminist theory, which attributes women's oppression to patriarchal control of women's biology and reproduction, Hartmann describes a "dual-system" theory for socialist feminism in which capitalism and patriarchy are two distinct but interacting systems of oppression. Unlike Marxist feminism, which Hartmann claims is "gender blind" and fails to specifically describe the situation of women under capitalism, and radical feminism, which fails to identify the material base of the patriarchal control of women, socialist feminism seeks to explain how both systems interact to subjugate women in both reproduction and production. More recent scholarship in socialist feminist theory expands the focus on capitalism and patriarchy to include the "notion that gender, class, and racial/ethnic relations [also] constitute an interlocking system of oppression" (Calasanti & Zajicek, 1993, p. 121).

Production, Reproduction, and Interlocking Oppressions

Production is often defined as creation and that which is accomplished in the public sphere. Reproduction, on the other hand, is that which is produced in the private sphere. Defined from a male viewpoint as maintenance work, reproduction is assigned less value that production.

Socialist feminists generally identify two realms of oppression related to production and reproduction: (a) women's segregated employment in low-paying jobs, and (b) the domestic labor of women and the economic, social, and cultural significance of that unpaid labor. Their focus is often on the interaction of the two. Socialist feminists also ground their work on how themes in production and reproduction differ by race, culture, ethnicity, and other sites of diversity. This allows for, according to Calasanti and Zajicek (1993), "the theoretical sensitivity needed to embrace the complex ways in which relations of domination interlock in people's lives" (p. 122). For example, socialist feminists, like other feminist schools of thought, write of the dialectic between production and reproduction; in other words, how work in one sphere affects work in the other. However, socialist feminists are more alert to the growing numbers of women who work in both spheres out of economic necessity, and emphasize the variations of women's lives by race and other factors.

A socialist feminist analysis, in contrast to liberal feminist theory, sees the role of the state in the continued oppression of women in both spheres. According to Naples (1991), a socialist feminist scholar, the state and its subsequent social policies contribute to women's oppression in five ways. These include: (a) using gender-neutral language to mask women's oppression and impoverishment; (b) stigmatizing household forms that differ from the male-headed, two-parent household; (c) controlling the work of reproduction; (d) maintaining women in paid and unpaid caretaking roles that are devalued both ideologically and economically; and (e) fragmenting social life in state policy (p. 25). Consequently, most socialist feminism's energies do not focus on any expectations that the system or the "state" will be the sole source of help for women.

Using this framework, Naples critiqued the Family Support Act (FSA) of 1988 and identified a number of ways in which patriarchal social relations are embedded in the FSA and how the state continues to enforce women's oppression and poverty. First, the FSA uses gender-neutral language, ignoring the obvious that it is women who are the primary caregivers of children and that it is men who are often negligent in making payments for their children's survival. Second, the FSA stigmatizes different households such as lesbian, or single-headed, emphasizing instead the two-parent patriarchal nuclear family. Third, women's reproductive rights are challenged by invasions of privacy and limited access to abortion. Fourth, women's work as family caregiver is made invisible due to family ethic ideology. Lastly, the connections between work in private and public spheres are ignored by family policies.

Although not her focus, Naples' analysis can be extended to the issues that surround caregiving and economic security across the life span, especially in later life. For example, Quadagno (1988) examined the linkages between both spheres that result in women having less access to private pensions compared to men. Moreover, and as was discussed in chapter 1, women's reproductive activities have resulted in women's penalization in both private-sector and public-sector pension schemes. A socialist feminist perspective alerts us to these linkages, and also integrates the ways in which race/ethnicity and class have placed older women, especially working-class and minority women, on the lowest rings of the financial ladder.

In contrast to production, domination in the domestic realm centers around women's unpaid reproductive labor. This includes childbearing; the physical and nurturing care of infants, children, and the aged; and the domestic duties associated with the household. The popular phrase "a woman's place is in the home" has its roots in the sexual division of labor which assigns women to the domestic realm. This sexual division of labor is also the source of women's subordination upon which socialist feminists focus. Such unpaid (or low-paid) labor has economic, social, and cultural significance, ultimately benefitting men at women's expense. By keeping women economically dependent on men, and serving as "rewards" in the private sphere, men become more compliant, due to their sense of responsibility and need for salaries to support their families (Hartmann, 1981).

But, avoiding an "either/or" argument, socialist feminism also sees the potential benefits in the work women provide at home that can result in a consciousness that is "holistic, relational, contextual and life affirming" (Donovan, 1996). It is these values, according to Donovan, that provide a base in which to critique patriarchy and capitalism. Nonetheless, the household work women provide gives men their supremacy. One solution is for housekeeping and childrearing work to become more collective social industries. But an orientation built on gender alone fails to help this analysis. For, if working-class women continue to provide these tasks to more privileged women, then such tasks, along with the women that perform them, will remain devalued and underpaid. The primary breadearner in most middle-class heterosexual families—the male—may hold the power at work and at home, but many working-class women and women of color rarely hold power in either sphere. In truth, as long as the division of labor exists by gender and race, work alone will not solve the problem of social injustice.

Another strategy at times advocated by socialist feminists to render childrearing and housekeeping more equitable has been "wages for housework." This would, according to MacKinnon (1989), "empower women within the home by demystifying the naturalness of their work. . . . By attacking women's economic dependence upon men, it proposes to alter the balance of advantage in the family" (p. 67). This strategy is considered controversial among many feminists, and will be discussed further in the following chapter.

Mitchell (1966) speculated that progress toward women's liberation is slow because of the socially useful roles that women perform in childrearing. In applying this reasoning to the unpaid caregiving provided by older women, we see that it is not only men who exploit the unpaid labor of women. Medical systems, social services, and many professions also depend on the unpaid labor of women to "fill the gaps" in service. This injustice must be addressed through policies and programs that support both women and men in their caregiving roles as a societal responsibility. Other supportive examples of women-centered policies and programs would ensure there are choices in whether or not caregiving is provided; promote solutions to the continued circumstances which force women and older women into caregiver's roles; and ensure that older women are not economically penalized for providing such care (Hooyman & Gonyea, 1995). In general, socialist feminists were overdue in grasping the fact that caregiving occurs across the life span, especially among the daughters and wives who provide the bulk of elder caregiving.

More recently, socialist feminism theorizes around what Calasanti and Zajicek (1993) refer to as the "paradigm of domination," similar to P. H. Collins' (1990) "matrix of domination." This concept emphasizes the ways in which age, gender, class, and racial/ethnic relations are interlocking forces of oppression (Calasanti & Zajicek, 1993). According to Calasanti and Zajicek, there are two theoretical concepts critical for socialist feminist thinking here. First is racial formation—the definition, formation, and weight assigned to race for meaning by social, economic, and political forces. The second concept applies this understanding of race formation to gender. Somewhat similarly, political, economic, and social forces also historically structure the meaning of gender relations. Therefore, and based on these two concepts, a sole focus on gender is not the goal of socialist feminism. Rather, the authors theorize that socialist feminism extends a relational understanding of the "structuring of class, race, and gender [as conceived] . . . as social processes through which class, and race/ethnicity historically structure the concept of gender, and simultaneously as processes through which class and race/ethnicity also acquire their specific meaning in the context of gender relations" (p. 122). Writings in contemporary socialist feminism reflect a greater concern with these intricate and complex factors as they impact on all women's well-being.

SOCIALIST FEMINISM AND AGING WOMEN

A growing number of gerontologists and socialist feminists are beginning to tackle women's aging issues from a socialist feminist perspective (see Blieszner, 1993; Calasanti, 1993; Calasanti & Zajicek, 1993; Dressel, 1988; Estes et al., 1984; Stoller, 1993). According to Calasanti and Zajicek (1993), there are five crucial areas of contributions that socialist feminists can make to gerontology and to older women. They include "analyses of (1) patriarchy and the paradigm of domination; (2) gendering processes within organizations; (3) production and reproduction as delineated by the dialectical relations between private and public spheres; (4) the family; and (5) the gendered welfare system" (p. 121). Stoller (1993), for example, in discussing caregiving from a socialist feminist perspective, describes it as an exploitation of "obligation, structured by the gender-based division of domestic labor, the invisibility and devaluing of unpaid labor, occupational segregation in the workforce, and an implicitly gendered work place" (p. 166). Arguing against women's essentialist nature to care, feminist socialists see caregiving as but another example of women's oppression. Many therefore resist all efforts to "reward" women with governmental payments if it keeps them providing this societal function at great cost and consequence to them. Other socialist–feminist scholars have studied such diverse topics as widowhood (Blieszner, 1993) and pension coverage (Hills & Tigges, 1995) from this perspective.

A socialist feminist approach to the study of widowhood, according to Blieszner (1993) "includes the interacting influences of gender, class, and race/ethnicity as reflected in the notion of the paradigm of domination" and attention to the "influence of capitalism and patriarchy on widowhood" (p. 172). She exposes a number of design flaws in how widowhood is studied, noting that research usually examines its relationship to well-being, mental health, and loneliness. Rarely studied are the economic consequences of widowhood to women and the "structured conditions associated with the economic dependence of women on men and their inadequate financial preparation for widowhood" (p. 175). Additionally, while research has studied the impact of class and race on the gender division of labor in marriage, the effects of these factors on widowhood are generally ignored. Such a focus leads to a victim stance on widowhood. Rather than taking an "either/or" approach to the study of widowhood, Blieszner notes that women may be more self-sufficient due to their socialization and the gender-based power relations and divisions of labor in the home in household tasks. Also, research too often conceptualizes women as the "other," with married women considered the norm. More-over, widowed men are generally ignored, in part because they are less numerous than widows. A socialist feminist approach does not agree with men being ignored—women are not the only ones who grieve. The relationships between lesbian and gay lovers are also absent from study. Thus, research that is nonfeminist often takes a limited analysis to widow-hood, seeing it as a static point in time and not contextualized by race, economic, or other factors. As argued by Blieszner, a socialist perspective on widowhood allows for increased focus on the economic consequences on widowhood, while also addressing topics such as self-sufficiency and the diversities of the experiences inherent in both widows and widowhood.

DIFFERENCE AND COMMON GROUND

As with other feminisms, there are some agreements and disagreement between these two schools. Earlier radical feminist theories grounded their focus in the effects of patriarchy on women's general well-being, while socialist feminist theories focused on the consequences of capitalism. Radical feminists are more attuned to differentials of gender hierarchy and power, while socialist feminists are more attuned to differences among women, with a sharper focus on class issues surrounding patriarchy and capitalism. In looking at the connections between radical and socialist feminisms, Young (1981) believes that the latter must develop a single theory out of the best insights of Marxism and radical feminisms, which can then comprehend capitalist patriarchy as one system that oppresses women. Hartmann (1981), on the other hand, contends that socialist feminists must "organize a practice which addresses both the struggle against patriarchy and the struggle against capitalism" (p. 32). More recently, Calasanti and Zajicek (1993) assert that socialist feminism is a perspective that can allow aging to be studied in a more inclusive manner, noting the diversities that exist in the aging process. Socialist feminists' focus on multiple and interlocking oppressions extends a critical understanding to the lives of men. This is because, as these authors note, "socialist feminists' focus on women is based on the premise that thinking from women's lives allows us to understand the realities of women's and men's economic and political situation" (p. 120). To analyze gender relations, both men and women must be included in a model that employs "divergent interpretative frameworks sensitive to power relations and the divisions of labor which traverse private and public spheres" (Calasanti, 1993, p. 280). In contrast, radical feminism has focused more on strategies of women organizing for women, and has taken somewhat of a more essentialist view of women. In contrast, socialist feminism has viewed the organization of all oppressed groups as the goal, as well as focusing on the linkages between all oppressions.

Each theory is concerned with the exploitation of women and how to stop it. Their strategies to end oppression have at times varied, but have also coalesced. Both recognize, although with different emphases, the patriarchal sex-gender system and the capitalist class system. The problems that surround gender-neutral language in social policy are acknowledged. Understood is how alternate family forms have been penalized by the state. Both disagree with liberal feminism, arguing that it is not the loss of equal opportunity that leaves women without rights and oppressed. While both schools also agree that caregiving and poverty are problematic for women, the needs of aging women have generally not been their focus. Moreover, radical feminists' focus over women's control over their bodies did not extend to women's control over their health over the life span, i.e., menopause, age-specific diseases, and so on. And, as we mentioned earlier, such a focus could begin needed discussions on women and men's control over their own dying process that can benefit both sexes and all ages.

Taking a larger view, Gibson (1996) suggests that this lack of attention to older women by Marxist, socialist, and radical feminists has resulted in a preoccupation with older women as social problems and with the social construction of inequality. In other words, the socialist and radical preoccupation with reproductive labor, paid labor, and the sex services provided by women results in a neglect of aging women who, divorced from such elements, do not "fit" into such analyses. This, as suggested by Gibson, has led to the present theoretical incapacity of feminism to incorporate issues about age. Recent writings by a number of socialist feminists have begun to correct this problem.

CONCLUSIONS

Radical feminists see patriarchy as the root of women's problems. Individual and collective change is sought, as well as "woman-centered" conceptualizations of women's lives. Women have benefitted from radical feminism's attention to issues such as violence against women in both the public and private spheres, and women's rights to choose their own lifestyles. Contributions from the dominance approach to understanding oppression expose the ways in which women's lives have been subjugated and sexually segregated in exploitative ways. Radical feminism calls not only for women to be freed from providing childbearing and childrearing responsibilities, but also to an end to gender hierarchy in all its forms. Nonetheless, it does not include a life-span perspective in its critique of society. With its earlier interest in women's biology, "age" is not considered. Issues of forced caregiving, sexual harassment, or violence against older women are ignored. Socialist feminism, on the other hand, views women's problems more as a manifestation of the larger social world that is both capitalistic and patriarchal. Socialist feminists are, historically, more equipped to understand the effects of both capitalism and patriarchy in explaining women's oppression, and are also more attuned to issues of race, class, heterosexism, and—more recently—age. Their recent literature is beginning to address age with thoughtful analyses.

Implications of Feminist Theories: Strategies for Change

Present Strategies for Equality: A Feminist Critique

To be honest with you, I think that [educating women about inequalities about income in later life] is important, but you have got to force Congress to do something about this. It is absolutely outrageous that we have not.

—Representative Mary Rose Oakar, May 22, 1990,
in a hearing before the Select Committee on Aging,
U.S. House of Representatives

Equality and justice are American myths. In 1776, equality was declared throughout the land. For many it wasn't so. In colonial and postcolonial times, women, Native Americans, and ethnic minorities, as well as White men who owned no property, were without most legal rights and generally considered "nonpersons" (Jansson, 1991). In a land intolerant of diversity, "justice and freedom for all" had a hollow ring. In 1870, the Fifteenth Amendment to the Constitution awarded universal suffrage to men, but women struggled until 1920 to earn theirs. As women soon realized, however, legal access to the voting booth did not automatically result in increased rights, power, and privilege.

Historically, feminists have advocated for women's right to a just and equitable life. Their strategies to reach this goal have not always been, however, in concert with one another. This chapter will discuss the present theoretical conceptualizations, and public policy and legal strategies recommended by feminists for achieving women's justice, security, and autonomy. Understanding the importance of sociohistorical time and changing influences on the nation's Zeitgeist, the present conservative agenda, will also be discussed. Although clearly not feminist, this perspective nonetheless has important implications for older women's equality and well-being.

POLICIES AND DIRECTIONS OF THE NEW RIGHT: THE CONSERVATIVE AGENDA

Since the 1970s, a number of conservative political and religious groups have actively become involved in the political process. Collectively known as the "New Right," they exert their presence in debates over abortion, secularism in public schools, sex education, gay and lesbian rights, affirmative action, defense spending, and welfare reform. Some proponents of the New Right, according to an article in *Time* magazine (Thurow, August 19, 1996) seek to "demolish the welfare state, including Social Security, and roll back federal powers over business and the states" (p. 46). A number of groups claim to be members of the New Right, including the Christian Coalition and the National Right to Life Committee. Among women, the conservative agenda has been the domain of a number of groups affiliated with the New Right, such as the Eagle Forum and Concerned Women for America.

Proponents of the New Right generally support the "family ethic" and define the "correct" family as the nuclear heterosexual patriarchal family, basing this on a White middle-class American norm. Conservative ideologies long for a return to what they view as a more simple time in the nation's history, when White males ruled the community and their homes, and when women and minorities were subordinate to them in both the public and private spheres. In the conservative quest to reconstruct the moral superiority of the traditional White patriarchal family, however, the historical, class, economic, and racial issues of contemporary families are ignored.

Conservative ideologies, policies, and programs generally bifurcate work in the home—the private sphere—from work in the labor market—the public sphere. Although the former has traditionally been the domain of women, the latter is viewed as the domain of men. However, women should not be confused; they are subordinate in both. Conservative ideologies ignore the fact that women are found in the public sphere nearly as often as men, albeit in segregated, lower-paid employment. Instead, it is the work in the public sphere held primarily by men that has market value.

This ideological framework reinforces traditional gender roles and the gender division of labor, at least for privileged women. Nonproductive labor (i.e., work in the home, the nurturance of children, support of the husband, and so forth) is judged valueless in the market. Activities such as these are not without intrinsic value—their value, however, is nonmonetary. Instead, the work women provide in the home is normative, descriptive, and expected of who women are by definition of their gender. Because such gender roles are considered normative for most middle-class women, conservatives believe that it is as proper for men to go out and work as it is proper for women to stay home. Subsequently, women's "work" does not have to be financially compensated—it is just what women "do." It follows, then, that women's work in the home is made invisible (L. V. Davis, 1994b).

Not only have work and family responsibilities been sexualized (men work, women stay home), but such activities are also hierarchized. In other words, when women do work outside of the home, their work earns less in monetary value compared to men's work. This is evident in men earning a higher income compared to similarly situated women, as well as data that document women's continued segregated places of employment. Women's work is also "racialized." In other words, women of color are expected to provide work in the home and in the low-paid market place. In contrast to conservative theorists, feminist arguments around the "family ethic" or familism believe that defining women's roles and responsibilities in this way has serious economic consequences for many women (see Abramowitz, 1992; Hooyman & Gonyea, 1995; Miller, 1990).

The News Right's beliefs surrounding gender roles and the gender division of labor influence national opinion. But apart from the coverage in the media, there is very little research on the New Right's influence on social policy on the national, state, and local levels (Midgley, 1990). This is curious, since the New Right has taken strong positions on a number of areas of national policy such as health care, race relations, and poverty. Over the last decade, a number of books have attempted to correct this by examining the New Right's views on contemporary social problems (Abel, 1987; Bruce, 1988; Ford, 1991; Jorstad, 1987) and how the nation should solve them.

There exists some haziness among various factions of the New Right in relation to social welfare. While some advocate for a complete end to social welfare, others contend it may have some limited value when and if it is offered as a last resort. Other factions of the New Right, notably the Christian Coalition, look to the Bible for their answers. Among the New Christian Right, according to Midgley (1990): "There can be no legitimate separation of the religious and secular domains. There is only one truth, which is the truth of the scriptures as interpreted by fundamentalist Protestant theologians. This truth should govern all human affairs including matters of social policy. It is through Christian teaching that we will find peace" (p. 400).

The New Right is more apt to blame the nations's woes on what they perceive as the unraveling threads of society's moral fabric. Moreover, it is the family, primarily women, that should be responsible for the health, education, and welfare of its members. Members of the New Right typically call to a return to traditional American values. In truth, the majority of Americans are supportive of "family values." The point of debate is often over the definition of "family," whose values speak for "America," and how much diversity is tolerated with the definition of such concepts.

Regardless of the varying factions, feminists note that the goals of the New Right are much more political and in synch with one another. The New Right aims to keep women in unpaid or underpaid positions so that they may continue to serve patriarchy and capitalism with their free work (Abel, 1987; Arendell & Estes, 1991). What such groups have in common is that they are antifeminist, antigay, anti-Communist, antiabortion, anti-sex education, antipornography, fearful of men's seeming loss of power and authority in the family, and against government-funded child care and welfare spending. Conversely, they are promilitary, pro-prayer in school, and in favor of an expanded church role in social welfare, as opposed to an expanded federal government role (Abbott & Wallace, 1992; Conover & Gray, 1983; B. Gould, 1990; Liebman & Wuthnow, 1983; Marshall, 1991).

THE NEW RIGHT'S FIGHT AGAINST WOMEN, WELFARE, AND LIBERALISM

According to feminist author and social activist Andrea Dworkin (1988), the New Right movement in the United States

> is especially concerned with opposing equality as a social goal. It stands against what Margaret Papandreou [American feminist and wife of Andreas Papandreou, former Prime Minister of Greece] has called "the democratic family," a family not based on the subordination of women but instead on equality, cooperation, and reciprocity. It stands against all programmatic efforts to achieve racial and economic equality. It stands against sex equality as idea and as practice. It seeks to destroy any movement, program, law, discourse, or sentiment that would end, injure, or undermine male dominance over women. The contemporary Right in the United States [is for] authority, hierarchy, property, and religion; democracy is what it is against. (p. 193)

In placing middle-class women who stay at home—the "good mother"—on a pedestal, the conservative agenda faces a dilemma in explaining their mean-spirited attacks against stay-at-home poor younger women as mothers (see Gilder, 1981; Murray, 1984, 1988). If "good" women stay home and raise the children, ideologically speaking, then one wonders why poor welfare mothers who do just that receive so much wrath. Why must a poor mother receiving welfare leave her children with others so that she can work a minimum-wage job? And how is it that decreasing or limiting aid to single mothers with children, which will result in increased numbers of poor children, is now viewed as a major political strategy for strengthening families?

Advocates of such "welfare reform" advocate for decreased benefits to the nation's neediest. The Personal Responsibility and Work Opportunity Reconciliation Act of 1996 was historic legislation in that it abolished the 61-year-old federal entitlement program, Aid to Families with Dependent Children (AFDC), and replaced it with Temporary Assistance to Needy Families (TANF). Supporters of this change argue that women who receive financial assistance through TANF, for example, even those with small children, should do the opposite of young privileged middle-class mothers. They must go out and take a job (any kind will do), while the middle-class woman should stay home to take care of hearth and home, usually resulting in her dependence on a male. Such inconsistencies in the conservative ideology, regardless whether the program is AFDC or TANF, support male domination over women, and White women over women of color. Lest poor women think they will earn respect and equality if they work outside the home, they only need to read conservative literature to know that their increasing numbers in the work force have been blamed for the decreasing number of jobs and men's insecurity in the work force (see Gilder, 1981; Murray, 1984). In essence, women are the scapegoats for a global economy. However, should poor women stay at home and not work, then they are parasites on the social welfare "liberal" state. Rather than thanking these women for providing the day-to-day care that their children's often absent fathers do not, the New Right attributes much of the federal deficit on poor mothers who receive public welfare benefits. Because of the sexist and racist nature of the attacks on the poor, attaching the nation's financial woes to poor women is a sure-fire way to take attention away from the nation's real problems of corporate restructuring, growing poverty, international drug trafficking, escalating crime rates, and a national mindset that escalates profit at any cost into a religion.

Poverty is viewed by conservatives as a result of personal failings, not structural disadvantage. Problems with the dual labor market, segregated employment, and the lack of comparative worth for women are inconsequential, as poverty is not caused by these issues.

From a life-span perspective, regardless of whether one is a recipient of public assistance or a more economically favored middle-class wife, nearly all women will end up with responsibilities for another kind of caregiving—caring for aging relatives. The conservative agenda is unrelenting here as well. Just as there is no need for a national child care policy, neither is there a need for a national long term care policy. Caregiving, whether it is for the young or the old, is viewed as a reflection of appropriate family values, and women should provide it free of charge and with a smile. Conservatives are not heartless—they do recognize that assistance is sometimes needed. The solution, however, is to look to churches and church-sponsored organizations, rather than federally supported legislation and programs (Jorstad, 1987).

Eisenstein (1981) hypothesizes that the reason the New Right attacks working mothers to the extent that they do is because the movement knows that working women have the potential to transform society. This is because "as women begin to understand the sexual bias in the marketplace . . . and continue to bear the responsibilities of housework and child care as women, they begin to voice feminist demands for affirmative action programs, equal pay, and abortion rights" (p. 78). In short, women begin to advocate and demand their equal rights. And since both liberalism and feminism seek "individual autonomy, independence, freedom of choice, equality of opportunity, and equality before the law" (p. 79), the New Right fears for the life of patriarchy. They couch their concerns, however, with well-orchestrated and well-articulated worries over the breakdown of the family. Liberalism, with its "welfare state," and feminism have simply got to be discredited.

THE CONSERVATIVE AGENDA, THE AGED, AND OLDER WOMEN

The New Right's attacks on aging policy have most often focused on issues of intergenerational equity and the proper role of government in social welfare. A number of conservative think tanks have led the charge against Social Security, most notably the Heritage Foundation, the Cato Institute, and groups such as Americans for Intergenerational Equity (AGE) and the Concord Coalition of the 1990s (Hudson, 1996). Those who attack Social Security have framed their argument as one generation (the aged) robbing children of their future because of the greed of the previous generation (Thurow, 1996). Other arguments have focused more of their attention on critiquing the appropriate role of government in providing for its citizens. Scholars note that such assaults are in reality thinly disguised attacks on social welfare (Hendricks, 1996; Hudson, 1996; Quadagno, 1996). Suggestions by conservative think tanks to privatize Social Security, or require income-eligibility requirements (means-testing), will have stark repercussions for the poor and near-poor aged, and will do little to make life better for poor children. I will return to this discussion in chapters 7 and 9.

In contrast to intergenerational fighting, a feminist analysis, together with a life-span perspective, documents the reciprocity between and among generations, and places responsibility for the nation's economic deficits on a number of global factors, rather than blaming the aged. Some of these alternate causes, according to Hooyman and Gonyea (1995), include "the worldwide economic upheaval, the decline in real wages for American workers, gender inequality in the labor market, and social policies that penalize nontraditional families" (p. 174).

In earlier chapters, I outlined the major issues impacting older women surrounding economic security, health issues, and caregiving that are further complicated by this nation's lack of adequate social welfare policies to prevent, address, and correct problems in them. What we saw from our discussion were the ways in which these issues interconnect with one another. Poverty in later life, one of the most troubling areas for women and policy analysts, is directly related to poverty in the earlier years. Ageism only adds to this risk of being poor and old. But the conservative agenda is presented with a conceptual and political dilemma if it attempts an explanation of older women's higher rates of poverty when compared to their male counterparts. If the vast majority of older women today, especially White middle-class older women, lived a life that mimicked the desired conservative agenda (e.g., stay at home in a long-lived marriage to one man), then how can their poverty be explained? Likewise, if older minority women and working-class women mimicked the work patterns of White men, spending their adult years in the work force as well as providing for the home front, then why are they the poorest of the poor?

It is relatively easy to see how the conservative agenda might suggest that poor older women are themselves to blame for their own poor financial status. Perhaps they just didn't save enough. Did they shop too much? Did they take one too many cruises? The myth of the wealthy widow is in sharp contrast to her actual economic status, a result of many of the factors that were discussed in chapter 1. Among these are restricted educational opportunities, limited educational attainment, no credit in Social Security or pensions for the years spent caregiving, segregated employment, and jobs that pay lower wages due to not only segregated employment but discrimination.

Herein lies the dilemma for the conservative agenda. If the fault of the older woman's poverty is not with the older woman who stayed home and raised the family, or who was employed in the work force in addition to caring for her family, then it must be structural. So the conservative agenda is in a quandary. They must look at structural inequalities such as sexism and racism as causes for poverty in younger women, combined with the force of ageism among aged women. But, rather than reach such a conclusion, the needs of older women are for the most part ignored. Issues of adequacy and equity for aged women are rarely, if ever, of concern to the conservative agenda. The causes of older women's poverty rate little attention or importance. In fact, many conservative writers deliberately mislead the public in pointing out the riches held by the "older population" (Ferrara, 1995; Thurow, 1996), when they know quite well that such figures do not speak for the vast majority of aged women, specifically older minority women, as well as working-class older men. Their sometimes disguised arguments to dismantle the Social Security system are justified in their eyes, as the White male aging experience has been universalized as speaking for all older people. Older White males do have higher retirement incomes than women and people of color. But to critique Social Security based on the wealth of the privileged few negates the poverty and near-poverty situations of working-class men and women, most older women, and women of color. Conservatives argue, instead, that because "older people" are wealthy enough, they shouldn't need such economic insurance and assistance. And this includes older women.

Conservatives see nothing wrong with the present system whereby older women receive retirement benefits most often as a dependent to a husband. Perhaps such an economically driven political analysis works quite well if one's marriage to a wealthy man never ends in divorce, a premature death, or loss of family fortune due to poor investing. Neglected, however, are other groups of women—the never-married, the divorced, working-class, and gay and lesbian older women. The conservative agenda does see the importance of connections between the private and public sphere, but only for men.

This point should be explained further. The conservative agenda understands all too well that a heterosexual working man benefits when he has a homemaker wife who stays home, raises the children, does the food shopping, picks up his clothes from the cleaners, supervises or does the yard work, and arranges their social calendar. This is because, as was previously discussed, the conservative agenda defines women's work as "nonwork," which then allows the man to serve capitalism to his best abilities. A "good wife" can assist a husband with a promotion at work by fulfilling household duties, for in doing so, the man is "freed up" to do double duty at work. The conservative agenda does understand the connection between the private and public spheres. But it refuses to see how staying at home for most women throughout their adult lives negatively impacts on their financial security in later life. Subsequently, neither do most conservatives comprehend the real value of social welfare programs, such as Social Security and Supplemental Security Income (SSI), that attempt to offer some economic protection to aging women. The second arena that presents problems for older women, also discussed in chapter 1, is the specific health concerns faced by older women. The lack of research on older women is associated with their inadequate and inaccessible health care. This deficiency of research on women, and more specifically older women, appears to be of little interest to the conservative agenda. It may be that, according to their view, the study of men provides relevant information about women as well. Ironically, as conservatives have always stressed the differences between the sexes, it is interesting that there has not been an outcry to study older women "as different" from men. Most feminists strongly suspect that this lack of attention and inadequate funding of women's health is due to the idea that aged women are not seen as worthy of the expenditure of funds.

Furthermore, conservative policies fail to uncover relationships among poverty, discrimination, and poor health. It blames women for their poor health, and fails to see their lives from a life-span perspective. These policies do not admit that a history of inadequate or nonexistent access to health care, poor nutrition, and poor health status in the younger years leads to poor health status in later life. And, as discussed at the start of this chapter, neither is a long term care system called for, since women provide this function. Neglected is the fact that while women do provide the bulk of long term care, men also care and are hurt by the lack of services as much as women. Rarely at issue among legislators are basic questions of social philosophy and social justice for those who need care the most.

The third issue that is problematic for women, and related closely to health and long term care, is caregiving. A number of feminist writers have expressed their concerns over the conservative agenda's definition and treatment of the family and caregiving in policy and social welfare (Arendell & Estes, 1991; Estes & Swan & Associates, 1993; Hooyman & Gonyea, 1995; Spakes, 1989). Conservatives define caregiving in terms of a normative and descriptive role for women and as an individual and family responsibility as opposed to a societal one. Thus, caregiving is not related to the devaluation of domestic and personal care labor, and certainly not related to social justice. The conservative agenda does not ignore the gendered nature of caregiving, but defines it as the right role for women across their life span.

In fact, the functionality of assigning women to caregiving is recognized as being beneficial and cost-efficient to society. Families are the cornerstone of eldercare in this nation (Estes & Swan and Associates, 1993).

Among the frail aged, 80% are cared for by families, not institutions (Leutz, Capitman, MacAdam, & Abrahams, 1992). Given that the average cost of nursing home care costs approximately $60,000 annually, and that 95% of such care is funded by Medicaid and family funds, the potential cost savings to government in the care women provide is astronomical (i.e., by keeping elders out of nursing homes) (Arendell & Estes, 1991).

It follows, then, that a number of strategies urge women to provide this care while ignoring the realities of family restructuring—most notably the increase in single families, decreases in income, motivation, geography, and other factors. These combined influences make it increasingly difficult for women to provide such care, and when they do, it is often at great cost to their personal well-being and financial health (Browne & Braun, 1997). A number of assumptions fall into the conservative approach. However, an analysis that looks at the relationships among caregiving, income, and health for younger women, and then ties these factors to the poverty rates of older women, is rarely considered in policymaking.

Caregiving Strategies

Congress has contemplated varying ways to credit families for the care of elderly dependents. Legislation attempts to wrestle with the increased need for eldercare, and the decreased availability of caregivers, primarily women, to provide it. Each year, increasing numbers of families look to the government for help, while the government, in its devolutionary fervor, looks more and more to the family to provide the much-needed assistance. What families are finding is that ever-decreasing levels of government assistance are available to them. All contemporary policies, notes Barusch (1995), look to place more burden on families. Where, she asks, are the plans or legislation to take burden away?

Barusch recently reviewed a number of national and international policies developed to deal with the issues that surround income, caregiving, and justice. A number of nations provide options to caregivers, such as retirement income credit for caregiving and payment for caregiver services. However, her review of policies in 33 countries concludes that each strategy can have adverse consequences for elderly people and their families, especially aged women. She specifically critiques three approaches to increasing family care of elderly persons that have been or are being tried in this country: filial support legislation, incentives for family caregiving, and service rationing.

Filial responsibility or support mandates via legislation an adult child's financial responsibility for his or her parents should frailty result in the need for government assistance and when parental resources are limited or nonexistent. More than 30 states now mandate legislatively some form of filial support (Bulcroft, Van Leynseele, & Borgatta, 1989). When elders become frail, the government assistance they most rely on is Medicaid. With filial piety laws, an adult child's income can be considered for their parent's eligibility assistance. Fortunately, at this time, Medicaid excludes family income, since the government has found that administering such filial piety laws are financially costly, and may be detrimental to family relations (Abel, 1987; Newman & Stuyk, 1990). Women, however, should not be lulled into apathy by the gender-neutral language of filial support legislation, as these laws are built on the expectations that women will provide the actual care of frail older adults.

Another strategy seeks to provide cash payments to caregivers to compensate them for wages lost from caregiving. In other words, family caregivers who leave a job to provide elder caregiving would be paid for their efforts with government funds, somewhat akin to a small salary. Keigher and Murphy (1992), for example, found in their study of nearly 50 poor and near-poor caregivers that a small monthly payment (less than $250) was viewed positively by women caregivers. Clearly, buying rice and bread is not an academic issue. Nonetheless, a dollar-for-dollar exchange in caregiving and work may be neither imaginable nor realistic. It is more likely to see that cash payments will result in limited numbers of employees being able to afford leaving a job to care for Mom or Dad. Rather than cash benefits, others argue for tax benefits to be allocated to caregivers, such as are provided by a number of nations. But tax benefits, although easier to administer than cash, have their own problems with issues of equity and equality; those with the greater incomes receive the largest benefits, with the lesser or no benefits going to those with lower incomes. Tax benefits may, however, encourage those who already provide care to keep doing it for a while. Idaho and Arizona are two states that presently provide more hands-on-support and cash payments to family caregivers.

The third alternative examined is the rationing of services. This residual approach limits the medical and custodial care available to caregivers by withdrawing and decreasing services as a governmental cost-savings strategy. This strategy responds to the often-voiced concern of conservatives that increased services will result in an "out-of-the-woodwork" phenomenon: that families will abdicate their own responsibilities for the aged, thus driving up the costs for care. But recent research does not support this conclusion (Noelker & Bass, 1994; Tennstedt, Crawford, & McKinlay, 1993). In the end, rationing denies services and places more of a burden on families, that is, women.

Arendell and Estes (1991) suggest that the neoconservative philosophy of the New Right conflates capitalism and patriarchy in its attempt to rationalize its increasing spending expenditures on national defense rather than social welfare. A number of gerontologists have added that any discussion of caregiving policies must be framed within the context of the present desire for less government, competing demands for funds, and concerns over the federal deficit (Dychtwald & Flower, 1989; Hooyman & Gonyea, 1995).

Strategies rarely discuss the economic consequences to women of caregiving. These include loss of Social Security and pension rights in their own names that guarantees poverty to so many older women in later life. Neither do they define caregiving for what it is—a gender division of labor. Subsequently, the nation is not prepared to deal with the burgeoning numbers of ill, frail, and disabled citizens in any way other than to depend on women. Unfortunately, policymakers, even those who do not view themselves as members of the New Right, have used the conservative agenda's emphasis on traditional values to encourage women to continue to provide such care when the actual goal is cost containment. But costs associated with caregiving exist. The real question is who should pay for them. Furthermore, as long as conservative ideology refuses to see women's work in the home as work, women's efforts will be financially neglected and exploited in the home, and devalued in the workplace. And all of this will be considered "normative," and therefore not in need of any governmental intervention or change.

Thus, the conservative agenda, with its variations, seeks to maintain those elements of patriarchal society that are strong and re-establish those that have lost ground in the past 20 years. They do so ideologically and in public policies that generally ignore women and older women's life situations and histories. Women have made some progress in their lives over this same time period, but how such changes may influence the older women of tomorrow is not at all clear. The majority of older women today grew up and raised their families in a society that was far more patriarchal than it is today, and yet their poverty rates remain shocking. Neither patriarchy nor the conservative agenda have protected them. In the end, the conservative agenda holds out little promise for future generations of older women.

THE LIBERAL AGENDA: FEMINIST STRATEGIES

In contrast to the conservative agenda, feminist legal scholars and social welfare advocates recognize that male forms of power over women are embodied in individual rights in the law and social policy (Abramowitz, 1992; MacKinnon, 1989; Miller, 1990; Olsen, 1991), and that this must be corrected. Feminists have continued to debate and argue over how to make women's lives equal to men's and to end their subordination. Liberal feminist theory desires to bring women into the mainstream. Radical feminists, with a focus on patriarchy and domination theory, demand that women's subordination to men be ended, and that they be freed from the demands of forced reproduction and from violence. Socialist feminists, in contrast, pursue a classless society. Postmodern feminists, on the other hand, argue for a deconstruction of the term "woman"—and reject universal truths about gender. Somewhat similarly, multicultural feminists advocate for a "multiple consciousness" of women (Cain, 1991), while seeking a vision for social justice and solidarity among women and people of color.

Equality is guaranteed by the Constitution's Fourteenth Amendment which promises equal protection under the law, promising that no state shall "deny to any persons with its jurisdiction the equal protection of the law." Its neglect of women specifically resulted in the unsuccessful efforts to pass the Equal Rights Amendment (ERA). Interestingly enough, there are some similarities between philosophies of the New Right and liberalism. Both espouse equality of opportunity. What they disagree on is who should be equal to who, what is wrong with society, and the welfare state's role in causing or correcting society's problems. Feminist theorists, in contrast to conservative ones, understand that inequalities of race and gender exist and are reflected in the nation's poverty rates. Feminists also understand that criticizing the welfare state will not erase the nation's inequalities.

In the past 15 years, feminists have concentrated on a number of different strategies to promote equality among women. More often than not, these strategies have been aligned with liberal thought. These have commonly come to be known as: (1) equal rights or treatment, or gender-neutral strategies; (2) equal opportunity or effect (or special protection) strategies; and (3) the beginnings of a third strategy that seeks a more transformative approach to improving women's lives. In "The Sex of Law," legal scholar Frances Olsen (1991) presents a framework that I believe is helpful in describing present legal strategies for women's equality.

Olsen (1991) begins with five premises:

1. Most of Western society thought is centered on dualisms: rational/ irrational, active/passive, abstract/contextualized.
2. These dualistic pairs divide the world into contrasting spheres.

3. These dualisms are sexualized—half are considered masculine and half are considered feminine.
4. The dualisms are not equal (i.e., what is considered masculine is considered superior to what is considered feminine).
5. Law is identified with the male side of the dualisms.

She proceeds to identify two current strategies for gender equality. The first is to oppose the sexualization but not the hierarchization of the male/ female dualism, or the gender neutral approach. The second path opposes the hierarchization but not the sexualization, or special protection. A third strategy, suggested by a number of feminist legal scholars, offers a new approach to the study of women's lives.

A great deal of scholarship has argued about which strategy is best (Abramowitz, 1992; Baron, 1987; Hess, 1985; MacKinnon, 1989; Majury, 1993). This next section is an analysis based on Olsen's work, along with that of other feminist legal and social welfare theorists. It is followed by an alternative strategy, presented in chapters 6 and 7, that incorporates themes from feminist, gerontology, and life-course literature—a feminist life-span perspective on aging and a feminist age analysis. Feminist frameworks can be used as tools to build on women's strengths while advocating for an end to their oppression on individual and structural levels.

GENDER-NEUTRAL STRATEGIES: OPPOSE SEXUALIZATION

The path of liberal feminism is to oppose the sexualization of the male/ female dualism while struggling with identifying women with the favored (male and rationale) side. The message for women is: Be the same as men (i.e., rational, assertive); the strategy is to advocate for gender-neutral policies and programs. In gender-neutral strategies, women are viewed as the same as men, and so require equal treatment with them. Laws and policies should reflect this sameness. Taking gender into account in any way is seen as problematic for the long term advancement of women. Rather, men and women should be treated the same. Women have fought for and earned some benefits from this strategy.

But men and women are not the same, as is evident in pregnancy, women's differing morbidity and mortality patterns with age, and their greater longevity. Gender is not just a variable, but structures women's lives across the life span. Nonetheless, the path to equal opportunity, according to the liberal strategy, is through improved access to education, careers, income, and health care. However, as MacKinnon argues, when "sameness is the strategy for equality, a critique of gender hierarchy looks like a request for special protection in disguise" (1989, p. 233). With regard to aging women, the "sameness" strategy doesn't take into account the difficulties faced by older women entering the job market for the first time after decades of childbearing, nor does it question the overall structure of capitalism and patriarchy in the oppression of women.

The study of older women's lives provides an opportunity to understand the meaning of gender-neutral strategies and their consequences to women. The liberal focus on individualization and private responsibilities does not accurately reflect well on older women's lives. It is not only feminists who are becoming sensitized to this understanding. In a hearing before the Subcommittee on Retirement Income and Employment of the U.S. House Select Committee on Aging (1992a), Representative Sherwood Boehlert made this statement:

> Taken at face value, America's retirement system is gender-neutral and appears to provide adequate vehicles to obtain security during the golden years. Nothing overtly discriminates against one sex. Yet a closer look at our retirement system uncovers a host of pitfalls that adversely affect a woman's ability to secure a sufficient retirement income for herself. (p. 9)

Boehlert discussed a number of issues that were presented in chapter 1: the fact that caregivers are penalized when leaving the work force by the zero years that are added to their benefit computation period; the wage gap between men and women that continues to exist, in part because of women's family responsibilities; women in full-time employment whose wages continue to lag behind men's—a result of the kinds of jobs women find available to them, the lack of comparative worth, and discrimination— and the changing American family that no longer typifies what Social Security had in mind. Representative Boehlert asks a good question of society: "What kind of message does our retirement system send? Marry rich and stay married as long as possible? Or work, but don't leave the work force to raise your child or care for an elder, or your contribution to Social Security will be worthless?" (1992a, p. 9).

Gender-neutral strategies focus on equal rights for women, not equal opportunity. But gender-neutral strategies neglect the fact that pensions are based on men's work patterns, with no credit given to the childbearing and caregiving years when unemployed. Furthermore, men's later years are not the same as women's, for it is in their mid- and later years that they are often at their peak in earnings, benefits, and prestige. Neither do men have to face the double standard of aging, thereby appearing in a more positive light than women (Gottlieb, 1989; Sontag, 1972).

As was discussed in chapter 1, eligibility for pension benefits is often based on family status. But as Abramowitz (1992) notes, pension benefits based on spouse status are risky business and can be taken away. Private pensions are no better. Women have limited access to private retirement benefits, and even when covered, women receive less than men (Abramowitz, 1992). Furthermore, women often lose their financial and health care benefits after divorce. Yet to change the law under this strategy would appear to give preferential treatment to women—rather than be an attempt to correct a lifetime of sex discriminatory practices and ideas. Finally, gender—neutral policies assume that the state and society are neutral in their treatment of gender—a dangerous statement for older women that ignores their financial, housing, and health dilemmas. When reading Congressional reports from the last 20 years on the status of older women, one is at first impressed with the amount of work that has gone into these discussions. But a deeper analysis demands outcomes that go beyond reports to legislators.

Gender-neutral reforms may be either preventive or remedial. Preventive reforms address the worsening and regressive nature of the nation's economy. These include efforts to strengthen the redistributive function of Social Security, as well as present efforts to increase the minimum wage and enforce the Family Support Act of 1988 and the Family Medical Leave Act of 1993. Remedial efforts include those designed to strengthen the nation's safety net, such as changes embodied in the 1992 recommendations of the Supplemental Security Income Modernization Panel and a number of suggestions by the Older Women's League.

The issue of Social Security's dual entitlement clause is a good example of the problems of gender-neutral strategies and laws. Social Security is supposed to be gender-neutral—by its wording, it is intended to protect men and as well as women. But the term "dual entitlement" is a misnomer. Women are entitled to collect benefits as a spouse or in their own name from their own work records—not both. The married woman who has worked her 35 years in the paid labor force and has contributed to her own Social Security finds that she can collect her earned benefits based on her own employment record or as a dependent—not both. This is not dual entitlement. Due to lower wages, segregated employment, part-time work, and years out of the work force, many women find that obtaining retirement benefits based on 50% of their husband's earnings actually results in a larger benefit than that based on their own work histories. So, a number of inequalities exist in this gender-neutral policy. For one, a working woman often collects the same as the woman who stayed home who did not pay into the system. The lesbian older woman does not have dual entitlement, and must receive her retirement income based on her work history alone. This is regardless of whether or not she has been in a long term relationship. The minority woman's spouse may not live to the age 65 to reach his retirement benefits. Ignored are women who are not married, or who are divorced or single. In brief, the effect of such a policy is discriminatory because it ignores the way that women's material world differs from men's.

Furthermore, and perhaps most important, there is a problem with the definition of "work." Present definitions of work exclude much of what women do in the home. Women's work in the marketplace is also devalued. Nonetheless, gender-neutral strategies do not advocate for structural barriers to be erected for women in the work force. The development of such strategies (as in special protection laws for pregnancy) are believed by some to actually sell equality short in the long run (MacKinnon, 1989; W. Williams, 1993).

Gender-neutral strategies also ignore the effect of the privatization of caregiving on one's income. When long term care services are not available to assist caregivers, it remains a family (i.e., woman's) response. These strategies also ignore the fact that women remain in segregated employment that nearly guarantees poverty in later life. To change this, policies must make older women's lives central to any analysis. What older women have to say about caregiving and their financial, health, and social statuses is essential in formulating more gender-responsive policies.

For example, present policies have ignored the negative effects of the lack of research on aging women's health, and the effect of living 7 additional years has on their economic and physical health. Present work and retirement policies disadvantage women because their work constraints (i.e., taking lower paying or part-time work to accommodate family responsibilities) and, for middle-class women, their more frequent interruptions in the work force result in limiting their earnings. And since Social Security and private pensions continue to be wage-based, women's retirement income is less than men's. Moreover, the fact that many women of color and working-class women are employed at the bottom of the employment pyramid, with their wages subsequently constrained throughout their lives, affects their retirement. But this disadvantage is ignored by gender-neutral policies. But in negating women's realities, they are unable to alleviate or prevent the material conditions of older women's inequality. That is because such interventions would appear to be a violation of rights if women are treated differently from men. As legal scholar Lucinda Finley (1993) notes, gender-neutral strategies obliterate the connections between power and knowledge construction. She says:

> To keep its operation fair in appearance, . . . the law strives for rules that are universal, objective, and neutral. The language of individuality and neutrality keeps law from talking about values, structures, and institutions,

and about how they construct knowledge, choice, and apparent possibilities for conducting the world. Also submerged is a critical awareness of systemic or institutional power and domination. . . . The majority talks in the language of neutrality—of color blindness, and of blind justice. . . . The dissent, which cries out in anguish about the lessons of history, power, and domination, is open to the accusation a that it speaks in the language of politics and passions, not law. (p. 574)

It is equal rights, rather than special protection, according to this school of feminist thought, that hold the most promise for women. What looks like equality is often just not so, however (Krieger & Cooney, 1991). Equal treatment works best when women's lives are similar to men's, but most women's lives are not like men's. As we have shown, women's concrete material world remains different from men's. In contrast, special protection—the second strategy to be discussed in the following section—seeks to provide protection to all women precisely because they are different from men.

SPECIAL PROTECTION/PRIVILEGE APPROACHES: OPPOSE HIERARCHIZATION

In contrast to gender-neutral strategies, the liberal special protection strategy rejects the hierarchy of the male/female dualism established by men and accepts the identification of women with moral behavior and emotionality while declaring the value of such traits. Difference is thus valued, not negated. Similar to the cultural feminist or essentialist argument, it seeks to accommodate women's historical and cultural differences. The message is that women are different from men; the strategy is the special benefit rule, or special protection. This strategy exists to value and compensate women for what they are or have been made to become by social inequality (MacKinnon, 1989). Equal opportunity, as opposed to equal treatment, is the goal.

Pregnancy has been a major issue for those seeking special protection. If women are the same as men, and therefore should be provided the same rights, then how should pregnancy be placed in this equation? Advocates of special protection argue that any view of pregnancy as a disability like any other ignores the effect of pregnancy and childrearing on women's lives. Moreover, the view that pregnancy is a disability, rather than life-affirming is also a male view. Thus, special protection rejects equal treatment's "formal equality model" in favor of an equal opportunity model. Instead, "positive action" is needed for pregnancy via specific benefits that will ensure that women are not disadvantaged if pregnant when employed (Krieger & Cooney, 1991).

A number of critiques have been leveled against the special privilege doctrine. Some blame women's inequalities not on the faults of gender-neutral strategies, but on the limits of litigation and legislation. According to legal scholar Wendy Williams, what is really needed is social change that realigns gender roles in the family and the workplace (1993). Further critiques of special protection claim that difference historically has been used to exclude women from choices. And, as a number of feminists have argued, such special "protection" via promotion of "difference" can "protect" you right out of a job (MacKinnon, 1989; W. Williams, 1993). Difference has also been used to categorize jobs by male or female, and the jobs listed have been far from equal in prestige, power, salary, or benefits. As many have noted, and as gender-neutral proponents fear, a dual system of rights leads to differential treatment. Eisenstein (1984), for one, warns that special protection legislation is contradictory at best, since it constrains women's choices in order to ensure their domesticity, thereby enforcing male/female "difference." Wendy Williams (1993) thus recommends that women focus on achieving equal rights and avoid constructing structural barriers such as those proposed by special privilege advocates.

Special protection legislation has generally ignored older women's issues, and yet, special protection laws hold some potential for improving the lives of older women. This is because to be different from men is both normative and descriptive of the present cohort of older women. The majority of today's older women married—especially upper- and middle-class women—stayed home, and raised children with the expectation that their husbands would take care of them financially throughout their lives. Rarely was divorce, disability, or widowhood a planned reality. Few of this cohort have income benefits based on their own work histories. Special privilege and private pensions do not reward caregiving responsibilities by crediting women's work history, and antidiscrimination mandates are both relatively new in the lives of older women. They are also rarely enforced. The end result of women's concrete life events is that women are often poor in later life.

This issue has been discussed with regard to caregiving. On one hand, feminists argue that to compensate women for providing caregiving tasks only reaffirms gender-role stereotypes and prevents long term structural change. On the other hand, the vast majority of caregivers (75%) are women, most often the poor, near-poor, and middle-aged. Is this not a case for special protection? Is the lack of long term care policies not gender discrimination?

Ironically, although they are not protected as family caregivers, neither are women financially protected should they work outside of the home. The majority of employed women remain in low-paying and low-prestige jobs, often with no retirement benefits and in unsafe and unprotected conditions. If such a picture is considered normative, then it ensures poverty for older women. No feminist can accept the argument that women choose to have low pay with minimal benefits and a lower quality of life.

Gender-specific reforms in the form of special protection legislation are generally preventive, offering the promise of security to later generations of women. Some preventive approaches could teach women about financial management and retirement planning. Others, such as pay equity, address structural forces in the labor market that weaken women's financial positions. Still others, such the proposed earnings-sharing plans and child care plans, offer a modicum of security to enable women to fulfill their caregiving responsibilities. Health care reform can also serve as an antipoverty strategy, protecting women from catastrophic health events, even as it provides some support for long term care and prescriptive drugs. The Women's Health Initiative discussed in chapter 1 is yet another example of specific protection that aims to study the effects of women's lives on their health—a topic severely neglected in past research. Gender-specific strategies can demand a re-evaluation of the allocation of research dollars. Since in 1994 there were three elderly women to every two elderly men and five oldest-old women to every two oldest-old men (United States Bureau of the Census, 1996), should not funding for research be weighted more heavily toward the study of older women?

In sum, there are a number of political and philosophical approaches to the "fair and just" treatment of women. Both gender-neutral and special-privilege strategies attempt to ensure women's access to that from which they have been excluded, while also valuing their strengths, regardless of whether such strengths are a consequence of who they are or who they have been forced to become as a result of their second-class status. However, both strategies fail to address the gender division of labor as the cause of women's oppression; the intersection of the multiple layers of oppression by gender, age, race, income, and sexual orientation; and the role of the state in addressing inequality. The function of the state, whether as a vehicle for social control, an avenue for empowerment, or as a provider of crucial economic support, continues to be debated (Ackelsberg & Diamond, 1987). An all-inclusive strategy may not be the answer if such a strategy does not acknowledge differences in women's lives. Instead, what is actually needed is to reconceptualize citizenship and equality.

Mcirvin Abu-Laban (1981) offers a somewhat more optimistic view about the lives of future aging women due to their growing economic independence, their increasing place in the work force, a greater tolerance for homosexuality and other family forms, and expanded reproductive freedoms. Nonetheless, she also warns that the potential antifeminist backlash, together with an expanding conservative and fundamentalist religion, suggests the possibility of a future return to a version of the status quo ante. She writes:

> To the extent that contemporary conservative religious movements embody restrictions which constrain women's access to prestige mechanisms other than those based on age-linked attractiveness or derived from a husband, to the extent that they restrict women to wife-mother roles as the only meaningful and appropriate roles, then future women of advancing age will be exceptionally vulnerable to declines in status, and, as well, vulnerable to several forms of socio-emotional deprivation. (p. 95)

Abu-Laban predicts that forces countering ageism may have better results than those countering sexism. In taking an international and historical view, she notes that prestige for older men has never guaranteed the same for older women. There are no assurances that the improvement to the aged's lot will mean a better life for women. The countering conservative movements aim to impose and mandate traditional values with respect to women's responsibilities in the home, and these may halt or even reverse the progress made.

In the end, both gender-neutral and special-privilege strategies offer some limited hope for some groups of women, but they generally ignore older women's lives. We turn now to more recent debates and to a different perspective that seeks to move older women to center stage in social policy and in social welfare debates.

TRANSFORMATIVE FEMINIST LEGAL ALTERNATIVES

Contemporary discussions by a number of feminist legal scholars have provided compromises to some of the issues that continue to perplex feminists regarding the benefits and limitations inherent in gender-neutral and special protection legislation and polices. While these discussions have not focused on aging women, they do suggest a number of interesting possibilities for social welfare and older women. Legal scholar Herma Kay (1993), for example, suggests that we adopt an "episodic analysis" which would limit differential treatment for the concrete, specific, "female" experiences, such as pregnancy. Could this view be adapted on behalf of older women's specific health needs, or would their needs be labeled as pathology? Would differential treatment acknowledge women's work histories, or would male work patterns and retirement paths still be the referent for women?

Diana Majury (1993) suggests another way out of this dilemma of gender-neutral and special-privilege strategies. Namely, we should look at equality as a strategy, rather than a goal for achieving justice. A new language of equality, she adds, will aid in discussions around the concepts of domination and oppression. Majury asks how we can get away from what she calls "the prototypical dilemma" in feminism equality debates, whereby "any attempt to specify and respond to the many inequalities to which women are subjected elicits accusations that one is reproducing or perpetuating those inequalities. Conversely, to treat women under a gender-neutral approach is to be accused of ignoring her world" (p. 267). Taking a somewhat postmodern approach, Majury warns against ignoring the complex and multiple differences among women, and seeks a strategy that looks instead at commonalities. Women's lives are characterized by power dynamics, psychological and sociological histories and traits, cultural norms and expectations, and social institutions. Therefore, the pursuit of a perfect equality theory may in itself be detrimental. Instead, equality-based policies and legislation should move away from male/ female and move toward the concept of advantage/disadvantage. Somewhat similarly, and within this approach, we call for a reconceptualization of age that moves away from young/old and focuses instead on advantage/ disadvantage across the life span. Such a reconceptualization may help to diffuse intergenerational friction.

Other feminist scholars believe that the feminist search for equality theory should be abolished altogether (Cain, 1991; MacKinnon, 1989; Majury, 1993). Finley (1993), for example, suggests that when we see job segregation as discrimination, family caregiving as a gender division of labor, and health care as biased, more of women's experiences are brought into the law and validated. While Finley does not specifically focus on aging women, her views can be seen as challenging feminists and others to see gender issues across the life span.

TOWARD A FEMINIST LIFE-SPAN PERSPECTIVE ON AGE: A FEMINIST AGE ANALYSIS

Feminism grapples with a number of issues ideologically and politically in its quest to improve women's lives. Aging women must be included in this feminist debate. Regardless of whether women are the "same" or "different" from men, they are not equal to men in their later years, for they enter old age with different life and work histories, a result of cumulative advantages and disadvantages. For many of the reasons discussed in this book, women are more often poor in later life than are men. To counter such distressing data, the disparities in pay between men and women must be faced. Discrimination by gender, age, race, class, disability, and sexual orientation must be stopped. Present legislation to do so must have some teeth. The very fact that women live 7 years longer than men and have differing social responsibilities in the care of children, the sick, and the aged should require more gender-focused research and some gender-specific legislation. Some ideas in these areas will be discussed in greater detail in chapter 7.

But any analysis on women, power, and aging must delve much deeper to improve older women's lives. Women do receive lower retirement incomes compared to men's as a result of low wages, discrimination, fewer opportunities for education throughout their lives—for some—an intermittent work history, and policies that do not acknowledge women's lives. What must be continuously examined among other issues is why women earn less than men in the same or comparable positions. It is not just because they are in segregated employment, because even women in the same professions as their male counterparts earn considerably less than comparable men (Hammer & Browne, 1991). This is neither equality nor justice.

In this chapter, we have discussed some of the ways in which gender equality is a neglected topic in conservative agendas. In contrast, legislative equality is most often viewed from a liberal perspective in two distinct ways. First, equality is linked to rights and equal treatment. Conversely, the second view is a focus on equality of effect. These are challenging issues that continue to be debated in feminist circles and are beyond the scope of this book. Their ideas, however, point us toward a different and hopefully a more expanded view of equality for old women.

What we realize is that policies are made not by women, but men's understanding of women. How is it, then, that older women's experiences as aging women, as caregivers, as workers, and as citizens, can be included in the debates over health care and long term care reform? How can older women's poverty be an integral part of the discussion on what form that Social Security, Supplemental Security Income, or housing assistance should take? How can older women's oppression be seen as a reflection of male definitions of women's beauty and worth? How can older women be encouraged to define themselves? How can older women's physical and mental health needs be made essential in research? How can we celebrate the strengths that exist among older women? Can we examine the connections among the multiple issues that impact on women's lives?

One place to start anew is in the formulation of policy built on women's lives. And yet care must be exercised in building policy on "women's lives" if such a view does not embrace women's strengths, oppressions, paths of resistance, and diversity that are influenced by multiple factors. The plurality of voices among women must not be lost, and neither should one type of woman be a referent point for defining "woman." A way must be found to balance the need for difference, recognizing at the same time those common themes that exist in aging women's lives that can build toward solidarity. Rather than one strategy, what may be needed is a focus on specific and concrete manifestations of inequality, and more respect for women's diverse experiences in real-life situations, as opposed to rhetoric. Can we identify older women's needs and recommend appropriate strategies with the goal of fairness while continuing to support more short-term reform and realistic strategies if helpful? If we believe in holistic analyses, why not?

Present strategies for change acknowledge that political and structural changes are needed to change women's lives. A feminist analysis understands that a different paradigm is needed in the conceptualization of work and productivity, power and empowerment, and the role of the aged in society. We must now turn our feminist analysis to the needs of older women. A feminist analysis sensitive to older women disagrees with a public-burden approach to aging that states that the aged are a problem to society (Peterson & Howe, 1988; Thurow, 1996). Neither does it believe that social welfare services to the nation's people are a public burden to the nation's coffers. The need for care is not necessarily built on an age trajectory. Instead, the aged live a life of change and growth like members of other age groups, composed of varying shades of dependence, independence, and interdependence at varying times of life.

Patrice Diquinzio and Iris Marion Young (1995) add their thoughts to the importance of feminist theory, ethics, and social policy as a strategy to improve women's lives:

> Bringing feminist ethics to social policy thus has the effect of focusing a gender lens on policy. A feminist approach to policy issues asks about the differences between men and women that neutral policy evaluation has failed to notice. Normative approaches to this gendering of policy often reveal the need for contextual applications of principals and methods, and for understanding the plural identities that claim most people's lives. Feminist approaches also need to show that simple alternatives between formalized equality and special treatment, or allowing or forbidding actions,

do not address policy issues involving sexuality and the sexual division of labor. (p. 7)

CONCLUSIONS

A feminist analysis critiques conservative ideologies for not serving the interests of all women. It exposes the relevance and some of the shortfalls of gender-neutral and special protection strategies in correcting and alleviating women's oppression. In the end, what feminism can offer is a greater awareness of women's lives and experiences across the life span. Feminists seek justice and freedom for all and an end to all other oppressions. We now turn to a further examination of the elements of a feminist life-span perspective on aging, one that seeks to broaden the discourse on feminism and gerontology to better the lives of women as they grow old.

A Feminist Life-Span Perspective on Aging

> Throughout their entire life cycle, women's daily existence and long term aspirations are restricted by discriminatory attitudes, unjust social and economic structures, and a lack of resources in most countries that prevent their full and equal participation.
>
> —Report of the Fourth World Conference on Women,
> Beijiing Platform for Action

In earlier chapters, I outlined some of the contributions, limitations, and problems associated with feminist schools of thought and other, nonfeminist, frameworks and ideologies in understanding the life situations of older women. In this chapter, I introduce a framework, incorporating ideas from previously developed feminist, gerontologic, and social work themes and frameworks, that attempts to specifically respond to aging women's needs. In this framework, I continue the critiques begun by a number of feminists, gerontologists, and social workers on the effectiveness of public and private polices (see Abramowitz, 1992; Hooyman & Gonyea, 1995, Kingson & Schulz, 1997; Miller, 1990; Van Den Bergh, 1995). But, unlike most other work, the focus here is on the lives of aging women.

WHY WE NEED A FEMINIST LIFE-SPAN PERSPECTIVE ON AGING

As a philosophical perspective, feminism is both a way of visualizing and thinking about situations, and an evolving set of theories that attempts to explain the various phenomena and causes of women's oppression

(Van Den Bergh & Cooper, 1986). At its most elementary level, it is a critique of gender oppression, but it is also concerned with the interlocking nature of all oppressions (Anzaldua, 1981; P. H. Collins, 1991; Hartmann, 1981; hooks, 1984; Jaggar, 1988; Lorde, 1984; MacKinnon, 1987, 1989; Zinn, 1990).

As was discussed in previous chapters, feminists view gender more as a social than a biological construction. Feminists understand that men and women's lives are defined and shaped by social mores, mandates, expectations, and changing advantages and disadvantages throughout the life cycle. The existence of multiple feminisms in the literature, while enriching the feminist discourse, has not shed much light on the lives of aging women. In responding to this neglect, we introduce a feminist life-span perspective on age as a tool to examine the lives of aging women, and to reconceptualize age issues from older women's voices.

We discussed in earlier chapters some of the major schools of thought in contemporary feminism. Regardless of their varied theoretical leanings, feminists do have a point of agreement with one another—that is, women's inequalities must end. Nonetheless, the existence of multiple feminisms makes defining a feminist life-span perspective on aging a challenging task. Fortunately, the writings of a number of feminist scholars, some discussed in previous chapters, identified themes that guide the development of this framework. Here, I will provide a brief review of some of the key issues in theories discussed in chapters 2, 3, and 4 that I believe have implications for aging women.

Traditional liberal or equality feminists attribute women's plight to their inequality to men, and have strongly advocated for increased rights for women in the public sphere. Speaking more clearly from the voices of White middle-class women, they have been sharply criticized for ignoring working-class women, women of color, and other marginalized women. In the process of universalizing and homogenizing women on a White middle-class model, they have failed to consider difference among women. As many of its theorists were younger women themselves, their issues gave preference to their own concerns—mothering, work and job equity, sexual harassment, and domestic violence, to name a few. In the absence of a life-span perspective, many liberal feminists failed to see how these issues continued into women's advanced years, nor did they discuss the impact of ageism on women. More recently, a number of liberal feminist theorists have begun this discussion of women and age by sharing their own experiences with age and the aging process (see Friedan, 1993; Greer, 1991; Pogrebin, 1996).

With its focus on individual rights and access issues, liberalism and liberal feminist theory have significantly influenced gerontology thought and practice. In fact, a great deal of gerontological study has undertaken a liberal or gender-neutral approach to the study of aging. Unfortunately, this has too often translated into a neglect of women in both the policy and practice arenas.

The women-centered approaches of cultural or essentialist feminists, on the other hand, celebrate and honor women's differences from men. Women's poverty, neglected health needs, caregiving responsibilities, and lowered social status are labeled more as individual than as sociopolitical issues. The essentialist discussion of women's caring responsibilities has focused more on women and children rather than caring over the life cycle. Nor have such discussions focused on how social welfare reacts, responds, or promotes men and women's socially and culturally defined gender roles. Critics of cultural feminists, however, have noted that institutionalizing difference may well rationalize the continuance of the status quo, with serious ramifications for women with age. This focus on difference has resulted in decreased emphasis on understanding the dynamics of gender oppression, women's multiple and interlocking oppressions, and the need for structural changes in the nation's sociopolitical structures, and more of an emphasis on celebrating women's "culture" as different and on a higher moral plane compared to the culture of men.

Multicultural and postmodern feminisms also criticize "essentialist" feminism for its universalizing of women's traits. Black feminists and other multiculturalists have taken White feminists to task for their exclusionary practices and theories. A point of agreement of both multicultural and postmodern feminists is that they seek more inclusive and less homogeneous feminist theories and methodologies that specify multiple voices and alternate sites for building knowledge. Both feminisms extend a critical eye toward universalizing theory and give more attention to specificity and diversity among women. While multicultural feminism has a more political aim and agenda and looks to solidarity as a possible strategy with other women and men, postmodernism has focused more on knowledge construction and deconstruction (A. Hartman, 1992). In its pursuit to deconstruct the category of "woman," postmodernism has encouraged necessary critical thinking in both feminism and gerontology, but has also critiqued the development of simple theory that could explain women's oppression. As with other feminist theories, neither multiculturalism nor postmodernism have focused on aging women, although a number of feminist gerontologists have begun to adopt a postmodern stance in their writings and arguments (Laws, 1995; Ray, 1996).

Finally, we briefly discussed radical and socialist feminisms. Radical feminists have sharply critiqued patriarchy and its effects on women. Some radical feminists, while also guilty of homogenizing women, see more clearly than others that women's problem is inequality, not difference. For all of their brilliant and groundbreaking work on issues such as violence against women, pornography, and women's control over their bodies, radical feminists did not extend their work to the lives of aging women. Socialist feminists, on the other hand, have contributed to an understanding of the economic status of women, as well as the economic relationships that exist between men and women. Equally as important, they have examined women's economic status from a life-span perspective, noting poverty's cumulative impact on women's lives. Socialist feminists have generally been more attuned to women's oppression by both capitalism and patriarchy, and have recently begun to critique a number of issues related directly to aging women—retirement, widowhood, and pension coverage. Their writings, similar to those of radical feminists, reflect a greater understanding and acknowledgment that state power is based on male interests as opposed to the liberal view of the state as a gender-neutral institution.

The preceding chapter also outlined the conservative world view of women's place in society and two feminist legal and political strategies presently used to promote equality among women. Conservative ideology stresses individual rights and responsibilities, and women's natural and secondary role in the family as caregiver and nurturer. Conservative strategies have most often called for a return to the patriarchal, nuclear family, and limited governmental assistance. Although aging women are rarely discussed, implicit within the conservative ideology is the idea that women will be protected by the family as long as they abide by its rules. Sadly, we saw in previous chapters that this is not so. In contrast, the approaches most often advocated for by liberal and liberal feminist theorists are gender-neutral and gender-specific strategies, reflecting a stronger view of government's role in promoting social justice.

Gender-neutral strategies seek women's rights and access to society's resources. Yet, by refusing to acknowledge women's differences to men, they ignore women's varying life status. Their desire is to speak for equality for all, but their writings and analyses neglect the life situations of women as they age. Similar to other feminisms, the force of ageism as a source of oppression for women is absent in most gender-neutral discussions.

In contrast, gender-specific strategies normalize women's life situations more as "difference." Subsequently, most of the writings on gender-specific strategies focus on issues relating to women's societally defined and dictated roles, expectations, and the consequences to such roles such as pregnancy and self-defense against family violence. One unintended result is the continuation of the status quo, as "women's roles" as nurturers of society are seen as not only descriptive but normative.

Ideas found within a feminist perspective on aging reject the conservative ideologies as well as liberal feminist strategies discussed in the previous chapter—the sexualization and hierarchization of male/female, young/old and White/non-White dualisms. Acknowledged instead is the value in the rights of all aging women in the private and public spheres. Recognizing that patriarchy and the gender division of labor are the problems in both the home and the market, a feminist age perspective or approach views changes in social structure, along with women's histories of resistance, empowerment, and strengths, as the solution. This perspective benefits from the incorporation of other feminist themes and methods—women's inequality to men and oppression throughout their life span; the emphasis on holistic, as opposed to bipolar and hierarchial thinking; women's celebration of difference; women's diversity and their multiple and interlocking oppressions; and the value of deconstruction in exposing universal truths about older adults as falsehoods. From this feminist framework, the contributions as well as the problems of both gender-neutral and special-privilege strategies are identified. Thus, it seeks justice from the state as only one of its strategies, since it understands that gender-neutral and gender-specific policies are impossible to achieve within a patriarchal system, especially one that operates under the false assumption that its gender values are unbiased. It is primarily these ideas that distinguish a feminist analysis from other liberal and gerontologic frameworks.

ELEMENTS OF THIS PERSPECTIVE

In addition to feminist theory's major influence on this perspective, I integrate literature from three other distinct and yet at times overlapping areas: (a) a life-span approach that also examines the social construction of age and cohort influences on the life course; (b) the work of gerontological scholars that take a critical stance toward the present state of gerontological knowledge; and (c) the work of feminist social workers who seek social justice for people of all ages. What feminism, gerontology, and social work have in common is a shared commitment to the importance of political change in social welfare and in social institutions, norms, and values to ensure older women's well-being.

The idea that people's lives are intimately connected and woven with the lives of others has been discussed by a number of feminist and nonfeminist theorists, especially in the literature of the life course (Elder,

1985; Riley & Waring, 1976; Settersten & Hagestad, 1996). A life-span approach, somewhat like a life-course paradigm (Riley, 1996) considers not only people as individuals, but people as they exist in groups, their relationship to social structures and power, and, ultimately, their relationship to social change (Antonucci, 1994; Riley, 1981, 1985; Riley & Riley, 1989). As Matilda White Riley (1996) explains, "people's lives can only be fully understood as they influence, and are influenced by, the surrounding social structures (of roles, primary groups, nation states, and other social and cultural institutions)" (p. 256). A life course explanation highlights "the influences of earlier lives that anchor diverse trajectories in old age" (O'Rand, 1996, p. 232). And, as noted by a number of scholars, inequality actually worsens with age (Crystal & Shea, 1990; Dannefer, 1987). Also acknowledged are the forces behind women's social location, their sociohistorical period, and their personal biography in shaping individual life and aging experiences (Stoller & Gibson, 1994).

Second, this perspective incorporates present knowledge in gerontology, together with its critiques, and the ways in which ageism affects women as they age (Arendell & Estes, 1987; Gonyea, 1994; Gottlieb, 1989; Hess, 1985; Hess & Waring, 1983; Laws, 1995; Lopata, 1987; Ray, 1996; Stoller & Gibson, 1994). Studies in gerontology have provided important data that aging is not, no matter what some may say, "all in one's head." Changes are real and exist; there are declines with age that must be addressed, as well as new avenues for growth and pleasure. What gerontological study tells us, then, is that aging is neither as good nor as bad as we may think. And yet, for all of its many contributions, gerontology finds itself doing a rapid "catch-up" on women's issues, thanks to the scholarly and advocacy work of a number of feminist gerontologists. Still, the focus of gerontology is aging and older adults, not women specifically. In contrast, ideas in a feminist life-span perspective on aging examine the developmental and other changes that occur to women in later life that may have followed them across the life span in the biological, physiological, social, and psychological spheres.

The third major influence of a feminist perspective on aging is from the social work knowledge base. Numerous social workers have embraced feminist concepts in theory, practice, and research (Abramowitz, 1992; Bricker-Jenkins & Hooyman, 1986; B. G. Collins, 1986; L. V. Davis, 1985, 1994; Gonyea, 1994; K. H. Gould, 1989; Gutierrez, 1990; A. Hartman, 1990; Morris, 1993; Laird, 1994, 1995; Swigonski, 1993; Van Den Bergh & Cooper, 1986; Wetzel, 1976, 1986). More recently, feminist social workers have begun taking a feminist social work perspective to gerontology (Crawley, 1994; Hooyman & Gonyea, 1995; Miller, 1990). The ideas for this perspective, then, come from many voices already spoken. What I hope to add to the work of these theorists and their frameworks is a specific focus on the needs of aging women, their unique challenges and triumphs, society's role in providing them with advantages and disadvantages across their lifetime, thoughts toward social justice for aging women, and ideas for a new epistemology on women and aging.

Furthermore, and borrowing from postmodernism, ideas from a feminist life-span perspective on age use the principles of deconstructionism to critique concepts often applied to older adults and to women. Deconstructionism demands suspicion of gerontology content when developed from a privileged male standpoint. Postmodernism emphasizes the complexities within gender and that the construct called "woman" can not be universalized and homogenized. Additionally, concepts such as retirement, health, caregiving, and work must be reconceptualized with the voices of previously marginalized people included in that reconceptualization. These kinds of critiques can be terrifically valuable. Nonetheless, postmodernism remains somewhat problematic, because it takes away from efforts toward solidarity since the category of older women is suspect.

Ideas in this perspective are thus clearly influenced by postmodern approaches to knowledge creation. We turn a critical eye to traditional categories of analysis and the present knowledge of gerontology. Equally influencing this perspective, however, are the contributions by radical and socialist feminisms, whose focus on women's concrete and economic lives increases our sensitivity to the oppressions from sexism, ageism, racism, and other discriminatory forces. We see that, regardless of age, women's most critical needs are in their economic and health statuses and their safety. Unfortunately, data on the lives of aging women's economic and health status alert us to their often difficult lives.

Like a number of other gerontologists, we acknowledge that aging affects both genders, and that many of the issues impacting on aging women also impact on men. The difference with this analysis is that, while we acknowledge that men age, and that race and class impact on men's life chances as they do women, this perspective focuses on women's experiences with age. Ultimately, we seek a better old age for women and men.

To ensure older women's needs are addressed, we seek a more woman-centered perspective for recognizing that women's economic and health status, caregiving responsibilities, and unmet social needs are outcomes of political, economic, and social forces that have essentially followed them throughout their lives. With ideas from this analysis or perspective, I begin to outline women's issues in ways that document the multiple forces of domination on their lives and their interlocking nature with one another. This perspective also acknowledges that ageism brings a different layer of oppression for women, one that looms ever larger with each advanced year. What is essential to this perspective is this desire to draw more attention to women's view of aging in their own words, one that documents and celebrates their strengths and resistance to oppression. Also included is the celebration of differences and voices between men and women and among women. This next section will elaborate further on the components of this perspective as interrelated ideas that build on each other.

The following ideas and themes adapted from many scholars and thinkers lead us to this somewhat tentative and still evolving feminist life-span perspective on aging. This perspective was first published as a chapter in Nan Van Den Bergh's book, *Feminist Social Work Practice in the 21st Century* (1995). It has changed since the publication of that chapter, and it will undoubtedly change again. Nonetheless, its elements include, in addition to present knowledge in gerontology and a critical (deconstructive) examination of that knowledge:

1. women as an oppressed population across the life span;
2. the added oppression from ageism;
3. diversity, domination and resistance;
4. the call for political strategies for change;
5. power, empowerment, and strengths;
6. visions of solidarity;
7. the need for holistic and ecological thinking;
8. expanded and alternative research methodologies.

INEQUALITY AND OPPRESSION ACROSS THE LIFE SPAN

A beginning place for this perspective is the acknowledgment of women's oppression and women's inequality to men across the life span. Few today argue that men and women's lives are the same, or that women's lives are more economically or politically stable compared to men's. As a group, women spend their lives poorer than men, regardless of age. Women, notably upper- and middle-class women, have traditionally been relegated to work in the private sphere—caring for children, husbands, and elder relatives. When women do work in the public sphere, they often continue to work in segregated work sites. This is especially true for working-class and minority women. Furthermore, they earn approximately 70 cents to every dollar made by men. Income parity by gender has not yet been attained. Regardless of whether women are restricted to the private or public sphere, their power is limited in both. The financial status of women is even more striking when one examines the poverty levels of women that White patriarchal society has so often ignored or treated disrespectfully—single mothers, women of color, lesbian women, and aging women.

A feminist perspective, then, focuses on the structures that promote inequality and the "difference that difference makes" (MacKinnon, 1989) on a structural and political level as opposed to an individual level. Furthermore, and borrowing ideas from radical feminists, a feminist age approach views the state's commitment to alleviating or correcting women's disadvantages as contestable. As one example, the Equal Economic Opportunity Commission's record for enforcing affirmative action cases on behalf of women has been under attack by many feminists. Even with the numerous policy changes over the past 25 years, the most recent census data inform us that women remain in segregated, low-paid employment, and are at higher risk than men for underpaid work.

Using this perspective, we see a lifetime of inequities between men and women directly attributable to patriarchal ideology and practice. Recognized is that age only exacerbates most women's risk for poverty, poor health, and social devaluation. Regardless of their age or color, women face discrimination in employment and remain for the most part, as we have discussed, in segregated employment sites. They continue to be targeted for sexual harassment on the job and are victims of violence in and out of their homes. Furthermore, women have yet to experience equal pay for equal work, and continue to be assigned by both their families and society to provide unpaid caregiving responsibilities to children, the sick, and the elderly.

As opposed to believing that such facts represent women's correct "place" in society, feminists understand that gender is a social construction that rarely benefits them (Hess, 1990). As Janice Bohan (1993) explains, gender does not reside "in the person but exists in those interactions that are socially construed as gendered" (p. 6). Therefore, we begin, as many feminists do, in understanding that certain traits attributed to women (i.e., passive, nurturing) are nothing more than qualities socially ascribed to women by the social structure, and not "essential" characteristics. Moreover, such socially dictated roles and responsibilities have both good and bad implications for women with age. As MacKinnon (1989) argues, the true name for women's condition is sexual inequality, not difference, whether affirmed or denied.

OPPRESSION FROM AGEISM

This perspective also incorporates relevant gerontology data. However, and as noted previously, much of what is known about gerontology comes from the study of primarily White men. This perspective looks suspiciously at data based on men's experience as speaking for the experiences of older women. In viewing women's oppression from a life-span perspective, the additional larger issue of ageism is acknowledged. Ageism is bigotry, discrimination, and prejudice that has real political and economic consequences for women. As a term coined by Dr. Robert Butler in his Pulitzer award winning book, *Why Survive? Growing Old in America* (1975), "ageism" is defined as:

> the process of systematic stereotyping of and discrimination against older people because they are old, just as racism and sexism accomplish this with skin colour and gender. . . . Ageism allows the younger generation to see old people as different from themselves, thus they subtly cease to identify with their elders as human beings. (p. 12)

In addition to the lifetime of problems and issues that affect women as they move through the life span, mainly as a result of sexism, women's gender inequalities are exacerbated both by advanced age and by ageism in policies and public sentiment. Divorce laws, age discrimination, nonresearched health concerns, and demeaned physical appearance individually and together challenge older women's attempts to age with dignity. They are expected to provide free care to both the young and the old, or to be invisible. With regards to their economic status, older women have about half the income of older men, and older women of color have even less income than older White women. The majority of older widows have incomes that fall well below $10,000. For many older unmarried women, Social Security remains their sole income source. One consequence to their dismal economic state is that women compose the majority of older recipients of Supplemental Security Income (AARP, 1993). One of the few arenas open for women to achieve privilege is through their physical appearance and their ability to reproduce. As patriarchal society can not equate age with either of these traits or abilities, older women become seen as "the other." The result is that many older women report feeling invisible and discounted. And yet, what we have learned well from multicultural feminisms is that oppression alone does not define one's authenticity. Where there are sites of domination, there are also sites of resistance. Individual and collective paths of caring and defiance to domination also articulate a self-determination that leads to authenticity.

DIVERSITY, DOMINATION, AND RESISTANCE: MULTIPLE VOICES

One's status in life is determined not by personal biography alone, but by social, cultural, and political forces and structures. In Eleanor Stoller and Rose Gibson's excellent contribution, *Worlds of Difference: Inequality in the Aging Experience* (1994), the authors explain that it is not only what one has experienced or accomplished in life that defines one's place and worth in society. Social, cultural, and political–historical forces and structures also influence the quality of one's aging.

"Social location," according to Stoller and Gibson, refers to the social hierarchy into which one is born. It is also based on personal and social attributes, such as gender, race, and class. Social location results in varied advantages and disadvantages, and shapes one's world and aging experience. In contrast, the historical period refers to those conditions that people experience at a particular chronological age. Certain historical periods relegate women to certain roles that have limited their life chances, and have increased their likelihood of experiencing negative life events. Finally, personal biography is how one adapts to social location and historical period. It is identity. The older woman who was never allowed to continue her education because "education was not important for a girl" can not be blamed for not having a well-paid profession that cushions her retirement years. Likewise, the older Black woman born prior to the civil rights era has had different life advantages and disadvantages compared to her 20-year-old granddaughter. In other words, women's lives are a function of their gender and other influences. Some older women have flourished in patriarchal society; the majority have not. The matrix of domination is complex, for a woman may be privileged due to her class but disadvantaged due to her gender. Some may escape racism, but all women do not escape sexism. If women live long enough, neither will they escape ageism. Understanding these various influences on aging helps to minimize comparisons that are limited by only gender or age.

Therefore, we seek out and listen to the diverse and multiple voices of women due to such political and social forces. We are critical of a singular voice of women, and yet continue to seek out those experiences that weave common threads among women. Themes evident in multicultural and postmodern feminisms uncover women's many shapes and colors, and aid in our understanding that women's inequality is shaped by the multiple intersections of race, class, age, ethnicity, and sexual orientation. Through these diversities, strategies can be found to counter oppressions. For example, tensions that exist between being a woman and being old, being a woman of color and being a feminist, and so forth, can be used as alternative sites for the development of new theory on women growing older. Diversity theories alert us to the tremendous cost of racism on the lives of older women, and also allow for a better understanding of the multiple and interlocking levels of oppression and their relationships to one another (P. H. Collins, 1991). Silence, then, is heard not necessarily as agreement, but as a potential site of resistance and dissent.

As we have stated, oppression alone does not define a person. Neither is ageism the only defining factor of an older woman. Not ignored are the strengths that older women hold from a history of life experiences, both good and bad, from resisting oppression, and from their connections to other peoples and issues.

CALL FOR POLITICAL AND STRUCTURAL CHANGE

Feminists believe that the "personal is political," and so value social change. Patriarchy and capitalism have shaped women's lives, relegating them to limited power in either the public or private spheres. What we have seen is that many of the nation's policies are predicated on women's being assigned gender roles and lower status. It is this understanding of the forces of domination in women's lives that ensures one's ability to see the value in advocating for structural and political changes to challenge domination. As Bricker-Jenkins and Hooyman (1986) note, there are no private solutions to women's issues. A feminist analysis that focuses on aging women recognizes the essential need for a paradigmatic shift for caregiving, health care, social lives, and work.

For example, neither private nor public policies consider that many women's work histories differ from men's, whether due to intermittent work histories, employment that offers no pension coverage, or part-time work with no benefits. Furthermore, policies rarely acknowledge what women in the home do as "work," and therefore do not compensate it, either with income or retirement benefits. Neither are those making public policy particularly sensitive or aware of the forces of sexism, racism, ageism, and other sites of oppression. A feminist life-span perspective on age can help to uncover what is problematic for women as they age, that is, bias in Social Security and pensions, and discrimination in employment due to interlocking oppressions, ageism, and for some, the effects of a lifetime of racism and homophobic acts. This perspective more broadly adds to the continuing discussion on rights, entitlements, citizenship, and inequality. Ideas from this perspective challenge practices and policies that negate women's worth and advocate for those that applaud their strengths while acknowledging life's difficulties. Thus, older women are credited as contributors to the political world, as opposed to only casualties of the system.

POWER, EMPOWERMENT, AND STRENGTHS

New conceptualizations of power and empowerment are required for this perspective. By moving away from victimization, women's empowerment, authenticity, and strengths are acknowledged and validated. As a process, activity, and a skill, empowerment is used by people and professionals to effect individual, social, and political change. A traditional conceptualization defines empowerment as a conflict model, with a goal of both increased personal control and political power for individual gain. Such definitions have been oriented toward domination and competition. In contrast, feminist definitions view empowerment more as the capacity and energy found in connections, and as potential for working toward the collective and community good. Rejecting negative views of older women, empowerment replaces such denigration with the uplifting words of older women themselves.

The number of books written by older women is growing at an unprecedented rate. Not surprisingly, older women authors educate others about the joys, the challenges, and the difficulties related to aging and to women. Uncovered are the negative stereotypes directed against older women, replaced by strategies that can be undertaken to minimize, counter, and prevent them. Moreover, this perspective examines the relationships between empowerment and authenticity.

There are many ways to be empowered and authentic. Examples can include the process by which older women define themselves, when they engage in individual and collective acts of political activism, and when the connections between all forms of domination are exposed.

VISIONS OF SOLIDARITY

This perspective, rooted in women's lives, seeks a vision for older women that is inclusive and transformative. Nonetheless, searching for commonalities without essentializing women is a difficult road to walk. We are reminded of Catherine MacKinnon's words: "Women's commonalities include, they do not transcend" (1989, p. 88). Although we hope for unity, we court solidarity, recognizing those issues where women's voices can converge, and those when race and class, not gender, may be primary organizing forces. The quest for solidarity also includes desired alliances between younger and older women through empathy, understanding, and honesty. However, in the past, feminist theory has been guilty of homogenizing women to a White middle-class mode, in part as a strategy to augment numbers and show strength as well as a reflection of racism in feminism. This strategy resulted in a weakening of feminism through the exclusion of so many voices. Multicultural feminism exposed the inadequacies of this model. From multicultural and postmodern feminisms, we have come to question realities and universal truths. We seek common themes when they exist.

Still, in feminism's efforts to speak for all women and in its quest for unity, what must be recognized is that some groups of women are left out of the discussion. By acknowledging differences as well as similarities among women, feminist age theory can become accountable to both racism and ageism within feminist theory. It can also develop strategies that are both critically reflective of the movement itself and inclusive of all women. As Angela Davis (1990) notes, it is in the allowing for difference among women that solidarity becomes possible. Accordingly, we recognize that specific issues may sometimes welcome more coalition-building as a strategy, rather than a solidarity based on a the needs of a universal woman.

A HOLISTIC AND ECOLOGICAL PERSPECTIVE

I noted previously that both feminist and nonfeminist theorists have written of people's lives and their relationships to one another and things. This perspective, characteristic of most feminist writings, embraces a holistic and ecological perspective and looks to linkages between the young and old, between races, between men and women, and between the healthy and the frail. Feminists view capitalism and patriarchy as distinct and yet related causes of women's oppression (Hartmann, 1981). Feminists reject those aspects of dualistic thinking that separate the public and private spheres, with women relegated to the private spheres (with their work economically devalued) and men to the public (with men's work economically valued in the marketplace). Instead, this perspective sees value in both spheres, as well as perceiving women's minimal power in either sphere. Rather than an either/or analysis, feminists advocate for the "both/ and" approach, emphasizing new conceptualizations of work, citizenship, and community. Feminist theories, especially those from women of color and aging women, inform us about "the interlocking nature of oppressions that are structured on multiple levels, from the individual to the structural, while a part of a larger matrix of domination" (P. H. Collins, 1991, p. 230).

In looking for connections among issues, we direct our attention to the reciprocity between and among generations, rather than to artificial barriers that prevent the building of relationships. The linkages among social, political, and economic issues and their impact on the life chances of women throughout the life cycle are also viewed as critical components to improving older women's lives. Thus, we examine again in the following chapter the economic and health status of women, their caregiving responsibilities and social roles, and the connections between these factors. This time, however, we use a feminist age analysis to uncover problems and suggest some possible solutions to women's most serious challenges.

Examples of some of these linkages among issues include: caregiving across the life span and women's poor wages and poverty levels; income and health care accessibility and adequacy; the gender division of labor and poverty; capitalism, patriarchy, and violence in the home; race and poor health; ageism and demeaned social status; and deindustrialization and poverty. Feminism understands that norms and behaviors established in one sphere, public or private, are reflected in the other sphere. For example, the devaluation of women is acted out in violence against women in their homes and sexual harassment on the job. Among aging women, their devaluation is evident in the absence of pay or low pay for home caregiving. Assignment of women to caregiving is replicated in both the public and private spheres, with women's assignment to unpaid family caregiving and to low-paid caregiving jobs in the community, whether as professional nurse or paraprofessional home care worker (Leutz et al., 1992). The valuing of women primarily for their physical beauty and for their reproductive skills does not impact on only the public or the private sphere. Women find their devaluation occurs in both with advanced age.

EXPANDED AND ALTERNATIVE RESEARCH METHODOLOGIES

What is usually characterized as traditional research, or quantitative methodologies, is associated with positivism. While a number of feminist researchers have used and still use this scientific method to identify and correct gender differences in theory and practice, other feminists note that a fundamental problem exists with the isolation of variables from their context (Swigonski, 1993). Social gerontology researchers are also critiqued by postmodern gerontology and critical gerontology scholars for their adoption and reliance on positivism. Gerontology researchers have, for the most part, labeled gender as a descriptive variable, rather than a central and defining factor in describing and explaining older women's life situations. As Gibson (1996) warns:

> The fact that the experience of being old and female is one characterized by lower income, greater disability, better social support, higher social participation, greater continuities, widowhood, and extreme old age—or, in other words, some coherent sense of what it means to be old and female as distinct from old and male—somehow disappears from such analyses. (p. 443)

In contrast, feminist research's focus on is on women's lives. It desires to hear their multiple voices and to have women define their own issues. This quest becomes its method, and the social reality of a situation is its research agenda. A feminist methodology is used by those who support the political aims of the women's movement for women's equality and freedom of choice in living their lives. According to Shulamit Reinharz (1992), themes often found in feminist research include the following:

> errors and biases feminists perceive in scientific research; the impact of feminism on the disciplines, the philosophy or epistemology of feminist research and whether feminist research constitutes a new or impossible paradigm, . . . the relationship between feminism and methodology, and criticism and praise about specific instances of feminist research. (p. 5)

Ray (1996) outlines a number of areas in which feminist research offers a unique contribution to gerontology and feminist methodology. Her suggestions add to directions for a feminist life-span perspective on aging. Feminist research, she adds, focuses on the role of the observer and the observed, understanding that researchers have standpoints, even when unknown to them. She argues for a closer relationship between research and practice to contribute to knowledge-building on behalf of women. Other elements of feminist research, according to Ray, are that it is generated from women's life experiences, and that it is interpretative, interactive, critical, and change-focused. To this end, she provides the following questions that guide the development of new theory on women and aging: "Are the findings of and by women? Is it self critical; does it challenge existing assumptions and data? Is its focus on changing the inequalities of women's lives?" (p. 676).

Although acknowledging that positivism is not the answer, most feminists realize that relativism is not, either. Relativism emphasizes that produced specialized thought is not only valid but truth. However, both positivism and relativism "minimize the importance of specific location in influencing a group's knowledge, the power inequities among groups that produce subjugated knowledge, and the strengths and limitations of partial perspectives" (P. H. Collins, 1991, p. 235). In contrast, feminist methodologies address the fact that power inequities and gender domination exist, and are reflected in research and in political and economic realities that affect women's lives. A feminist methodology can help to address these issues by taking into account the specific life experiences of women that culminate in a stressful old age, but that also recognizes their strengths and contributions. In this way, suggests Gibson (1996), the inaccuracies and silences about aging women can be corrected.

Thus, ideas found in a feminist life-span perspective view gender as a construct that provides women with advantages and disadvantages throughout the life cycle. More specifically, a feminist research methodology incorporates a holistic view of women's lives and identifies strategies to change the status quo and improve aging women's lives. Feminist theory sees the value in multiple ways of knowing. It identifies the inadequacies of positivism, with its focus on objectivity and rationality, and recognizes that science is neither objective nor necessarily rational. Feminist research is skeptical of book knowledge as "the written truth," because women know that their voices (and silences) have not been heard or recorded in any representative or normative fashion. Left out of the center, women have found alternative "locations" to speak their words and express their feelings—poems, drama, critical essays, and other forms. Therefore, we seek to locate and hear the voices of old women and support their validation in these and other forms, not as different from men's, but as legitimate in their own right.

CONCLUSIONS

Ideas from this perspective lead us in the direction toward a feminist epistemology on women and age further articulated in chapter 9. An epistemology examines the nature and scope of knowledge as well as its limitations (P. H. Collins, 1991). An epistemology of women and age requires that the lives of older women are best understood when viewed as a result of both opportunities and limitations and strengths and disabilities, together with the added force of ageism. Recognizing that older women are relegated to marginalized status in this nation, we seek to document and validate older women's thoughts, experiences, and lives while also acknowledging the larger contributions that older women can make in the dismantling of distorted myths and untruths about women and other oppressed people. We seek varied and expansive sites to best understand how knowledge of older women can be learned and shared. A new epistemology of women and age insists that feminism pay attention to and respect older women's voices. Welcoming new data on old age, we extend a critical eye to gerontology and feminism both for their concepts derived from male perspectives and for their exclusion of older women respectively. For varied reasons to be elaborated on further in this book, a new epistemology of women and aging suggests that feminism may be aging women's strongest hope for a just old age. Finally, thoughts toward a new epistemology seek to document empowered action and paths of resistance used by older women, as it advocates for structural change to benefit the present and future lives of all women.

A Feminist Age Critique of Present Paradigms and Policies

> Feminism does not see its view as subjective, partial, or undetermined but as a critique of the purported generality, disinterestedness, and universality of prior accounts.
>
> —Catherine MacKinnon

> We do not need to share common oppression to fight equally to end oppression . . . we can be sisters united by shared interests and beliefs, united in our appreciation of diversity, united in our struggle to end sexist oppression.
>
> —bell hooks

Critiquing the ways in which gender and gender relations are developed and culturally promulgated and maintained continues to be a major task of feminism. Feminists challenge established norms around women, seek to actively construct more positive and realistic images of women, and advocate for new opportunities for women. An important focus for feminists has been to examine the nation's policies for the ways in which they shape and respond to women's lives. In this chapter, I discuss and critique public and private policies that affect women's economic and health status, caregiving responsibilities, and social lives, using ideas from a feminist life-span perspective on aging—a feminist age analysis. Their critique underscores the need to examine how women's lives are different from men's as a direct result of their biology, gender norms, strengths, and inequalities. These differences, which are cumulative across the life span, result in an aging experience that is more challenging for women than it is for men. Elements from a feminist life-span perspective on aging, presented in the previous chapter, also acknowledge the multiple and interlocking forces of oppression on women throughout their lives. It is understood that not all women enter old age with the same resources as a result of varying advantages, as well as multiple sites of oppression and resistance. Moreover, the effects of age-ism, as a form of domination, are emphasized as forces that ultimately color all women's prospects for a just old age. I steer away from an androcentric perspective that views older women as only problems to society. Such a view ends up, as Gibson (1996) warns, ignoring the "problems that society poses for older women . . . as the problems that old women pose for society take hold" (p. 434). I offer this feminist age analysis, then, as a tool to critique "what is" and move us in the direction of "what could be" on behalf of aging women.

I argue in this chapter, as do other feminist thinkers, that public and private policies, as decisions made by individuals and by society, are directly attributable to patriarchal ideology. Consequently, these policies wrongly reflect a view of aging women not as citizens but as dependents and, ultimately, as costly burdens to society. Feminist analyses examine women's lives from sites of contribution, strength, and oppression. A feminist age analysis extends this analysis to consider how patriarchal notions of older women have influenced and continue to influence social policy. Moreover, ideas from this analysis underscore the connections among work, economic status, caregiving responsibilities, and social status across the life span; the relationships among poverty, oppression, and poor health; and the connections between economic/political forces and women's well-being. Ideas found within this analysis advocate for struc-tural changes to benefit women's lives and suggest that a new paradigm is essential in framing these lives, one that acknowledges the strengths that exist among older women. Furthermore, the need for new conceptual-izations of power and empowerment is emphasized, with a focus on women's aging. Ideas central to a feminist age analysis also suggest that solidarity is a key political strategy to promote social justice. In this analysis, I acknowledge a number of trends that reflect aging women's diversity—their greater numbers in the work force, the increasing numbers of divorced and single women, the growing ethnic diversity among the nation as a whole, especially the aged, and the many years women spend as widows. Finally, in this chapter I look to methodologically creative and rigorous studies, together with other sources, that focus on the lives, tribulations, and contributions of all aging women. A feminist age analysis, built on women's realities, not myths or assumptions, should lead to political strategies that support women. For this to happen, we must hear what aging women have to say.

A FEMINIST AGE CRITIQUE OF ECONOMIC POLICIES

In this section, I critique economic policies that impact on older women from a feminist age analysis. Feminists, of course, are not the only ones who have sharply criticized the ideological underpinnings that have framed retirement and other public policies as based on gender-role stereotypes (Leonard & Nichol, 1994; U.S. House Select Committee on Aging, 1990a, 1990b, 1992a, 1992b, 1992c). A number of values and beliefs that reflect the ideology of the "family ethic" have come under scrutiny by feminists: (a) that women are dependent and men are independent (the breadwinners) as opposed to viewing marriage as an equal family unit; (b) that women are natural nurturers, observed in caregiving assigned to women and by the lack of retirement work credits for women as caregivers; (c) that there are few connections or linkages between the private and public spheres; and (d) that the patriarchal family is the preferred family form.

In chapter 1 we discussed the Social Security Act of 1935. This Act was designed to reward the typical upper-and middle-class family of the time, in which the male was a breadwinner and his wife was his dependent within a marriage that was only to end with the death of one of the partners. White, middle-class women generally followed gender-role expectations by focusing their energies on the private sphere, as opposed to the public sphere, and by taking care of their families. Unlike today, few middle-class women worked full-time out of the home, primarily because the financial burden of the family was firmly placed on the man's shoulders while care of children, the sick, and the aged were the responsibilities of the woman. When middle-class women did work, more often than not it was in part-time, segregated and low-paid employment, and with years taken off for family caregiving duties.

In contrast, the economic profile of working-class and most ethnic women, detailed in previous chapters, clearly shows that these two groups of women were never excluded from the demands of both the public and private spheres, only from the rewards. Unfortunately for women, the benefit formula established in 1935 for Social Security has not changed sufficiently to reflect the numerous demographic and societal changes affecting women today and our growing awareness of the diversities among women. Neither have private pensions supported most women's work patterns. Finding and agreeing on the public and private sector solutions that will ensure a poverty-free old age for older women are issues that have yet to be resolved.

Elements from a feminist life-span perspective on age that we draw from in this section include: (a) women as an oppressed population across the life span and their added oppression from ageism; (b) women's cultural and lifestyle diversities; (c) the need for political and social change to improve older women's lives as well as the lives of the future cohort of older women; and (d) an ecological/holistic view of women's lives that looks to the connective threads among their economic, health, caregiving, and social statuses.

As an example, we discussed in previous chapters the fact that caregiving has serious economic ramifications for women. With feminist age analysis on caregiving we acknowledge that women both receive and provide care. For many, caregiving is an act of love, whether it is in providing care to a spouse or other family member, providing paid care to the frail and disabled, or as volunteer in the community. As in the case of spousal caregiving, however, public policies directly and indirectly support gender-role stereotypes by binding marital status to public or private pension benefits and investment capabilities via the income of a husband and by not crediting years of providing child care or elder care responsibilities in either public or private pension plans (Abramowitz, 1992; Gottleib, 1989). Furthermore, and as Abramowitz cogently points out, women who follow such traditional definitions are generally rewarded financially more than women who are employed outside of the home. For example, the present cohort of the oldest-old married women typically benefit from their husband's more generous Social Security and private pensions' benefits, compared to their divorced counterparts who collect a retirement benefit based on their own work history. Divorced older women must also have been married for at least 10 years to collect benefits in their former husband's name. Moreover, widows often receive smaller benefits if their husbands die before the retirement age of 65 years. In short, being outside of the traditional White nuclear family headed by a man has serious financial consequences for women throughout their lives, but even more so as they age.

An adequate retirement income depends on the earned income from Social Security, private pensions, and personal savings in a woman's own name or name of spouse. As was discussed earlier, strategies to find the right balance among these three that provides for a decent status of living for older women have been forthcoming, but an agreement on which strategy to take has been difficult to reach at best. The following section reexamines Social Security, private pensions, employment policies, and savings for their availability and accessibility using elements of a feminist age analysis.

SOCIAL SECURITY AND SUPPLEMENTAL SECURITY INCOME

The divorce rate has risen, the number of women in the paid labor force has grown, and women's roles have changed since the enactment of the

Social Security Act of 1935 (Rodeheaver, 1987; U.S. House Select Committee on Aging, 1992a, 1992b). Although Social Security was never designed to be the sole retirement income of Americans, the majority of older women rely primarily on it, and the amount received is rarely sufficient for health and financial well-being. In truth, the characteristics of both the American work force and the American family have changed dramatically since 1935. Should the future see no changes in the premises underlying Social Security (women as dependent, men as breadwinners, narrow definition of the family, penalization of caregiving with limited dropout years, and no credit for caregiving) and if sex segregation, race, and age discrimination in the work force continue, women's financial security will continue to be less adequate than men's.

Social Security may be an entitlement program, but, as noted earlier, entitlement programs are not synonymous with universal access or adequate care. Divorced and minority older women—whose work histories are more similar to White men's, at least in number of years worked—find that discrimination, segregated employment, and lack of access to private pensions have dire ramifications for their economic survival. Furthermore, the present cohort of older women is most vulnerable to cuts in the nation's safety net of services such as old age assistance programs due to their low income, or limited or nonexistent work histories. The need for financial assistance, whether through the Supplemental Security Income program or housing assistance, becomes even more important to members of these latter two groups. This is because, historically, old age assistance from the means-tested SSI program has been more vulnerable to cuts than has Social Security. Cuts in programs such as SSI impact more on ethnic women than White women (Torres-Gil, 1990).

Social Security was built on the dual issues of equity and adequacy. But, for many reasons, among them the high rate of poverty that persists among aging women, "achieving adequacy and equity standards for [aging women] remains one of the unmet social goals by the framers of the Social Security system" (Holden, 1997, p. 101). In part, this is because Social Security was developed on the base of earned rights, not universal eligibility. In this way, equity emphasizes worker's contributions over those who have been defined as noncontributory, such as dependents. The system is also based on the concept of adequacy. Simply put, it is how income meets needs. In contrast to equity, adequacy seeks to provide a minimum income base for older workers and their spouses. This results in higher income workers receiving greater benefit amounts compared to those lower wage workers, and lower income workers receiving a higher return on their investment. Just how do these issues affect the retirement income of women?

One critical issue for Social Security for women revolves around the issue of dual entitlement. This clause states that a dependent spouse, usually a woman, must choose between receiving her pension on her own work history or receiving a benefit as a homemaker and spouse. At the present time, a two-earner couple often receives the same (or less) retirement income from Social Security compared to a one-earner couple with comparable life earnings (U.S. House Select Committee on Aging, 1992b). Adequacy in this case emphasizes provision of minimal benefits to retired workers, children and elderly wives of retired workers, elderly widows of insured workers, and children and widows of deceased workers. Considering the high levels of poverty among older women, the fact that 74% of the nation's poor elderly are women, and the high numbers of older women living just above the poverty threshold are evidence that do not provide any assurance that the adequacy goals of Social Security are being met. Although it is hoped that future cohorts will benefit from laws that have made pensions and survivor provisions for divorced and widowed women more accessible, benefit adequacy may undermine such gains for working women (U.S. House Select Committee on Aging, 1992a, 1992b). Thus, a number of reform strategies have been recommended, although not yet enacted, to promote equity for working spouses and ensure adequacy for the homemaker and elderly widow (see Burkhauser & Smeeding, 1994; U.S. House Select Committee on Aging, 1992b, 1992c).

Reform proposals have generally focused on marital earnings sharing to replace the dual entitlement clause. Marital earnings strategies would combine the couple's earnings during their marriage and divide them equally, with each spouse receiving a benefit based on 50% of the marital earnings plus any individual earnings before and after the marriage (Bandler, 1989). As Bandler states, this strategy "recognizes marriage as an economic partnership, reduces benefit disparities between spouses, provides homemakers protection, and increases benefits for many divorced workers" (p. 309). Advocates for equity reform hope that the marital earnings strategy will provide a more just distribution of resources for working women and two-income couples. However, critics claim that such changes will help the upper-income two-income couple at the expense of the homemaker; cut benefits for one-income couples and divorced men; eliminate all family entitlements; cut many benefits for the young family; penalize low-benefit couples; and lower benefits for older adults (U.S. House Committee on Ways and Means, 1985). In contrast, those favoring adequacy reforms advocate preserving the financial security of the worker and family members, regardless of whether they are employed outside of the home, and have focused on entitlement gaps and inadequate benefits. Critics of adequacy reform claim that any changes will help the homemaker and elderly widower, but not employed women. As Holden (1997) cautions: "Reforms linked to the combined final average earnings of both spouses could cause the gender neutral program to be work-neutral as well. A system that has explicitly rejected rewarding particular patterns of individual earnings should also be neutral with regard to the patterns of earnings between spouses" (p. 103). The debate continues about how to preserve adequacy for elderly widows, families, and low-benefit couples and equity for dual income couples (Kingson & O'Grady-LeShane, 1993; Sandell & Iams, 1994).

A thorough evaluation of proposals that aim to improve women's lives is essential prior to adapting and enacting any new policies. Evaluation requires a critique of the assumptions on which these policies are based. Rather than view older women as a homogeneous group, for example, aging women are seen as a diverse population. It is recognized that any structural change to Social Security will have winners and losers. One strategy is to target those who are in the most financial need of benefits, rather than assume that one's work history will offer income protection to all. At the same time, feminists realize that targeting the poor holds some inherent political dilemmas. There are no public welfare sacred cows, and targeting financially needy older women who are recipients of social insurance programs will be a difficult tightrope to walk for policymakers who favor a strong involuntary and government-controlled Social Security system. In the end, the road to making Social Security into a means-tested program may undermine its much needed citizen support (Kingson & Schulz, 1997).

To its credit, Social Security has adapted, albeit slowly, to a number of demographic changes. Amendments have liberalized its definitions of the family, increased flexibility in retirement age, and expanded benefits for divorced spouses. Social Security has a number of positive biases, including the fact that it is involuntary and inaccessible until retirement age, regardless of need. This inaccessibility eventually helps the poor in a protective way by preventing earlier withdrawals of funds to help children or for other reasons. Female workers also make greater use of the weighted, progressive benefit that helps those in lower wage brackets (Bandler, 1989). However, it still does not lift women from the ranks of the poor. Other strategies to eliminate the inequities in the Social Security system have been proposed by the Older Women's League. In a hearing before the U.S. House Select Committee on Aging, they offered the following recommendations:

1. Provide dependent care.
2. Eliminate the seven-year waiting requirement for disabled widows.

3. Working widows who delay receiving benefits should be given delayed retirement credits (DRC's) in addition to widow benefits.
4. The earning limit should be eliminated for people with limited earnings who have minimal or no private pensions.
5. Caregivers of disabled spouses should be treated as if they were caring for an adult disabled child.
6. Eliminate the two-year waiting period for divorced spouses over age 62.
7. The persisting problem of inequities in benefits between most one and two-earner families must be reexamined and rectified. (U.S. House Select Committee on Aging, 1990b, pp. 57–60)

Also supported by the Older Women's League are the findings from the Technical Committee on Earnings Sharing, a Washington, DC feminist advocacy and policy group. Their plan, known as the Modified Earnings Sharing Plan, recommends that marriage be defined as a economic partnership. In this way, the financial contributions of homemaking would be recognized, lending some protection to those who provide unpaid labor in the home (Miller, 1990). Women who stay at home would be able to have a Social Security record in their own name, since married couples would share their earnings for future Social Security benefits. Moreover, the stay-at-home spouse could also earn disability benefits in his or her own name, something not presently available. Other recommendations from the National Women's Law Center include permitting additional dropout years and endorsing modifications in special minimum benefits (U.S. House Select Committee on Aging, 1992c). These recommended changes acknowledge a critical point: that entitlements are, after all, only socially, politically, and economically constructed structures that can and do change with shifting values and mores, legal interpretations, new administrations, the national Zeitgeist, and more. As was stated earlier, entitlements are not synonymous with universal rights or access, although they are probably the closest approximations to such rights that we have today. But the disparities in benefits by race, gender, and the interlocking forces of gender plus race point to the fact that, even with entitlements, not all receive "just and equitable" benefits.

A different reform strategy to improve older women's economic status is to focus on the Supplemental Security Income program, a public assistance program administered by the Social Security Administration. Specific proposals have suggested that SSI payments be raised. This strategy would be especially helpful to those who are divorced, who are only entitled to 50% of an ex-husband's earnings after age 65, and to those who have not worked long enough to earn an adequate benefit on their work history and earn a pension. Recommendations to be considered for SSI were voiced in a hearing before the U.S. House Select Committee on Aging's Symposium on women and retirement:

1. Increase SSI benefit level from the current 75% of poverty to 120% above poverty over a five year period.
2. Eliminate the one-third income reduction in benefits for recipients living in another's home.
3. An increase in the amount of assets allowed.
4. A lowering of the age requirement from 65 to 62 years.
5. Enhanced efforts to extend work incentives.
6. An increase in Social Security administrative staff to handle backlog of unprocessed disability applicants. (1992c, pp. 100–102)

None of these strategies have yet to be enacted. Other voices, like Barusch (1994), argue that it is only through maintaining and improving those services as part of the "safety net" (programs and services such as food stamps, Medicaid, and public housing), together with SSI, that older women's economic status will be protected. Barusch states:

Today's lower income women will not benefit from Social Security reforms designed to address the inequities confronted by dual-earned couples. Nor will their status be improved by introduction of caregiving credits. Within America's program for income maintenance in retirement only one intervention might enhance the quality of life for those who today must choose between food and rent: raising the safety net. (p. 183)

Divorced and widowed older women are most at risk for poverty, along with those with limited work histories and/or work in low-paid jobs, which describes the majority of older women today. For such women, pension reform will provide only limited assistance. Rather, the government's continued and expanded commitment to a "safety net" for poor older women is needed. This will require a commitment to the benefits achieved from a liberal welfare state, a difficult task in these economic and political times. Unlike Social Security, however, the poor have low usage rates of SSI. Barusch suggests that the following may improve access to such safety-net services: simplifying application forms and other procedures, expanding actual benefits, increasing program availability, and improving staffing.

PRIVATE PENSIONS AND SAVINGS

Private pensions are criticized for being inaccessible to men and are even more inaccessible to women. This is especially true for minority aging women. Private pensions are necessary to meet the financial needs of older Americans, and yet, as previously discussed, men's work histories and types of employment result in men receiving private pensions more often than women. Two important pieces of legislation briefly mentioned in chapter 1 that have attempted to provide some protection to aging workers are the Employment Retirement Income Security Act (ERISA) of 1974 and the Tax Reform Act of 1986.

The Employment Retirement Income Security Act is aimed at stopping retirement funding abuse. However, it does not make pensions mandatory, and rarely protects the marginalized worker. Instead, protection is most often offered to employees who are long term, full-time, well-paid, and who work for large industrial employers. Rarely do women and ethnic minorities fit this profile. ERISA covers traditional pensions (i.e., not IRAs) and private pensions, and not pensions from the state, county, and federal governments where women are more often employed. Furthermore, benefits to a survivor are only 50% of the worker's benefit. And, at present, ERISA does not require the division of plan benefits under divorce.

The Tax Reform Act of 1986 is another key bill aimed at helping women and minorities. It mandates that private plans subject to ERISA (other than multi-employer plans) must provide vesting after 5 years or an equivalent-graded schedule. Multi-employer plans are allowed to vest benefits in 10 years (U.S. House Select Committee on Aging, 1992b). The vesting requirement exceeds the time most women remain in one job, however. The minimum vesting period is 5 to 7 years, but the average women works in one job only 4.3 years, and unlike Social Security benefits, private pensions are not portable. Furthermore, although a sufficient savings account is surely helpful, it is difficult to save for one's retirement if one has made a minimal income throughout one's lifetime.

A number of principles from a feminist life-span perspective on aging can help to underscore the connections between race, gender, and discrimination on pension availability and the annuity amount. We see clearly how older women of color are least likely to have pensions, even though their work history in length of time worked is similar to that of White men. Reform strategies have advocated amending ERISA to make it mandatory and involuntary like Social Security, including 401K plans as a supplement; requiring the division of pension benefits upon divorce; reducing the vesting period to 1 year; requiring spousal consent to all options; and eliminating pension integration (U.S. House Select Committee on Aging, 1989, 1992a, 1992b, 1992c). These policies and their proposed changes can be beneficial to some women. However, it is doubtful that these and other reform strategies will be helpful to the majority of women as long as they are based on work patterns that are rarely the norm for minorities, women, and women of color. Moreover, pension coverage does not provide much protection to the divorced woman who was married less than 10 years to her former spouse.

A decent retirement income is still based, for the most part, on wages earned while in the labor force. Because of this, women, especially working-class women and women of color, will continue to be left behind economically until gender and race discrimination are no longer tolerated.

EMPLOYMENT POLICIES

The absence of family-related policies to support the employed seriously impacts on working women (Hooyman & Gonyea, 1995; Tennstedt & Gonyea, 1994). Increasing numbers of women are finding that they are "doing it all" but with fewer resources and less support. Given women's concrete life experiences, and the relationship of such life experiences to retirement income, a number of proposed strategies aim to improve their economic security in later life. A feminist age analysis underscores the difficulties that exist in the ability to retain, keep, or advance in a job when one provides care to a dependent sick child or frail older adult. With a feminist age analysis we understand that, even among women with sufficient financial security that allows them to hire someone to provide caregiving, that "someone" is more often than not another woman—a woman of color, one who is poor or near-poor, and one who must go home and continue nonpaid caregiving when her paid caregiving responsibilities are done.

The fact that women are increasingly in the work force is well recognized. Also widely acknowledged is the fact that child care remains the primary responsibility of women. Still, a national family policy has yet to be developed. As a result, programs to support child care are severely limited by both ideological beliefs and financial constraints. As we note in chapter 1, the Economic Recovery Act's allowance of flexible spending accounts is a step forward in permitting employees to use their pretax income to pay for child care. However, such benefits offer the most benefit to middle-and higher-income families and workers. For the most part, families, especially lower-income families, continue to rely on informal care, often other female family members, to care for their children. With feminist age analysis, we recognize the fact that should they be able to afford formal child care, the preschool and day care workers women rely on are also predominantly female and underpaid.

Also discussed in chapter 1 was the 1993 Family and Medical Leave Act, which provides for some parental leave and some leave time to provide caregiving responsibilities to family members. Women enthusiastically embraced this policy as one of the nation's first to recognize the relationship between the family and work responsibilities that especially fall on women. However, a feminist critique of this act requires that we examine its purpose. According to the FMLA, it seeks:

1. to balance the demands of the work place with the needs of families, to promote the stability and economic security of families, and to promote national interests in preserving family integrity;
2. to entitle employees to take reasonable leave for medical reasons, for the birth or adoption of a child, and for the care of a child, spouse, or parent who has a serious health condition;
3. to accomplish the purposes described in paragraphs (1) and (2) in a manner that accommodates the legitimate interests of employers;
4. to accomplish the purposes described in paragraphs (1) and (2) in a manner, consistent with the Equal Protection Clause of the Fourteenth Amendment, minimizes the potential for employment discrimination on the basis of sex by ensuring generally that leave is available for eligible medical reasons (including maternity-related disability) and for compelling family reasons, on a gender-neutral basis; and
5. to promote the goal of equal employment opportunity for women and men, pursuant to such clause. (Public Law 103-3, 107 Stat.6-7)

A feminist age analysis acknowledges the strides this policy has made, and yet we also see its shortcomings in promoting equality. For one thing, the leave is unpaid, with the result that the allowable 12-week leave time remains the unreachable dream for many families. For single parents, it is all but an impossibility. Among married couples, it is the woman who usually takes the "leave," as her wages are typically less than that of her husband. Furthermore, businesses with fewer than 50 employees are exempt from having to provide FMLA benefits. And, as we have seen, women and persons of color are more often found employed in small rather than large businesses. The very fact that small businesses are exempt from participating in the FMLA contradicts the stated purpose of the FMLA, which is to "promote national interests in preserving family integrity" (Public Law 103-3, 107 Stat.6-7).

One of the more problematic components of this policy is in its definition of "family" as the traditional family. Those couples living together, good friends who are in fact surrogate families to one another, and gay and lesbian couples are excluded from receiving such benefits. Single parents, primarily women and one-fourth of the nation's households, are not officially excluded, but find in reality that they can rarely take unpaid leave. Furthermore, there exists an interesting and illogical theme within the FMLA that reflects the lack of connective threads between the public and private spheres within this policy. That is, while the economic costs to business for providing this leave are seen as a public concern, the costs to family caregivers remain in the private sphere. In contrast, we see the limits of the public/private sphere argument within the FMLA that relate to the conceptualization of dependency and caregiving. We also pay attention to the value of language, and suggest that "unpaid elder care" should become more a part of our vocabulary.

In sum, the FMLA takes a gender-neutral approach to social policy reform, and in doing so negates the gender-specific nature of caregiving work. By adopting a patriarchal definition of family, many alternative family structures are ignored. Similarly, Eve Feder Kittay's (1995) analysis of the Family Medical Leave Act also argues that its limitations

> are traceable to an ideology of reciprocity and equality that continues to push dependency concerns back into the domain of the private, that is, to a conception of dependency concerns which still fails to recognize the extent to which addressing these needs are a matter of the social cooperation required for a well-ordered and just society. (p. 19)

And, by pitting job security against caregiving tasks, it continues to ignore the fact that both work and family well-being constitutes the health of a nation. Kittay (1995) offers this suggestion: "We need to shift our vision and see society as constituted by the nested dependencies that require a concept of justice between persons who are equal in their connections but unequal in their vulnerability and for whom a notion of *doulia*—of caring for those who care—is central" (p. 24).

The life-cycle nature of discrimination against women, the added impact of ageism, and the relationships among deindustrialization, a stagnant economy, and the poverty of women and people of color are paramount in a feminist age analysis. Thus, changes in women's economic status will require personal and political strategies, and thoughtful attention must focus on how any modified and new programs would be financed. Such discussions are beyond the scope of this book. Readers are encouraged to read the Congressional Symposium on Women and Retirement, U.S. House Select Committee on Aging (September 24, 1992c) for an excellent analysis of some of these issues.

Another critical employment reform strategy is to support the Equal Employment Opportunity Commission (EEOC) in making a greater commitment to investigate race, age, and gender discrimination. This is because, and as noted by O'Rand (1996) in her insightful discussion of cumulative advantage and disadvantage throughout the life cycle, "government intervention at later ages cannot fully compensate for the longer term patterns" (p. 233). Although it remains controversial, the goals and strategies of affirmative action policies are usually supported by women and by minorities because they have seen the benefits of its programs. Class action suits and other legal mechanisms could result in better funding for affirmative action programs, an end to segregated employment, increased attention to ageism in employment, and the beginning of serious attention to comparable-worth issues. Other employment options worth mentioning include employment policies that provide wage and job equity (job parity for full-and part-time workers and an increased minimum wage) as well as compensation equity (pension, health insurance, and family-responsive options). Moreover, small businesses should not be excluded from pension policy changes, as women work primarily in small business. Additionally, caregiving credit could be given toward one's retirement in public and private pensions for both men and women.

Taking a broader look at employment assumptions about women's roles in the private and public spheres, we look holistically at these issues and grasp the connections among work, economic status, and caregiving responsibilities. It is possible for employee benefits to support women and men in the work force with family responsibilities, rather than continue with the present lack of such benefits that can result in increased strain and eventual job displacement. The number of companies, however, that provide family-care and elder-care benefits to their employees, while growing, remains shockingly small. As men also provide caregiving, the absence of such benefits hurts them as well. Also not lost in our analysis is the fact that ageism hurts women's chances for employment, retention, and promotions.

The goal of a feminist age analysis, then, is to focus on women's economic status in later life and to ensure that all older women have an adequate income as a result of their rights of citizenship, as opposed to rights based on their roles as wife, mother, or caregiver. The problem, then, is not that women work or don't work, or for that matter, that women retire. Men both work and retire. The problem is that, as we have stated, women earn less income in their working years due to the multiple factors and results of segregated employment; an intermittent work history for some; punitive pension policies that punish women (and men) for taking time off from work to provide caregiving; and the effects of sexism, racism, heterosexism, and eventually ageism. The solution lies in recognizing that any retirement program that is based on wages throughout one's life will only replicate earlier injustices. As Gibson and Allen (1993) note: "Attempts to improve women's coverage are commendable, yet they do not address the wider structural issues wherein the dominant system of providing adequate income in old age is premised on the life long work-force participation patterns of a minority of the aged population—men" (p. 90). Both women and men must plan for their own retirement years. However, the prevention of poverty in old age will depend on not only their personal actions, but on the elimination of discriminatory work and hiring practices throughout their working years, and on a benefit package that recognizes people's worth as contributory citizens in their multiple and varied forms.

OLDER WOMEN AND SOCIAL SECURITY: RECENT DEBATES

Recent debates and discussions over the future of Social Security often focus on two potential dilemmas: (a) the relationship between Social Security and the national deficit and the growing numbers of older adults, and (b) the decreasing numbers of working adults to support the former at the expense of the latter. Possible solutions have included means-testing and privatization of Social Security (Quadagno, 1996). But how would such changes impact on aging women?

Means testing would require proof of low-or lower income status as a program eligibility requirement for benefits. On the face of it, this would appear to hold a minimal problem for women, since most older women would "pass" such a test. And yet means testing remains controversial. A summary of a meeting of the Odyssey Forum (1996), a group of policy experts and scholars, examined the role of government in social welfare and concluded that a change to mean testing for benefits would erode public support, act as a disincentive to private retirement savings, and undermine the dignity of beneficiaries who paid into the system throughout their working years. In the long run, such changes could harm more women if Social Security is not strong.

The second "solution" for Social Security is privatization. The idea behind privatization is that it will be better economically for individuals to voluntarily enter into a private pension plan, perhaps a nongovernment plan, instead of the compulsory Social Security program. And yet this solution too has a number of problems. First, it would shift the investment risk to individuals with no insurance that their financial benefits would be protected. Second, it ignores the fact that many lower income adults would be neither economically able to enroll in such programs nor possessed of the financial savvy to ensure a high and consistent rate of return. Notes scholar Jill Quadagno (1996):

> There is no evidence that privatization of benefits would increase savings, and no evidence those private investments would provide an adequate

substitute for Social Security benefits, at least for lower income workers. Rather, past experience suggests that, unless highly regulated, people would likely to withdraw them and use them as family needs arose. (p. 391)

She further explains that if higher income workers opted out of the system, then there would be fewer subsidies for lower income worker benefits.

A strong economic base for the nation is essential, but blaming the nation's declining economic growth on Social Security or other entitlement programs is inaccurate and irresponsible. Rather, Quadagno (1996) suggests that other reasons be examined for the nation's economic woes, such as: "foreign competition [that] has reduced the domestic market for mass-produced goods, U.S. owned multinational corporations [that have] helped to erode the domestic wage base and reduce unemployment, and the rising deficits [that] have increased interest rates and reduced investment capital" (p. 398). In reality, Social Security adds nothing to the national deficit. The dependency ratio, so-named because it supposedly tracks the changing proportion of children and older adults in the population, frames its arguments in terms of intergenerational warfare. In other words, the growing aging population will rob children of their future (Ferrara, 1995; Peterson & Howe, 1986; Thurow, 1996). But as Eric Kingson suggests, "The age dependency ratios tell only a part of the story . . . [since the dependency ratios] . . . may be partially offset by economic growth, lengthened work lives and the relative decline in the number of children" (cited in American Society on Aging, 1996b). Other scholars like Harry Moody (1994) add that the combined dependency ratio (government support for children and the aged) "has actually declined since 1960 and is projected to continue declining until after 2010, when it begins to rise only modestly again" (p. 196). As Moody thoughtfully points out, the real issue for policymakers should be to ensure that both children and the aged are supported by public policy.

Similar to a number of liberal and gerontology theories, the ideas from a feminist age analysis lend themselves to see attacks on Social Security as part of a broader attack on the nation's social insurance and public welfare programs by conservatives and elites who would like to see the dismantling of what they see as "the social-liberal state." Among conservatives, the so-called "long arm of government" is seen as detrimental to the nation's economic health, unless it is used to provide subsidies or bailouts to tobacco and defense industry giants.

But Social Security, although not perfect, can change and has changed to meet the financial needs of its beneficiaries. It protects the nation's most needy families and disabled, as well as older adults. Social Security is the only source of retirement income for many older women. Means-testing, which will weaken its national support, and privatization will not protect them from poverty. This is not to say that reform is not needed or necessary. After all, if reform is not managed, benefits may be cut and premiums may be increased. And, as previously noted, changes such as these will have a disproportionate negative economic impact on older women. Still, prior to changing or dismantling such a system, citizens should seriously ask themselves if they want to live in a society that ignores its most vulnerable, and that in effect punishes people for growing older and for the decisions they have made about caring for others.

A FEMINIST AGE CRITIQUE OF CAREGIVING POLICIES

STILL A WOMAN'S ISSUE

One of the more troubling areas for women today, especially midlife and older women, is their assignment as sole caregiver of the young, the chronically disabled, and the aged (Brody, 1990). As shown in this and previous chapters, caregiving has serious and specific economic repercussions for women. Women who stay home to raise their children, or who leave a job in midlife to care for aging parents, find that they accrue neither public nor private pension benefits for providing such care. Women who work part-time to allow themselves time with their families often end up in lower paid jobs with limited access to private pensions. Working-class and poor minority women are more apt to serve in both roles, but with fewer resources. Moreover, should aging women desire to re-enter the work force, they often find that their limited marketable skills result in their hire in low-paying service or clerical positions (Hooyman & Kiyak, 1993). This plays out in an average monthly retirement benefit for older women that is approximately 58% that of older men (U.S. Bureau of the Census, 1990a, 1990b). The consequence of such interrupted, delayed, limited, or eliminated work force participation is often near-poverty status for many older women (Quadagno & Meyer, 1990; U.S. Bureau of the Census, 1993a). While many can hope to gain access to pensions via their marriage status, as we have seen, such claims on another's pension are precarious at best (Abramowitz, 1992).

With a feminist age analysis, we avoid a masculinist/conservative view that defines caregiving as both normative and descriptive for women. At the same time, the positive aspects of caring for both women and men are not ignored (Kramer, 1996). We also recognize that women may choose to provide caregiving, that women both provide and receive care-giving from other women and men, and that caregiving, far from being "free," has costs and consequences.

A feminist age analysis, using elements from a feminist life-span per-spective on aging (a) examines caregiving through the lens of sexism and ageism; (b) makes diversity of the family, the caregiving experience, and of the nation key concepts; (c) reconceptualizes caregiving holistically, as women both give and receive care, looking at its connections to other aspects of women's lives; (d) acknowledges the strengths of caregivers and sees the potential for solidarity among women as one strategy for ending exploitation; and (e) advocates for political and social change to make caregiving more equitable. In embracing women's views of empowerment, we also acknowledge that women want the choice to provide the care, as well as the choice to receive it. As Gibson and Allen (1993) argue: "To deny women (and men) who choose to care for a disabled person the right to do so (with adequate support) is to indulge in a privileging of public over private values consistent with an earlier androcentric stage of feminist analysis. [Instead, it is] adequacy of provi-sion in both arenas is the key policy direction to be pursued" (p. 86).

A FEMINIST AGE ANALYSIS OF CAREGIVING POLICIES

As a whole, society does not give much attention to what women do and the ways in which they are not compensated for their contributions. Conservative strategies, discussed in chapter 5, follow the family ethic ideology, whereby women's natural role is in the home serving the family. Consequently, the conservative focus has been to increase the family's responsibilities of caregiving while providing some minimal assistance. Two liberal feminist responses were also summarized in chapter 5— special-privilege and gender-neutral strategies. Neither appears to differ that much from its conservative counterpart. The special-privilege argu-ment seeks to value and compensate women for their roles, but ultimately reinforces the status quo. At present, it aims to restore the family ethic—in other words, women should remain as caregivers, as it is congruent with natural abilities and growing needs. Themes from special-privilege policies are evident in the absence of a national long term-care policy, the use of women as government's main strategy to help control the costs of long term care, and the poor pay of those providing caregiving as a career (England, 1990). In contrast, the gender-neutral strategy aims to support people in their caregiver roles by providing services. In its efforts to be gender neutral, it ignores the fact that the vast majority of caregivers are women. In doing so, it neglects the point that caregivers are often poor because no credit has been given by either public or private pensions to their years spent caring for children and aging relatives. A feminist age analysis extends beyond special-privilege and gender-neutral responses and sees caregiving for what it is—a gender division of labor. Therefore, in this analysis, we question the reasons for assigning only women to such caregiving duties, and critique the effects of sexism and ageism that promulgate such thinking in a patriarchal society.

Historically, social welfare has categorized people as either worthy or not worthy, based on compliance with the family and work ethic. Ironically, however, what defines a woman as worthy in the younger years (especially White middle-class women) is too often translated into economic insecurity in the later years. The social promise of economic protection is rarely fulfilled. The woman who enters the work force after years of childrearing faces not just gender, but age (and perhaps race) discrimination. The woman who decides to leave her job to care for an aging relative finds that her caregiving years result in a depressed effect on her retirement benefits, especially if she has had a low and moderate earning history (Kingson & O'Grady-LeShane, 1993). The connections between many of these issues are a critical focus of a feminist age analysis.

With a feminist age analysis, we understand that women cannot play the caregiving game and win their financial security. Abramowitz' (1992) compelling analysis of how policies have regulated the lives of women describes succinctly how women have been penalized—intentionally or not—for both complying and not complying with the family ethic; that is, staying home and having children. And, as we have seen, the other categories of women—husbandless women, childless women, married working women, and lesbian women—often receive fewer retirement benefits than married women in traditional homemaker roles. Low wages, whether due to years of unpaid caregiving, or low-paid employment, still translate into low retirement income. The result is that many homemakers do better financially by collecting their Social Security benefits as dependents, with their "security" dependent on another's work history as well as commitment to the relationship.

This discussion benefits from the insightful analytical work of Nancy Hooyman and Judith Gonyea in *Feminist Perspectives on Family Care: Policies for Gender Justice* (1995). These authors examined family caregiving across the life span of the disabled, the mentally ill, and the frail aged and found four underlying assumptions in present long term care policies that impact on women's caregiving roles. These include: (a) the care recipient, as opposed to the family, is the target of services; (b) a belief in the superiority of community care; (c) a medical definition of dependency; and (d) privatization and informalization of care. Hooyman and Gonyea convincingly argue a number of points with which many health and human service workers are all too familiar: that it is not only the aged, but their families, that often need the assistance; that community care is not always the "best for the elder," and sometimes not even the cheapest; that dependency can be emotional and social, in addition to physical and medical; and that the term "informal care" actually refers to the unpaid care provided by women. Their analysis also reminds us to avoid the false dichotomies that exist around caregiving that ignore the reciprocity surrounding caregiving. With a feminist age analysis, we understand that families both receive and give care across the generations and throughout life, and that caregivers demonstrate numerous strengths in its provision.

Diversity is another key element in a feminist age analysis. Acknowledged are the many changes in American family life that have developed over the past 30 years, such as the changing definitions of family, women's increasing presence in the work force, the growing numbers of older citizens, and the increasing ethnic and cultural diversity of our citizens. Hence, most feminists do not believe that the traditional nuclear family should be the sole norm on which sound social policies are founded. Neither should policies be based on ideologies that place women as the family's natural caregiver and that ignore the reciprocities of care between caregiver and care-receiver. Instead, both traditional and alternate family types are valued and legitimized and deserving of services and benefits. Not only is there diversity found in family types, but there is great diversity of the caregiving experience itself, reflecting changing gender norms, expectations, obligations, and cultural and ethnic variations. And, while ethnic/cultural diversities of the nation impact on varying caregiving styles and preferences, it nonetheless remains true that women continue to be the primary caregivers of the aged (Braun & Browne, 1998).

Caregiving is important in building the social fabric of a moral society. Using ideas from a feminist age analysis, we also recognize the diversity of the caregiving/care-receiving experience. Thus, principles from a feminist age analysis seek to support all types of families that provide such care via public policies that recognize the importance of assistance and resources to lessen the burden. We recognize the intersection of other factors, notably age and race, with caregiving and care-receiving. Caregiving, after all, is provided not just to husbands but lovers, friends, children, and grandchildren (Minkler et al., 1993). Although a feminist age analysis supports choices in caregiving, we also realize that poor women do not always have the same choices that middle-class women do when it comes to caregiving. In truth, working-class and increasing numbers of middle-class women do both—they provide caregiving and they work outside the home. Private long term care insurance plans and solutions will not offer them any relief or assistance. For those below or slightly above the poverty line, receiving a tax credit when one purchases long term care services will have no impact on their income, as they in most likelihood will not be able to buy such services to begin with. Moreover, caregiving that is not economically reimbursed will not be embraced by the majority of men. Perhaps it is time that women ask why they continue to accept this financially and socially denigrated role. To move toward a feminist social welfare policy requires that women seek a stronger voice for political action with a variety of strategies: solidarity and linkages with other women, membership in nonhierarchical organizations and community action groups as well as with the traditional power sources, and exchanges and alliances with sympathetic men. More specifically, a new vision for caregiving demands that social welfare move beyond developing programs for female caregivers and instead advocate for a comprehensive national long term care policy with an adequate funding base to support all caregivers.

In avoiding an androcentric view of caregiving, we look holistically and understand that caregiving can be both a labor of love as well as one that has serious consequences to women, especially with age. A feminist age analysis of women's financial security in later life must not only critique women's work patterns that prevent/diminish benefits, but also examine women's caregiving patterns across the life span. As Quadagno and Meyer (1990) posit, we must question why women are punished for doing what society said they should do, that is, providing care. Although some hold out hope that more equitable changes in the Social Security Act will result in improved financial status for women, others disagree. According to Hooyman and Gonyea (1995):

> Although changes to the Social Security law would be highly useful, there are obstacles to using Social Security as the primary vehicle through which to correct gender-based inequities in the labor market. The strongest obstacles are the contributory nature of Social Security and the fact that Social Security is based on the assumption that caring work in the home is not of value to the marketplace, despite the female caregiver's innumerable contributions to societal well-being. (p. 249)

Another strategy for women is to build solidarity around the caregiving issue. We recognize unfair burdens placed upon the family, and see that few women will escape some responsibility in this area. It is projected that the burdens on women will only increase at a time when services are increasingly less affordable and available. Hooyman and Gonyea (1995) advocate for women to begin work toward developing caregiver coalitions as one strategy for gender justice. A feminist organization for caregivers would recognize the intersections of gender with race in women's lives and styles of organization, and the critical importance of women working together. Local and national coalitions would follow feminist values. Among these would be a "validation of women's experiences as caregivers of the chronically dependent, interconnections among women's multiple roles, the importance of legitimizing caregiving work, recognition that the personal is political, and empowerment as both a goal and means to attain the goal" (p. 346).

The real issues that surround caregiving are those of money and the role of government and families (i.e., women) should be in providing such care. The problem, as I have stated at the onset of this section, is not the movement toward community-based care. Rather, the problem is the lack of adequately funded long term care services that can support any caregiver—male or female—in providing such tasks. When caregiving is examined more closely, for example, we find that 80% of the frail elderly are cared for by families, not by institutions. Federal and state governments are quite aware that, at an average cost of $60,000 annually for nursing home care of which Medicaid is the primary payee, the "free" informal care provided to the frail by women is a real cost-saver to the nation. A feminist age analysis understands that such care is not free, but has real costs and consequences to women.

This is one reason why men and women may conceptualize government interventions in very different ways. Women are usually more in favor of government assistance because services can make their lives easier. The gender gap in politics may well exist, according to feminist social critic Barbara Ehrenreich (1996), because politicians, primarily male, ignore the needs of children, the frail, and the aged, and women's concrete realities of caring. Not surprisingly, they also neglect the needs of women as the nation's caregivers. This is why liberal feminism has not been successful in changing the face of long term care. Liberal feminism, predicated on an individualistic approach to women's issues, has historically led to supportive rather than structural system changes. We do not blame liberal feminism for the fact that the nation has privatized both child care and long term care. But women are the majority of caregivers to both the young and the old, and it is hard to see how liberal feminist approaches will solve the issues regarding caregiving by ignoring this fact or by supporting individual changes. If the lack of an available and affordable child-care and long term care system makes life difficult for so many women, is not the nation's unwillingness to develop such a system a form of gender discrimination?

Therefore, gender-responsive policy changes in caregiving must acknowledge the unfair burden placed on women by society's abdication of those who require care, a consequence of both sexism and ageism. Importantly, and as a beginning, a gender-fair policy would stop caregivers from being penalized in the Social Security system. In the present system, workers are allowed to drop 5 years of low earnings or no earnings in their benefit calculation. As women usually leave the workforce for an average of 11 years as a result of caregiving, this allowable dropout time does not provide them with the help they need, nor does it reflect their material lives. Other countries, like Canada, have dropped all caregiving years from benefit calculation. A number of bills have been previously proposed in Congress that would add more dropout years. Such a change would not be without cost, and to date Congress has not been willing to support such legislation. This is clearly shortsighted, given the impact of the aging population, the increasing numbers of grandparents raising children, and the impact of the AIDS epidemic on women's and men's work and caregiving patterns. Continued neglect of this issue will only increase women's chance for poverty in later life.

But could a potential political solution ever be reached that would be feasible in these economic times? Many think that the answer is a resounding "yes." According to figures from a 1992 report from the House Select Committee on Aging, an option providing 5 additional caregiving years would cost about $120 million over the first 5 years and a 0.24% taxable payroll over the long range. And providing only three additional dropout years would not appreciably change the short-range costs, but would reduce the long-range cost to 0.16% of taxable payroll (U.S. House Select Committee on Aging, 1992a). So, although there is a way out of this current policy dilemma, the nation's will appears to be absent. Most women employed in the legitimate workforce do earn disability and survivor's insurance benefits in their own names if they work. Unfortunately, these benefits still do not address the issues of adequacy and equity for women. And, as the same report notes, what of the 7.8 million older women, mostly immigrants, who receive no Social Security benefits due to their work as domestics?

Although saving federal dollars on the backs of women is a bargain, it is also amoral. One might even be swayed to support such a policy of penalizing caregiving, even an implicit one, if women were then taken care of medically and financially for providing such a cost-saving function to the government. But, as we have seen in data from census and other reports, women are in fact financially penalized in their retirement years for absence from the work force in their earlier years, even if they have provided 20, 30, or 40 years of caregiving to children, aged parents, and the ill. For these older women, their poverty is directly related to years out of the workforce providing caregiving. For others, notably working-class women and women of color, their poverty is additionally related to low wages, segregated employment, and discrimination. They are not afforded even the luxury of "dropping out," because they work for survival. Therefore, groups like the National Women's Law Center, the 1980 National Committee on Social Security, and the Technical Committee on Earnings Sharing advocate for the special minimum Social Security benefit to be increased so that women with little or no earnings because of caregiving responsibilities can have some protection against poverty (U.S. House of Representatives, 1992b, 1992c).

Caregiving raises ideological, ethical, and programmatic issues for those who work with the aged: How can women not be exploited when there are not enough long term care services? A number of reform strategies have been suggested: a reexamination of eligibility rules for pensions to include caregiving credit; the reeducation of men and women to promote caregiving as a family and community responsibility; the expansion of community-based services; increased caregiver training and education; and support from employers for family-friendly, responsive services and benefits (Allen, 1993; Zarit et al., 1980). Programs to help caregivers may, at first glance, appear gender neutral. Social policies that appear gender neutral in intent are not gender neutral in impact, however (Abramowitz, 1992; England, 1990; Moon, 1990). As England argued (1990), "gender-neutral policies may influence choices already shaped by sex role stereotypes, thus perpetuating gender inequities" (p. 10). We must analyze closely any program that works to keep women as caregivers with little assistance, while offering them classes to better "cope" with their stressors associated with caregiving and inadequate payments for their services.

PRESENT DEBATES ON CAREGIVING

Major debates on caregiving and elder care today center on: (a) strategies to keep costs down; (b) whether or not government interventions lead to families relinquishing their care to formal services; and (c) if families should be paid with governmental funds to serve as caregivers. According to Rivlin and Wiener (1988), the federal government has devised various strategies to keep costs down while encouraging families to do more. One has to do with tightening Medicaid's eligibility criteria. Medicaid pays for the care of the majority of those residing in nursing homes. Added restrictions on Medicaid eligibility requirements result in fewer opportunities for families to get relief with their caregiving, and when caregiving is no longer a viable option. By refusing to increase the payments and length of time for payments for home care reimbursements, families are also told quite clearly that the care of the aged is their responsibility.

The passage of the Omnibus Reconciliation Act (OBRA) of 1983, with the establishment of the Diagnostic Related Groups (DRGs) for Medicare recipients, has also passed care back to families. Such policies have resulted in what professionals refer to as elders being discharged "sicker and quicker." In other words, where once a frail elder would be cared for in the hospital, such care is now being shifted more and more to the family—regardless of their willingness or ability to provide such care. Using a feminist age analysis, we can more easily see that cost containment in health care, welfare reform, and the lack of a national long term care policy are just three ways to tell the family, primarily women: "You do it! Caregiving is your job. However, don't expect to get paid for it or supported in your old age for your years of providing it."

Furthermore, there is the fear of the "woodwork effect." In other words, this is the idea that families will provide less caregiving or informal care as more publicly supported services are available. But such fears have generally been proven unfounded by recent research. Instead, services have been found to support, not supplant, the assistance provided by primary caregivers (Noelker & Bass, 1994; Tennstedt et al., 1993).

The third debate focuses on payment for caregivers (see Capitman & Yee, 1996; Keigher & Linsk, 1996). Hooyman and Gonyea (1995), for example, suggest that, since reforming Social Security to be more responsive to caregivers appears unrealistic, other types of payment for caregivers should be considered. Supporting the financial health of caregivers is a worthwhile goal. Indeed, programs that provide financial support to caregivers are evident in most industrialized nations. Payments are viewed by some to hold some promise for equity for women. The argument appears to be something like this: Since the reality is that women are the primary caregivers and will probably continue to provide this care, then society should at the very least reimburse them, even minimally, for their work. However, since women's work has and continues to be devalued economically, such "payments" can hardly be expected to result in any kind of adequate wage. Capitman and Yee (1996) make a different but related point concerning the availability of home services, noting that home care labor supply shortages are primarily a result of inadequate reimbursement and exploitative labor practices. Paying caregivers an inadequate "wage," then, will not alleviate any kind of caregiver shortage. These authors further agree that family care payments would hardly help women since it is men, not women, who usually have "more access to family caregivers because women outlive men, and spouses are the principal providers of family care to the aged" (p. 154). Payments to caregivers may actually end up being counterproductive if they "reduce the potential for meaningful coalitions and successful political strategies among the disabled" (p. 156). Perhaps more important, and since both women and men provide caregiving, a better tactic may be to guarantee an adequate retirement income package for all.

A solution using ideas from a feminist age analysis begins with the understanding that caregiving must be analyzed within a framework based on women's status in a patriarchal society throughout their lives. It defines the problem not as caregiving itself, but the lack of available and affordable home and community-based and institutional long term care services.

Among the political strategies discussed, I look with some suspicion at payment to caregivers by states based on filial piety laws, although I agree that payments may well provide some tangible relief to those who most need it. Gibson (1996), while noting that such payments are contradictory to feminist aims, also admits that "even its admission into the public agenda would recognize the immense burden of unpaid labor care which falls disproportionately on women" (p. 93). In the end, a focus on whether or not to financially reimburse women for their caregiving functions may be a limited discussion. Such "payment" continues to relegate women to this role, rather than addressing the real issue of caregiving—the inequities surrounding society's gender division of labor, and women's relegation to caring for others across the life span—a function that appears to increase, not decrease, with age.

From an administrative perspective, filial policy laws have rarely been enforced for numerous reasons. First, the definition of "filial piety" is not consistent. Is it emotional care, financial care, or both? Further, any savings from such laws are highly questionable. Nonetheless, the fact that such laws remain "in the books" in more than 40 states (Hagestad, 1987) should be alarming to every woman. A feminist age analysis leads to questions about government's role in defining not only family but the filial responsibilities of adult children. Should adult children be mandated to support their parents financially, emotionally, and socially? A thoughtful response is voiced by Carroll Estes and her colleagues in *The Long-Term Care Crisis: Elders Trapped in the No-Care Zone* (1993). These experts in health care and long term care policy question the present focus on cost containment for neglecting the real issue surrounding caregiving and long term care: that is, development of a sound funding mechanism to meet the needs of frail and needy citizens.

Using ideas from a feminist age analysis, we do not see caring and caregiving as the problems. Neither does a feminist age analysis seek to favor the public or the private sector's role in caregiving. Rather, the problems surrounding caregiving revolve around the following: the assignment of caregiving to women; the rules that have ignored or punished women's contributions to family life; the nation's neglect of family policies; and the lack of community-based and institutional services (Browne, 1994; Hooyman & Gonyea, 1995; Stoller, 1993). Paying women to be caregivers, similar to the Marxist-feminist call for "wages for housework," may actually result in a "step-back" for women's progress by a confusing attempt to value what has always been devalued by society. Instead, a new vision for caregiving demands that we advocate for a comprehensive universal health care plan and a national long term care policy to support all citizens. In avoiding an either/or level of analysis, a feminist age perspective understands that gender justice is not in an adversarial position to caring. With its emphasis on empowerment and responsibility, we also ask why women continue to maintain this role. According to England (1990), caregiving raises contradictions and dilemmas that must be understood in light of women's commitment to this role, the power of social relations, and the continuation of the nations' gender policies that relegate women to nonpaid family labor. Cost containment associated with community care only works if there is an unpaid caregiver willing and able to provide the needed care. Home care only works if one has a home. Neither are without cost and consequence to someone.

A FEMINIST AGE CRITIQUE OF HEALTH CARE AND LONG-TERM CARE POLICIES

Advocates for health care and long term care reform have generally attacked the present system for its lack of accessibility, its high costs, the lack of health research on aging women and minorities, and its inequitable distribution (Estes et al., 1993; Hooyman & Kiyak, 1993; Zones, Estes, & Binney, 1987). Rather than provide a description of illnesses and health issues faced by women, we consider the socioeconomic and cultural factors that surround a specific health issue and examine the extent to which societal expectations of and charges placed on women lead to their health problems.

One major focus in health care today is on the evaluation of payment alternatives for health care for older adults and developing new funding models (Rivlin & Wiener, 1988; Takamura & Seely, 1994). As we discussed in chapter 1, older adults generally rely on a mix of Medicare, Medicaid, private health insurance, and private savings to pay for their health and long term care needs. Medicare, while designed primarily with acute care needs in mind, nonetheless covers 45% of health care spending for the elderly overall. It provides less, however, in the area of covered benefits for long term care services (National Academy on Aging, 1996). Additionally, the anticipated Medicare Health Insurance Trust Fund short-fall, expected in the year 2001, is resulting in numerous proposals before Congress to increase the premiums on middle-class and upper-income older adults. Options presently discussed include raising payroll taxes, changing premiums and copayments, expanding managed care, and re-examining cost sharing to effect the use of certain services (National Academy on Aging, 1996). Medicaid, the state and federal funding medical insurance program for indigent people, accounts for 71% of government spending for nursing home and home care (Rivlin & Wiener, 1988). For many of the reasons previously discussed, older women often turn to Medicaid to pay for their long term care needs. It is imperative that any Medicare or Medicaid proposals that are given serious consideration be evaluated with the profile and needs of older women in mind.

The costs of health and long term care are a national concern. There is some evidence that the Diagnostic Related Groups (DRGs) and other tightened eligibility rules for Medicare recipients have brought down some costs of medical care, but there appear to be increased costs to the family. Feminists understand quite well that cost control and welfare reform policies result in the family taking full responsibility for caring. And, as we have seen, "the family" has become a euphemism for "women." Thus, a feminist age analysis incorporates a number of elements from a feminist life-span perspective on aging in its critique of the present health care and long term care systems that are incorporated in the following discussions. Among these are: (a) women's oppression across the life span, and the added influence of ageism on women's lives; (b) women's diversity; (c) a holistic view that looks for connections among issues and sees the importance of prevention in health care; (d) the need for political strategies for change; (e) the key role of empowerment in women advocating on behalf of their own health; and (f) the critical importance of research that focuses on sex-specific problems with age.

HEALTH CARE AND LONG-TERM CARE POLICIES AND PROBLEMS

Few would argue that women's health care needs have been adequately researched, addressed, or managed, regardless of age. From feminism came the idea that women's health was important in and of itself and that women should be empowered to take control of the knowledge about their well-being and treatments to improve their health. Women seek not only the information that allows them to make informed decisions for their health, but also access to affordable health care when they need it. Whether it is acute or long term care, a feminist age analysis makes issues of quality care, affordability, and accessibility fundamental to any discussion on women's health, especially for previously ignored groups of older women—older women of color, the never-married, divorced, and the oldest-old. In order for health care to be effective, a feminist age analysis recognizes and incorporates the diversities of women in its demands for women-focused research and a responsive and responsible health care system that offers a continuum of care from prevention to end-of-life supports. For example, Black women are more prone to heart disease, and yet the lack of clinical studies on this population has led physicians to recommend interventions whose efficacy may be questionable with this population. And low-income women and women who live alone are disproportionately being stricken with Alzheimer's disease, with the concomitant need for increased long term care services at a time when such services are threatened with serious cutbacks.

In contrast to acute care, long term care was defined previously as those types of care and services provided to frail persons of any age who need sustained care to manage the daily activities that they can no longer provide independently. This inability to maintain some level of independence can make one vulnerable and at risk for poor physical and emotional health, and institutionalization. In the absence of a national long term care policy, a majority of the nation's elderly rely on Medicaid to help pay for long term care services. It is not surprising that few are happy with the program, since it was never intended to become the nation's "de facto" long term care program. With Medicaid, services are often restricted, and many physicians and facilities are hesitant to take Medicaid patients, as the reimbursement is substantially less than what they would receive with a private-pay patient. Medicaid's income eligibility requirements are designed to help the poor, not the middle-class, even though many middle-class Americans turn to Medicaid for help. The topic of long term care is a concern for both men and women, but more so of women, who are its chief consumers and providers. Equal access to affordable health services should be available to all regardless of ethnicity, age, gender, and sexual orientation. As we have seen, however, health care utilization rates among minority elderly women differ from those of their White counterparts. Unexpected health care and long term care costs remain a major source of worry for many Americans.

The relationships between "the family ethic," women's assignment to unpaid caregiving responsibilities, and the absence of a national long term care policy are essential in analyzing present policies. With a feminist age analysis, we understand the connections among the growing needs for long term services, the lack of present services, and the increased call for family caregivers to "pick up the slack" created by the first two factors. Subsequently, the rights of women are neither promoted nor protected when a health care industry shifts this burden of care from the public to private sectors, when the public sector slashes services to aging adults and their families, and when both private and public policies indirectly mandate that women leave work to provide care to family members, and then penalizes their pension benefits for doing so. Long-term care, in contrast to high technological care, is primarily personal care provided in home or custodial settings. It does not have the exorbitant expense tied to sophisticated high-tech care, and yet public policy continues to find ways to not support caregivers (Hooyman & Gonyea, 1995). Thus, we see the total cost of caregiving to women—not only the financial repercussions of lost wages and benefits as a result of being out of the labor force, but the emotional costs of isolation and exhaustion as well.

The years of providing long term caregiving and being under-or unemployed as a result of this caregiving can wreak havoc on anyone's retirement income, as we have discussed at length. But the situation is worse for women and minorities, due to their generally poor wage histories as a result of segregated employment and low wages. Women continue to receive (and accept) the clear message that they should be caregivers. Unfortunately, the message they never receive is that such roles and functions will impact on their financial status; nor do they always understand the relationship of their financial status to receiving accessible and quality health care.

At a recent Women's Health Conference in Honolulu, I observed the following creative and empowering strategies of a group of women who were advocating for the state to pass a social insurance program for long term care. The women, dressed as fortune tellers, provided free "readings" to women. The all-too-true scenario they presented was this:

> You stay at home to take care of your spouse and your children, his parents, and your parents as they become frail. You work out of the home intermittently, or at a job with much less pay than your husband's. Your husband tells you he will take care of you, but as he ages he needs long term care. You have no benefits in your own name and you sadly find out that benefits in someone else's name can be taken away. The expenses of the nursing home where you place your husband after years of providing

caregiving at home leaves you with only a small amount that the government allows you to keep under the spousal impoverishment plan. Ironically, you have spent your life caring for others; now there is no one to care for you. Or perhaps you are divorced, or never married. Your situation is no better. (The Family Hope Coalition, 1994)

From the look on women's faces as they had their "fortune" told, these women's advocates had effectively made their point. The nation's present family policies that relegate women to lower-paying jobs and nonpaid caregiving duties have serious consequences to their health and well-being in old age. And women, especially poor, working-class, and minority older women, must be made aware of these facts.

The financing of long term care is a hotly contested issue. The debate often focuses on where the financing should be placed—in the public or the private sphere. Partly in response to the shortcomes of Medicare and Medicaid, more and more companies are entering this debate by offering private long term care insurance. However, their products are relatively untested, often inaccessible to all elders with certain ailments, and not financially affordable for the majority of those who could use this coverage. Not surprising then, Medicaid has remained as the "de facto" funding base for long term care. And yet, in these fiscally austere times, poverty-targeted programs are most at risk by legislators. This is because poverty-based benefits stratify on the basis of gender and race in addition to class. As Meyer (1994) argues, "The U.S. long term care system stratifies by default to the extent that U.S. social policy fails to take steps to alleviate gender and race inequalities generated by the social and market forces" (p. 12). She found that women and some minorities, more than White men, relied on Medicaid and that such benefits were received not because eligibility was easier for them, but because they were poorer. Consequently, as Butler (1994) warns, "New ageists are referring to women when they talk about denying health care to the elderly" (p. 7).

Even when social policy has attempted to respond to aging women's needs, the lack of understanding of women's lives leaves such policies ineffective. As an example, the 1988 Medicare Catastrophic Health Care Act, repealed the following year, retained a provision that allows the community-based spouse to have a monthly payment of at least 150% of the federal poverty line and one-half of the $12,000 of the couple's income, whichever is the greater amount. In this way, the Spousal Impoverishment Plan, as it is called, attempts to help married women and men avoid the problem of having to spend all of their assets to become eligible for Medicaid in order to pay for long term care. But according to Meyer (1994), spousal impoverishment remains primarily a woman's problem for a number of reasons. Men are three times more likely to leave an impoverished spouse in the community compared to women. Furthermore, the present older cohort, unlike many younger couples, placed marital property in the husband's name only. Thus, all of the couple's properties were deemed the property of the husband, which not only determined Medicaid eligibility, but resulted in all assets being made available to the institutionalized elder. Additionally, lesbian older women have no legal recourse to their spouse's assets and health insurance. Finally, Black and Hispanic older women are widowed earlier than White women, leaving them without spousal support for more years. Hence, there is little evidence that older women, especially minority older women, have had their financial picture improved with the enactment of the Spousal Impoverishment Plan (Meyer, 1994).

As of this writing, the national debate on health care waxes and wanes. In the wake of new and daily assaults on quality health care, a feminist age analysis remains committed to the concept of universal access for all Americans that includes long term care. Given the differences in longevity between men and women, the financial difficulty in attaining long term care, and the nation's reliance on women's unpaid caregiving, health care reform is especially essential for women. Without a provision for long term care funding, Medicaid remains an unworkable primary funding source for long term care. As for quality care, it may be argued that, since the majority of nursing homes are occupied by older women who have their care reimbursed by Medicaid, such policies have hardly been unworkable or discriminatory for them. Such an argument, however, would ignore the fact that those on Medicaid often receive less than adequate care, due to reimbursements that are less than the reimbursement from private paying patients. It also ignores the lack of available caregivers for these women who were probably caregivers themselves, as well as their forced isolation from society as a result of living in a nursing home.

In the absence of a social insurance model for long term care coverage, Meyer (1994) makes a number of suggestions for improving long term care that may offer some limited assistance to aging women. Among these are that Medicaid make its eligibility guidelines more sensitive to the needs of minorities and older women; that income ceilings and personal need allowances be set significantly higher than their present rate; and that reimbursement procedures be prevented from being discriminatory. Other strategies include expanding Medicare coverage to include more long term care services, and to make community care comprehensive enough to reduce caregiving burdens on family members, the majority of whom are women.

While there remains no national policy on long term care, there appears to be some movement toward support of private pay long term care insurance. A recent change from the Health Insurance and Portability Act of 1996 will offer some assistance to those who own such plans. Beginning January 1, 1997, purchasers of such plans may deduct the cost of long term care premiums from their taxes, similar to other medical expenses (Kleyman, 1996). Considering the high costs of long term care insurance, it is safe to say that lower-and most middle-class families and older women will find this an empty gesture.

PRESENT DEBATES IN LONG-TERM CARE

Cornman and Kingson (1996) argue that the current debates about long term care funding have framed their questions too narrowly, limiting the focus to questions on the nation's capabilities to continue to fund its aging programs and policies, and if those programs cannot be funded, how those programs can be reduced. Dialogues such as this one discuss the nation's spending on older adults in the same breath with the federal deficit, the trend toward smaller government, and the desire for cost containment in government services, insinuating a relationship among these issues. Discussions, often lively and intense, can be potentially beneficial as they foster a clearer understanding of the issues. But, according to Cornman and Kingson, what is often heard are the following limited questions: Who should pay for long term care? Who should provide it? And, finally, how can we contain its costs?

Rather than begin the discussion with these and other similar questions, these authors suggest that we begin our inquiry with broader questions for developing aging long term care policy and discussions that incorporate the importance of values in policymaking. Imagine if the goal of a public education system was to contain costs, rather than educate the young in a safe and good-quality environment. Somewhat similarly, any discussion on long term care of the frail should proceed with a dialogue that examines the nation's values that "drive the debate" (Cornman & Kingson, 1996). Data on aging and older adults have been fruitful over the past three decades, and knowledge on the frail aged and caregiving is now voluminous. What we have not done is to articulate the nation's values that ultimately influence and direct public policy. As Cornman and Kingson wisely and prophetically add: "Without an established context our national dialogue will be void of values which respond to such basic issues as the meaning and purposes of life, individual and societal responsibilities, and even the kind of society the people of this country desire for people of all ages" (p. 15).

A feminist age analysis offers some ideas, then, for what a more just and equitable caregiver and long term care policy could look like. It would incorporate women's lifelong disadvantages in its policies, and would in fact seek to correct the most serious examples of such oppressions at every stage of the life cycle (Gibson, 1996). Long-term care would not be built on family assumptions about roles and behaviors. And, regardless of race, ethnicity, class, or sexual orientation, all women would be entitled to quality health care. Justice, as noted by Gibson (1996), is not achieved as long as it is women who bear the brunt of the social, emotional, and financial costs of caregiving and the related lack of long term care services.

Public policy develops from both the economic state of the nation and of the world, and from the nation's values. Without question, each factor influences the other. But, when present long term care issues are framed under the cost-containment umbrella, the results bring an equally limited response. Preventing institutionalization as a goal for long term care may, for example, be incompatible with the family's ability to provide compassionate and adequate care. Instead, values that speak to support of the family cannot favor policies that seek to transfer long term care responsibilities to already overworked families. Rather than limited discussions and debates, the nation's dialogue will benefit from discussions on commonly held values that speak to the public good, the reciprocity and connections between the generations, and the morality of supporting families as the "right thing to do." A preferred feminist debate would ask, instead: What is the right thing to do when people need health care, regardless of age and gender?

A RESEARCH AGENDA FOR AGING WOMEN

The lack of research on women remains especially troublesome. In chapter 1 we discussed the growing awareness that women's health needs have been neither adequately conceptualized nor addressed by practitioners or researchers. Feminists bristle at the idea that the study of aging men's health concerns has provided answers to questions about aging women's health. They decry the fact that women have too often been excluded from observational and clinical studies, even when the issue being studied has great importance to their well-being. Feminists are critical of health research that has too often had a focus on reproductive health issues while rarely studying other areas, such as menopause and women's health after age 60. Feminists and numerous gerontologists advocate for more research findings on women to be translated into healthy practices and accessible health care. Furthermore, as health care has rarely empowered them, women seek a more active role as participants in promoting and maintaining their own health (Sharp, 1995; Webb, 1986).

A feminist age analysis advocates for the inclusion of women in research studies, especially aging women, as they are and will remain the majority of the aging population. Favored are research methods that acknowledge the existence of power inequities, gender and other forms of domination, and those that speak from women's voices. From a feminist age analysis, women are not viewed from a disease perspective. In other words, while acknowledging that differences between men and women exist, women are not pathologized for these differences. Ideas from a feminist age analysis insist that interventions on women's health be based on their well-being, not profits, and that women have a say in their own health care.

One area that remains controversial for menopausal and postmenopausal women is estrogen replacement therapy (ERT). Women have always experienced menopause, but very little is known about its biological, psychological, behavioral, or social aspects. As was discussed in chapter 1, hormone therapy is now being prescribed for menopause, for its possible positive long term effects in preventing heart disease, osteoporosis, and other ailments. And yet the absence of randomized clinical studies on the efficacy of ERT should be alarming to the 40% of women in the ages between 45 and 60 who have taken it. As women don't normally die of menopause, a feminist age analysis urges women to take caution and do their own research prior to taking a medication that may increase the risks for endometrial and breast cancers. Although some studies have concluded those taking ERT lowers cholesterol levels and may produce some protection against heart disease, others warn that ERT may increase the risks for breast cancer by as much as 70% for women between 60–64 years (Colditz et al., 1995).

Feminist researchers have taken a critical look at such recent research. For example, in evaluating studies that have focused on the efficacy of ERT, participants often appear to be a healthier sample at midlife (i.e., White, middle-class, educated, of slim build, with already lower risks for heart disease) than the average woman. This bias in sample selection may result in data that are skewed toward showing positive benefits of ERT.

A number of other feminist authors have begun to question women's treatment by the health care industry. Two recent books focus on menopause and the broader topic of women and health care. In Sandra Coney's new book, *The Menopause Industry: How the Medical Establishment Exploits Women* (1994), the author warns that it is still too early to know if ERT is beneficial to women or not. *Unequal Treatment: What You*

Don't Know About How Women Are Mistreated by the Medical Community by Eileen Nechas and Denise Foley (1994) is another book that informs its readers about how women have been ignored and poorly treated by research and by nonresearched treatments and procedures.

The National Institute of Health's Women Health Initiative hopes to correct many of these problems. Begun in 1991, it is presently studying 140,000 middle-aged and older women over a 10-year period in a controlled study that will examine the effects of dietary and estrogen therapy and treatment on menopause and specific disease processes. Women should follow data from these and other studies closely. In the meantime, books like authors Lissa DeAngelis and Moly Siple's *Recipes for Change: Gourmet Wholefood Cooking for Health and Vitality at Menopause* (1996) provide useful information on natural methods for health promotion. Women can also take heed from what Dr. Christianne Northrup, author of *Women's Bodies, Women's Wisdom: Creating Physical and Emotional Health and Healing* (1995) has to say about women growing older:

> In our ageist culture, many women, instead of believing in their capacity to remain strong, attractive, and vital throughout their lives, instead come to expect their bodies and minds to deteriorate with age. Thus, we as society collectively create a pattern of thoughts, behaviors, and fears that makes it much easier to manifest the worst physical reality. We can't reverse our collective cultural negativity about menopause and aging overnight. What we can do is consider ourselves pioneers in a new frontier—one in which menopause and aging will be redefined. (p. 435)

Thus, we critique the present health care system and advocate for a research agenda that places aging women's needs on the national agenda and examines women's needs in their own right. Gender-specific concerns such as menopause, geriatric malignancies, osteoporosis, breast cancer, incontinence, and neurological degenerative diseases should be points of study. Moreover, education is viewed as having an empowering function for women in taking charge of their own health from birth to death. Also emphasized is the need for professionals to be trained in working with aging women from a normative and a gender-specific perspective. The political and social climate affects older women's health. Therefore, the need for vigilant attention to these forces on local, state, and national levels is essential to protect women's health.

TOWARD A NEW EPISTEMOLOGY ON HEALTH AND WOMEN

Women's unique health histories and status present challenges to adequate health care delivery. And yet any feminist age analysis is careful to document the strengths women bring to aging, and seeks to identify, acknowledge, and replicate models of empowering approaches women have taken on behalf of their own health. Borrowing ideas from Black feminist thought, we acknowledge the need for a fundamental paradigmatic shift in an epistemology of aging women and health. Ideas from a feminist age analysis see the effects of interlocking systems of oppression faced by women, and especially older women of color, lesbian women, those in poverty, and the never-married, to their financial, health, caregiving, and social lives. Understanding the political and social climate with respect to health care and women's health is critically important. As Angela Davis (1990) states in speaking about the lives of Black women: "We have become cognizant of the urgency of contextualizing Black women's health in relation to the prevailing political conditions. While our health is undeniably assaulted by natural forces frequently beyond our control, all too often the enemies of our physical and emotional well-being are social and political" (p. 55).

Hence, we see the need for a variety of different political and empowering strategies to improve women's health. One example of a woman's self-help project is the Atlanta based National Black Women's Health Project that has, since 1981, brought women together to learn and teach others about health issues for themselves and their families. It utilizes a variety of techniques such as self-help groups and community organizing for group empowerment. Paula Doress-Worters and Diana Laskin Siegel's book, *The New Ourselves Growing Older: Women Aging with Knowledge and Power* (1993), written in collaboration with the Boston Women's Health Book Collective, is another example of an empowering self-help woman's group that has educated women about their health. Other women's groups, like the Red Hot Mamas, have adopted these and other models. What women have learned is that doctors need to be challenged about their assumptions about menopause and other aging-related health concerns, and that women must pay increased attention to their well-being. In the process of empowerment, women become more knowledgeable consumers, and demand an end to inequalities in research, policy, and practice. Feminist practice in health care can include many other strategies. Among those offered by Sharp (1995) are for medical schools to strengthen their curricula in geriatrics, with a focus on older women; and for physicians and other health care professionals to continually assess themselves for ageist thinking and discriminatory behaviors. Others note the importance of education, not only for health care providers about the needs of older women, but education for older women themselves. Through empowered actions, women can better learn to negotiate the health care system on their own behalf (Webb, 1986). The message for health care workers, then, is to share their knowledge with older women and to respect them. Webb (1986) also advocates for the development of alternative structures to provide health care, such as collectives, in addition to continued efforts toward working within existing structures for change.

Age adds a new dimension to women's lives, and further provides an opportunity to expose the ways in which women, as they experience various life transitions, may end up unknowingly exploiting other women. For example, in an article in a Sunday newspaper (Creamer, 1995), an article listed the top 20 union executives in Honolulu and their salaries. None were women. Underneath this article was another one, with the headline "Poverty hits aged women worst." In another section of the paper on the same day, an article described how insurance companies are encouraging hospitals to release women who have just given birth after 24 hours as a cost saving. The article described one woman who was happy to go home early. Who saw the irony in the beginning of the article: "With her mother-in-law waiting at home to help with the new baby, Coriann M. could hardly wait to get back there after giving birth July 11"? The older woman is no doubt providing free labor. One only hopes that she is doing so willingly, that this is an isolated incident that does not jeopardize her employment if she works, and that she can financially afford to do so. If not, there is a good chance that she will end up without sufficient retirement income and poor.

With a feminist age analysis, we see the connections between these issues and women's chances for a just old age. Without a responsive and universal health care policy, women will continue to be excluded from health care coverage due to life patterns, responsibilities, and policies that ignore both of these areas.

Far from being secondary to the health care system, social welfare has a critical role in documenting the inadequacies of the health care system and how social policies have kept women poor. It will be the responsibility of social welfare to design, advocate, and implement more inclusive, affordable, and effective health and long term care models that incorporate women's specific financial and health concerns while documenting their preferred models of support. For example, a more enlightened and critical perspective would underscore the potential ramifications of filial piety laws on women's well-being and health. A gender-fair social welfare system should not reproduce the values of a racist and sexist state that prevent women, especially poor and minority women, from receiving the health care they deserve.

Fortunately, all is not a disaster where it concerns women's health. There is actually some good news with regards to health care policy and gender research. Women are finally being included in clinical studies, although most results will not be known until well into the 21st century. There is also increased focus by feminists on the procedures and methodologies used by researchers to evaluate women's health. For aging women's health to reach its potential, the nations' health and long term care research agenda must continue to promote the interests of all women via sound research methodologies and practices. New empowering strategies that build on women's strengths and knowledge are advocated for by women. Feminist age analyses have helped to underscore the relationships among these issues for women—caregiving, work, health status, and poverty. A feminist age analysis questions the axioms that women's bodies are the same as men's, and that the lack of research on women is therefore inconsequential; that menopause is a disease or a deficiency; that there is no relationship or a minimal relationship between income and health care, and that health care can save money off the backs of women's labor from caregiving. Further acknowledged are the special problems of older women, especially older working-class women and women of color, in accessing affordable and quality health and long term care services.

In summary, we see that the goal of a feminist age analysis on older women's health is to understand and improve their health via the study of sex-specific diseases and ailments, as well a those diseases that affect both men and women, but women differently. The problem is not that women are different from men, but that women have both similar and dissimilar health needs and patterns compared to men that are important to study in their own right. The solutions lie with a health care system that is both adequately and fairly funded, universal in its accessibility, and offering high-quality care. Both women and men will benefit from such a system. Additionally, women need more funded research on women's health issues; new and revised health care policies that incorporate new research data on women's health into policies and practices; an awareness of the differences and commonalities that exist among women; a system that refuses to be built on assumptions about family and women's roles, and, finally, knowledgeable health personnel who refuse to take ageist attitudes toward aging women.

A FEMINIST AGE CRITIQUE OF OLDER WOMEN'S SOCIAL REALITIES

Women's gender roles throughout their life span, discussed in earlier chapters, are primarily associated with family roles. Social norms and expectations and social policies, based on assumptions about such roles, often leave women disadvantaged in later life. Feminist theory has exposed women's prescribed gender roles as social constructions, as opposed to the biological and functional arguments that emphasize the naturalness and functionality of such roles for society's well-being (Franks & Rothblum, 1983; Glenn, 1987). In contrast, feminist theory questions the paradigm that makes "woman" only synonymous with "mother," "wife," and "caregiver." Aging theory has also begun to question such paradigms. Data from Celia Hurwich's study of older women, for example, suggests that these women did not adopt or define themselves by traditional sex-role stereotypes and prescriptions. She found that each of her subjects led an extraordinary, productive, creative, and meaningful life.

> Perhaps the traits these women share of trust, risk-taking, adaptability, nonconformity, and the ability to live in the present were important in fulfilling developmental stages of life. [It is, she adds] . . . our attitude and relationship to our life's experiences [that] colors our approach to aging—whether we experience growth, change and aliveness, or boredom, retreat, and statis. (1982, p. 177)

In contrast to conservative doctrines that often define women by their traditional sex-role functions, we use the following elements from a feminist life-span perspective on aging to critique assumptions about older women: (a) women's oppression across the life span and the added influence of ageism; (b) women's diversity; (c) the need for empowering strategies; and (d) the opportunity that solidarity can offer women-to-women relationships. These themes are integrated in the following sections.

To begin with, a feminist age analysis underscores the fact that not all aging women have lived oppressed lives as a result of patriarchal society. Data, however, do not support the contention that the majority of older women flourish in that environment. With a feminist age analysis, we also understand that not all older women are or were married, and recognize that society differentially rewards women based on race, class, and other social dimensions. Thus, we question policies that make women deserving of benefits and services pending their acceptance of the family ethic, those dominant American social norms based on capitalism, patriarchy, and White supremacy that articulate women's work and family roles (Abramowitz, 1992). We argue that women are deserving of equality and services not because they are good (i.e., nurturing) but because they have earned these rights as citizens. Hence, any reality that denies women their rights and insists on their subordination should be sharply rebuked and discarded.

WOMEN'S ROLES AND WORTH IN OLD AGE

Patriarchal society dictates that the signal important role for young adult and middle-aged women is that of wife and mother. It is to them that society looks for the maintenance of the physical, emotional, and social health of the family. Some women have been responsible for the financial health of their families as well. The feminist critique of the patriarchal family grows out of the conviction that it is the family that is the fundamental vehicle for creating and maintaining women's oppression (Glenn, 1987). A feminist age analysis, however, avoids the simplistic dualisms that often result in women having mixed emotions and hearing contradictory messages about the family. In truth, the family is neither all bad nor all good. Families can and do bring great joy and satisfaction, and for some women, family life can also bring financial rewards. However, the family also places unfair burdens and financial risks on other women, especially with age. Social welfare rarely attempts to change the basic paradigm about women's roles in the family and more often than not ends up choosing compensatory strategies, as opposed to those that may alleviate the roots of injustice.

As we have seen, caregiving is a role that places numerous burdens on and has serious consequences for women. Feminists have argued for women to have the choice of being mothers—but rarely do women have the choice over whether to be a caregiver. The frail aged, the majority of whom are women, are themselves often providing care to an elderly husband. At present, some services provide superficial support to women when they are providing care, but even this support often disappears when the caregiver's "charge" has died. Who provides for the aging woman when she is alone, when her worth is so dependent on her giving care to someone else?

A number of feminists have begun to question another role for which older women are well-known—that of grandmother. As Russell notes (1987), what typically comes to mind when we think of the aging woman is a fulfilled older woman, surrounded by her loving family. What is not remarked upon is the fact that her fulfillment has been achieved through perpetual work for others. Barbara Macdonald, writing about women, aging, and ageism in *Look Me in the Eye* (Macdonald & Rich, 1983) articulated her views about the role of grandmother in this way: "Each time we see such a woman as "grandmother," we dismiss the courage of her independence, we invalidate her freedom. We tell her, in the face of her own choices, that her real place is in the home" (p. 105). Older women's work in the home, or in the home of their children taking care of their grandchildren or as babysitters to others' children, is rarely acknowledged or respected. Macdonald adds:

> But today, the role required of her in familia is "grandmother." It does not matter to the master how much she may have longed for the day when she would be freed from children's demands; freed to listen not to their voices; but to her own. If she is indifferent to her grandchildren or impatient with them—if she is convinced that her own last years are just as important as their early ones—then her usefulness to the master threatens her very survival. She can be called senile, and tamed with drugs. To see an old woman as "grandmother" is to join the master in defining her as a woman whose right to exist depends on her loving and serving us. (pp. 105–106)

As we have stated earlier, caring for others, whether it is a lover, a husband, a child, or a grandchild, can bring great joy. Aging women contribute a great deal to the family through their prescribed gender roles. However, a feminist age analysis does not define or view older women by these roles. Instead, if we listen to what older women have to say about being a mother, grandmother, or caregiver, we understand more clearly that this is not the only way they wish to define themselves. There is more to experience with aging than providing for others.

A NEW VIEW OF AGING WOMEN

A preferred strategy is to look to older women and how they define themselves. For those who are grandmothers and caregivers, we see clearly that the same system that can reward middle-class wives who stay at home does not reward women for their work as caregiver and grandmother, regardless of how important or functional it is for society. We refuse to see older women as ineffectual or to define them by these gender-role expectations. Instead, we see older women as examples of survivors who have contributed much to society and who have developed numerous paths of resistance to a society that is generally not supportive of them. We look to a new conceptualization of women, power, and empowerment. In actuality, life-affirming empowerment strategies are played out every day by women in every community and on many levels, including that of personal biography and awareness and struggle. As noted by Ackelsberg and Diamond (1987):

> Women, especially poor women and women of color, cross those supposed boundaries (between the public and private spheres) continually in the process of carrying out their domestic chores. They are the ones who

negotiate with landlords, markets, and agents of the state such as health care providers and welfare officers. (p. 523)

Similarly, we see older women's paths of resistance in their work in churches, in their communities, and as consumers. Furthermore, women are learning the value in sharing their paths of resistance to oppression with others. Documenting such voices not only helps to legitimize them, but counters the negative beliefs and obviates the sharing of incorrect messages about aging women. Younger women in turn can find their own paths of resistance by learning about other women's strategies against oppression and by having the courage to develop their own.

Correcting images about aging women is essential, as popular perceptions shape social policy and subsequently social welfare. In *Two Old Women* (1993) Velma Wallis has written a strong example of aging women's strength and courage in the face of adversity. Wallis tells the tale of two elderly Athabaskan women who are abandoned in the wilds due to cultural tradition and in response to their tribe's pending starvation. The old women are at first too stunned to function. They end up surviving and becoming stronger in the process. It is a wonderful story of empowerment and the strengths and potentials of age. Janet Roebuck (1983) offers another way of viewing older women—as revolutionary. Roebuck illustrates how older women have already demonstrated their abilities to adjust and grow with time—today's aging woman could have been born in a log cabin, she has experienced two world wars, and today uses her voice to dictate to her computer. Roebuck suggests that the study of older women in Western society can help us to "clarify our visions of the past and future and provide us with appropriate models for survival in a less than ideal world" (p. 249).

We have previously discussed the negative ways in which older women are portrayed in both literature and in the media (see AARP, 1996b; Bailey et al., 1993; Vasil & Wass, 1993). The picture of strong older women, however, flies firmly in the face of a conventional wisdom that emphasizes aging women's weakness and ineffectiveness. There is increasing evidence that older women have numerous strengths, but this does not fit the stereotypes about aging women, and so they are ignored or explained in bizarre fashions. For example, older men commit suicide at a rate three times that of older women. Canetto's (1991) review of gender variations in suicide among the aged found that male researchers, instead of hypothesizing that women may adjust better to aging than men, have explained this phenomenon as pathology—aging women cling to life when they should not! Instead, we acknowledge women's documented greater longevity, their stronger coping skills, and their expanded network of supports as strengths worthy of celebration.

Another role for women is that of the beauty or decorative art. Rather than accept women's worth as tied to her physical appearance, ideas from a feminist life-span perspective on aging urge women to self-define themselves in their own image, to put an end to self-loathing, and to find new ways of looking at connections to others. We stop blaming women for growing old, and instead celebrate the process. In truth, women have always engaged in numerous survival strategies that they have developed. Some choices women make are rational, given the reality of their situation. To understand this, we take a broader look at women's lives and their economic, health, and caregiving statuses. For example, keeping a "youthful" appearance, rather than viewed as a fight against time, is often a realistic response to help one retain necessary employment in an ageist society that makes older women expendable. In contrast to a feminist life-span perspective on aging, most of the "How-to books" recommend a more individualistic approach to aging, rather than a structural one. While an individualistic approach encourages older women to become adaptable and flexible in their attitudes, learn how to make necessary changes, wear the "right clothes," and be alert to new work opportunities and career training programs in order to find a good job in mid-or later life, a feminist life-span perspective on aging is aware that such strategies will rarely work if the older woman is not granted a job interview. Advocated for, instead, is an end to age and gender discrimination as a more productive strategy.

According to Reinharz (1986), perspectives in feminism and gerontology provide a much-needed antidote to the belittling of women's appearance and communication patterns. Communication-building, life review, and cultural education are all consciousness-raising activities for developing self-definition and authenticity in later life. The goal is often that of building connections to other living things and the real-life issues people face. This perspective is evident in much of Florida Scott Maxwell's writings. In *The Measure of My Days* (1968), the author, in her 80s at the time, said it best as she spoke about the need for connection and exclaimed the following:

> So I still care! At my age I care to my roots about the quality of women, and I care because I know how important her quality is. The hurt that women have borne for so long may have immeasurable meaning. We women are the meeting place of the highest and the lowest, and of minutia and riches; it is for us to see, and understand, and have pride in representing ourselves truly. Perhaps we must say to man "You create us when you love us, but you destroy us both when you stress our inferiority. The time may have come for us to forge our own identity, dangerous as that will be." (p. 104)

In seeking connections between women, we are not blind to the betrayals among women—between White and minority women, between younger and older women, between heterosexuals and gays. By exposing it and learning its roots, women can realize they are not each other's enemies. True, there is little solidarity between younger and older women, and between women of different races and cultures, and it won't develop if this reality is denied. The process of solidarity can begin this process when older women stop being ignored, patronized, or romanticized, either as grandmother, wise sage, or old crone. Age must be confronted, but respectfully, realistically, and with both anticipation and sadness.

Here again women need to listen to the voices of older women that offer a different and compelling view of aging than the one presented in the popular media. In Hurwich's study (1982), one of the women had this to say: "There are compensations at all ages. I think my compensation is being old enough to say whatever I please, being old enough to do whatever I please" (p. 172). Macdonald (Macdonald & Rich, 1983) is another author who offers an expanded perspective on observations of one's aging that is neither all positive nor negative:

> I like growing old. I say it to myself with surprise. . . . There are days of excitement when I feel almost a kind of high with the changes taking place in my body, although I know the inevitable course my body is taking will lead to debilitation and death. I say to myself frequently in wonder "This is my body doing this I cannot stop it I don't even know what it is doing. I wouldn't know how to direct it. My own body is going through a process that only my body knows about. I never grew old before, I never died" . . . And then, I realize, lesbian or straight, I belong to all the women who carried my cells for generations and my body remembers how for each generation this matter is ending is done. (p. 19)

A feminist age critique of women's social roles views women's life situations with age as both reflective of oppressions, strengths, and intensities. Many women fear growing older. The problem is not that men and women's appearances change with age. Rather, it is society's denigration of the aging process that has resulted in aging being seen in such a negative light. This is not to say that a feminist age analysis adopts a romantic view of age. Problems and challenges very much exist, and social policies rarely prevent or correct them. Nonetheless, a feminist age analysis refuses to advocate for a "forever young" philosophy. Age has its own experiences and opportunities, and to disavow them denies growth and possibility.

We also acknowledge that many of women's roles across the life span lie in the provision of caring—regardless of whether such care is paid, not paid, low-paid, or voluntary. A feminist age analysis questions what are considered universal truths about women's places in society. The relationships between the lack of community and institutional services to increased demands on women to provide more caring are laid bare. While acknowledging the pleasures and contributions that can exist in the provision of such care, society's present long term care system is "parasitic" on the backs of older women to provide it (Gibson & Allen, 1993). Accordingly, we advocate for a strong government presence in long term care only when its principles are feminist in nature, and when it is built on women's voices.

CONCLUSIONS

A feminist life-span perspective on age provides a number of factors to scrutinize when examining women and aging—a feminist age analysis. Some of its key elements include recognition of oppression across the life span of older women, the negative impact of ageism on older women's lives, and the influences of social, cultural, and political forces on women's lives. It also recognizes women's lifetime of inequities and the relationships between women's roles, sexism, racism, homophobia, and classism to their poverty. It realizes, as Glenn has argued, that the debate over women's place in the family is really about women's place in society (Glenn, 1987), and what she is worth. Focusing on the relationships and the interdependence between the family and women's roles, feminist age analysis provides a foundation for understanding women's impending poverty in later life.

In taking more of an ecological view, we see clearly the relationships that exist among economic statuses, caregiving responsibilities, and health in the later years. Likewise, we recognize the serious impact that a lifetime of segregated employment, absence of actual and enforced affirmative action, and gender-role discrimination have on a woman's retirement income, and seek to advocate for changes in social welfare that have encoded gender-role prescriptions into policies that ultimately hurt women. Such a perspective uncovers the dynamics of power and control in the formulation of social policies, and their consequences for aging women. It makes it clear that positive change must be accomplished on the policy level, and that such change will not come easily and without advocacy. Rather than seeing older women as victims or burdens, we gain a new perspective from older women and a new respect for them as contributors and empowered survivors.

Thus, we rethink how gender and age are viewed and how social welfare both contributes to and compensates for women's oppression. We ask: If aging women planned the social welfare agenda, what would be its features? As we begin to develop some ideas toward an epistemology of women and age, some of this thinking starts with the work of various other feminists and critical gerontologists. Recognized first would be the fact that older women do not usually become poor with age, but have had a lifetime of multiple and interlocking layers of disadvantages that need correction. Hence, the well-being of all women would be a focus of such a new epistemology. Also acknowledged would be the ways in which ageism hits men and women in negative ways, but also the ways in which it affects older women more harshly and earlier than men. Third, increased research on women's experiences with age and sex-specific diseases and ailments would be strongly advocated for. Fourth, older women's strengths, documented by stronger social supports, greater longevity, and better coping skills compared to men, would encourage a more positive view of women's social roles in later life. The potential of empowerment and solidarity would be viewed as two strategies to foster personal and political change on behalf of aging women. Fifth, more clearly understood would be how the ideology of the family ethic has played out in social welfare policies and practices to the detriment of aging women's physical and economic well-being. Lastly, the nation's social welfare policymakers would be challenged to develop policies to ensure a decent life for older women.

Advocacy on behalf of the aged helps to refine and test a rethinking of feminist theory by showing ways in which it has been conceptualized without regards for the aged and the aging. In turn, advocacy with and on behalf of aging women can challenge gerontological theory to refocus its direction on the majority of the aging, older women. In the final analysis, feminist frameworks such as this one assist us to see older women's lives from a lifetime of experiences, opportunities, and oppressions. Women's problems are a result of gender inequality across the life span, and not of their sex difference from men. We understand the following. As long as women are relegated to the home and nonpaid caregiving of the young, the ill, and the aged, they will be exploited. The continuation of basing women's pensions on men's wages and male work patterns will only result in their continued poverty. When aging women's health needs are ignored, nonresearched, or pathologized because they are different from men's, they will receive inadequate health care. When women are only valued for their youth-defined beauty and reproductive functions, older women will not be respected. And, when gender is segregated from age, race, and sexual orientation, the needs of all women will be marginalized and neglected.

Empowerment and Older Women

Let younger people anxiously inquire, let researchers tie themselves in knots with definitions that refuse to stick, the middle-
aged woman is about her own business, which is none of theirs.

—Germaine Greer

One of the most important foci of social welfare is the empowerment
of oppressed people to participate in the decisions that impact on
their lives (Sheafor, Horejsi, & Horejsi, 1988; Solomon, 1976).
Empowerment has been defined as a process (Gutierrez, 1990); an intervention (Parsons & Cox, 1989; Solomon, 1976); and a skill (Mandell &
Schram, 1985) benefitting such diverse populations as those with AIDS
(Haney, 1988), nursing home residents (McDermott, 1989), and the seriously ill adolescent (Price, 1988). Empowerment has also been viewed
as an especially appealing strategy for women. It has been described as
a strategy to assist re-entry women (Towns & Gentzler, 1985), abused
women (S. Hartman, 1983), divorcing women (Ricci, 1985), and women
of color (Gutierrez, 1990). The definition of "empowerment," however,
remains ambiguous and vague (Hegar & Hunzeker, 1988). What has been
neglected is a critical analysis of empowerment's basic premises and
underlying meanings, and how the conceptualization of empowerment
shapes interventions.

Also neglected is the examination of the concept and practice of empowerment with older women. As noted in chapter 1, they are significant
consumers of social welfare services as a result of the number of problems
faced with advanced age—multiple chronic health problems, low incomes,
barriers to health and human services, and assignment to caregiving duties
(Minkler & Stone, 1985; Stone et al., 1986; Verbrugge, 1989). This chapter
will discuss and contrast varying definitions of empowerment; describe
what is problematic in the definitions for empowerment practice with

and on behalf of older women; and, finally, offer thoughts toward a reconceptualization of empowerment to better meet their needs.

POWER AND EMPOWERMENT DEFINITIONS

Empowerment is derived from the traditional definition of "power"—"the ability to do or act; capability of doing or accomplishing something; political or national strength; the possession of control or command over others; and legal or official authority" (*Random House College Dictionary*, 1988, p. 1039). "Power" is often used synonymously with force, strength, authority, jurisdiction, control, and command. Van Den Bergh and Cooper (1986) note that in most traditional models, power is seen as a finite commodity to be controlled, particularly in determining the distribution of rights, resources, and opportunities. Similar to its root, empowerment is defined as "to give power or authority" (*Random House College Dictionary*, 1988, p. 434), lending itself to a view that it is synonymous with the possession of control, authority, or influence over others, as well as the help provided to assist one to gain control over one's life. In contemporary society, empowerment is a popular term, with its emphasis on individual self-assertion, upward mobility and personal advancement, or the psychological experience of being powerful (Bookman & Morgen, 1988). The basic underlying principle here is that empowerment is often conceptualized as an individual experience, primarily promoting individual, not the collective good, or increased political power for individual gain.

Empowerment has been characterized similarly and differently by social work and feminist literature. Social work readings have basically defined empowerment in three ways: as an intervention and product, a skill, and a process. Solomon (1976) popularized the term of empowerment in the 1970s and defined it as an intervention and strategy. Her definition of empowerment, supported by Hegar and Hunzeker (1988) and McDermott (1989), describe both traditional and creative social work interventions and strategies that are especially effective with oppressed populations. Others have defined empowerment differently, viewing it as one of the major skills and responsibilities of those working in social welfare today (Mandell & Schram, 1985).

Others characterize empowerment more as a process than a product—a process in which people are assisted to help themselves (Gutierrez, 1990). Pinderhughes' definition of empowerment (1983) is the individual feeling of increased power and the capacity to influence the forces which affect one's life space with less of a focus on changes in structural arrangements

(1983). Gutierrez' work in empowerment with women of color also views empowerment as a process but with a somewhat different focus. Her definition is one by which individual empowerment contributes to group empowerment, and in which increases in group power enhance the functioning of individual members (1990). Still others have examined the concept of empowerment and advocacy. S. Chandler (1990), for example, supports the growing role of mediation in social work, and suggests that empowerment may be replacing advocacy because of the adversarial nature of advocacy which is not congruent with the mediation process.

Feminist theory has also defined empowerment in diverse ways (P. H. Collins, 1991; Humm, 1992). Common themes can be drawn from the literature, however. Bookman and Morgen (1988), writing in *Women and the Politics of Empowerment*, use the term "empowerment" to describe "a spectrum of political activity ranging from accounts of individual resistance to mass political mobilizations that challenge the basic power relations in society" (p. 4). Their definition examines empowerment as a process aimed at the macro level for "consolidating, maintaining, or changing the nature and distribution of power in a particular cultural context" (p. 4). Achieving good is aimed more at the collective than the individual.

In *Money, Sex, and Power: Toward a Feminist Historical Materialism* (1985), Nancy Hartsock analyzed leading feminist theorists for their views of power and empowerment. One such theorist, Dorothy Emmet, defined power as a creative energy in contrast to the traditional definition of domination, coercion, or personal advancement. Taking a broader view than Bookman and Morgen (1988), Emmet saw power as being operationalized in many arenas other than the political, including the arts, ideas, and relationships. Hannah Arendt, another political feminist theorist, agreed with Emmet that power is not coercion and personal upward mobility; instead, it is the exercise of capacity and potential, and could be explained in its relations between people. Power, and therefore empowerment, springs up, according to Arendt, whenever people come together and act, and its legitimacy comes from the act of creating community (Arendt, 1958).

Patricia Hill Collins (1991), in writing about Black feminist thought, suggests that empowerment begins with self-definition and notes the relationships among thought, action, and empowerment. Audre Lorde (1984), a feminist author/poet, also critically examines issues surrounding the concept of power and empowerment. Empowerment, according to Lorde, begins with the recognition of acceptance of difference in our society. Her challenge to society is to deal with the differences imposed by race, sex, age, sexuality, and class head-on, as opposed to ignoring such differences and homogenizing all women. Lorde echoes Emmet in defining power as a creative energy, force, and potential. Empowerment can thus shift away from divide and conquer to define and empower (Lorde, 1984) and from overpower to empower (Van Den Bergh & Cooper, 1986). It is also viewed as a process in which to "lift" other oppressed people, not only women (A. Davis, 1990).

Power and empowerment, then, are reconceptualized by feminists as processes more than things, with a focus more on power as energy, potential, self-definition, and competence rather than domination, coercion, and competition. Hartsock (1985) sees the common thread in their understanding that power is a process "rooted . . . not simply in womens' experience but by the systematic pulling together and working out of the liberatory possibilities present in that experience" (p. 259). Thus, the aim of having power over another is to liberate the other, rather than to dominate and kill.

Postmodern feminists also see that liberation can empower, especially when the experiences of those who have been marginalized are valued and affirmed and they have the opportunity to tell their own stories (A. Hartman, 1992). A feminist conceptualization of empowerment can be thus summarized as the process of liberation in self and others, as a life force, a potential, a capacity, growth and energy, and where one works toward community and connection responsibly, as opposed to working primarily toward one's individual good.

To summarize, the social welfare literature has diverse ways of describing empowerment. It has been defined as a process, an activity, and a skill effecting change in various populations. Its purposes are equally far-ranging, from the capacity to influence the forces which affect one's life space for one's own benefit, to a view of empowerment as a political process benefitting many. A more traditional conceptualization defines empowerment as a conflict model, with a goal of both increased personal control and political power for individual gain. Such definitions often have an orientation toward competition and domination. In contrast, a feminist definition views empowerment more as a capacity and energy found in connections, and a potential working toward the collective and community good. Social welfare appears to draw its definitions from both traditional and feminist definitions. I suggest in this chapter that elements of various definitions are indeed necessary to be truly inclusive of the needs of older women.

CRITIQUE OF PRESENT CONCEPTUALIZATIONS

Before I offer thoughts toward a reconceptualization of empowerment for older women, it is necessary to examine what may be problematic in some of the definitions discussed. A traditional definition of empowerment focuses on domination and control, individual gain, and upward mobility. For many reasons, more structural than intrapsychic, these characteristics or traits are rarely experienced by older women. Such definitions are constrained for them by the ways in which their gender, race, class and historical time limit their access to economic resources and political clout. This conceptualization, clearly out of reach for many older women, makes it difficult to see their strengths and needs from anything but a victim perspective. Subsequently, it lends itself to a "blaming the victim" mentality, ignoring older women's personal biographies and the influences of societal messages and structural forces that relegated women to the home or to menial and poorly paid employment.

Unknowingly, the strengths of older women are neglected if a conceptualization of power and empowerment is one of domination and control, as opposed to capacity and relatedness. In reality, these concepts are not exclusive of one another. Moreover, stressing independence and individual good, as opposed to the more feminist ideals of interdependence and societal good can result in interventions that miss the mark. For example, many social welfare policies and programs have overlooked the interdependence—the reciprocity of giving—of the aged, and have ignored the qualities of relatedness and connection (Rodeheaver, 1987).

In contrast to a traditional conceptualization, feminist conceptualizations of empowerment often begin with social relatedness, energy, capacity, and an emphasis on community good. Empowerment has been defined in four of the major paradigms underlying current feminist praxis: feminist-liberal, multicultural feminism/diversity, radical/socialist, and postmodernism. As we discussed in chapters 2 and 5, the feminist-liberal view is actually two views. The first negates difference between men and women while the latter, referred to as cultural or difference feminism, or essentialism, values difference between men and women (MacKinnon, 1989). The first view, the "women are the same as men" argument, has been criticized for not acknowledging the many differences that exist between men and women, especially as they age. Furthermore, the claim that women are the same as men too often makes maleness and masculinity both the reference point and the desired state of being. Power then becomes domination. In contrast, essentialism describes women as having core qualities that are nurturant, peaceful, cooperative, and have a moral political consciousness (Chodorow, 1978; Gilligan, 1982).

Discussed in earlier chapters were some of the problems with cultural feminism, or essentialism. Some of these are worth reiterating, as they impact on aging women's potential for empowering thought and action. K. H. Gould (1989), for example, eloquently argues that those who label certain qualities or traits as feminine may be "bottling old wine into new bottles." In other words, attributing certain core qualities of nurturance and caring to women by nature of their sex does not allow for an analysis of how women's presumedly distinctive consciousness can be conditioned by history, culture, race, or class (K. H. Gould, 1989). The result is a false homogenization of older women that ignores the often tragic life situations of older women of color (Dressel, 1988). Another problem lies in attributing certain natural qualities of nurturing only to women, with the end result of a societal view of women as natural and (unpaid) caregivers. By emphasizing this so-called "natural" role of women to be caregivers of young, infirm, and old people, present policies that do not give economic credit to such responsibilities are promulgated and endorsed, with scant attention given to the serious health and economic ramifications of caregiving. Still another problem with essentialism for older women is in its almost exclusive emphasis on the values of community and connection. This perspective ignores the reality of domination and force that exists and which must be counteracted through advocacy and legislation in areas that need attention—the fight against age and sex discrimination, and the promotion of issues like parental leave, family care, and job parity for women.

Gould's critique of essentialism ends up providing some support to the second, third, and fourth paradigms: the multicultural/diversity, radical/socialist, and postmodern feminisms. These perspectives attempt to correct some of the problems with the liberal-feminist stand by noting the diversity of women and women's experiences and the need for political and linguistic change. While the multicultural/diversity and radical/socialist perspectives often emphasize the role of multiple and interlocking historical oppressions and women's economic status respectively, the postmodern feminists "highlight/foreground/emphasize/insist" on multiple layers of difference (Sands & Nuccio, 1993, p. 492). But these perspectives have traps as well that may impinge on women's empowerment. In short, they suggest that the social relations of power are so fundamentally structured in American society by the interaction of gender, race, and class that women's struggle for empowerment cannot be understood without making these factors central to analysis (Bookman & Morgen, 1988). This analysis can lead to challenges in building solidarity among older women.

Furthermore, Sands and Nuccio (1993) view postmodern feminism from a diversity perspective and claim that this perspective provokes the need for reconceptualizations of many social work assumptions. If knowledge and power are one, as suggested by the postmodernist philosopher Michel Foucault (1980), then social welfare advocates must take notice of their conceptualizations in their knowledge base, but also must re-examine how knowledge is conceptualized and retrieved. Postmodern feminism, for all it adds to our understanding of the hegemony of ideas and how knowledge is subjugated, is criticized for its emphasis on difference to the exclusion of solidarity, thereby ignoring the need for coalitions that can pursue collective ends.

A major criticism of postmodern feminist thought is its inability to do more than deconstruct gender inequality, as opposed to offering a new and transformational perspective on gender relations (Caraway, 1991). The diversity that exists among women can lend to question: How realistic is it to find common goals and political action strategies for women as a group, when there are so few similarities among them? Empowerment among women, however, can be reconceptualized to incorporate themes of difference and acknowledgment of social inequality. Caraway (1991) supports such a stand. Nonetheless, she warns of the chances feminism takes in a focus on difference alone: "While diversity should be embraced, the lessons of realpolitik tell us that fragmented agents which don't congeal into wholes at certain strategic barricades likely will get vaporized" (p. 4). Angela Davis (1990), for one, acknowledges the critical importance of difference, but does not see it as excluding some form of multiracial unity. She writes of the many issues that coalesce among women: safety for children, world peace, and nuclear disarmament, to name a few. In the end, relegating gender to a matter of difference or sameness—whether compared to men or women—disguises the reality of gender as a system of social hierarchy and an inequality (MacKinnon, 1989). Ultimately, the underlying meanings in varying definitions of empowerment suggest that a reconceptualization of the term should be considered for on behalf of older women.

TOWARD A RECONCEPTUALIZATION OF EMPOWERMENT FOR AGING WOMEN

In writing about the lives of Black women, P. H. Collins (1991) explains how their resistance to oppression occurs on three levels: the level of personal biography; the group or community level contextually created by race, class, and gender; and the systematic and larger level of social institutions. Taken together, Collins' understanding of the matrix of domination and the broad themes from traditional social work and feminist definitions of empowerment lead to these thoughts on a reconceptualization of empowerment for, with, and on behalf of older women. Included in this reconceptualization are the need to include the components of authenticity, connection and relatedness, the collective and community good, and the reality of social power to combat social inequality—women's reality.

VALUE OF AUTHENTICITY

Authenticity is defined as the quality of being genuine, or as "entitled to acceptance or belief because of agreement with known facts or experience" (*Random House College Dictionary*, 1988, p. 91). Emanating in the private, personal space of an individual woman's consciousness, authenticity is a result of courageous thought and action that requires that one be self-defined (P. H. Collins, 1991). To be authentic requires not only speaking and hearing one's voice, but accepting that one's voice has value. The glorification of what is male in this society has for too long repressed, trivialized, or ignored women's voices. Similarly, the current emphasis on youth all too often blinds us to the possibility of age. The interaction of ageism and sexism has all but silenced many aging women's voices. Fortunately, this is changing. Therefore, what must be discovered is what age and aging can really look like (Friedan, 1993).

In *The Change, Women, Aging and Menopause* (1991), Greer notes that women can no longer meet the needs of patriarchal society by reproducing and being sexual, and so they find themselves without a self-view. The more unauthentic women are to themselves, the more they have assimilated male patriarchal values. What age can offer women, suggests Greer, is the opportunity to realize how they have been valued for their reproductive abilities and sexual favors. What women must do, then, is to deconstruct this false vision of women because it is unauthentic, and define themselves. She writes:

> The woman ejected from the feminine subjugation by the consequences of her own aging can no longer live through others, or justify her life by the sexual and domestic services that she renders. She must, being in free fall, take a long look at the whole landscape that surrounds her and decide how she is going to manage to live in it, no matter how chill the wind that buffets her ill-equipped person. At first she may cling to her old life, trying to claw back something of what she poured into it so unstintingly, but eventually, her grieving done, her outrage stilled, she must let go. Only if she lets go can she recover her lost potency. (pp. 373, 374)

According to Greer, old age is a time of great change and potential. The older women must, in effect, redesign herself in her own vision—a vision that is neither phallocentric nor ageist. This quest for authenticity is clearly another form of empowerment. Through acts of real courage, the older woman defines herself and demands her visibility by refusing to be society's "other" anymore. Self-definition in itself can be an act of true resistance and power. Our quest, then, must be to: (a) listen to older women—what is their view of themselves?; (b) read the works of older women—Florida Maxwell, May Sarton, Barbara Macdonald, Betty Friedan, and others come to mind; and (c) hear their standpoint—what could the social welfare agenda look like if older women developed and directed it?

In short, we actively participate and demand from others a new vision for aging and aging women. This process is potentially exciting, as self-growth always is, but it can be made less so when one is worried about basic survival. An acknowledgment of this reality is not falling prey to what Wolf (1994) has described as victim feminism, when women seek power through a definition of helplessness and powerlessness. In contrast to this view is one that acknowledges the life choices, societal expectations, and the structural barriers that have shaped the lives of all women throughout their lives and that too often results in poor health, low self-esteem, and poverty.

Listen to how one of the authors of *Growing Old Disgracefully: New Ideas for Getting the Most out of Life* (Hen Co-Op, 1993), describes what authenticity means to her:

> I no longer lie about my age. I have come out of the closet. I say how old I am and it feels just right. I like calling myself an old woman—it makes me feel strong and wise and important. . . . Other people sometimes seem embarrassed when I say I'm old. They're quick to reassure me that I'm not really old, as if it were some horrible disfigurement, or a disease they are worried about catching, like being (heaven forbid) single, which I am again by choice. My life is far from perfect and I have much to learn, but I feel more authentic than ever before. I'm growing old disgracefully and enjoying each step along the way. I am 63 years old. (pp. 51–52)

VALUES OF CONNECTION AND RELATEDNESS

A great deal of feminist literature deifies the values of connection and relatedness, regardless of whether they are values inherent to women biologically, or are a result of women's adaptations to their secondary status in a patriarchal society. The ability to identify the value placed on connection and relatedness by older women will allow us to see connection and friendships, as opposed to domination and conflict, as sources of power and strength for older women. We see that their connection to their history through their grandmothers is another form of empowerment.

A reconceptualization will also result in a re-examination of definitions of successful aging that use control and independence as the markers of successful aging, in contrast to relatedness and interdependence (Rodeheaver, 1987). Nursing home residents who march to their administrator and advocate for change are one example of empowerment, but this is only one form. Although knowledge and appreciation of assertiveness are important, the presence of support systems may be the critical factor in successful aging (Berkman & Syme, 1979).

A more critical view of empowerment will assist us in recognizing the potential dangers in the essentialism argument, that is, that women are "natural nurturers." Caring, as noted by Baines et al. (1992), must be seen as both a source of women's strength and oppression. Present policies built on such beliefs continue to take advantage of women by expecting them to be unpaid caregivers regardless of the economic and health ramifications to the caregiver. In actuality, caregiving can end up being hazardous to one's health.

A belief in the value of connection and relationships can result in the development of interventions that support the empowerment of the individual and can contribute to group empowerment (Gutierrez, 1990) and societal change (Kuhn, 1991; Kuhn & Hessel, 1977). Ann Weick (1994) has this to say about the relationship between personal power and power for the community good:

> Knowing that one has the ability to re-image her life is a fundamental aspect of personal power. To see things differently, to name things in new ways, is a source of power that is not given by others. It is a power, however, that can be shared with others, so that the act of seeing differently moves naturally into the realm of collective action. Once it is discovered and possessed, it serves as the seedbed for all other imaginings. (p. 226)

A new direction in interventions would not negate the value of strategies that teach older women ways to fight the forces of oppression. A new direction could add interventions that support friendships, community connections, self-help, support groups, family support (including financial) and education, and peer counseling. All hold the possibility of turning personal power into collective power.

There are numerous ways in which to feel such a sense of empowerment. The authors of *Growing Old Disgracefully: New Ideas for Getting the Most Out of Life* (The Hen Co-Op, 1993), themselves all in their 60's, for example, found that the beginning of their own empowered action came when they began to share their stories. For these women, growing old "disgracefully" means finding ways to break established patterns and seizing the opportunities to choose their own directions:

> Women in general, and old women in particular, have had our voices silenced or distorted in so many ways that it is sometimes difficult to think of words that express what is important to us. When we finally start to say them aloud, we release ourselves from the restrictions that have been put on us by others. We are reaffirming that our lives are important. . . . It was the process of speaking and being listened to that was empowering. As we recounted things we had done in our lives, we began to appreciate that even though we had followed ordinary patterns, we had accomplished more than we had given ourselves credit for. (pp. 5–6)

A focus on empowerment and authenticity will result in new questions about services. For example, since friendships and other primary relationships are more common that marriage among older women, should marital status continue to be the major eligibility criterion for income security and assistance, access to health care, and other services?

COMMUNITY AND THE COLLECTIVE GOOD

A third way to make empowerment more inclusive will be to emphasize the community and collective good. A growing number of older women become socially conscious as many, especially White older women, begin to experience discrimination for the first time. Rather than a focus on the self, many begin to extend their energies toward social change. Friedan, now in her 60s, expressed it this way: "It would be a violation of our own wisdom and generativity to empower ourselves in age only for our own security and care—it would be the denial of the true power of age" (1993, p. 635). Thoughts on community and the collective good lend themselves to a reevaluation of the causes of women's oppression from a personal analysis to a political one. An older woman may be admonished for not budgeting correctly, or for not planning for her own old age adequately enough, rather than having her poverty understood as a result of a lifetime of sex and race discrimination. Realistically, we need to ask ourselves just how far $560, the average monthly income of older women, can reach today. Such an understanding would encourage more macro-interventions for women throughout their lives that advocate for pay equity, family leave policies, subsidized housing, and comprehensive and universal health care that includes long term care. Similarly, a social worker who recommends that an older patient be cared for by a 57-year-old woman needs to understand and explain the economic ramifications of such a decision to this woman, while advocating on the legislative level for caregiving policies that are equitable and fair. P. H. Collins (1991) offers encouragement to all women who strive to be empowered through connectedness and community activism. It is through persistence, she says, that this journey from "silence to language to action" will evolve.

Older women have been involved in numerous activities to promote social justice. The Older Women's League is but one example. This national organization was formed by aging women to provide a forum for advocacy on behalf of other aging women.

Reconceptualizations argue against the use of simplistic definitions of older women. There are differences imposed by age, race, culture, sexual orientation, and other factors, and homogenizing women ignores these and other differences. Widowhood does not mean the same thing to all older women, and neither does forced employment and retirement at age 65.

THE REALITY OF SOCIAL POWER

The fourth element in a reconceptualization of empowerment requires the acknowledgment of gender hierarchy and social inequality for women throughout their life cycles. While connections and friendships are critically important at any age, the road toward social equality will require transformational social and political change in the epistemology of gender relations. Interpersonal power is not social power. A reconceptualization of empowerment cannot ignore the stark economic and health realities that exist for many older women, especially the very old, women of color, and working-class women (Allen & Pifer, 1993; Older Women's League, 1986). Friendships and community, while critical for well-being, cannot make up for inadequate nutrition or shelter. Instead, advocacy and legal action are the necessary strategies. While acknowledging the diversities of women's lives, women must find the bond to join forces with other women to advocate for change on behalf of all women. As bell hooks (1984) noted, "Solidarity strengthens resistance struggle" (p. 44). But rather than bonding because of "shared victimization," hooks suggests that it is through "political commitment to a feminist movement that aims to end sexist oppression" that solidarity can occur (p. 47). We cannot have a serious discussion of empowerment without discussing authenticity, valuing connections, the community, and the collective good, but such a discussion would be incomplete without a clear understanding of the sociopolitical and economic factors related to an awareness of women's inequality. At the same time, overcoming injustice and bigotry can be empowering actions by themselves.

OLDER WOMEN AND EMPOWERMENT MODELS

Recording other women's history of resistance and empowerment strategies provides evidence of a rich history of persistence and success. A brief examination of women's preferred styles and models of empowerment, both past and present, can add further assistance in thoughts toward a reconceptualization of this term. The work of Dorothea Dix on behalf of the mentally ill is but one example of what is possible when a belief in community is demonstrated with moral actions. Jane Addams, a relentless crusader for the poor, established settlement homes based on her belief in community and justice. The political activism of Ida B. Wells is another example of a courageous woman who, in seeing the connections between racism and sexism, fought for women's rights and fought against the Ku Klux Klan. These women's conceptions of empowerment stressed community and the collective good.

There are numerous contemporary examples. Laurie Shields, who co-authored *Women Take Care—The Consequences of Caregiving in Today's Society* with Tish Sommers (Sommers & Shields, 1987), is yet another illustration. In 1975, Shields was what many social workers would have labeled a displaced homemaker or a woman-in-transition. Widowed and in her early 50s, she found that society had little use, interest, or concern for a 50-year-old widow with limited training and who had not been in the labor force for 30 years. She refused to see such attitudes against her as personal, however, and instead viewed them as political—a result of living in a sexist and ageist society. To address such injustice, she began three movements—for displaced homemakers, for midlife and older women, and for caregivers. Lou Glass, former president of the Older Women's League (OWL), stated that Shields never saw her problems as hers alone, but those faced instead by millions of women (Stauffer, 1989). Shields' empowerment style reflected strength, the collective good, and connections between women.

Today, the list of older women who daily demonstrate their convictions and courage is endless. Maggie Kuhn, the late founder of the Gray Panthers, well-known as an advocate to end ageism, spoke out against all oppression and injustice (Kuhn & Hessel, 1977). Her growing awareness of ageism led her write of the interrelatedness of all oppression. Shimeji Kanazawa, a well-respected advocate for older adults in Hawai'i, came to her advocacy role after her experiences as a Japanese American woman led her to redefine discrimination in a broader context. She speaks for all ages of every race and color. The heart-rending story of Beulah Donald's victory over the Ku Klux Klan after they murdered her 19-year-old son is a lesson in courage and love. Marie Rogers, an 83-year-old Native American, speaks out on behalf of helping Native American elders live healthy, productive, and independent lives. And we look to women like Frannie Peabody, of Portland, Maine, who in her 90s cofounded an AIDS hotline, and Helen Endicott's work with the nuclear disarmament movement.

Women are also bonding together as they seek to understand and prepare for their own aging. One example is the Red Hot Mamas, an organization that fosters education and exercise among women in their mid- and later years. It began as a grassroots reaction among women who were dissatisfied with the information they were receiving from their physicians on menopause and aging. Today, there are now Red Hot Mamas chapters in more than 30 states. The work of these and other women are important to document, for they speak to the value placed on authenticity, well-being, connection and relatedness, and the community and collective good. Their empowerment could best be characterized as actions that stem from a moral stance that creates meaning in living. Other examples are women's work in social movements such as civil rights, welfare rights, labor, and peace (Blumberg, 1990; West & Blumberg, 1990a, 1990b).

CONCLUSIONS

A reconceptualization of power and empowerment must take full account of women's diverse lifetime experiences. We reject the simplistic and dualistic conceptualizations of empowerment, with its focus on the powerful or the powerless. In contrast, we see the multiple roots of oppression and strengths faced by women of all ages. While numerous professions have stressed looking for clients' strengths, all too often the forces of ageism and sexism have resulted in a view of older women as weak, passive, and disagreeable. Unknowingly, traditional definitions of empowerment may lend themselves to support of such a view.

The growing numbers of older women in our population suggest the importance of initiating a new discourse on the needs and abilities of older women, their preferred styles of empowerment, and the implications for the greater society's good. It is true that aging women are significant consumers of social welfare benefits and programs. Service utilization tends to be associated with increased age, functional limitations, social isolation, and those who live alone—categories that more often than not characterize older women than men. But we do not look at older women through a lens of pathology. As we begin to examine gender and aging more closely, so too must the concept of empowerment be examined—and society's assumptions about women, their roles, and their strengths.

PART FOUR

Aging Women and Feminist Theory

Thoughts Toward a New Epistemology of Women and Aging

How can ageism be defined by women; how can we develop clear vocabulary and theory: Can we afford to ignore it?

—Baba Copper

Incorrect and negative images of older adults continue to pervade society in its myths, expectations, and norms. For reasons previously discussed, women fare even worse than do men in their advanced years as a result in part of public policies that disadvantage women throughout their lives, from a society that all too often mentally and physically abuses those less able to defend themselves, and from women's sense of worth that has been defined by male narratives regarding beauty and reproduction. Explained by a male epistemology that distorts their life experiences with motherhood, the family, and in the workplace, women ultimately find their needs ignored. Defined by their physical attributes and their ability to reproduce and be sexual beings, women find their worth declining after age 30 or so—earlier than do men. Too often, the woman who has aged out of the reproductive years is seen as surplus, extra, a public burden.

Earlier chapters detailed the extent to which age brings challenges to women's financial security, health, caregiving roles, and social status. A feminist life-span perspective on aging was offered as a tool to reconceptualize issues around women and aging and to critique public and private policies that impact on women's lives. As we have seen, public and private policies are too often predicated on an ideology which assigns a second-class status to women and relegates women to home responsibilities and to segregated places of employment. The result has been advantageous for some women, but devastating for the vast majority.

Far from seeing older women as victims, what I wish to document in this chapter are the contributions, activism, and sense of community that are attributable to older women. I believe that age presents women with an opportunity to formulate new perspectives on age, gender, and power, and their intersections with one another. This is because the increased marginalization of women in their advanced years actually aids them in critiquing society from what Lorde (1984) described as an outsider/insider perspective. I suggest this for a number of reasons. When we examine the effects of sexism on women across the life span and the effects of ageism on older adults, we can begin to expose society's narratives on older women so their true images can emerge. I also argue that it is through an analysis of the myths and assumptions about aging women that some of the pitfalls of patriarchal reasoning can be laid bare. I offer these thoughts toward a new epistemology of women and age with four purposes in mind: (a) to help form more realistic and potentially more respectful views of aging and old women; (b) to expose some of society's narratives on oppressed peoples; (c) to find sites where oppressions converge; and (d) to help highlight and navigate the potential that solidarity holds for older women and other marginalized persons.

Briefly outlined and described in previous chapters were several themes from liberal, multicultural, postmodern, radical, and socialist feminist theories. Each focuses on the meaning of gender in society. Given their varied and valued perspectives, we also note that feminist theory has generally and historically ignored age and aging women. Nonetheless, I argue that feminist theory, with its focus on women's strengths and political action, its identification of multiple oppressive forces directed at women throughout their lives, its emphasis on women's diversity and commonalities, and its capacity for critical thinking and rethinking, holds the greatest potential for advancing new thinking about aging in society. To this end, a feminist life-span perspective on aging, presented in chapter 6, sought to reconfigure the existing feminist paradigm from the contributions and omissions of these and other feminist theories and to extend these theories on behalf of aging women.

Aging woman's contributions, endured oppressions, and paths of courage and resistance are a pivotal focus of this perspective. Rather than viewing aging women's problems as a byproduct of ageism alone, we understand that women's oppressions follow them across the life span. Incorporating much of what aging research has contributed to the understanding of aging processes, we also turn a critical eye at findings that have been based on the lives of the privileged. Although age-based oppression affects both women and men, we believe that there must be an awareness that oppression impacts on women earlier than upon men and with more serious economic consequences. Also emphasized in this perspective or framework were components that:

- Emphasize the sociocultural, historical, and political forces that both define oppression and that forge self-definition;
- Incorporate women's diversity into a definition of "woman";
- Advocate for personal and political change to improve women's status;
- Reconceptualize power and empowerment;
- Adopt a holistic and ecological perspective to the study of women and women's issues, linking them to other oppressions;
- Seek opportunities for solidarity with other women and men; and
- Search for new and alternate methodologies in practice, policy, and research.

I used this perspective to critique a number of both existing and proposed public and private policies of great concern for older women's economic and health status, caregiving roles, and social lives. This is a feminist age analysis. What follows are a number of thoughts regarding the realities and limitations of ideology, practice, and policy for a gender-just world, in particular for women as they grow older. By listening to older women's voices, together with feminist and gerontologic writings, a new way of thinking about, learning from, and living life as an older woman begins to take shape. Thus, feminist theories provide some beginning ideas for an epistemology of women and age.

EPISTEMOLOGY AND OLD WOMEN

Epistemology is the study of knowledge and the philosophical issues that surround knowledge and truth. Feminists and postmodernists have understood the critical importance of understanding whose "knowledge" is legitimized by society, whose is not, and who "tells us what we are to know." More than 50 years ago, Simone de Beauvoir warned that society's denial and denigration of older adults results in the true aging process being unrecognizable. Therefore, one strategy to make aging recognizable is to deconstruct the myths and substitute such untruths with women's own words, presented through a variety of genres. Such efforts allow us to begin the work necessary to describe an epistemology of women and age—a new feminist age theory.

Gerontologists focus on the study of the aging process and see older adults neither as all victims nor examples of productive, happy older adults. Profoundly influenced by the European positivistic scientific method, gerontologists often seek answers to questions about health and quality of life issues, whether it is degree of nursing home use among the frail or levels of life satisfaction among community-based dwellers. Most agree that ageism has harmed older adults. Feminists, on the other hand, focus primarily on women. They perceive women's lives as characterized by certain advantages and disadvantages, but always hurt by sexism. While critical of age theory that is gender-neutral in both design and intent, feminists have been slow to address the needs of aging women. Gerontologists, while disappointed in feminist theory's neglect of aging women, also must admit that they themselves have not been trailblazers in gender studies.

There are a number of commonalities that exist between feminism and gerontology. A number of authors have begun to examine the compatibility of these two fields of study (see Gibson, 1996; Gibson & Allen, 1993; Laws, 1995; Ray, 1996; Reinharz, 1986). Borrowing ideas from poststructuralists, both fields understand that age and sex are socially constructed phenomena that are also based on some biological processes. Each is defined, shaped, and influenced by social and power relations that involve a hierarchical structure with views enforced by violence, myths, and societal expectations. According to Shulamit Reinharz (1986), feminists and gerontologists share a philosophical desire to "create a social consciousness, a social theory and a social policy which will improve the life chances of a special group" (p. 87). They tend to choose research, education, and political struggle as strategies to improve women's and older adults' lives. While acknowledging the role of oppression in the lives of both older adults and women, feminists and gerontologists also recognize their strengths, and the critical role of activism in changing socially dictated roles, social structures, and policies that limit their participation.

Within the ranks of feminist and gerontology theorists, different political strategies are espoused. Some call for segregation policies and practices, believing in a "culture" of gender and age, while others recommend integration with the greater society as the preferred challenge. More recently, both feminists and gerontologists have begun to emphasize the diversities that exist in their ranks. Aging women have benefitted from the knowledge bases of both gerontology and feminism, with some limitations based in areas neglected by both disciplines. Thus, thoughts toward a new epistemology on women and age draw and expand from both of these areas of study, but with attention to the needs and concerns of aging women.

What I suggest here are six major themes that influence the development, shaping, and sharing of knowledge of and about women's aging. First, a new epistemology of women and age argues that the study of women is essential and key to understanding the aging process. Therefore, it aims to deconstruct and dismantle the negative myths about older women that pervade not only scholarly work but the popular media, replacing them instead with the thoughts and writings by older women. Moreover, the negative force of ageism directed against older adults, especially older women, is recognized. And yet, on a broader level, ageism is viewed as a potential force to expose society's dominant narratives on oppression and as a means to dismantle patriarchy.

There are a number of other potential themes to this epistemology. I propose that ageism, clearly a negative force, can also be viewed as a new tool to uncover oppressions as interlocking and connecting forces instead of disparate entities. Caregiving, a third theme, is recognized as a major focus of women's lives that influences the creation and validation of both society's view of women and of women's own world views. Caregiving is also conceptualized as a site of intersecting oppressions. Fourth, the need for a feminist age theory is presented as an alternative to the present gender-neutral approach to the study of age. Fifth, the importance women place on authenticity in old age in legitimizing their voices and knowledge is acknowledged as a necessary ingredient for redefining their relationships with other women and with society. Finally, an epistemology of women and age advocates for new conceptualizations of power and empowerment. It locates the many power bases that exist within and among aging women. Emphasized here is the importance of individual self-definition and the value of authenticity for seeing the "potentials of age." Moreover, the need for individual and structural change is articulated as essential in ensuring a more just and equitable life for women with age.

The following section examines these components more fully. They are offered as a beginning place for exposing some of the problems with society's definition and treatment of women, especially as they grow old. Ultimately, the creation of new knowledge of older women is its goal. A more balanced view of age sees older women neither as all victims nor all examples of successful aging. Aging women face numerous problems, and yet our great-grandmothers, grandmothers, and perhaps mothers died in childbirth, worked the fields, and faced harassment and jail as they battled to earn women's suffrage—none trivial activities. Older women do face a myriad of problems, but the view that only tragedy stalks their lives is untrue. Throughout this chapter, the voices of older women describe their lives and share their thoughts, replacing other narratives that present older women as weak, passive, and incompetent.

Given these themes, we also bear in mind that old age in population aging—the aging of the world's population—is a relatively new development. The look backward by aging women is a phenomenon just beginning to be studied among women, feminists, gerontologists, and social welfare advocates. Before population aging became a reality, we did not have the opportunity to engage in age-based analyses. Therefore, this analysis is also influenced by historical and cohort factors.

AGEISM: A TOOL TO UNDERSTAND GENDER AND POWER RELATIONS

> We need to begin the systematic examination from a feminist perspective of the issues involved in women's aging, the condition of old women and our society's ageism. As the pervasiveness of ageist thinking becomes apparent, both in our culture and in the feminist movement itself, we will need to carefully scrutinize many of our basic assumptions attitudes and values. (Healey, 1986, p. 61)

When health research began to study men and women, it was found that sharp and distinct differences can exist between the sexes. Women menstruate, they are capable of giving birth, and as they age, they face issues related to menopause, breast cancer, and heart disease. Nonetheless, women were neglected in many of the nationally funded studies on age and health. While many explanations have been advanced by primarily male researchers, what cannot be ignored is the fact that sexism is a major cause of this omission.

In addition to sexism, ageism is recognized as a critical problem for aging women that must still be corrected. Ageism was defined earlier as discrimination and bigotry directed against older adults because of advanced years. It is aimed at both women and men, but at women earlier than men, for a number of reasons. As women grow older, they must struggle against societal interpretations that equate aging with loss and infirmity. Indeed, some interpretations and myths have become part of society's core narratives about not only aged women but aged adults and other oppressed peoples as well. These narratives are hardly gender, race, or age-neutral, but are defined to keep certain groups powerful. Hence, there are narratives that depict women as hysterical, minorities as less intelligent, older people as confused, and aging women as a burden to society. On the other hand, some narratives see the aged as an increasingly powerful political force. Nonetheless, as the nation continues to experience a changing political and social Zeitgeist, the needs of older women are only beginning to be documented.

In contrast, the study of aging and ageism from a feminist life-span perspective offers women, including younger, privileged women, the opportunity to begin to see the illogic in patriarchal–masculinist thought. The study of ageism also presents an opportunity to build and nurture solidarity with others. By studying aging myths and societal assumptions, we begin to understand the many ways in which older women have come to be devalued. In turn, women of all ages can become sensitized to the ways in which they may be complicit with dominant society's denigration and exploitation of older women.

In general, most male narratives on aging women can be summed up as viewing older women as sexless, undesirable (other than as a free workhorse), incompetent and a burden, and as competitors of other women—both young and old. For example, the prevalent narrative assumes that the older woman is sexless and undesirable after age 30 or 40—unless she can "pass" as a younger woman. An epistemology of women and age refuses to accept youth as the preferred and perhaps only prescription for beauty or sexuality. But, more than that, ideas in a new epistemology give us a window to expose patriarchal thinking.

For example, the rape of a 75-year-old grandmother reveals the fallacies in the masculinist definition of rape as sexual. Older women are raped every day, as are infants and young children. But if the 75-year-old woman is not sexy to the 40-year-old male, as the masculine narrative tells us, then rape must be seen for what it is—an act of violence, degradation, and anger. The male narrative attempts to have it both ways, but it cannot. In other words, masculine thinking says women are raped because they are alluring creatures tempting men beyond their self-control, rather than understanding rape as violence against women. Simply put, according to the patriarchal argument, it is the woman's fault. But the same masculine thinking says that older women are not alluring. How, then, can the rape of older women be explained? While tragic, the rape of older women helps to expose misogynist thinking, and to expose the power relations between men and women that too often explode in violence.

Aging exposes a myriad of other narratives about old women. As an example, all older women are portrayed as being financially "well off" or, conversely, as incompetent and weak. We have already discussed women's high risk for poverty with age. The very fact that older women survive their later years in a society that ignores and devalues them substantiates just how courageous and persistent they actually are! If women are incompetent and weak, how do they manage to survive 7 years longer than men, with so little with which to survive? If women are so incompetent, why are they handed the role of caregiver for the next generation, the sick, and the frail?

Another narrative questions women's abilities to maintain friendships with other women because of their competition with each other over men. A narrative such as this one ignores and trivializes women's friendships, both new and those maintained over generations, which tend to be the glue that sustains them in adversity. Women continue to help other women financially and emotionally across the life span, even as they themselves survive on minimal retirement incomes and absent or inadequate pensions. Such a narrative also ignores the needs of aging lesbian women, for whom "the man" was never the prize sought. The importance of friendships and alternative sources of affection and love become clearer when one considers the following: the numbers of women who are gay; the fact that the average age of widowhood is 57 years of age in this country; and that women's life expectancy is now in the mid-80's.

Still another widespread narrative describes older women as burdens to themselves and society—rather than saying the truth: that older women are employees, volunteers, wives, mothers, grandmothers, and friends. Women spend more than half of their lives caring for children and aging parents as nonpaid or low-paid workers. Seventy-five percent of caregivers to the frail are wives, daughters, and daughters-in-law. The male narrative does not introduce into the discussion any serious thought on who is served by women's free labor. But women are not burdens, because they provide free caregiving. As I have argued elsewhere, aging women should receive equitable treatment compared to others expressly because they are citizens, not because they are caregivers.

Rather than conceiving them as a burden, we use ideas from a feminist age analysis and challenge society's views and assumptions about older women. In truth, backing ageist views of older women limits not only older women's lives, but all women's futures. Ageism, neither desired nor deserved, can nonetheless be used as a method to expose the inequalities that exist in relationships and the societal assumptions that are false and harmful to more than the aged and older women. Thus, aging offers the opportunity for a greater and expanded understanding of oppression, and can lead to the further questioning of other narratives on oppressed populations.

The present debate on generational equity is another example of faulty masculinist thinking which must be deconstructed (see Callahan, 1990; Ferrara, 1995; Thurow, 1996). "Generational equity" refers to the conceptualization of complex public policy issues as conflict between generations (Minkler, 1991). Older adults, usually portrayed as a homogenous and economically privileged group, are depicted as causing the nation's budgetary woes because of selfish and reckless demands for entitlements in Social Security, Medicare, and other programs. The conflict is usually framed as pitting "greedy geezers" against the nation's poor children. Gerontologists Eric Kingson, John Cornman, and Barbara Hirschorn (1986) explain the limitations in what the term "generational equity" has come to mean:

> Equity between generations, while certainly desirable, is a very limited criterion on which to base the distribution of scarce resources among those with competing claims. Even if all parties could agree on what constitutes a fair distribution of resources among generations, achieving such a balance would not necessarily meet many of the nation's goals for social justice. For example, it would not guarantee: 1) that poor citizens would be provided with minimally adequate resources; 2) that non poor citizens would be protected from the risks of drastic reduction in their standard of living due to factors beyond their control; or 3) that all citizens would be afforded equal opportunity to achieve what their potentials allow. In short, as Binstock, a professor at Case Western Reserve University, has observed, the current preoccupation with equity between generations "blinds us to inequities within age groups and throughout our society." (p. 2)

Although appearing to advocate for the needs of children, this debate in reality blames the poverty rate of the nation's children, unquestionably a national disgrace, on the retirement incomes and health needs of older adults. Some older adults do well financially, but they are far from the majority. The average Social Security income of older women is about half that of older men, and, as a group, Black older women live on less than $3,000 a year. Because the majority of older adults are women, the arguments expressed among generational equity advocates against the aged will impact on women more than men. It may be argued that present economic and social welfare policies are contradictory and paradoxical, which depersonalize human suffering. Economic policies are usually insensitive to their impact upon less privileged persons and the poor. Production, productivity, and profit are of central concern, and anything that diverts resources from making this possible is problematic. A feminist age analysis is aware of these points. But more than this, a feminist age analysis sees many policies as also pornographic and misogynist for the ways in which they assign women the task of unpaid care of children, the sick, and the aged throughout their lives; penalize them financially for doing so; assign them to segregated, poorer-paying worksites; and then blame them and their meager Social Security payments for children's poverty and the nation's budgetary troubles.

AGEISM AND UNDERSTANDING INTERLOCKING OPPRESSIONS

> To begin to understand ageism is to recognize that it is a point of conver-
> gence for many other repressive forces. The violence of men against women
> and against weaker, less powerful men. The lifelong economic and social
> status of women. Capitalism's definition of productivity and who can
> engage in it, and its indifference to those it forces to be "unproductive".
> Contempt for the physically challenged. Enforced and institutionalized
> heterosexuality and the family, which confine women to male-defined roles
> and economic dependencies. And inevitably racism . . . (Macdonald, 1983,
> p. 61)

Older women face the effects of ageism and sexism, and some face racism
and heterosexism as well. Data on women's economic status help to
expose the multiple roots of poverty and oppression. As we have discussed,
it is not only poor younger women who become poor older women, but
many middle-class women join the ranks of the poor in later life. With
each advancing year, growing numbers of women begin to see how
superficially they are valued (or devalued, as the case may be) for something outside of themselves (namely, their youth). This understanding
allows some to begin to comprehend how race, ethnicity, class, and sexual
orientation are used by the dominant society to devalue others according
to equally superficial categories. In other words, the roots of oppression
are exposed, and with this awakening comes the realization that one's
oppression is a part of a larger picture of domination and inequality.

Nonetheless, I do not argue here that older women are more oppressed
than others. As Audre Lorde emphatically and poetically voiced, we should
not be interested in developing a hierarchy of the oppressed. Instead, we
look at the "interlocking forces of oppression" (Treichler, 1986, p. 60),
"intersectional oppressions" (Crenshaw, 1990, p. 199), or what P. H.
Collins (1991, p. 222) refers to as "an overarching structure of domination"
as explanatory frameworks for understanding the phenomenon of oppression. We also see the connections between and among the various sites
of oppression as opposed to only their differences or similarities. We
extend our feminist analysis to see who fully benefits from multiple layers
of oppression, and how the knowledge of those oppressed comes to be
ignored and devalued. In discussing the lives of African American women,
P. H. Collins (1991) notes how the study of various oppressed populations
can help reconceptualize thinking about ideologies, social welfare, and
real people's lives:

> Afrocentric feminist notions of family reflect this reconceptualization pro-
> cess. Black women's experiences as bloodmothers, other mothers, and

community other-mothers reveal that the mythical norm of heterosexual, married couple, nuclear family with a non-working spouse and a husband earning a "family wage" is far from natural, universal, and preferred but instead is deeply embedded in specific race and class formations. (p. 223)

She voices her view this way as to the benefits of seeing oppressions from an interlocking perspective:

Replacing additive models of oppression with interlocking ones creates new possibilities for new paradigms. The significance of seeing race, class, and gender as interlocking systems of oppression is that such an approach fosters a paradigmatic shift of thinking inclusively about other oppressions, such as age, sexual orientation, religion, and ethnicity. (p. 225)

Aging exposes the relationships and differences between and among all sites of oppression. The late Maggie Kuhn, founder of the Gray Panthers, offered this much earlier comment: "I've come to see all injustices, no matter how small or seemingly unrelated, as linked." Kuhn (Kuhn & Hessel, 1977) also shared her special insights about the ways in which oppressions are indeed interlocking:

In this age of self-determination and liberation, many groups are struggling for freedom. All these struggles are linked in the worldwide struggle for a new humanity. Together they have the potential for a new community-based social justice system of human compassion and selfhood. Old people have a large stake in this new community—in helping to create it and extend it. The winds of change are impelling and empowering. They can free us or destroy us. (p. 13)

Unfortunately, feminist activists have not always understood ageism as an interlocking force with other sites of oppression. Speaking to participants at a 1985 Women's Studies conference, feminist activist and author Barbara Macdonald called for attendees, primarily younger women, to look at their own ageism and rethink their work's focus: "Has it never occurred to those of you in women's studies, as you ignore the meaning and the politics of the lives of women beyond our reproductive years, that this is male thinking? Has it never occurred to you as you build feminist theory that ageism is a central feminist issue?" (1986, p. 21). Younger women are not immune to falling prey to society's negative images of aging women. Sensitized to the negative results of sexism, many have nonetheless ignored ageism. Macdonald continues:

Thus you who are younger see us as either submissive and childlike or as possessing some unidentified vague wisdom. As having more soul than you or being over-emotional and slightly crazy. As weak and helpless or as a pillar of strength. As "cute" and funny or as boring. As sickly sweet or dominating and difficult. You pity us, or you ignore us—until you are made aware of your ageism, and then you want to honor us. . . . None of these images has anything to do with who we are—they are the projections of the oppressor. (p. 24)

Unable to see older women's contributions as well as dilemmas, younger women fail to acknowledge and appreciate older women. They also end up refusing to participate in their own aging. But such denial of self prevents one from learning from and appreciating those who have come before. It also builds barriers to the needed preparatory planning work for one's own later years.

Interlocking oppressions are sometimes not seen until they are experienced first-hand. Personal experiences with oppression often result in an individual seeing the world differently. While in her late 80's, Florida Scott Maxwell (1968) exclaimed:

Suddenly, I see what I did not see before. I have felt all my life exactly as those who ask for equality. The real need is for honour, often not deserved, desired the more when not deserved. Our cry sounds as though we had been demeaned, and while we are demanding "Our rights" we are saying, "Do not demean us for our differences, self-shame is hard to bear." (p. 105)

As Maxwell learned, ageism presented her with an opportunity to understand interlocking oppressions. Women who had privilege due to youth and beauty may begin to understand—many for the first time—that they were privileged. In their younger years, their youthful vigor and beauty were not viewed as detriments. They may have even used these attributes, even unconsciously, to achieve some power. But with age comes change. Women who were never excluded from power and privilege—or so they thought—find it painful to be ignored, to be made invisible, and to have their economic status diminished and threatened. They discover what really happens when they cross the line of acceptable behaviors. And for women, unacceptable behavior is to look old. Healey (1986) explains what this has to do with aging and ageism:

Having spent our lives estranged from our own bodies in the effort to meet that outer patriarchal standard of beauty, it is small wonder that the prospect of growing old is frightening to women of all ages. We have all been trained to be ageist. By denying our aging we hope to escape the penalties placed upon growing old. But in doing so we disarm ourselves in the struggle to overcome the oppression of ageism. (p. 60)

Other women become more powerful because of their cumulative life experiences. Additionally, and as Greer has written about so well, some women feel freed from having to factor in beauty as their reason for living. Still, it is unfortunate that privilege is often not acknowledged as such until it is taken away. When it is lost, it is finally seen for what it is—a privilege, and not a birthright. The illusion of protection vanishes and women see through the aging process their shared fate with other women and marginalized persons. While painful, it is in the sharing of similar problems that building blocks can be gathered for solidarity. Therefore, the experience of ageism can help to expose society's narratives on the harmful effects of discrimination. The more privileged who thought that minority persons' view of oppression was "in their heads," that ethnic groups were "too sensitive," or that one's oppression was somehow "deserved due to some inferiority" learn the fallacies of their earlier thinking, as they too eventually fall victim to discrimination. Understanding the connections between issues allows us to see the legitimacy in fighting against sexism, ageism, and racism as "pieces of the same puzzle."

What Macdonald suggests is that age provides an opportunity to open ranks, rather than close them—an opportunity to build solidarity. Healey (1986) presents this analysis of Macdonald and her own thoughts:

> I subscribe to Macdonald's view that "age in our society gives us a second opportunity (or places the demand on us, if that is how it feels) to finally deal with our difference, if we have not done so before; to move out of that safe harbor of acceptability". Here the difference we have to deal with is our own aging. Neither to run from being old nor to succumb to being more acceptable as a "young old." We have the opportunity to deal with what is different, special, unique about being older and old, to find a belonging with other women as they examine the issue of aging, no matter what their age. (p. 62)

A new epistemology of women and age acknowledges sexism and other oppressions that women face. Yet it is the interlocking of oppressions that present more serious barriers to survival than one site alone (P. H. Collins, 1991). To see ageism, racism, or heterosexism in feminism's ranks is on one level appalling, for it exposes the conceptual and methodological apparatus of the dominant society that is present in feminist thinking. It may well irritate and anger many, for it exposes our complicity. On the other hand, acknowledging feminist theory's contributions, as well as its problems, can mark the beginning of its historical recovery, accountability, and vision for aging women. It can also work toward a new awareness of a place for solidarity with aging women and other oppressed peoples.

One of the contributors to *Growing Old Disgracefully: New Ideas for Getting the Best Out of Life* states it this way:

> It is the vocabulary of the Women's movement which provides the women of my generation with the means to redefine old age for ourselves and in our own terms. Ageism is an oppression just as racism and sexism are, or the oppression of one class by another. It is from the Women's movement that women like myself draw our strength and inspiration to fight all these oppressions. I still—almost—believe it is a movement to change the world! (Hen Co-Op, 1993, p. 80)

CAREGIVING AS A CENTRAL THEME IN WOMEN'S LIVES AND AS A SITE OF INTERSECTING OPPRESSIONS

> The source of your ageism, the reason why you see older women as there to serve you comes from the family.
>
> —Barbara Macdonald

Policymakers generally see caregiving as a woman's issue. It is more accurately a family and societal one. As I have discussed throughout this book, caregiving is a responsibility across the life span, and an everyday experience for most women. Indeed, it can be said that women's lives are characterized by caregiving, regardless of whether or not they are employed outside of the family, regardless of what kind of family the woman has—as a single, lesbian, or widowed woman—and regardless of whether her status is nonpaid, volunteer, or poorly paid. Moreover, and despite egalitarian protestations from the "New Man," women provide double duty in both caregiving and housekeeping responsibilities in increasing numbers, and with escalating frustration. But, what is also true is that while women provide care, they also receive it. For, when older women become frail, it is women—either paid or low-paid—who will care for them.

Patricia H. Collins (1997) has recently extended her work on Black feminist theory and oppression to the study of the family as a site of intersectional oppressions. Somewhat similarly, what I suggest here is that elder caregiving may be viewed as a site of and an illustration of "intersectionality." For, when we examine more carefully the issue and phenomenon of caregiving through a feminist age lens, we see quite clearly the ways in which the intersecting oppressions of gender, race/ethnicity, class, and sexual orientation come into play.

For example, in examining gender and caregiving, Gibson and Allen (1993) note the lack of attention directed at spousal caregiving. In part, they hypothesize that this lack of attention is based on the idea that couples share caregiving responsibilities in a reciprocal manner. In other words, common knowledge dictates that when the wife becomes frail, the husband provides the needed care, and vice versa. It was probably assumed that there was an inherent fairness to spousal caregiving; hence, the apparent lack of research attention on the subject. But, citing evidence gathered in Australia, Gibson and Allen dispute this notion of shared care. In this research study, even when the woman became frail and disabled, half still prepared the meals for the nonfrail spouse, and one-third still handled the housework responsibilities. On the other hand, men took greater responsibility for home maintenance tasks. While women provided most of the household tasks (i.e., meal preparation, housekeeping, and errands) for frail husbands, the reverse was not true. When it was the wife who was frail, smaller numbers of men prepared meals, provided housekeeping, and did errands. This is even more unjust, suggest Gibson and Allen, when one considers the work that women do must be done daily (i.e., meal preparation), while the work men do (i.e., fixing a leaking faucet) can be put off for months. This nonreciprocity in the sexual division of labor is rarely researched, and is complicated by the fact that women live longer than men, leaving them without even the minimum assistance men provide.

Gibson and Allen also found that marriage appears to offer protection from institutionalization, more so to men than women, in part because "men are either less willing or less capable of maintaining a dependent spouse in the community" (p. 83). As they correctly conclude, it is woman's labor that maintains older couples in their own homes, with great savings to the public coffers. Therefore, Gibson and Allen recommend the rejection of gender-neutral concepts such as interdependence and caregiving. Instead, terms such as these should be revisited using a feminist age analysis, so that their social policy implications can best be understood:

> The use of such concepts as the interdependence of couples in old age, coupled with the devalued nature of women's private sphere responsibilities (exemplified by the relative invisibility of old women's "normal" domestic responsibilities) obscures the non-reciprocity of women's situation in old age, and fails to recognize the extent to which social provision for the aged is parasitic upon the labor of old women. (p. 84)

Examining the existing patterns of service delivery and expenditures as distributed by sex provides further evidence for caregiving as a site of interlocking oppressions. Gibson and Allen, for example, found that gender differences exist in the kinds of services needed and used. Services women need the most appear to be the ones least available to them. The types of care women do not do for themselves and men do (e.g., home maintenance) are the services least provided by agencies. In contrast, the types of care men do not do and women do (e.g., housekeeping, meal preparation) are the services most often provided (Gibson & Rowland, 1984). Similarly, the lack of respite and transportation services impacts more on women than men, because these are the services that most caregivers (i.e., women) need. Curiously enough, the majority of professionals who work with the aged are women.

Furthermore, when levels of disability are factored in, males consume a disproportionate share of community-based (home) and institutional services. This is not to deny that the majority of service beneficiaries are old women, but, rather, "that men receive access to such services more easily, because of their perceived incapacity to care for themselves" (Gibson & Allen, 1993, p. 87).

Additional illustrations of caregiving as a site of interlocking oppression are apparent with the examination of financial payments to caregivers. Policies established by a number of different nations and states to fund caregivers rarely make spouse caregivers eligible for such payments. Since women are the majority of spouse caregivers, they bear the brunt of the inadequacies of such eligibility policies. In essence, then, the present system of services reinforces and even replicates, rather than corrects, women's disadvantages and men's advantages across the life cycle.

This reliance on women's caregiving, combined with the notion that men are "natural recipients of care," and women are "natural nurturers of care," has led to what Gibson and Allen refer to as a social welfare system that is "parasitism on women" and is "phallocentric" in its service delivery system (1993, p. 79). In other words, a long term care system has been built on the free care of aging women, and is responsive more to men's needs than to women's. What is critical to note, according to Gibson and Allen, is that such a model:

> forestall [s] the development of a plausible, equitable, and adequately funded range of services catering to the diversity of situations, problems, and preferences of aged women and men. Furthermore, the relatively more politically powerful minority of the aged, men, have little objective in such a re-orientation. Within prevailing circumstances, their meals are still cooked, their clothes washed, the house cleaned, the shopping done, and their illnesses nursed by wives and/or female relatives, just as they were throughout earlier phases of the life course. . . . To challenge the distinct

unmet needs of older women is inevitably to challenge the allocation of resources and its basis in sexual politics and sexual economics. (p. 89)

Thus, women, more so than their male counterparts, note the connective threads that weave among what they do at home, what they do at work, and the appalling lack of affordable long term care services. They understand quite well that, regardless of what the conservative agenda and the masculine ideology may say, caregiving is work, and it is demanding work at that. Most women recognize that society supports them in doing work in both spheres, but with minimal, grudging assistance. Conservatives and masculinists may wonder what the problem is with having women serve as caregivers. In contrast, a feminist age analysis sees a socially defined gender division of labor that relegates women to these tasks, and understands how the lack of government-funded services in long term care poses a real problem for women and has material consequences for them. Women must grasp the connection between staying at home and an inadequate retirement—when their retirement income is based on their limited work history. Increasing numbers of women see the connections between their income throughout their lives and their devaluation at home and in the marketplace; between low income and having an inadequate retirement income, between caregiving responsibilities and work/career advancement, and between women's low income and the impoverishment of their children. A feminist age analysis understands that the family is a social unit that benefits society, and that while caregiving is humane and important, taking advantage of caregiving women is immoral.

The intersectionality of gender/race/ethnicity, class, and sexual orientation is also exposed when paid caregiving is analyzed using a feminist age perspective. While research has not extensively focused in this area, relationships have been found between class, income, and caregiving, or informal care. In general, one's level of income has an inverse relationship to the use of formal services. In other words, the higher the income, the more one can and often does rely on paid, formal care. But since older women are more poor than older men, they are less able to pay for such care. When it comes to race variations in caregiving, alternate hypotheses have been offered to explain why various racial groups rely more on informal care than Whites, ranging from cultural values, traditional roles, and discriminatory practices (Braun & Browne, 1998). This topic warrants further attention and discussion.

Somewhat more research has begun to investigate the relationships that exist between paid nonfamilial caregivers—home care providers—and the recipients of such care, as well as the influences of race and class on these relationships (Aronson & Neysmith, 1996; Baines et al., 1992). Home health as an industry is expanding primarily as a means to cut public spending and to increase profits in the health care industry (Aronson & Neysmith, 1996). Numerous professionals are employed in this industry— physicians, nurses, physical therapists, social workers, and others. On the positive side, technology has made it possible for people to be cared for in more natural and home environments and for more conditions to be demedicalized. Rather than professionalizing what does not need to be performed by professionals, we can be cared for and assisted by others in many of our day-to-day activities. Few would argue against the benefits of being cared for in one's own home by loved ones. Nonetheless, this increased attention on home care has also led to an escalating need for paid home care workers, those usually employed in the home health industry who provide a wide range of paid caregiving services to frail older adults. Home care workers, in contrast to home health care workers, are often considered low-skilled, are low-paid workers, and are more often than not women of color, working-class women, and immigrant women. Aronson and Neysmith (1996) write:

> Their low status and vulnerability are the result of the intersecting disadvantages of gender, social class, and race. As a labor force, they are made up of women with few marketable skills and occupational choices, and they are also drawn from the ranks of immigrant and visible minority populations. . . . Thus, their positioning reflects historical continuities between the subordinate status of domestic service and human service work. (p. 61)

Aronson and Neysmith suggest that these workers, because of their race/ethnicity and social class, are exploited. Their work is devalued and their bargaining power weakened because the location of their work is in the privacy of old people's homes. The implication—for the worker, the care receivers, and the family caregivers—is that members of each group are in jeopardized positions due to the lack of respect for the worker, lack of an adequate pay scale for women, and the rarely discussed influences of racism, classism, and other oppressive forces impacting on the caregiver-care receiver relationship. As with other segments of society, it would be unrealistic to believe that race, social class, and gender biases do not surface here. The conflicts that can and do occur between care recipients and caregivers, that of more privileged and less privileged women, are also found in other domestic work (Glenn, 1985, 1992). As Aronson and Neysmith warn:

> In future research and political activity, it will be important to recognize how home care workers, elderly service recipients, and family caregivers

are, together, caught and disadvantaged by the work transfer, by the public discourse in old people's needs and women's work, and by the systematic depersonalizing of home care labor. The likelihood of losing sight of the potential for solidarity is considerable as the potential for conflict among women looms large. . . . It will be important that we recognize that the origins of these oppressive dynamics lie, in large part, in the structuring of health and social policies and in discursive and managerial practices that limit elderly person's entitlements and shift responsibility for meeting their needs to unpaid or poorly paid women. (p. 75)

The relationship between caregivers and care recipients can be even more problematic because ours is a heterosexual-dominant society. Gay and lesbian paid caregivers often face job discrimination in hiring and job retention. Gay caregivers are further marginalized, as insurance and government policies do not recognize long term relationships not sanctioned by marriage. Moreover, gay and lesbian couples usually are not eligible for each other's health insurance policies, family medical leave policies, and other benefits.

While acknowledging the numerous problems surrounding caregiving, we also recognize that many women do choose to provide care, whether it is as a paid, low-paid, or nonpaid caregiver, and many more receive care. The voices of those receiving care are less often heard, and rarely studied. In truth, the lack of a long term care policy responsive to older women leaves both care recipient and caregiver vulnerable and needy. An epistemology of women and age can not ignore this fact. The problem, as I stated in chapter 7, is not that women provide caregiving, nor is it the trend toward home care and community-based care of the aged. Many older women probably will benefit from the caregiving of another woman, if they can in fact remain in their own homes. The problem is the lack of available and affordable long term care services in both the community and in institutions that places great burdens on caregivers, and that results in the isolation of both caregivers and care recipients. A new epistemology does not, therefore, see caregiving as a problem, even though it is quite aware of the harm created by public and private employment pensions to women who take time off to provide such care. And, although changes in ideological thinking about women's roles must be applauded, older women as both caregivers and care recipients will suffer in the absence of an equitably, adequately funded community-based long term care system. Likewise, the problem is not that women have more career options available to them, and so may not be as available as in previous times to provide caregiving. As we have seen, women are continuing to provide these tasks. Rather, an epistemology of women and age defines the problem as the present system that has not chosen to provide adequate and affordable long term care services to frail older adults.

In addition to expanding an awareness of sites of interlocking oppressions, the theme of caregiving in women's lives provides some potential benefits. Caregiving, as suggested by Donovan (1996), can generate greater awareness of the uncertainties in life, which in turn can result in a life view that is less dominating and more holistic than a masculinist view, and in an ethic that "is non imperialistic, life affirming and that reverences the concrete details of life" (p. 173). It is not that women or men, as caregivers, are "better people" than noncaregivers. Rather, caring for the frail reveals the many vicissitudes of life that can result in one's awareness of those less able in a way that is neither blaming or judgmental. Conversely, not lost in this analysis is the fact that caregiving can and has led to some reacting abusively.

In a somewhat similar vein, caregiving may actually provide women new opportunities to consider the role of government in relation to the needs of its citizens. For example, social critic Barbara Ehrenreich (1996) suggests that the gender gap in politics is actually a reflection of male and female differences in family caregiving. She makes note of the relationship between political inclinations and caregiving by gender. Most men, she describes, even those with families of their own, spend more of their time in a "special guy world" characterized by sports and personal purchases. She says, in contrast,

> Women have tended to stay firmly embedded in the nexus of intergenerational dependencies—doing more than their share of the child rearing, for example, and of the caring for elderly and maundering parents. . . . Naturally, the diverging life situations of men and women favor divergent political ideologies. Cut off from the daily contact with the weak and needy, and hypnotized by the zero-sum ethic of televised sports, men were bound to be seduced by the social Darwinism of the political right, with its vision of the world as a vast playing field for superstar line-backers and heroic entrepreneurs on leave from the Fountainhead. Women, on the other hand, are more likely to have a vested interest in the notion of human interdependence: that we are not freewheeling nomads of free-enterprise ideology but vulnerable beings held together by mutual need. Thus to the residents of guy land, government often looks like the 50-ft third grade teacher from hell, taxing and regulating and otherwise spoiling the fun. But to a woman sandwiched between children and parents, the "Nanny state" is not a Republican pejorative but rather an extension of herself. Dump Granny out of the nursing home because the Medicare budget is too high, and who is going to change her Depends? (p. 36)

Caregiving thus provides for a different perspective on human capital as—even children, the sick, and the frail—are recognized as having value.

Men and women who provide care see the uniqueness and strengths of individuals well beyond a reliance on physical and/or economic definitions. Women, because of their prescribed (not natural) caregiving roles, tend to appreciate the largely inescapable relationship of dependent and independent behavior to the human life cycle more than do non-caregivers.

FEMINIST AGE THEORY

In looking back at her life, the 80-year-old Florida Scott Maxwell found herself trying to understand why men must feel superior to women: "I still do not see why men feel such a need to stress [women's supposed inferiority]. Their behavior seems unworthy, as though their superiority was not safe unless our inferiority was proven again and again. We are galled by it, even distorted by it, mortified for them, and forever puzzled" (1968, p. 100). More recently, a number of feminists have extended this line of questioning to ask why society, and why feminists themselves, have generally ignored the needs of aging women. Somewhat similarly, a small but growing number of gerontologists have also begun to inquire as to why aging and feminist studies have neglected this population. Some look at both influences. Healey, for one, asks herself and her readers: "How did it happen, this totally denigrating picture of old women? To understand this phenomenon we must look at sexism, for ageism is inextricably tied to sexism and is the logical extension of its insistence that women are only valuable when they are attractive and useful to men" (1986, p. 59).

An epistemology of women and age sees value in a feminist age theory, one that does not take a gender-neutral approach to the study of age as have so many gerontological theories. And, unlike most feminist theories, it neither ignores age nor makes youth the referent point for aging women or men. It refuses to accept the privileged male point of view which is prevalent in gerontological theory. Neither does feminist age theory assume that older men and women are alike, nor does it assume that all older women are alike. Instead, feminist age theory acknowledges certain broad areas of concern—namely, that women suffer from poverty more so than men, have gender-specific health concerns, and face multiple oppressive forces throughout their lives. Therefore, social welfare policies and programs must be constructed to address these and other needs while aiming to correct inequities.

A feminist age analysis studies gender similarities and differences with age, focusing on older women and including the diversity among them. Its analyses point to older women's strengths, and yet are not blind to the many issues that face older women, not the least of which are poverty and discrimination. Unlike most gerontological theories, feminist age theory rejects gerontology's fascination with and absolute dependence upon the positivist discourse and scientific validation methodology as the only avenues to seeking out women's stories.

A feminist age analysis documents the ways in which older women's voices and advice have been ignored in the political process. In national debates, their voices have often been silenced and outweighed. Discussions on income distribution, child care, family violence, and health care debates rarely include their perspectives, even though their life stories provide a wealth of information that demand their inclusion. Until recently, they have been neglected in nationally funded health studies, leading to their health needs being misunderstood and ignored. At best, their life experiences and perspectives are an afterthought in policy formulation. Subsequently, both private and public sector policy initiatives rarely have resulted in an improved life for the majority of older women, in sharp contrast to many older men.

As a departure, a feminist age analysis validates the importance of women's voices and lives, using new, alternative genres and methodologies as tools to study them. A feminist age analysis does not engage in this pursuit without also acknowledging the inherent dilemma in seeking out aging women's voices. This is because the knowledge of oppressed groups, often subjugated knowledge, is never far from the power of the group that formulated and conceptualized it (P. H. Collins, 1991). Knowledge by and about older women can be compromised by the inherent interests of the power elite involved in formulating and conceptualizing such knowledge. So, while older women's voices may be subjugated knowledge, their views bring a valued alternative perspective and methodology for the examination of society's narratives. According to Collins, "Subjugated groups have long had to use alternative ways to create independent self-definitions and self valuations and to rearticulate them through our own specialists" (1991, p. 202). Thus, it is critical to search for women's voices in poetry, short stories, and plays—places other than traditional academic discourse, and often published in smaller publishing houses. When they inform quantitative reports from sources such as the Bureau of the Census, epidemiological studies, and qualitative research, much more can be learned about aging women's lives.

The diversity found among older adults requires that we study aging from diverse perspectives. Ageism cannot be understood in isolation from sexism, racism, classism, and heterosexism. Borrowing ideas from feminist postmodern thought, feminist age theory questions the idea of universal aging and the terms "older adult" or "older women." What is understood is that the life situations of older women are compelling arguments for why their lives must be studied, and why social policies must be reexamined for their consequences for older women. Furthermore, women's unique health profile is viewed as a major reason why older women should be studied, as opposed to a reason for their exclusion. And while research on older men does not provide answers to our questions about older women, we see how a gender-neutral approach to the study of age also has not aided men's aging. As Calasanti and Zajicek (1993) note, it is not only women who "have gender." Thus, we must talk about the entire aging population. What is needed are assurances that aging information must factor in and be informed by data, information, and experiences pertinent to women.

Appropriating ideas from both postmodernists and cultural feminists, a feminist age theory seeks to clarify the importance of language. Worth further elaboration is gerontologist Martha Holstein's (1992) feminist critique of the concept of productive aging, for it underscores the significance of language and feminist methodology in promoting well-being for both sexes. Recent discussions on productive aging often correlate it with work and worklike activities (Birren, 1985; Butler & Gleason, 1985; Moody, 1988). This is not an entirely negative thing, for associating older adults with work may reduce some age-related barriers to employment, in the end helping both men and women alike. But, as Holstein suggests, a focus on productivity can end up devaluing relational activities—so characteristic and descriptive of women's lives, and of a growing number of men's—across the life span.

A number of feminists have offered theoretical critiques of the cultural meaning of aging. Some have been discussed in earlier chapters (de Beauvoir, 1972; Friedan, 1993; Greer, 1991). Cultural understandings of age, according to Holstein, "legitimate roles and norms appropriate to the last stage of life . . . and address the fundamental contributions inherent in old age" (p. 18). Holstein argues that gerontologists have embraced a masculinist definition of productive aging, one that builds on images of health, success, and wellness from a male referent point. Thus, she believes, assumes a narrow work-oriented, financially driven definition, one that holds negative connotations and consequences for older women as it negates socialization and nurturing activities such as caring for children and elders. Such a definition also leads to a questioning of the worth of those who are unable to work; that is, the severely disabled, the homeless, as well as some retired persons. A work-focused definition of productive aging has potential negative consequences for all older adults, insofar as it aligns socially acceptable behavior to traditional notions of work, rather than the inherent dignity of age and the moral value of caring for the aged. With or without intent, such a view devalues the financially uncompensated activity carried out by women and retirees.

While not disputing the potential positive aspects of such a definition (there can, after all, be joy in work), Holstein fears that efforts to quantify older adults' contributions to the greater society—as in volunteering or other ways of proving their "worth"—may be used by gerontologists to silence others who see older adults as burdens. But, Holstein argues that doomsayers, members of the New Right, and neoconservatives who believe that the aged are taking food from the mouths of children because of their selfishness and greed will not in all likelihood be swayed by such arguments, since their goal is much more drastic—ultimately, the dissolution of the social welfare state.

A feminist age critique inherent in feminist age theory benefits all older adults, not only older women. Some views of productive aging, warns Holstein, "can easily become another vehicle to obscure diversity, establish new standards for an acceptable old age, and list heavily toward meeting someone else's vision of social and economic needs" (p. 23). In contrast, feminist age theory seeks older women's perspectives on how to conceptualize productive aging. For example, a focus upon paid employment negates contributions by many older women whose lives have not been characterized by such roles. Likewise, homogenization of all older women neglects the fact that working-class and minority women work because of financial necessity, not necessarily for self-fulfillment. Even today, the majority of older women find work in only 20 of the Department of Labor's 400 categories. More often than not they are the sales clerks, bookkeepers, service workers, secretaries, and nurse's aides (U.S. Department of Labor, 1991b), all jobs which offer generally lower salaries with minimal or no benefits. Most women assume such jobs for their sheer survival. But by linking social welfare benefits to work, policies may further relegate women to low-paying jobs which benefit business, not women. Again, we turn to Holstein:

> By conflating the availability of such low-wage work with the larger, value laden goal of a productive aging society, less sympathetic voices can transform what may be an economic necessity for an older woman into a newly honored social norm. . . . A narrow view of productivity can become the captive of those who wish to de-legitimate income support programs. By emphasizing health and vigor, by pointing to the availability of jobs (without consideration of the quality of those jobs), and by ignoring the inherent gender biases of such a strategy, a job-oriented view of productivity can be used politically to threaten the already tenuous economic status of older women. (pp. 24, 25)

In helping to build the foundations for new images of productive aging, older women provide us with a broader definition of productivity. Narrow definitions do not lend themselves to labeling as "productive" the retired worker, the 35-year-old mother who stays at home to raise her children, the 25-year-old disabled student, or the 63-year-old woman caring for her 87-year-old mother with Alzheimer's Disease. Who should define such work as nonproductive? While not negating those who must work for pay, there are other ways to contribute to oneself, family, and society. Holstein further suggests that aging women contribute to the reconceptualization of aging because of "affiliative histories, their flexibility learned in their years of balancing home/work and other demands, their ability to deal with ambiguity and complexity, and their continued potential for growth once they have more freedom" (p. 29). Holstein's feminist critique proposes that the following should be included in a new definition of productive aging: "a new emphasis on personal relationships and life fulfillment; value of work well done for its own sake; the norm of helpfulness to others; and an emphasis on care and responsibility" (p. 29). She suggests a number of social welfare policy recommendations, some already discussed in chapter 7. Among these are assistance to lower-income people to seek relief through the Age Discrimination in Employment Act; education, so that older women know that they are part of a protected legal class; caregiving credit in public and private pensions; and new research that examines consequences of health policies for older adults.

Feminist age theory seeks to hear out and validate what older women say about their lives. A balanced perspective acknowledges the varied experiences of women with age and seeks out their commonalities and differences, and the benefits and burdens among women based on their material world. In emphasizing diversity, we avoid a single perspective of normality for aging women. Critical of male narratives, we question common assumptions about age-related issues and conceptualization of terms such as "work" and "productivity" from a male standpoint. And yet we also acknowledge the need to develop theories on aging based on some generalizations about older women's lives. In the end, feminist age theory understands that women's self-definitions and world views must lead the way for woman-sensitive policies which improve the lot of women and men alike.

AUTHENTICITY AND POWER

Younger is not better; it is simply different. Embracing one's years means that old is good. Not better, just different than young. Years are an accumula-

tion of experience that one does not deny, either in the changes they have
made upon our enduring bodies, the lines they have furrowed on our faces,
or the quirks and strengths that have forged into our personalities. Typical
uses of the words young and old ignores the disadvantage of youth and
emphasize the negative aspects of age. (Copper, 1986, pp. 50–51)

In chapter 8, authenticity was defined as self-definition and genuineness.
To move towards a more realistic vision of age, older women must insist
upon their own visibility. Feminist theory argues that women must define
themselves and hear one another's stories. A new epistemology on women
and age extends this point by striving to understand how older women's
denigration came to be and the purpose it serves, exposing the way it
manifests itself in the social structures of the family, the political, and
the economic worlds, and by documenting older women's strategies that
resist discrimination and denigration. As we noted elsewhere, age discrimination does not transcend other sites of oppression. Instead, nearly all
older women's lives are marked by cumulative disadvantage and advantage
based on historical, cultural, and other factors. Some women do enter old
age with privilege; still, the scale rarely tips in their favor. Therefore,
older women have had to resist internalizing society's negative views and
opinions. We can begin anew when we listen to the words of older women,
and document the value they place upon self-definition and self-validation
with advancing age. In the previously mentioned anthology on women
and aging, Healey (1986) articulates what aging means to her:

What does it really mean to grow old? For me, first of all, to be old is to
be myself. No matter how patriarchy may classify and categorize me as
invisible and powerless, I exist. I am an ongoing person, a sexual being,
a person who struggles, for whom there are important issues to explore,
new things to learn, challenges to meet, beginnings to make, risks to take,
endings to ponder. Even though some of my options are diminished, there
are new paths ahead. (p. 62)

And, in the same anthology, Margaret Randall (1986) describes the process
of her own aging as akin to a journey, as she begins to learn more about
herself. Aging is about:

A changing mind, a changing set of values (or values that firm themselves
up somehow)—becoming stronger as they at the same time become less
rigid—I can understand how in this way of life we have created for ourselves, THINGS do become palpable "signs" of change. The clothing I
wanted as a young woman is no longer important to me. The gadgets only
clutter my life. My focus is much more centered. More and more I spend

time trying to understand the so many moments or passages I once let pass me by in relative abandon. . . . It seems to me now that I am almost always alone. Alone in a way I cherish. As much if not more than I cherish "being with" those I love . . . I no longer have patience for the things I once even cultivated, for reasons I then accepted unquestionably. It is as if suddenly everything is made of glass, and I can see through objects and words and gestures and expressions in a way I never could before. (p. 128)

Rather than a theme of loss, disability, and death, an epistemology of women and age expresses the opinion that opportunity with age also exists. While not ignoring the very real losses that can and do occur with age, Paula Doress-Worters and Diana Siegel, authors of *The New Ourselves Growing Older: Women Aging with Knowledge and Power* (1993) have this to say:

In the second half of life, many of us have an opportunity to pay attention to ourselves and our own needs and aspirations, perhaps for the first time. The added years we gain with increased longevity can be ours to grow spiritually and intellectually. Midlife is often spoken by women in metaphors of birth and rebirth, a time to nurture our talents, casting off the external criteria by which we may have devalued ourselves and blossoming in new ways. (p 437)

Authenticity requires that older and younger women face each other and examine their distrust and resentment. Younger women must take responsibility and hear the anger and disappointment from older women who have felt betrayed by younger women's co-option with masculinist thinking, so evident when they often unwittingly join patriarchy in the denigration of older women. Older women must recall their own earlier struggles to survive in a male-dominated society that too often resulted in their adoption of masculinist points of view. This realization can build empathy and sympathy between the generations. Both must recognize that life is a continuum. The dualistic conception of age pits young against the old, and with it comes lost opportunities for women's solidarity. Baba Copper (1986) articulates:

The natural alliance that old women have a right to expect with mid-life women will not emerge until all women begin to recognize the pitfalls of age passing. Separating the perspective of the barely passing older women from some of my concerns as one who no longer is able to pass has taken all my confidence and a great deal of hindsight. The mid-life woman feels increasing pressure—internal and external—about aging as well as the rejections of ageism. It is natural that she rushes forward to define the problem. In asserting her power over the insights of the older woman—the complaints, the accusations of ageism, the naming of the universal hatred of the old women, she unconsciously silences the inherent radicalism of the only one who can really tell her how it really is. (p. 56)

A first step toward a more positive and yet balanced view of age is for younger women to acknowledge that their fears of aging and their ambivalence toward aging women are but symptoms and consequences of their own masculinist thinking that denigrates the old. This is not to argue that these fears are always unrealistic. In contrast, the ability to see older women as contributors to the greater community encourages all women to view aging for its triumphs as well as its challenges. In turn, aging becomes a far from depressing subject. It is in this realization that younger women can begin to fight ageism on both individual and structural levels and begin the needed work toward building solidarity. In rejecting negative attitudes toward the aged, younger women actually help themselves by starting the process of planning and preparing for their own older years in a realistic fashion and by respecting themselves as aging women. Older women must fight against their own ageist ideas as well. The late Tish Sommers, co-founder of the Older Women's League, said it well when she argued that liberation will only come when [we as older women] "start to like ourselves and other older women" (1993, p. 429).

The fears about growing older that are prevalent in society get in the way of authenticity with age. Gloria Steinem, in *Moving Beyond Words* (1994), optimistically declared her thinking at age 60: "I found this newer state of being, refusing to take a back seat and insisting on pushing everything a little further. . . . A growing more radical with age" (p. 11). But she also discusses her worries over writing a chapter on "Doing 60"—would younger women even want to read it? It is not an unfair question. How many women, younger or older, have friends and colleagues whose age spans differ from their own by more than 10 years? What is needed, according to Letty Cottin Pogrebin's recent book *Getting Over Getting Older: An Intimate Journey* (1996), are more voices of older women to serve as role models, so that younger women can learn the potential and possibilities of age. To combat fears, there must be more talking between and among generations if we are serious about forging a better life for all women.

Another way to understand women's authenticity in later life is through their writing and documentation of their contributions and paths of resistance. Recall how Germaine Greer (1991) discusses authenticity in older women:

If we continue to see our own age through the eyes of observers much younger, we will find it impossible to understand the peculiar satisfaction of being older. If we can conquer our own lack of interest in ourselves and our kind, and turn to older women's writing about being older women, we will find stated again and again the theme of joy. (p. 383)

Fiction is another method to learn about older women. Author Barbara Frey Waxman (1990) coined the term "reifungsroman," or ripening, to refer to a new genre of fiction written primarily by older women about older women. According to Waxman, women's lives do not completely conform to male experiences and development as observed by male researchers, and so must be studied independently from men's lives. The reifungsroman, she describes, "rejects negative cultural stereotypes of the old woman and aging, seeking to change the society that created such stereotypes." Common themes found in this genre speak to women's authenticity in later life, their love for adventure and discovery, and their interest in developing new opportunities in relationships. They also

include themes of physical and psychic pain; loneliness, alienation from family and youthful society; self-doubt, feelings of uselessness; and grief over the loss of friends, mental acuity, and physical energy—there is, nevertheless, an opening up of life for many of these aging heroines as they literally take to the open road in search of themselves and new roles in life. (p. 16)

Rather than seeing aging as only decline, the reifungsroman writes of older women's inward journey to a greater understanding of their lives (Sarton, 1984). Waxman writes that older women

gradually come to terms with crucial decisions they made as youths; with past experiences, often sexual, that influenced their lives; and with their cultural roots. Then they try to chart a new course either into or through old age, which they embark on at the end of the work. Usually they have become revitalized, newly self-knowledgeable, self-confident, and independent before they move forward. If the protagonist of the reifungsroman dies at the end of the story, it is commonly after she has grown in a significant way. (p. 17)

And, finally, Greer eloquently elaborates on the ways in which aging can add a deepening understanding of authenticity and life's purpose with age. She speaks of women's spiritual journey with age, a journey that brings self-definition and authenticity.

The discontent of youth passes when you realize that the music you are hearing is not about you but itself. The important thing is not you listening to the music, but the self realizing form of the music itself. Then you can begin to understand the beauty is not be found in objects of desire but in those things that exist beyond desire, that can not be subordinated to any use that human beings can make of them. (1991, p. 377)

EMPOWERMENT, POLITICAL ACTIVISM, AND THE POTENTIALS OF AGE

Not all women come to terms with their increased life expectancy in ways that celebrate their aging. It is hard to be enthusiastic about age when one is hungry or frightened by society's indifference. A fear of aging makes it difficult to see aging as any thing but a calamity. The need for social justice and advocacy for those too tired to help themselves is a real task for women of all ages.

According to Tish Sommers (1993), the problem of older women is their isolation and lack of power:

> We know how to serve, now we must lead. We must recognize the strength and beauty of our own age group. We have been separated from each other by our dependency on men, and many of us because of ageism and sexism have avoided the company of older women. Polls show that older people hold the same negative opinion of their peers as the rest of the population. Yet older women like ourselves can provide us with great support in our later years. And if we are going to make changes on our own behalf and that of other older women, we must find each other. In the process we will discover our potential power. (p. 429)

As aging women begin to navigate the agescape, their own and the nation's, empowerment can be viewed as a major strategy for fighting ageism and other sites of oppression. Rather than deny aging, an empowered aging woman embraces the process, understanding that every stage in life has both problems and opportunities. The empowered older woman acknowledges the difficulties and challenges that can accompany age. As Greer so eloquently tells us, it is in these very challenges that difficulties must be faced and embraced for "the purpose of life is not to feel nothing" (p. 5). Hence, the resurgence of the very beautiful and emotionally powerful rituals organized by women that celebrate both old women and the aging process (see Fischer, 1995; Harrison, n.d.). To paraphrase Sommers, the problem is isolation, the solution empowerment. Combatting isolation requires that older women write about their life experiences and their experiences with their communities, and ensure their publication.

In this book, I argue for a more feminist definition of empowerment, one that equates the term with capacity, energy, and a belief in oneself. It includes being authentic to oneself, questioning society's assumptions that do not match with one's own, and recognizing and acknowledging the fact that society can present a hostile environment for older adults, especially aging women. An essential component, then, of empowerment is the need for advocacy for both personal and political strategies to address the reality of unjust social power. Empowered women accomplish this when they challenge society's assumptions about growing older as women. This can occur on the personal, spiritual, economic, and political levels. As increasing numbers of aging women join the ranks of the nation's poor, they can stop blaming themselves and feeling that their poverty is their unlucky lot in life. Instead, older women can begin to question the masculinization of wealth versus the feminization of poverty in this nation and around the world. In doing so, empowered thought can become political thinking and action on the local, state, and national legislative levels.

Empowerment also speaks to the potentials of age. Legal scholar Kimberle Crenshaw (1992) states that the empowerment of Black women is empowerment of the entire community. Likewise, so can the empowerment of older women have the potential to fight for gender justice and battle against other oppressions. Every woman knows that, notwithstanding an early death, she will grow older and be faced with a choice. She can fight the process of aging with all of her energies and resources, or she can use her energies for more constructive and broader purposes—for battles that are more worthy and winnable. Aging illustrates how women are all trapped by the current system. Therefore, it provides a strategy to resist and change it—if not for themselves, then for those who will come after them. In this way, aging can be viewed as generating a potential strategy to promote solidarity among women. Greer states that "we must not cast the old woman out but become her more abundantly" (p. 357). And Tish Sommers had this to say about the value and pride in being an older woman and the responsibility that comes with age:

> As older women, we have benefitted from the experience of the black movement, the women's movement, and the elder advocates. We reject the demeaning images of older women and the exclusion of older women from policy making for elders. We proudly claim our age and experience as demonstrating our right to live lives of dignity, activity, and involvement in our communities; decent health care and housing; an income sufficient to enjoy, rather than simply to endure, our later years; and the recognition that we are important members of society with much to contribute. (1993, p. 439)

Efforts taken toward building a socially just world can take place on many levels. Political activism is one method; poetry can be another. Sometimes, the two join forces. Dr. Ruth Harriet Jacobs' (1993) poem is a political act in its efforts to change society's view of aging women:

> Don't call me a young woman
> It is not a complement or courtesy but rather a
> grating discourtesy.
> Being old is a hard won achievement
> not something to be brushed aside
> treated as infirmity or ugliness
> or apologized away by "young women"
> I am an old old woman, a long lived woman
> I'm proud of it. I revel in it
> I wear my gray hair and wrinkles as bases of triumphant survival
> and I intend to grow much older . . .
> Don't call me a young woman
> You reveal your own fears of aging
> Maybe you'd better come learn from all of us wonderful old women
> How to take the sum of your life
> with all its experiences and knowledge and
> show how a fully developed life can know the joy of a past well done
> and the joy of the life left to live. (p. 5)[1]

Disputing the false compliment of being told she is a "young" woman, Jacobs challenges younger women to stop using their youth as the presumed referent point for aging women. She is proud of her years. It is not that Jacobs does not appreciate beauty in youth, but that she sees her own beauty and enjoys her own aging.

Documenting women's acts of resistance and refusal to buy into society's negative valuation of aging women can be political acts, lending themselves to collective identities and strategies with other women and men. In the political arena, rather than being thankful for the crumbs society throws her way, the empowered older woman yells "shame" to legislators and officials who seek to blame her for the nation's financial woes. She seeks out alternatives to spending energies on the latest "de-aging creme." Instead, she would rather take joy in being an "obnoxious" woman. In other words, she advocates, politicizes, and fights for justice

---

[1]From *Be An Outrageous Older Woman* (p. 5), by R. H. Jacobs, 1993, Manchester, CT: Knowledge, Ideas, and Trends. Copyright 1993 by R. H. Jacobs, PhD. Reprinted by permission.

for herself and for those who can not, because their own daily quest for survival saps their strength.

A good example in documenting the political strengths of older adults was the 1988 Medicare Catastrophic Health Care Act, repealed by Congress the following year after political fallout from some senior citizen groups. This Act would have provided additional health care coverage such as expanded acute care benefits and home care. However, it was opposed by higher income older adults because of a surtax to be paid by them, based on income (Hooyman & Kiyak, 1993). As is often the case, it was the voices of the more affluent who were heard. In contrast, a feminist age analysis understands that the voices of all women must be heard in these kinds of debates. But, regardless of whether or not one agreed with the outcome of this repeal, it was an example of what can happen when people are empowered to speak. Furthermore, empowerment calls for coalition-building between women and men and within and between age groups. Not entirely pessimistic, we see that laws and initiatives have the potential for improving women's lives across the life span. An example is the 1993 Family and Medical Leave Act. While elaborating on its limitations in chapter 7, we also note that it is a law that may well help both younger and older women, and that it was passed with primarily male votes.

This discussion on the potentials of age is not meant to engender a romanticized view of aging. Real-life worries exist about health and financial status, increasing dependencies, devalued physical appearances, and death. What a new epistemology of women and age seeks is a balanced view of aging. Women's subordination can be resisted by both personal and institutional change. Regardless of the strategy, however, a feminist age perspective acknowledges that change will not come about easily or quickly.

Women growing older tell us that new challenges, uncertainties, and opportunities come with age. The authors and contributors of *The New Older Woman* (Downes, Tuttle, Faul, & Mudd, 1995), for example, refer to this time of life as being members of the "bridge generation"—pioneers in the rediscovery of age. Regardless of one's age, we need to hear what older women have to say to themselves, to society, and to each other. What we learn is that, clearly, there is no one way to be. Some older women's lives, as we have discussed, are marked by a lifetime of difficulty. Others, like the Native American author Meridel LeSueur (1986), often exclaim joyously while in their 70's: "I am luminous with age" (p. 10). Still others find that age itself has minimal meaning; rather, other historical and cultural forces have taken precedence in self-definition and discovery, as Sarah and Elizabeth Delany humorously and warmly described their own aging in: *Having Our Say: The Delany Sisters' First 100 Years* (1993). Regardless of triumph or tribulation, aging women have much to share about their strategies for empowered survival. Their lessons are for all generations. Baba Copper (1986), for example, offers this sage viewpoint as a bridge to other generations and as a strategy for how to best prepare for their own aging as empowered women:

> But there are ways that all women can begin to prepare the way for the empowerment of themselves in the future, when they are old. The first step is for women to recognize that they have been programmed to hate old women and to deny them power. This brainwashing is so subtle that its eradication will take an effort equal to that which we have made and still must expend upon sexism. Further, this brainwashing extends down through our lives, making us fear the processes of our own bodies within time, so that our energies and attention are constantly undermined by ageist competition and self-doubts. These are attitudes and expectations that we can change now, if we decide to. Empowerment of women will come when we identify with women older than we are, not before. (p. 57)

The valuing of aging women's life contributions and experiences is in sharp contrast to the patriarchal devaluation of women. Increased documentation about older women, whether through studies, words, song, or other genres, results in making it easier to find positive comments about aging, and more particularly, aging women. Finding such subjugated knowledge is not easy in a society that more often that not negates aging women's contributions and ridicules their existence. Thus, we look to old women's voices as a corrective to begin a true re-examination of women's aging.

When Celia Hurwich (1982) interviewed older women for her study, she found 10 older women who contradicted the images of older women as frail and dependent. These women's lives were characterized by themes of aliveness, engagement in meaningful activity, nonconformity, adaptability, risk-taking, and a trust in themselves and their world. Their works were creative in the larger sense of expanding one's "being." Hurwich found her own work with these women exciting and liberating in that it could free younger women from their fears about growing older and becoming an older woman. There is much to learn from studies such as this one. Unfortunately, her San Francisco-area sample was composed of college-educated, White middle-class professional women who enjoyed greater social status, prestige, and a greater income throughout their lives compared to many other older women. Hurwich herself noted this bias, and recommended that future studies look at the diversities that exist among older women. To really hear older women's voices requires their documentation and legitimization in all shapes and colors.

CONCLUSIONS

An epistemology on women and age builds on both omissions and contributions of feminist and gerontology theories. As a start, it believes that the study of age must make women and women's diversity central to its analysis. We see how caregiving provides women with a different way of looking at their lives and of their world compared to men's. Women grasp the connective threads that exist between and among individual, family, and societal issues. Subsequently, caregiving is seen as a site of intersecting oppressions, rather than a site of only gender injustice. A new epistemology on women and aging acknowledges the interlocking nature of a lifetime of what are often multiple oppressions, the interconnections between ageism and all forms of oppression, the strengths and paths of resistance taken by women to fight inequalities, their value of authenticity, the need for political and social activism to make a difference, and the potentials of age. A new epistemology concedes that men's experiences have taken precedence over women's, and the young over the middle-aged and older woman. Therefore, rather than disavowing the fact that older women are and will remain the majority of the aged population, an epistemology of women and age advocates for a gender-focused approach to the study of age. Neither are the negative effects of ageism on both a personal and societal level ignored. But what I suggest is that women and older women's marginalization can help to develop a perspective and viewpoint that, more than educating society about gifts of age, can lead to efforts that build bridges toward solidarity with others, and offers a potentially more important role in helping to explore the illogic in masculinist thinking.

Recreating Visions for Older Women: Some Concluding Thoughts

Death is an inevitable outcome of life, but aging is a privilege.

—Germaine Greer

Some call it ecofeminism, some call it spiritual, some call it radical feminism but I call it possible.

—Bella Abzug

P
ublic policies reflecting demographic trends discussed throughout this book have tended to be meliorative in their strategies toward justice for women. In this concluding chapter, I attempt to look to the years ahead to suggest what the future may hold for the present cohort of older women and for younger women as they move through the life cycle. I will also suggest a number of additional thoughts to aid us in developing an epistemology of women and age and briefly summarize some of the major themes presented in earlier chapters.

TOWARD THE 21ST CENTURY

In the last 25 years, women have in fact experienced some notable successes through incremental changes in social policy. Changes in Social Security and pension vesting requirements have benefitted a number of women. Health care reforms, and to a more limited extent, long term care, remain on the nation's political agenda. It is more readily recognized that health care and long-term care should be rights of citizenship, although the form they take, along with their financing strategies, continues to be debated. An increasing number of women in the paid work force are earning their own retirement benefits, and there is an expanded awareness by feminists that advocacy efforts must acknowledge both the contributions and the needs of poor, working-class, and ethnic and minority women. On the political front, Judge Ruth Bader Ginsburg was selected for the United States Supreme Court, after a work history of representing the rights of women. The Family and Medical Leave Act of 1993 was passed, providing leave so that more working adults can retain their jobs when they must temporarily devote themselves to caring for a sick child or elder parent. A number of other laws—such as the Tax Reform Act of 1986—were enacted, which provide some protection for women in planning for their retirement years. More recently, Independent Retirement Accounts (IRAs) can be established by homemakers when the combined compensation of both spouses is at least equal to the total contribution. Previously, the amount that could be contributed by a nonworking spouse was only $250 annually. This change offers some hope that increasing numbers of older women can retire with pensions, savings, and dignity.

There is other good news. In the years after the debacle of the Anita Hill hearings, increasing numbers of women have entered politics, offering some hope for a more balanced view of women's voices. In the area of social welfare, the Administration on Aging's multimillion dollar Initiative on Older Women aims to increase government partnerships designed to address the specific needs and issues of older women, improve their capacity to contribute to society throughout their lives, and educate older women at the grassroots level about issues of import to them—income security, health, violence, housing, and caregiving. In the area of health research, the National Institute on Health has funded, through the Women's Initiative, the largest clinical and observational study to research health issues pertaining specifically to women. Moreover, it appears that society is slowly becoming more aware of the strengths of aging women as well as the challenges they face, in part due to the educational and political efforts of organizations such as the Older Women's League and the work of older women themselves. Still, the look toward the 21st century remains disheartening and lacking in prospects for fundamental change for women growing older. Many of women's problems—poor pay, poverty, violence, segregated employment, the "glass ceiling," discrimination—seem frustratingly intractable. Consequently, it is a challenge to be optimistic about the future of many young women as they move through the life span.

I say this for a number of reasons. First, the growth of the female-headed household is accelerating at an unprecedented rate, especially among young Black women (Ozawa, 1993). Many are single women, single mothers, and economically at risk. Low pay continues to make life difficult, and gender discrimination in employment, while illegal under the Equal Employment Act, is alive and well. Furthermore, many politicians and citizens alike believe that poor single women pose a serious threat to the nation's economy and to its moral fiber. Current and future erosions in the nation's safety net for poor, single, and working women are in some ways a response to this imagined threat (Ozawa & Kirk, 1996). Such changes will not increase women's chances for an economically viable old age.

Second, while women have made some advancements in entering the work force, 80% of women still occupy 5% of the nation's job categories of jobs (U.S. Bureau of the Census, 1990a, 1990b). The majority of working women are still employed in sex-segregated occupations, such as clerical, sales, and service (U.S. Department of Labor, 1991b). The move out of segregated employment is painstakingly slow, and, as discussed in chapter 7, retirement benefits continue to be built on wage-based formulas. For too many women, their low income in the paid work force is reproduced in their Social Security benefits. And, as has been elaborated on throughout this book, the majority of women continue to spend fewer years in the paid work force compared to men; change jobs more frequently; consistently earn less; and are more likely than men to work in part-time employment. Such work patterns are directly attributable to family responsibilities, discrimination, and limited educational opportunities. Ethnic and minority women, more apt to have work histories that resemble White men's, at least in years worked, face the additional burden of race discrimination on the job. Lesbian women still face social stigma and job discrimination from the heterosexual community. As we have seen, one result of these factors is that women are twice as likely to live in poverty than men throughout their lives.

Government reports on women's economic future are also pessimistic. A paper from the Women's Bureau, U.S. Department of Labor (1993), for example, provides this sobering "future" scenario on the status of a "typical" working woman who is presently aged 35 to 54 years:

> While her earnings place her above the poverty line, her chances of dropping below the poverty threshold increase dramatically should she become a female head of household. While fully insured by Social Security, she is not covered by an employer-financed pension or retirement. And, since she is employed in a traditionally female low-pay occupation, her Social Security payment will be woefully inadequate.

Third, the economic health of the nation will directly impact on the nation's willingness and ability to support entitlement and other programs for the aged (Torres-Gil, 1992). Indeed, it is only through a strong economy that the economic needs of older adults can be sustained, their health care needs met, and the burdens of caregiving alleviated. According to Fernando Torres-Gil (1992), three trends are influencing change in the United States: longevity, diversity, and the global economy. As he further explains:

> In the 21st century, demographics and aging will be just two of several forces shaping our lives and influencing our adjustment to the new aging. Events occurring overseas or across borders affect demographic and social trends. . . . Geopolitical and military actions will help or hinder our response to domestic matters. . . . History shows that in times of economic recession and depression, populations are less willing to assist others through the pubic sector. Advocates for the poor and disadvantaged have as much as stake in international trade and economics as do business and labor. (p. 166)

Fourth, the decline in manufacturing jobs and deindustrialization has led to the increasing use of part-time workers and leased employees for both men and women (Zinn, 1990). Such workers usually have no benefits, and 70% of all part-time workers in this country are women (whether by choice or through lack of an alternative). With deindustrialization comes downsizing, and age discrimination begins earlier for women than for men. The result is that women and minorities generally lose their jobs before White men.

Fifth, the business community, with some exceptions, has not taken a significant leadership role in promoting family-friendly options such as day care, elder care benefits, and family leave (Tennstedt & Gonyea, 1994; Trzcinski, 1994). According to data from the U.S. Department of Labor (1994), only 5% of all full-time employees in medium and large establishments have access to child care benefits; 10% have flexible benefit plans; 2% have paid maternity leave; and only 1% have paid paternity leave. In small establishments, the percentages are even smaller (United States Department of Labor, 1991a). Although companies like Eli Lilly deserve accolades for their family-friendly policies, projections that business will embrace expansive caregiving benefit packages that run across the life span and offer more than a referral service still remain to be fully realized.

Sixth, minority populations are projected to represent 25% of the older population by the year 2020, up from 13% in 1990 (AARP, 1993). The nation's race and class tensions continue to be problematic, with the passage of more punitive policies toward immigrants and the poor, the attack on affirmative action programs, and the escalating violence directed against non-White segments of society. It is not at all clear if social and economic resolutions between the classes, races, and generations will evolve in a positive direction. What is true is that the minority population in general, and women of color in particular, continue to occupy the lowest rings on the occupational ladder, and that the combination of the effects of racism, sexism, and eventually ageism leaves older women of color the poorest of the poor among the aged cohort. As suggested by Torres-Gil (1992), the nation's changing demographic face can lead to different scenarios:

> Economic disparity, disenfranchised youth, the changing workforce, ethnic diversity, and the need to rebuild America will be improved or worsened by our response to longevity, diversity, and generational claims. Diversity might, for example, cause us to recognize the basic needs of all, or might simply create more interest group competition for scarce public resources. Longevity might provide us a productive older population or create a drag on the national economy. Generational claims can lead to alliances or conflict between age groups. (p. 168)

Seventh, the ever-widening gap between the rich and the poor is perhaps one of the nations' more critical challenges. It is true that some are doing quite well in the present economy. Corporate profits rose dramatically in the 1980s and 1990s, from $526.9 billion in the fall of 1993 to $609.6 billion in the summer of 1995 (Hoechstetter, 1996). During this period, the executives of major corporations received unprecedented pay and benefit increases. At the same time, workers' wages dropped and companies downsized. Unfortunately, women and ethnic minorities have not been at the receiving end of this skewed bounty. A woman poor in her younger years, a woman getting no child support from the father to raise her children, a woman working in the "pink ghetto," a professional woman not earning job parity with her male counterparts—each of these will have a lower income and thus a lower retirement income compared to an older man. Where is society's will and commitment to ensure a better way of life for women?

Finally, the process of devolution, whereby the federal government limits its funding and leadership role in public policy and programs, has begun. The most vulnerable will be hit the most, at least until the baby boomers begin to retire and find services for them and their families inadequate. One hopes that they will advocate for a more responsive government. Devolution may provide some additional flexibility in the delivery of services but may also result in decreased funds for services. According to Jeanette Takamura, Assistant Secretary of Aging, Department of Health and Human Services, cited in *Aging Today* (American

Association on Aging, 1996b), the federal funding gap, together with states' desires to maintain the present state of funding, may lead to fewer resources for long term care. One result may be decreased funds for community-based services and nursing homes, exacerbated by inflationary effects. Since Medicaid funds not only elders but single parents, children, and the disabled, there may be intergenerational conflict fanned by devolutionists who will see this discussion as an opportunity to disguise the real problem—the absence of a noncategorical long term care program, along with the lack of a solid funding base for long term care services. Problems will continue, Takamura predicts, until society can come to terms with the undeniable need for reliable support for the frail and their families.

In contrast to present policy directions, and given women's greater longevity and present and future needs, a feminist age analysis advocates for women's voices to lead the way in policy and social welfare discussions. But, as a population that has historically been politically oppressed, will their voices be heard?

Nonetheless, there may be reasons for cautious optimism about older women's future. Feminist writings have helped us to more clearly understand the status of women in an inequitable and patriarchal society. The increased political roles of women offer another ray of hope. Technology may offer some assistance with changing and more flexible work schedules, assistance with caregiving, and more effective and accessible healthcare. Current societal trends, as noted by Abu-Laban (1981), suggest some promise for improvement in the lives of older women. Among these trends are increased access to prestige and status based not on physical attractiveness but on competence and desirability in the work force. Furthermore, women are beginning to prepare more for widowhood and singlehood. There is greater equalization of partner survivorship and new options for relationships, including those with other women, whether in close and long term friendships, lesbian relationships, or other preferred forms of relationships. Additionally, childlessness is an increasingly acceptable option and choice for women. On the down side, Abu-Laban points out that children may be less of a support, since there will be fewer of them. For childless women, there may be higher rates of institutionalization and fewer alternatives for receiving care in their own homes.

The major reason for optimism about older women, however, is due to groundbreaking work by older women themselves. As we have seen, today's older woman has both similarities and dissimilarities with those who came before her historically with respect to gender-role assignments, education, experience with discrimination, work history, and other factors. Aging women, demanding corrections to ageist and sexist myths, are insisting that their voices be heard and respected rather than ignored or patronized. What is also encouraging is that a growing number of policymakers, gerontologists, researchers, and social welfare advocates and professionals have adopted feminist themes in their practice aimed at improving not only women's and men's lives but in broadening the definition of citizenship in society (see Abramowitz, 1992; B. G. Collins, 1986; L. V. Davis, 1994; K. H. Gould, 1989; Hooyman & Gonyea, 1995; Morris, 1993; Laird, 1995; Van Den Bergh, 1995).

In the end, thoughts toward an epistemology of women and age were suggested that offered some tentative directions for rethinking our knowledge about older women, and for reconceptualizing the relationship between older women and social welfare. We introduce here to this beginning dialogue on women's aging three additional themes: (1) what it means to thrive as an older woman; (2) the naming of new political realities and strategies; and (3) the adoption of new genres of research and learning.

FROM SURVIVOR TO THRIVER

In earlier chapters, we discussed how age can add to the burden of women's oppression in a culture that glorifies youth as a major source of women's power. One counter-strategy is to examine older women's multiple oppressions in order to eliminate them and move society toward a utopian future without the stigma of old-age—deBeauvoir's "ageless society." A new vision of older women by women differs from that offered by the established social order. Older women speaking from their own feminist standpoint can fight the image of older women as "the other," and they can do this by recognizing the value in telling their own stories. Giving voice to life stories can bring a recognition of both contributions and strategies for resisting oppression across their lives. The authors from the Hen Co-op (1993), for example, found that this experience of sharing their stories activated their political side, helped to build community, supported them in risking change, and empowered their self-worth. By regaining their voices and history, women seek and share common experiences, and in this way, linkages to other women can be found. Similar to the way in which Black feminism declares the visibility of Black women and asserts self-determination as essential for empowerment, older women are declaring their visibility. As the concept of older women becomes more strong and positive, the possibility for a just world for women as they age can more readily be seen. In doing so, ageism for both women and men is combatted.

In seeking out older women's vision, it is easy to become enormously excited about the work that is already occurring in this area, much of it published in the past 5 years. Examples of this perspective, to mention only a few, include Marilyn Bell, *Women as Elders: Images, Visions, and Issues* (1987); Janet Chandler, *Why Flowers Bloom* (1993); Sarah L. Delany and A. Elizabeth Delany, *Having Our Say: The Delany Sisters' First 100 Years* (1993); Peggy Downes, Ilene Tuttle, Patricia Faul, and Virginia Mudd, *The New Older Woman* (1996); Colette Dowling, *Red Hot Mamas: Women Coming into Their Own at 50* (1996); Betty Friedan, *The Fountain of Age* (1993); Germaine Greer, *The Change: Women, Aging, and Menopause* (1991); The Hen Co-Op, *Growing Old Disgracefully: New Ideas for Getting the Most Out of Life* (1993), and *Disgracefully Yours: More New Ideas for Getting the Most Out of Life* (1996); Ruth Harriet Jacobs, *Be an Outrageous Older Woman: A R.A.S.P.* (1993); Sandra Haleman Martz, *When I Am an Old Woman, I Will Wear Purple* (1987) and *Grow Old Along with Me—The Best Is Yet to Be* (1996); Florida Maxwell's *The Measure of My Days* (1968); Letty Cottin Pogrebin, *Getting over getting Older* (1996); Catherine Rountree, *On Women Turning 60* (1997); Ruth Raymond Thone, *Women and Aging: Celebrating Ourselves* (1992); Barbara Frey Waxman, *From the Hearth to the Open Road: A Feminist Study of Aging in Contemporary Literature* (1990); and Frances Weaver, *The Girls with Grandmother Faces: A Celebration of Life's Potential for Those Over 55* (1996). As these authors detail what aging means to women as they grow old, their words become both celebratory acts of age as well as acts of political resistance against ageism, sexism, and other oppressions.

EMBRACING NEW POLITICAL REALITIES AND SOLIDARITY

For numerous reasons discussed throughout this book, feminist methodology adopts the belief that women's lives are not equal to men's (Hartmann, 1981; Hartsock,1985; MacKinnon, 1989). Women's problems are recognized as a result of a patriarchal and capitalistic system. The acknowledgment that state power is male power, including motherhood and all other institutions, helps us to better see the ramifications of social inequality on women's lives throughout the life cycle. As argued by Quadagno and Meyer (1990) and others (Abramowitz, 1992; Hooyman & Gonyea, 1995; Moon, 1990; Ozawa, 1993) gender inequality in later life is a function of market-derived inequities that accumulate during work years, the eligibility rules that determine benefits and penalize women, and the effects of a lifetime of racism, classism, homophobism and other sites of oppression. Therefore, there is a need for political and structural change.

The need for political activism has perhaps never been as strong as it is today. America's changing welfare policies and entitlement programs are under attack, and in fact some have crumbled. The attacks are not only directed against older adults and older women but the poor, many of whom are women, children, and the disabled. Primary among these problems is the nation's lack of moral commitment to care for the needy regardless of age. To date, the success of feminist, gerontological, and social welfare advocates in putting a halt to these so-called "reform" strategies has been questionable.

And yet, the fight to guarantee and protect entitlements and programs for the poor and needy must remain a worthwhile challenge. To this end, a strong political base is necessary to ensure people's rights are protected. Such a base will require new notions of solidarity among the disenfranchised as well as more powerful groups. Wishing that the political Zeitgeist will change and that such "welfare reform" will not happen will not make it so. Rather, aging women have an active role to play in this new political movement. What aging women tell us in their own writings is that many older women seek an expanded role in the political process because they are attuned to the interlocking and multiple nature of injustice; because of their awareness of diversity; because of their understanding of the life cycle; and because of their desired connections and continuity with the next generation.

In thinking about social welfare's responsibilities to the aged, a number of questions must be raised again. As examples, we can revisit how the most needy of the aged, primarily women, might be targeted with universal entitlement programs. A new political energy could be directed at asking why older women remain the most at-risk population for poverty, and why retirement benefits are so often tied to one's marital status. An understanding of the relationship between these factors allows the reader to dispute recent articles on women's poverty that blame their inadequate income in later life as a result of "fear of financial planning" or "an inadequate savings plan" as opposed to a lifetime of an inadequate income, which is itself a result of segregated employment, discriminatory wages, unfair divorce laws and eligibility rules for pensions, and ineffective, nonexistent, and at times punitive family polices. The conservative backlash, the economic times in which we live, the fiction of widespread intergenerational friction being fed almost to a frenzy by the media, and the consequences of these factors on the well-being of women of all ages are not lost to empowered older women. Understood is that political activism is a necessary tool that must counter the myths that incorrectly present a false image of older women to society. What is also appreciated, however, is that not all older women have the awareness and energy to enter the fight.

Multiple layers of difference and oppression illuminate the especially difficult time that working-class women, women of color, and homeless women experience as a result of gender, class, and race discrimination. From this awareness, feminist theories can acknowledge their exclusion in their literature, and the omission of discussions on older women as well. In doing so, it is more likely that a new feminist agenda can move women toward an uncharted solidarity based on the ending of women's oppression. Clearly, not to see ageism or racism when one sees sexism is a moral inconsistency. In truth, feminism will not reach its potential as long as it is exclusionary (A. Davis, 1990). As hooks (1984) so eloquently argues: "There can be no mass-based feminist movement to end sexist oppression without a united front—women must take the initiative and demonstrate the power of solidarity. Unless we can show that barriers separating women can be eliminated, that solidarity can exist, we cannot hope to change and transform society as a whole" (p. 44).

Others agree, arguing that all oppressions, not just ageism, must be stopped. The late Maggie Kuhn (1980) insightfully acknowledged how the political consciousness of older adults could result in increased solidarity among peoples: "If we can open up new life styles that enable us to function with power and authority and influence, then we are working for the survival of society as a whole" (pp. 225–226). She asked elders to rethink the economic structures that prevent them from continuing to work, suggested that they try more communal living, and encouraged residents of retirement villages and old age homes to become involved as voting members of these institutions, making policy and monitoring the performance of staff. Holstein (1992) offers another vision for aging women—as leaders and as social critics, based on their diverse and lifelong experiences. In the end, women's lives can serve to document not only their joys and accomplishments, but their unjust treatment. Their experiences and world views can act to restructure society to one that is more welcoming and accepting of diversity in all its shapes and forms.

NEW GENRES OF LEARNING

This commitment to recreate new visions of older women requires ingenuity and varied methodologies. Although the study of older women has greatly increased over the past 10 years, there is still a great deal we do not know about gender and age. We have suggested throughout this book that older women are a not a problem to society; rather, society can be a problem to older women. I submit that to learn more about aging women, a series of alternate methodological approaches, and the use of other forms of literature, including the incorporation of poetry, autobiographies, personal memoirs, journals, conference proceedings, and fantasy be used to document older women's strengths as well as their tribulations. These new forms of knowledge, as suggested by Lorde (1984) and others (P. H. Collins, 1989, 1991; hooks, 1984) can perhaps lead to a new vision of theorizing, policy formulation, and practice. Books briefly profiled in this book, and written by women of color and older women, have greatly strengthened our abilities to listen, to critique, and to understand the present order.

In chapter 9, we examined a new genre referred to as the reifungsroman, written by and about aging women, that attempts to educate and dispel other myths about aging women. In this genre, old age for women is a "time of discovery, liberation, and adventure, offering women an opportunity to form new ties, not just to reinforce old ones" (Waxman, 1990). Works such as Waxman's can end up weakening the well-recognized polarities between the young and the old. Women are hungry, she found, for a literary connection that allows them to connect with older women. In contrast to a focus on deterioration with age, this genre encourages a rethinking of the experience of aging, in both its glory and pain, but which has been especially burdensome for women. A rethinking of standpoints holds both a personal and political focus. As we look at older women's thinking and behaviors, an individualistic view of age is left behind as we instead gravitate toward a more collectivist one.

Strategies that help to learn more about older women are expanded to include more accessible writings such as poems, plays, journals, and short stories. Varied and alternate approaches also acknowledge the difficulties older women face in publishing their work. Not all of the society is interested in older women reclaiming their voices and silences. Leah Cohen, author of the realistic book *Small Expectations: Society's Betrayal of Older Women* (1984), for example, found that prospective publishers did not want to publish her book without "a happy ending." And, in the introduction to *The New Older Woman: A Dialogue for the Coming Century*, Downes and her coauthors (1996) note how the publishers and editors of major West Coast newspapers did not feel there would be sufficient interest in even a news article on aging women. One editor sent them this note: "No use for older women—even those who are new." A note from another simply said: "We'll pass" (p. xviii). Fortunately, these authors persevered because they refused to accept being ignored and patronized. Their journey, as our own, continues.

AN EPISTEMOLOGY OF WOMEN AND AGE

From these and other themes discussed throughout this book, I have offered a number of tentative directions to move us toward an epistemology of women and age. Such a charge requires a feminist standpoint—to see women's collective reality, one must know women's point of view. Acknowledging that "woman" begins with a small "w," we seek out and hear women's varied stories.

A feminist life-span perspective on aging was offered as a framework to explore women's oppressions, differences, and abilities, and to provide a way in which to analyze old age from the experiences of women. It transcends the chronological limitations imposed on women and the aged in the public and private spheres through a male epistemology. Ideas from this perspective make visible the view that age is a continuum, rather than a mechanism to separate or pit one generation against another. With its focus on the life cycle of women's oppression, we are critical of any policy, program, or law that does not address the social and economic realities of diverse women of any age in light of the nation's ills. Therefore, we advocate for women's equality in their younger years in decent jobs and wages, child support, housing, and adequate government transfer programs (Mulroy, 1995; Ozawa, 1993). We also acknowledge that women's later years are characterized by more dependency on public policy than are men's, and that public policy changes to limit benefits will affect women disproportionately.

Integrating additional ideas from feminist and gerontological theories, a feminist life-span perspective on age focuses on the following elements. In taking a life-span approach, we acknowledge that women's lives are characterized by both varying degrees and intensities of advantage and disadvantage across their lives that differ by historical forces, personal biography, race and ethnicity, class, and numerous other factors. We know that a picture of older women that ignores the multiple determinants of their oppressions and their multiple strengths is incomplete. We re-examine the relationships between gender, age, and power and uncover the negative stereotypes that are directed at women. In acknowledging the power differentials between the sexes, and the role of the state in setting forth such differences, structural and political change is recognized as paramount. At the same time, we note some of the problems with how power and empowerment are conceptualized, and look to older women's voices to give us a new direction.

Not content to only acknowledge difference and diversity, we actively seek out the multiple differences that exist among women, as well as their commonalities in various genres and alternate research methodologies. Searching for women's history through their own experiences, voices, and silences allows us to hear the needs of older women whom the male viewpoint finds especially problematic—the never-married woman, the older lesbian, the working-class older woman, the older women of color, the homeless older women, and the disabled. The potential for solidarity is examined. Borrowing from feminist theory, we oppose the binary and hierarchical approach that characterizes so much of Western thinking and instead look to linkages between and among women, between women and men, between the young and the old, between and among varied personal and political issues, and between women and society. Taking a more ecological view, we also look at the relationships among numerous and various factors to women's financial and health status, caregiving responsibilities, and social lives throughout their life span that culminate in a disadvantaged old age for too many women.

The ideas from this framework lead to a feminist age analysis. This analysis scrutinizes, evaluates, and exposes contradictions in the effectiveness of public and private policies in defining, shaping, and addressing the needs and concerns of aging women. As we discussed earlier, a feminist age analysis does not see older women as a problem for society; rather, it more accurately views society as a potential problem to older women. It questions the basic premises that underlie policies and is concerned with not only the rights of aging women but with justice for other oppressed populations. If justice means, as Kirp, Yodof, and Franks (1986) argue in their book, *Gender Justice*, enhancing choices for individuals and securing a focus on process rather than on particular outcomes, then a feminist age analysis questions, in contrast, if meaningful choices can be made within a patriarchal capitalistic society.

As a beginning, this perspective supports some of the liberal strategies of improving all women's access to careers, decent wages, education, and other opportunities that foster independence. But we move further and look toward a transformation in how gender and age are conceptualized. An epistemology of gender and age recognizes that women's problem is, as MacKinnon has said (1989, 1990), one of inequality, not difference, and that this will not change as long as a male epistemological stance is accepted.

Thus, a feminist age analysis advocates for justice for women of all ages, understanding that progress will not occur without a struggle and without solidarity with women and other marginalized persons, ultimately with the intention of creating a good life for all people, regardless of gender, ethnicity, and age. In the end, we understand that the well-being of older women depends not only on the quality of jobs available to them in their earlier years and whether or not they are given credit for staying home (or at least not penalized for providing such care in their public and private pensions), but an end to the division of labor and discriminatory work and pension policies and practices based on gender, age, race, class, sexual identity, and other factors. We call for an end to not only ageism, but all forms of oppression.

We listen critically and with some anxiety, therefore, to the present debate and discussions on entitlement programs that connects the funding of these programs to the nation's deficit. Some changes may be necessary for its solvency (Moon & Mulvey, 1996) and yet a gender-neutral approach to the discussion ignores specific economic issues faced by women and their linkages to women's health, caregiving, and social status. Accordingly, the dangers in the argument for making Social Security a means-tested program are more readily understood, for such a change will erode middle-class support for the program and result in making it more vulnerable to political and economic forces and changes (Skocpol, 1995). Such a change would impact on women and disadvantaged minorities more than on White men. Ironically, it will also impact negatively even upon these men, as they will find that the costs cannot be obliterated and shifted away. Furthermore, a feminist age analysis that realizes that both men's and women's lives are shaped, for good and bad, by social structure can increase linkages between the sexes with the understanding that both have unfair burdens placed on them. With its focus on diversity, we see racial oppression in society and among feminists—with an aim away from race-blind theoretical formulations (Dressel, 1988) and toward social justice by structurally addressing the roots of all oppressions (Abramowitz, 1992). Acknowledgment of the multiple experiences of women is central because it negates the portrayal of the aged as only a prosperous population. But, as stated throughout this book, neither does it portray all older women as victims.

Feminists often advocate for ameliorative strategies because they appear more feasible and palatable than radical ones, but will they be successful? In *Women on the Front Lines: Meeting the Challenges of Aging America* (1993), Allen and Pifer articulate the challenge as one of creating new policy initiatives that generally empower and integrate older women in our aging society. While one hopes that reform and integrationist strategies will address the needs of women, serious risks exist in asking a government insensitive to the needs of women to remedy the situation. On the other hand, it is essential that women become more involved in the social welfare policy arena, as outdated models of service and assumptions based on today's older population will not suffice (Silverstone, 1996). Instead, new approaches must be proposed to address the needs of the aged and other needy citizens. But, if history is a guide, these new ideas will not give much relief to aging women without their political activism.

This book examined four areas of concern for aging women—income, caregiving, health, and their social lives. A feminist age analysis recognizes women's lives across the life span reflect domination and inequality, and, on the other hand, achievement and possibility. It questions the basic premises that underlie public and private policies, and is concerned with not only the rights of aged women, but the rights of the poor and other populations. Furthermore, it seeks empowerment and solidarity as two strategies to end such separations by age. A feminist age analysis, assisting us to view older women's lives more accurately and clearly, leads to these tentative ideas for a new epistemology on women and age.

This attempt at a new epistemology of women and age underscores the importance of studying older women as critical for advancing gerontological and feminist theories so these theories may speak for older women and advance our understanding of age. It sees a lifetime of oppressions, usually multiple and interlocking, that culminate into disadvantage in aging women's lives. Additionally acknowledged is the difficult time ageism brings to older women and men. However, it also suggests that ageism can be used as a tool to understand gender and power relations more clearly. Ageism can also assist women and men in their understanding of oppressions as interlocking and connecting, rather than as disparate entities. Caregiving was recognized not only as a central theme in women's lives, but as a site where oppressions intersect with one another. While specific gender roles such as mother and grandparent can and often do bring great satisfaction and joy, an epistemology of women and age is keenly aware that such roles present injustices to both women and men, but more so women, whether they are wives, mothers, daughters, paid, low-paid, and not-paid caregivers, grandmothers, or volunteers. Importantly, it questions the male paradigm and masculinist narrative that women's place and worth exist only when she serves the patriarchal family as caregiver. The need for a feminist age theory was discussed. Authenticity was offered as an additional and alternative method for older women to achieve power. Ideas around empowerment, solidarity, and the potentials of age were suggested that may benefit not only older women but other marginalized populations. In the end, a new epistemology of women and age aims to form more realistic and respectful visions of aging women, expose some of society's narratives on other oppressed populations, find sites where oppressions converge, and highlight the potential that empowerment, authenticity, and solidarity hold for women with age. Although not denying the fact that ageism is a negative force, we instead choose to focus on women's strengths and the opportunities that can present themselves as a result of age in the dismantling of patriarchal thought and action.

Subsequently, these thoughts for an epistemology of women and age do not focus, as we stated earlier, on a "forever young" philosophy. Instead, age is viewed as a natural process, with its own lessons to be learned. It is health, vibrancy, connection to more than the self, respect from others, and aliveness that are desired, not necessarily youth. Women's issues such as financial security and health are essential to understand, not as different from those of men, but as an important field of study that can promote women's well-being. After all, it is through research that policies and practices can become more responsive to the varied needs of women. As Ray (1996) suggests, a goal for a feminist-oriented gerontology should be the liberation of all elders, especially women. In acknowledging the limited energies most people face in their daily struggles, we insist that older women's liberation not be at the expense of other marginalized persons.

Specifically, we offered a number of beginning questions toward a new epistemology of women and age. Rather than ask if employment policies can be made more responsive to the needs of women as caregivers, we can ask why the family is the responsibility of women. How can caregiving be incorporated into public policy without discrediting it? An epistemology of women and age redefines the definition of citizenship to conceptualize caregiving and work as both family and societal responsibilities, and to value both economically and in other ways the contributions of both caregiving and work to the family and the market. Thus, we advocate for the development of policies that address these issues from a perspective that recognizes caregiving as an economic, work, and as a community concern. Other questions are posed. For example, why do women have a better chance of receiving adequate benefits if their work history is similar to a man's, and how should this be changed? Given that the average marriage lasts only 7 years, should marriage continue to be an eligibility factor for pensions? Can we redefine health and well-being? Can we make women's health needs throughout their life span a priority research agenda? In truth, a new epistemology advocates for a reshaping of knowledge for and by aging women. Such an epistemology has yet to be fully articulated by older women themselves. Nonetheless, we take these early steps to seek answers to new questions about gender and power relationships that are embedded in our social, cultural, and political fabric.

In earlier chapters, we elaborated on the fact that women's worth, based on the family ethic and further influenced by racism, classism, and heterosexism, has serious consequences to their income and health status, caregiving roles, and social lives. Although some women may have benefitted from patriarchal society, most do not. Even those who have benefitted economically rarely find that these benefits continue with age. Not lost are Celia Hurwich's words, "I have never felt so free. Old age is the best time in life" (1982, p. 159). As numerous authors have written, the potentials of age are exciting. Age can be the greatest adventure. But we also recognize that these statements are not necessarily true for many older women, especially the old-old, working-class, minority women, and the never-married. When we examine the lives of older women more closely, the roots of their oppressions become more clear, and so should society's resolve to correct inequalities via personal and structural change. Growing old can be an opportunity, for the lives of aging women can offer a standpoint in which to critique gender, power, and age throughout the life cycle. Ageism, then, can move us toward authenticity in old age as we learn more about other peoples and injustice, oppressions, and, ultimately, more about ourselves. We are no longer indifferent to other people's pains or our own. In the end, the real gift of age may be in the opportunity it provides to work to end inequality via personal growth, coalition-building, and solidarity efforts for political change.

References

Abbott, P., & Wallace, C. (1992). *The family and the new right*. Boulder, CO: Pluto Press.

Abel, E. K. (1987). *Love is not enough: Family care of the frail elderly*. Washington, DC: American Public Health Association.

Abramowitz, M. (1992). *Regulating the lives of women: Social welfare policy from colonial times to the present*. Boston: South End Press.

Abu-Laban, S. M. (1981). Women and aging: A Futurist perspective. *Psychology of Women Quarterly, 6,* 85–97.

Abzug, B. (1996, October 27). Cited in "NOW celebrates activism with election year flair." *National Times*, p. 2.

Ackelsberg, M., & Diamond, R. (1987). Gender and political life: New directions in political science. In B. B. Hess & M. M. Ferree (Eds.), *Analyzing gender: A handbook of social science research* (pp. 504–525). Newbury Park, CA: Sage.

Alaska, K. (1994). *Income among older Americans in 1992*. Washington, DC: American Association of Retired Persons.

Allen, J. (1993a). Caring, work and gender equity in an aging society. In J. Allen & A. Pifer (Eds.), *Women on the front lines: Meeting the challenges of an aging America* (pp. 221–240). Washington, DC: The Urban Press.

Allen, J. (1993b). The front lines. In J. Allen & A. Pifer (Eds.), *Women on the front lines: Meeting the challenges of an aging America* (pp. 1–10). Washington, DC: The Urban Press.

Allen, J., & Pifer, A. (Eds.). (1993). *Women on the front lines: Meeting the challenges of aging America*. Washington, DC: Urban Press.

American Association of Retired Persons. (AARP). (1993). *A profile of older Americans, 1992*. Washington, DC: Author.

American Association of Retired Persons. (1994). *Facts about older women: Income and poverty*. Washington, DC: Author.

American Association of Retired Persons. (1996a). *A profile of older Americans: 1995*. Washington, DC: Author.

American Association of Retired Persons. (1996b). *Virtually invisible: The image of midlife and older women in prime time TV*. Washington, DC: Author.

American Medical Association, Council on Ethical and Judicial Affairs. (1990). Gender disparities in clinical decision making. *Journal of the American Medical Association, 266*, 559–562.

American Society on Aging. (1996a). How long can you live? Aging in the 21st century. *Aging Today, 17*, 5, 14.

American Society on Aging. (1996b). Two futures of aging: The entitlement debate. *Aging Today, 17*, 3, 5–6.

Amott, T., & Matthaei, J. (1991). *Race, gender, and work: A multicultural economic history of women in the United States*. Montreal: Black Rose Books.

Anderson, M. L. (1988). *Thinking about women*. New York: Macmillan.

Anderson, M. L., & Collins, P. H. (Eds.). (1992). *Race, class, and gender: An anthology*. Belmont, CA: Wadsworth.

Antonucci, T. (1994). A lifespan view of women's social relations. In B. Turner & L. Troll (Eds.), *Women growing older: Psychological perspectives* (pp. 239–269). Newbury Park, CA: Sage.

Anzaldua, G. (1981). La Prieta. In C. Moraga & G. Anzaldua (Eds.), *This bridge called my back: Writings by radical women of color* (2nd ed.) (pp. 198–209). Watertown, MA: Persephone.

Arendell, T., & Estes, C. L. (1987). Unsettled future: Older women, economics, and health. *Feminist Studies, 7*, 3–24.

Arendell, T., & Estes, C. (1991). Older women in the post-reason era. In M. Minkler & C. Estes (Eds.), *Critical perspectives on aging: The political and moral economy of growing old* (pp. 202–226). Amityville, NY: Baywood.

Arendt, H. (1958). *The human condition*. Chicago: University of Chicago Press.

Armitage, K. (1979). Responses of physicians to medical complaints in men and women. *Journal of the American Medical Association, 242*, 2186–2187.

Aronson, J., & Neysmith, S. M. (1996). "You're not just in there to do the work": Depersonalizing policies and the exploitation of home care workers' labor. *Gender and Society, 10*, 59–77.

Asian Women United of California. (Eds.). (1989). *Making waves: An anthology of writings by and about Asian American women*. Boston: Beacon Press.

Atkinson, T. G. (1974). *Amazon odyssey*. New York: Links.

Awaiakta, M. (1988). Amazons in Appalachia. In B. Brant (Ed.), *A gathering of spirit* (pp. 125–130). Ithica, NY: Firebrand.

Axinn, J. (1989). Women and aging: Issues of adequacy and equity. In J. D. Garner & S. O. Mercer (Eds.), *Women as they age: Challenges, opportunities, and triumphs* (pp. 339–362). New York: Haworth.

Bailey, W. T., Harrell, D. R., & Anderson, L. E. (1993). The image of middle-aged and older women in magazine advertisements. *Educational Gerontology, 19*, 97–104.

Baines, C., Evans, P., & Neysmith, S. (1992). Confronting women's caring: Challenges for practice and policy. *Affilia, 7*, 21–44.

Bandler, J. T. D. (1989). Family protection and women's issues in Social Security. *Social Work, 34*, 307–311.

Baron, A. (1987). Feminist legal strategies: The power of difference. In B. B. Hess & M. Ferree (Eds.), *Analyzing gender: A handbook of social science research* (pp. 474–503). Newbury Park, CA: Sage.

Baruch, G., Barnette, R., & Rivers, C. (1983). *Lifeprints: New patterns of love and work for today's woman*. New York: McGraw-Hill.

Barusch, A. S. (1994). *Older women in poverty: Private lives and public policies*. New York: Springer Publishing Co.

Barusch, A. S. (1995). Programming for family care of elderly dependents: Mandates, incentives, and service rationing. *Social Work, 40*, 315–322.

Bell, M. J. (Ed.). (1987). *Women as elders: Images, visions, and issues*. New York: Haworth.

Bell, M. R., Berger, P. B., Holmes, D. R., Jr., Mulvaney, C. J., Bailey, K. R., & Gersh, B. J. (1995). Referral for coronary revascularization procedures after diagnostic coronary angiography: Evidence of gender bias? *Journal of the American College of Cardiologists, 25*, 1650–1655.

Bell, M. R., Gill, D. E., Garratti, K. N., Berger, P. B., Gersh, B. J., & Homes, D. R., Jr. (1995). Long-term outcome of women compared with men after successful coronary angiography. *Circulation, 91*, 2876–2881.

Berkman, L., & Syme, S. L. (1979). Social networks, host resistance, and mortality: A nine-year follow-up study of Alameda County residents. *Journal of Epidemiology, 109*, 186–204.

Berman, P. W., O'Nan, B. A., & Floyd, W. (1981). The double standard of aging and the social siltation: Judgments of attractiveness of the middle-aged woman. *Sex Roles, 7*, 87–95.

Bhaskaran, S. (1993). Physical subjectivity and the risk of essentialism. In Women of South Asian Descent Collective (Eds.), *Our feet walk the sky: Women of the South Asian diaspora* (pp. 191–202). San Francisco: Aunt Lute Books.

Birren, J. (1985). Age, competence, creativity, and wisdom. In R. Butler & H. Gleason (Eds.), *Productive aging: Enhancing vitality in later life* (pp. 29–36). New York: Springer Publishing Co.

Blieszner, R. (1993). A socialist-feminist perspective on widowhood. *Journal of Aging Studies, 7*, 171–182.

Blumberg, R. L. (1990). White mothers as civil rights activists: The interweave of family and movement roles. In G. West & R. L. Blumberg (Eds.), *Women and social protest* (pp. 166–179). New York: Oxford University Press.

Blustein, J. (1995). Medicare coverage, supplemental insurance, and the use of mammograms by older women. *New England Journal of Medicine, 332*, 1138–1143.

Bohan, J. (1993). Regarding gender: Essentialism, constructionism, and feminist psychology. *Psychology of Women Quarterly, 17,* 5–21.

Bookman, A., & Morgen, S. (1988). *Women and the politics of empowerment.* Philadelphia: Temple University Press.

Braito, R., & Anderson, D. (1983). The ever-single elderly woman. In E. W. Markson (Ed.), *Older women: Issues and prospects.* Lexington, MA: Lexington Books.

Brant, B. (Ed.). (1988). *A gathering of spirit: A collection of North American Indian women.* Ithaca, NY: Firebrand.

Braun, K., & Browne, C. (1998). Cultural values and caregiving patterns among Asian and Pacific Island Americans. In D. Redburn & R. McNamara (Eds.), *Social gerontology: Selected readings.* Westport, CT: Greenwood.

Bricker-Jenkins, M., & Hooyman, N. (1986). *Not for women only: Social work practice with a feminist future.* Silver Spring, MD: NASW Press.

Brody, E. (1990). *Women in the middle: Their parent-care years.* New York: Springer Publishing Co.

Browne, C. (1994). A vision for practice with older women. *Journal of Applied Social Sciences, 18,* 5–16.

Browne, C. (1995a). Empowerment in social work practice with older women. *Social Work, 40,* 358–364.

Browne, C. (1995b). A feminist lifespan perspective on aging. In N. V. D. Bergh (Ed.), *Feminist practice in the 21st century* (pp. 330–354). Washington, DC: NASW Press.

Browne, C., & Braun, K. (1995). Cultural values and aging: Unpublished transcripts from a study, Cultural variations and values in aging. Honolulu, Hawaii: University of Hawaii Schools of Social Work and Public Health.

Browne, C., & Braun, K. (1996, March). Culturally-linked values on aging and their relationship to caregiving patterns. Paper presented at the 42nd annual program meeting of the American Society on Aging, Anaheim, CA.

Browne, C., & Braun, K. (1997). *What happens when a geriatric case management program closes?* Unpublished report. Honolulu: University of Hawaii Schools of Social Work and Public Health.

Brownmiller, S. (1975). *Against our will: Men, women, and rape.* London: Secker and Warburg.

Bruce, S. (1988). *The rise and fall of the new Christian Right: Protestant politics in America, 1978–1988.* Oxford: Clarendon Press.

Bryson, V. (1992). *Feminist political theory.* New York: Paragon House.

Bulcroft, K., Van Leynseele, J., & Borgatta, E. F. (1989). Filial responsibility laws. *Research and Aging, 7,* 374–390.

Burby, R. J., & Rohe, W. M. (1990). Providing for the housing needs of the elderly. *Journal of the American Planning Association, 56,* 324–340.

Burkhauser, R. V., Duncan, G. I., & Hauser, R. (1994). Sharing prosperity across the age distribution: A comparison of the United States and Germany in the 1980s. *Gerontologist, 34,* 150–160.

Burkhauser, R. V., & Smeeding, T. M. (1994). *Policy brief: Social Security reform: A budget-neutral approach to reducing older women's disproportionate risk of poverty.* Syracuse, NY: Syracuse University Maxwell School of Citizenship and Public Affairs/Center for Policy Research.

Butler, R. (1975). *Why survive? Growing old in America.* New York: Harper and Row.

Butler, R. (1994). Dispelling ageism: The cross-cutting intervention. In R. B. Enright, Jr. (Ed.), *Perspectives in social gerontology* (pp. 3–10). Needham Heights, MA: Allyn and Bacon.

Butler, R., & Gleason, H. (1985). *Productive aging: Enhancing vitality in late life.* New York: Springer Publishing Co.

Cain, P. A. (1991). Feminist jurisprudence: Grounding the theories. In K. T. Bartlett & R. Kennedy (Eds.), *Feminist legal theory: Readings in law and gender* (pp. 263–280). Boulder, CO: Westview.

Cain, P. A. (1993). Feminism and the limits of equality. In D. K. Weisberg (Ed.), *Feminist legal theory: Foundations* (pp. 237–247). Philadelphia: Temple University Press.

Calasanti, T. M. (1993). Bringing in diversity: Toward an inclusive theory of retirement. *Journal of Aging Studies, 7,* 122–150.

Calasanti, T. M, & Bailey, C. A. (1991). Gender inequality and the division of household labor in the United States and Sweden: A socialist-feminist approach. *Social Problems, 38,* 31–53.

Calasanti, T. M., & Zajicek, A. (1993). A socialist-feminist approach to aging: Embracing diversity. *Journal of Aging Studies, 7,* 117–132.

Callahan, D. (1990). Setting limits. In P. Homer & M. Holstein (Eds.), *A good old age: The paradox of setting limits* (pp. 23–35). New York: Simon and Schuster.

Canetto, S. (1991). Gender and suicide in the elderly. *Suicide and life-threatening behaviors, 22,* 80–97.

Capitman, J. A., & Yee, D. (1996). Should family members be paid to provide care to elderly relatives? No. In A. Schlarach & L.W. Kaye (Eds.), *Controversial issues in aging* (pp. 155–158). Boston: Allyn and Bacon.

Caraway, N. (1991). *Segregated sisterhood: Racism and the politics of American feminism.* Knoxville, TN: University of Tennessee Press.

Chandler, J. (1994). *Why flowers bloom.* Watsonville, CA: Papier Mache.

Chandler, S. (1990). *Competing realities: The contested terrain of mental health advocacy.* New York: Praeger.

Chodorow, N. (1978). *The reproduction of mothering: Psychoanalysis and the sociology of gender.* Berkeley, CA: University of California Press.

Chrystos. (1988). I'm making you up. In B. Brant (Ed.), *A gathering of spirit* (p. 153). Ithaca, NY: Firebrand.

Church, G., & Lacayo, R. (1995, March 20). Social insecurity. *Time Magazine,* pp. 24–32.

Cixous, H. (1976). The laugh of the Medusa. *Signs, 1,* 875–893.

Cohen, L. (1984). *Small expectations: Society's betrayal of older women.* Toronto: McClelland and Stewart.

Colditz, G., Hankinson, S., Hunger, D., Willett, W., Manson, J., Stampfer, M., Hennekens, C., & Speizer, F. (1995). The use of estrogen and progestin and the risk of breast cancer in postmenopausal women. *New England Journal of Medicine, 332,* 1589–1593.

Collins, B. G. (1986). Defining feminist social work. *Social Work, 31,* 214–219.

Collins, P. H. (1989). The social construction of Black feminist thought. *Signs, 14,* 745–773.

Collins, P. H. (1991). *Black feminist thought: Knowledge, consciousness, and the politics of empowerment.* New York: Routledge.

Collins, P. H. (1997, February). The ties that bind: Family values and race, ethnicity, class, and nation. Paper presented to the Hawaii Sociological Association. Honolulu, HI.

Conover, P. J., & Gray, V. (1983). *Feminism and the New Right: Conflict over the American family.* New York: Praeger.

Copper, B. (1986). Voices on becoming older women. In J. Alexander, D. Berrow, L. Domitrovich, M. Donnelly, & C. McLean (Eds.), *Women and aging* (pp. 47–57). Corvallis, OR: Calyx.

Coney, S. (1994). *The menopause industry: How the medical establishment exploits women.* Alameda, CA: Hunter House.

Cornman, J., & Kingson, R. (1996). Trends, issues, perspectives and values for the aging of the baby boomers. *Gerontologist, 36,* 15–26.

Corti, M., Williamson, J., Phillips, C., Rautaharju, F., Rautaharju, P., Ferucci, L., Brancati, F., & Fried, L. (1995). Cardiovascular diseases and diabetes. In J. Guralnik, L. Fried, E. Simonsick, J. Kaspar, & M. Lafferty (Eds.), *The women's health and aging study: Health and social characteristics of older women with disability* (NIH pub. No. 95-4009). Bethesda, MD: National Institute on Aging.

Coveney, L., Jackson, M., Jeffreys, S., Kay, L., & Mahoney, P. (Eds.). (1984). *The sexuality papers: Male sexuality and the social control of women.* London: Hutchinson.

Cox, E. O., & Parsons, R. J. (1994). *Empowerment-oriented social work practice with the elderly.* Pacific Grove, CA: Brooks/Cole.

Crawley, B. (1994). Older women: Policy issues in the twenty-first century. In L. V. Davis (Ed.), *Building on women's strengths* (pp. 159–178). New York: Haworth.

Creamer, B. (1995). Coming home. *Honolulu Advertiser*, D-1, F-1, F-3.

Crenshaw, K. (1990). A Black feminist critique of antidiscrimination laws and politics. In D. Kairys (Ed.), *The politics of law* (2nd ed., pp. 195–218). New York: Pantheon.

Crenshaw, K. (1992). Whose story is it anyway? Feminist and antiracist appropriations of Anita Hill. In T. Morrison (Ed.), *Racing justice, engendering power* (pp. 402–440). New York: Pantheon.

Crown, W. H., Mutschler, P. H., & Schulz, J. (1992, September 24). *The economic status of divorced older women.* Paper presented to the Congressional Symposium on Women and Retirement, Subcommittee on Retirement Income and Retirement, House Select Committee on Aging. Washington, DC: U.S. Government Printing Office.

Crystal, S., & Shea, D. (1990). Cumulative advantage, cumulative disadvantage, and inequality among elderly people. *Gerontologist, 30,* 437–443.

Cummings, S. R., Neuitt, M. C., Browner, W. S., Stone, K., Fox, K. M., Ensrud, K. E., Cauley, J., Black, D., & Vogt, T. (1995). Risk factors for hip fractures in white women. *New England Journal of Medicine, 332,* 767–773.

Daly, M. (1978). *Gyn/Ecology.* Boston: Beacon Press.

Dannefer, D. (1987). Aging as intracohort differentiation: Accentuation, the Matthew effect, and the life course. *Sociological Forum, 2,* 211–236.

Dasgupta, S., & Dasgupta, S. (1993). Journeys: Reclaiming South Asian feminism. In Women of South Asian Descent Collective (Eds.), *Our feet walk the sky: Women of the South Asian diaspora* (pp. 123–130). San Francisco: Aunt Lute Books.

Davis, A. Y. (1971). Reflections on the Black women's role in the community of slavery. *Black Scholar, 7,* 3, 5–10.

Davis, A. Y. (1981). *Women, race, and class.* New York: Vintage.

Davis, A. Y. (1990). *Women, culture, and politics.* New York: Vintage.

Davis, K. (1985). Health care policies and the aged: Observations from the United States. In R. H. Binstock & E. Shanas (Eds.), *Handbook of aging and the social sciences* (2nd ed.). New York: Von Nostrand Reinhold.

Davis, K., Grant, P., & Rowland, D. (1990). Alone and poor: The plight of elderly women. *Generations, 14,* 43–47.

Davis, K., & Rowland, D. (1991). Old and poor: Policy challenges in the 1990's. *Journal of Aging and Social Policy, 2,* 37–59.

Davis, L. V. (1985). Female and male voices in social work. *Social Work, 30,* 106–115.

Davis, L. V. (Ed.). (1994a). *Building on women's strengths: A social work agenda for the twenty-first century.* New York: Haworth.

Davis, L. V. (1994b). Why we still need a woman's agenda for social work. In L. V. Davis (Ed.), *Building on women's strengths* (pp. 1–26). New York: Haworth.

Day, A. T. (1991). *Remarkable survivors: Insights into successful aging among women.* Washington, DC: The Urban Institute.

DeAngelis, L., & Siple, M. (1996). *Recipes for change: Gourmet wholefood cooking for health and vitality at menopause.* New York: Dutton.

de Beauvoir, S. (1949). *The second sex.* New York: Vintage.

de Beauvoir, S. (1972). *The coming of age.* New York: Putnam.

Deevey, S. (1975). Such a nice girl. In N. Myron & C. Bunch (Eds.), *Lesbianism and the women's movement.* Baltimore, MD: Diana Press.

Delany, S. L., Delany, E. A., & Hearth, A. H. (1993). *Having our say: The Delany sisters' first 100 years.* New York: Dell.

Detre, K., Yeh, W., Kelsey, S., Williams, D., Desvigne-Nickens, P., Holmes, D., Jr., Bourassa, M., King, S., 3rd, Faxon, D., & Kent, K. (1995). Has improvement in PTCA procedures affected long term progress? The NHLBI-PTCA registry experience. *Circulation, 91,* 2868–2875.

Diamond, T. (1992). *Making grey gold: Narratives of nursing home care.* Chicago: University of Chicago Press.

Diquinzio, P., & Young, I. M. (1995). Introduction. *Hypatia, 10,* 1–7.

Donovan, J. (1996). *Feminist theory: The intellectual traditions of American feminism.* New York: Continuum.

Doress-Worters, P., & Siegel, D. L. (1983). *The new ourselves growing older: Women aging with knowledge and power.* New York: Touchstone.

Dowling, C. (1996). *Red hot mamas: Women coming into their own at 50.* New York: Bantam.

Downes, P., Tuttle, I., Faul, P., & Mudd, V. (1996). *The new older woman: A dialogue for the coming century.* Berkeley: Celestial Arts.

Dressel, P. (1988). Gender, race, class: Beyond the feminization of poverty in later life. *Gerontologist, 28,* 177–180.

Dworkin, A. (1981). *Pornography: Men possessing women.* London: Women's Press.

Dworkin, A. (1988). *Letters from a war zone.* London: Secker and Warburg.

Dychtwald, K., & Flower, J. (1989). Calling a truce in the age wars. *State Government News, 32,* 7–9. (Lexington, KY, Council of State Governments publication.)

Ehrenreich, B. (1996, May 6). Viewpoint: Whose gap is it anyway? *Time,* p. 36.

Eisenstein, Z. (1981). *The radical future of liberal feminism.* New York: Longman.

Eisenstein, Z. (1982). The sexual politics of the New Right: Understanding the "Crisis of Liberalism" for the 1980s. In N. Keohane, M. Rosaldo, & B. Gelpi (Eds.), *Feminist theory* (pp. 77–98). Chicago: University of Chicago Press.

Eisenstein, Z. (1984). Feminism and sexual equality: Crisis in liberal America. New York: *Monthly Review.*

Elder, G. H., Jr. (1985). Perspective on the lifecourse. In G. H. Elder, Jr. (Ed.), *Life course dynamics: Trajectories and transition, 1968–80* (pp. 23–49). Ithaca, NY: Cornell University Press.

Elder, G. H., Jr. (1994). Time, human agency, and social change: Perspectives on the life course. *Social Psychology Quarterly, 57,* 4–15.

Engels, F. (1942). *Origin of the family, private property, and the state.* New York: International Publishers. (Original work published 1884)

England, S. E. (1990). Family leave and gender justice. *Affilia, 5,* 8–24.

Erikson, E. (1963). *Childhood and society* (2nd ed.). New York: Norton.

Erikson, E. (1982). *The life cycle completed: A review.* New York: Norton.

Estes, C., Gerard, L., Zones, J. S., & Swan, J. H. (1984). *Political economy, health, and aging.* Boston: Little, Brown.

Estes, C., Swan, J. H., & Associates. (1993). *The long-term care crisis: Elders trapped in the no-care zone.* Newbury Park, CA: Sage.

Fahs, M. (1993). Preventative medical care: Targeting elderly women in an aging society. In J. Allen & A. Pifer (Eds.), *Women on the front lines: Meeting the challenges of an aging America* (pp. 105–131). Washington, DC: The Urban Press.

Falcone, D., & Broyles, R. (1994). Access in long term care: Race is a barrier. *Journal of Health, Politics, Policy, and the Law, 19,* 583–595.

Faludi, S. (1992). *Backlash: The undeclared war against American women.* New York: Anchor.

Family and Medical Leave Act (FMLA). (1993). Public law 103-3, February 5., 107, Stat. 6-29.

Family Hope Coalition. (1993). *Imagine . . .* Presentation at the Honolulu Women's Health Conference in Honolulu, Hawaii, June. Honolulu: Author.

Ferrara, P. (1995, December). The Social Security mess: A way out. *Reader's Digest,* 107–110.

Finley, L. M. (1993). Breaking women's silence in law: The dilemma of the gendered nature of legal reasoning. In D. K. Weisberg (Ed.), *Feminist legal theory: Foundations* (pp. 571–581). Philadelphia: Temple University Press.

Firestone, S. (1970). *The dialectic of sex.* London: The Women's Press.

Fischer, K. (1995). *Autumn gospel: Women in the second half of life.* New York: Paulist Books/Integration.

Flax, J. (1987). Postmodernism and gender relations in feminist theory. *Signs, 12,* 621–643.

Flax, J. (1990). *Thinking fragments: Psychoanalysis, feminism, and postmodernism in the contemporary west.* Berkeley: University of California Press.

Ford, D. E. D. (1991). Translating the problems of the elderly into effective policies. In E. A. Anderson & R. C. Hula (Eds.), *The reconstruction of family policy* (pp. 91–109). Westport, CT: Greenwood.

Forman, M. (1985). Social security is a women's issue. In B. Hess & E. Markson (Eds.), *Growing old in America: New perspectives on old age* (pp. 212–275). New Brunswick, NJ: Transaction.

Foucault, M. (1980). *Power, knowledge.* New York: Pantheon.

Franks, V., & Rothblum, R. D. (Eds.). (1983). *The stereotyping of women: Its effects on mental health.* New York: Springer Publishing Co.

Freeman, J. (1996). *Women: A feminist perspective* (5th ed.). Mountain View, CA: Mayfield.

Freeman, M. (1990). Beyond women's issues: Feminism and social work. *Affilia, 5,* 72–89.

Fried, L. P., Kasper, J. D., Simonsick, E. M., & Zeger, S. L. (1995). Disability: The spectrum of function in moderately to severely disabled older women. In J. M. Guralnik, L. P. Fried, E. M. Simonsick, J. D. Kasper, & M. E. Lafferty (Eds.), *The Woman's Health and Aging study: Health and social characteristics of older women with disability* (pp. 19–22) (NIH Pub. No. 95-4009). Bethesda, MD: National Institute on Aging.

Friedan, B. (1963). *The feminine mystique.* New York: Norton.

Friedan, B. (1993). *The fountain of age.* New York: Simon and Schuster.

Friedman, R. (1996). Boomers, ageism, health, and hope. Address before the 42nd Annual Program meeting of the American Society on Aging. *Aging Today, 17,* 3, 9.

Friedman, S. S. (1995). Beyond White and other: Relationality and narratives of race in feminist discourse. *Signs, 21,* 1–49.

Friend, R. (1990). Gaying: Adjustment and the older gay male. *Alternative Life Styles, 3,* 231–248.

Gambrell, R. D. (1987). Estrogen replacement therapy for the elderly woman. *Medical Aspects of Human Sexuality, 21,* 81–93.

Garner, J. D., & Mercer, S. O. (Eds.). (1989). *Women as they age: Challenge, opportunity, and triumph.* New York: Haworth.

George, L., & Gwyther, L. (1986). Caregiver well-being: A multidimensional examination of family caregivers of demented adults. *The Gerontologist, 26,* 449–456.

Gerstel, N., & Gallagher, S. (1994). Caring for kith and kin: Gender, employment, and the privatization of care. *Social Problems, 41,* 519–527.

Gibson, D. (1996). Broken down by age and gender: "The problem of Old Women" redefined. *Gender and Society, 10,* 433–448.

Gibson, D., & Allen, J. (1993). Parasitism and phallocentrism in social provisions for the aged. *Policy Sciences, 26,* 79–98.

Gibson, D., & Rowland, D. T. (1984). Community vs. institutional care: The case of the Australian aged. *Social Science and Medicine, 18,* 997–1004.

Giddings, P. (1994). The last taboo. In T. Morrison (Ed.), *Racing justice, engendering power* (pp. 441–470). New York: Pantheon.

Gilder, G. (1981). *Wealth and poverty.* New York: Basic.

Gilligan, C. (1982). *In a different voice.* Cambridge, MA: Harvard University Press.

Giroux, H. (Ed.). (1991). *Postmodernism, feminism, and cultural politics.* Albany, NY: State University of New York Press.

Glenn, E. N. (1985). Racial ethnic women's labor: The intersection of race, gender, and class oppression. *Review of Radical Economics, 17,* 86–108.

Glenn, E. N. (1987). Gender and the family. In B. Hess & M. Ferree (Eds.), *Analyzing gender: A handbook of social science research* (pp. 348–380). Newbury Park, CA: Sage.

Glenn, E. N. (1992). From servitude to service work: Historical continuities in the racial division of paid reproductive labor. *Signs, 18,* 1–43.

Glick, P. C. (1955). The life cycle of the family. *Marriage and Family Living, 18,* 3–9.

Glick, P. C., & Park, R., Jr. (1965). New approaches in studying the life cycle of the family. *Demography, 2,* 187–202.

Gonyea, J. (1994). The paradox of the advantaged elder and the feminization of poverty. *Social Work, 39,* 35–41.

Gottleib, N. (1980). The older women. In N. Gottleib (Ed.), *Alternative social services for women* (pp. 280–331). New York: Columbia University Press.

Gottleib, N. (1989). Families, work, and the lives of old women. In J. D. Garner & S. O. Mercer (Eds.), *Women as they age: Challenges, opportunities, and triumphs* (pp. 217–244). New York: Haworth.

Gould, B. (1990). Fear of feminism: The right wing and family values. *Social Justice, 17,* 136–145.

Gould, K. H. (1987). Feminist principles and minority concerns: Contributions, problems, and solutions. *Affilia, 2,* 6–19.

Gould, K. H. (1988). Old wine in new bottles: A feminist perspective on Gilligan's theory. *Social Work, 33,* 411–416.

Gould, K. H. (1989). A minority-feminist perspective on women and aging. In J. D. Garner & S. O. Mercer (Eds.), *Women as they age: Challenges, opportunities, and triumphs* (pp. 195–216). New York: Haworth.

Grau, L., & Susser, I. (1989). *Women in the later years: Health, social, and cultural perspectives.* New York: Harrington.

Greene, R. R. (1986). *Social work with the aged and their families.* New York: Aldine de Gruyter.

Greer, G. (1991). *The change: Women, aging, and menopause.* New York: Fawcett.

Grewal, I. (1993). Reading and writing the South Asian Diaspora: Feminism and nationalism in North America. In Women of South Asian Descent Collective (Eds.), *Our feet walk the sky: Women of the South Asian diaspora* (pp. 226–245). San Francisco: Aunt Lute Books.

Gullette, M. M. (1995). Inventing the "Postmaternal woman, 1898–1927": Idle, unwanted, and out of a job. *Feminist Studies, 21,* 221–253.

Guralnik, J. M., Fried, L. P., Simonsick, E. M., Kasper, J. D., & Lafferty, M. E. (Eds.). (1995). *The Women's Health and Aging Study: Health and social characteristics of older women with disability* (NIH Pub. No. 95-4009). Bethesda, MD: National Institute on Aging.

Gutierrez, L. (1990). Working with women of color. *Social Work, 35,* 149–154.

Hagen, J. L., & Davis, L. V. (1992). Working with women: Building a policy and practice agenda. *Social Work, 37,* 495–502.

Hagestad, G. O. (1987). Family. In G. L. Maddox (Ed.), *The Encyclopedia of aging* (pp. 247– 249). New York: Springer Publishing Co.

Hammer, H., & Browne, C. (1991). How big is the gender gap? *Hawaii Bar News,* 3–4.

Haney, P. (1988). Providing empowerment to the person with AIDS. *Social Work, 33,* 251–253.

Haraway, D. (1985). A manifesto for cyborgs: Science, technology, and socialist feminism in the 1980's. *Socialist Review, 15,* 65–107.

Harding, S. (1986). *The science question in feminism.* Ithica, NY: Cornell University Press.

Harding, S. (1988). Situated knowledge: The science question with feminism and the privilege of partial perspectives. *Feminist Studies, 14,* 575–599.

Harris, A. (1991). Race and essentialism in feminist legal theory. In K. T. Bartlett & R. Kennedy (Eds.), *Feminist legal theory: Readings in law and gender* (pp. 235–262). Boulder, CO: Westview.

Harris, M. B. (1994). Growing old gracefully: Age concealment and gender. *Journal of Gerontology, 49,* 149–158.

Harrison, C. (n.d.). *Wise woman croning ceremony: A celebration of age.* Unpublished paper.

Hartman, A. (1990). Aging as a feminist issue (Editorial). *Social Work, 35,* 387–388.

Hartman, A. (1992). In search of subjugated knowledge (Editorial). *Social Work, 37,* 483–484.

Hartman, S. (1983). A self-help group for women in abusive relationships. *Social Work with Groups, 8,* 133–146.

Hartmann, H. (1981). The unhappy marriage of Marxism and feminism: Towards a more progressive union. In L. Largent (Ed.), *Women and revolution: Discussion of the unhappy marriage of Marxism and feminism* (pp. 1–41). Boston: South End Press.

Hartsock, N. (1985). *Money, sex, and power: Toward a feminist historical materialism.* Boston: Northeastern University Press.

Harvard Women's Health Watch. (1994). Menopause, incontinence. *1,* 2–5.

Harvard Women's Health Watch. (1995). Menopause: Alternatives to hormone replacement. *1,* 2–3.

Harvard Women's Health Watch. (1996). Mitral valve prolapse. *3,* 4–5.

Haug, M. R., Ford, A. B., & Sheafor, M. (1985). *The physical and mental health of aged women*. New York: Springer Publishing Co.

Hazan, H. (1994). *Old age construction and deconstruction*. Cambridge, England: Cambridge University Press.

Healy, B. (1991, May 30). Hearing before the U.S. House Select Committee on Aging, Subcommittee on Housing and Consumer Interests. *Women at midlife: Consumers of second rate health care* (102-814) (p. 76). Washington, DC: U.S. Government Printing Office.

Healey, S. (1986). Growing to be an old woman: Aging and ageism. In J. Alexander et al. (Eds.), *Women and aging: An anthology by women* (pp. 58–62). Corvallis, OR: Calyx.

Hegar, R. L., & Hunzeker, J. M. (1988). Moving toward empowerment-based practice in public child welfare. *Social Work, 33*, 499–503.

Hen Co-op. (1993). *Growing old disgracefully: New ideas for getting the most out of life*. Freedom, CA: Crossing Press.

Hen Co-op. (1996). *Disgracefully yours: More new ideas for getting the most out of your life*. Freedom, CA: Crossing Press.

Hendricks, J. (1996). A review: Intergenerational relations: More smoke than fire. *The Gerontologist, 36*, 125–128.

Herzog, A. R., Holden, K., & Seltzer, M. (1988). *The health and economic status of older women*. Amityville, NY: Baywood.

Hess, B. (1985). Aging policies and older women: The hidden agenda. In A. Rossi (Ed.), *Gender and the life course* (pp. 319–331). New York: Aldine.

Hess, B. (1990). The demographic parameters of gender and aging. *Generations, 14*, 12–16.

Hess, B., & Waring, J. (1983). Family relationships of older women: A woman's issue. In E. Markson (Ed.), *Older women* (pp. 227–252). Lexington, MA: Lexington Books.

Hill, D. C. O., & Tigges, L. M. (1995). Gendered welfare state theory: A cross-national study of women's pensions. *Millbank Quarterly, 9*, 99–119.

Hillner, B. E., Penberthy, L., Desch, C. E., McDonald, M. K., Smith, T. J., & Retchin, S. M. (1996). Variations in staging and treatment of local and regional breast cancer in the elderly. *Breast Cancer Research Treatment, 40*, 1, 75–86.

Hoechstetter, S. (1996). Taking new directions to improve public policy. *Social Work, 41*, 343–346.

Holden, K. C. (1997). Social Security and the economic security of women: Is it fair? In E. Kingson & J. H. Schulz (Eds.), *Social Security in the 21st century* (pp. 91–104). New York: Oxford.

Holstein, M. (1992). Productive aging: A feminist critique. *Journal of Aging and Social Policy, 4*, 17–34.

hooks, b. (1981). *Ain't I a woman? Black women and feminism*. Boston: South End Press.

hooks, b. (1984). *Feminist theory: From margin to center.* Boston: South End Press.

hooks, b., & West, C. (1991). *Breaking bread: Insurgent Black intellectual life.* Boston: South End Press.

Hooyman, N., & Gonyea, J. (1995). *Feminist perspectives on family care: Policies for gender justice.* Newbury Park, CA: Sage.

Hooyman, N., & Kiyak, H. A. (1993). *Social gerontology* (3rd ed.). Needham Heights, MA: Allyn and Bacon.

Hudson, R. B. (1996). The changing face of aging politics. *The Gerontologist, 36,* 33–35.

Humm, M. (1990). *The dictionary of feminist theory.* Colombus, OH: Ohio State University Press.

Humm, M. (Ed.). (1992). *Modern feminisms.* New York: Columbia University Press.

Hurwich, C. (1982). *Vital women in their 70s and 80s: A study of ten selected women.* Unpublished master's thesis, Antioch University West, San Francisco.

Hynes, D. M. (1994). The quality of breast cancer care in local communities: Implications for health care reform. *Medical Care, 32,* 328–340.

Ingram, B. (1996). New data to reveal national costs of chronic conditions. *Aging Today, 17,* 5, 7.

Irigaray, L. (1980). When our lips speak together. *Signs, 6,* 69–79.

Irigaray, L. (1981). This sex which is not one. In E. Marks & I. de Courtivron (Eds.), *New French feminisms* (pp. 99–106). Brighton, UK: Harvester.

Jackson, J. (1985). Poverty and minority status. In M. Haugh, A. Ford, & M. Sheafor (Eds.), *The physical and mental health of aging women* (pp. 166–181). New York: Springer Publishing Co.

Jacobs, R. H. (1993). *Be an outrageous older woman: A R.A.S.P.* Manchester, CT: Knowledge, Ideas, and Trends.

Jaggar, A. (1988). *Feminist politics and human nature.* Totawa, NJ: Rowman and Littlefield.

Jaggar, A., & Rothberg, P. (1984). *Feminist frameworks* (2nd ed.). New York: McGraw Hill.

Jansson, B. (1991). *The reluctant welfare state.* Belmont, CA: Wadsworth.

Jorstad, E. (1987). *The new Christian right, 1981–88.* Lewiston, NY: Edwin Mellen Press.

Jovanovic, L., & Levert, S. (1993). *A woman's guide to menopause.* New York: Hyperion.

Kadi, J. (Ed.). (1994). *Food for our grandmothers: Writings by Arab-American and Arab-Canadian feminists.* Boston: South End Press.

Kay, H. H. (1993). Equality and difference: The case of pregnancy. In D. K. Weisberg (Ed.), *Feminist legal theory: Foundations* (pp. 180–189). Philadelphia: Temple University Press.

Keigher, S. M., & Linsk, N. L. (1996). Should family members be paid to provide care to elderly persons? Yes. In A. Sclarlach & L. W. Kaye (Eds.), *Controversial issues in aging* (pp. 148–153). Boston: Allyn and Bacon.

Keigher, S. M., & Murphy, C. (1992). A consumer view of a family care compensation program for the elderly. *Social Service Review, 66,* 256–277.

Kemper, P., & Murtaugh, C. M. (1991). Lifetime use of nursing home care. *New England Journal of Medicine, 324,* 595–600.

Kim, P. K. (1983). Demography of the Asian-Pacific elderly: Selected problems and implications. In R. L. McNeely & J. L. Cohen (Eds.), *Aging in minority groups* (pp. 29–41). Beverly Hills: Sage.

Kingson, E., Cornman, J., & Hirschorn, B. (1986). *Ties that bind: The interdependence of generations* (pp. 1–14). Arlington, VA: Seven Locks Press.

Kingson, E. R., & O'Grady-LeShane, R. (1993). The effect of caregiving on women's Social Security benefits. *Gerontologist, 33,* 230–239.

Kingson, E. R., & Schulz, J. H. (Eds). (1997). *Social Security in the 21st century.* New York: Oxford University Press.

Kirp, D. L., Yudof, M. C., & Franks, M. S. (1986). *Gender justice.* Chicago: University of Chicago Press.

Kittay, E. F. (1995). Taking dependency seriously: The Family and Medical Leave Act considered in light of the social organization of dependency work and gender equality. *Hypatia, 10,* 8–29.

Kleyman, P. (1996). New law boosts long term care insurance. *Aging Today, 17*(5), 1–2.

Kramer, B. (1996). Gain in the caregiving experience: Where are we? What next? *The Gerontologist, 37,* 218–232.

Krieger, L. J., & Cooney, P. N. (1993). The Miller-Wohl controversy: Equal treatment, positive action and the meaning of women's equality. In D. K. Weisberg (Ed.), *Feminist legal theory foundations* (pp. 156–179). Philadelphia: Temple University Press.

Kristeva, J. (1981). Women's time. In N. Keohane, M. Rosaldo, & B. Gelpi (Eds.), *Feminist theory: A critique of ideology* (pp. 31–54). Chicago: University of Chicago Press.

Kuhn, M. (1980). Grass-roots gray power. In M. M. Fuller & C. A. Martin (Eds.), *The older woman: Lavender rose or gray panther* (pp. 223–227). Springfield, IL: Charles Thomas.

Kuhn, M., & Hessel, D. (1977). *Maggie Kuhn and aging.* Philadelphia: Westminister Press.

Kuhn, M., Long, C., & Quinn, L. (1991). *No stone unturned: The life and times of Maggie Kuhn.* New York: Ballantine.

Laclau, E. (1988). Politics and the limits of modernity. In A. Ross (Ed.), *Universal abandon? The politics of postmodernism* (pp. 63–82). Minneapolis: University of Minnesota Press.

Laird, J. (1994). Changing women's narratives: Taking back the discourse. In L. Davis (Ed.), *Building on women's strengths: A social work agenda for the 21st century* (pp. 179–210). New York: Haworth.

Laird, J. (1995). Family-centered practice; Feminist, constructionist, and cultural perspectives. In N. Van Den Bergh (Ed.), *Feminist practice in the 21st century* (pp. 20–40). Washington, DC: NASW Press.

Lark, S. (1994). *The menopause self-help book*. Berkeley, CA: Celestial Arts.

Laws, G. (1995). Understanding ageism: Lessons from postmodernism and feminism. *Gerontologist, 35,* 112–118.

Leonard, F. (1991, September/October). The curse. *The Owl Observer*, p. 7.

Leonard, P., & Nichols, B. (Eds.). (1994). *Gender, aging, and the state*. Montreal: Black Rose Books.

LeSueur, M. (1986). Rites of ancient ripening. In J. Alexander, D. Berrow, L. Domitrovich, M. Donnelly, & C. McLean (Eds.), *Women and aging: An anthology by women* (p. 10). Corvallis, OR: Calyx Books.

Leutz, M. N., Capitman, J. A., MacAdam, M., & Abrahams, R. (1992). *Care for frail elders: Developing community solutions*. Westport, CT: Auburn House.

Lewis, M., & Butler, R. (1972). Why is feminism ignoring older women? *International Journal of Aging and Human Development, 3,* 223–232.

Lewittes, H. H. (1989). Just being friendly means a lot: Women, friendship, and aging. In L. Grau (Ed.), *Women in the later years* (pp. 139–160). New York: Harrington.

Liebman, R. C., & Wuthnow, R. (Eds.). (1983). *The new Christian right: Mobilization and legitimization*. New York: Aldine.

Longino, C., Soldo, B. J., & Manton, K. G. (1990). Demography of aging in the United States. In K. Ferraro (Ed.), *Gerontology issues and perspectives* (pp. 285–297). New York: Springer Publishing Co.

Lopata, H. Z. (1969). Loneliness: Forms and components. *Social Problems, 17,* 248–262.

Lopata, H. Z. (1979). *Women and widows*. New York: Elsevier.

Lopata, H. Z. (1987). Women's family roles in a life course perspective. In B. B. Hess & M. M. Ferree (Eds.), *Analyzing gender: A handbook of social science research* (pp. 381–407). Newbury Park, CA: Sage.

Lorde, A. (1984). *Sister outsider*. Trumansburg, NY: Crossing Press.

Luthra, P. (1993). Pati Dev. In Women of South Asian Descent Collective (Eds.), *Our feet walk the sky* (pp. 257–263). San Francisco: Aunt Lute Press.

Maas, H., & Kuyper, J. (1974). *From 30 to 70*. San Francisco: Jossey-Bass.

Macdonald, B. (1985). Outside the sisterhood: Ageism in women's studies. In J. Alexander, D. Berrow, L. Domitrovich, M. Donnelly, & C. McLean (Eds.), *Women and aging: An anthology by women* (pp. 20–25). Corvallis, OR: Calyx Books.

Macdonald, B., & Rich, C. (1983). *Look me in the eye: Old women, aging, and ageism.* San Francisco: Spinsters, Ink.

MacKinnon, C. (1987). *Feminism unmodified: Discourses on life and law.* Cambridge: Harvard University Press.

MacKinnon, C. (1989). *Toward a feminist theory of the state.* Cambridge, MA: Harvard University Press.

MacKinnon, C. (1990). Liberalism and the death of feminism. In D. Leidholdt & G. Raymond (Eds.), *The sexual liberals and the attack on feminism* (pp. 3–13). Elmsford, NY: Pergamon Press.

Mahoul, L. J. (1994). Battling nationalisms to salvage her history. In J. Kadi (Ed.), *Food for our grandmothers* (pp. 24–29). Boston: South End Press.

Majury, D. (1993). Strategizing in equality. In D. K. Weisberg (Ed.), *Feminist legal theory: Foundations* (pp. 264–275). Philadelphia: Temple University Press.

Malveaux, J. (1993). Race, poverty and women's aging. In J. Allen & A. Pifer (Eds.), *Women on the front lines: Meeting the challenges of aging America* (pp. 167–190). Washington, DC: The Urban Press.

Mandell, B., & Schram, B. (1985). *Human services: Introduction and intervention.* New York: John Wiley.

Manton, K. G., Patrick, C. H., & Johnson, K. W. (1987). Health differentials between blacks and whites: Report trends in mortality and morbidity. *Millbank Memorial Fund, 65*(Supplement), 129–199.

Marks, E., & deCourtivron, I. (Eds.). (1980). *New French feminisms.* Brighton, UK: Harvester.

Markson, E. (1983). *The older woman: Issues and prospects.* Lexington, MA: Lexington Books.

Marshall, S. E. (1991). Who speaks for American women? The future of antifeminism: American Feminism: New issues for a mature movement. *The Annals of the American Academy of Political and Social Science, 515,* 50–62.

Martz, S. H. (Ed.). (1987). *When I am an old woman, I will wear purple.* Watsonville, CA: Papier Mache.

Martz, S. H. (Ed.). (1996). *Grow old along with me: The best is yet to be.* Watsonville, CA: Papier Mache.

Marx, K. (1967). *Capital.* New York: International Publishers. (Original work published 1867)

Maxwell, F. (1968). *The measure of my days.* New York: Penguin.

Mazumdar, S. (1989). General introductions: A woman-centered perspective on Asian American history. In Asian Women United of California (Eds.), *Making waves: An anthology of writings by and about Asian American women* (pp. 1–22). Boston: Beacon Press.

McDermott, C. J. (1989). Empowering elderly in nursing home residents: The resident's rights campaign. *Social Work, 34,* 155–157.

Meyer, M. H. (1990). Family status and poverty among older women: The gendered distribution of retirement income in the United States. *Social Problems, 37,* 551–563.

Meyer, M. H. (1994). Gender, race, and the distribution of social assistance: Medicaid use among the frail elderly. *Gender and Society, 8,* 8–28.

Midgley, J. (1990). Review article: Religion, politics, and social policy: The case of the new Christian right. *Journal of Social Policy, 19,* 397–403.

Miller, D. (1990). *Women and social welfare: A feminist analysis.* New York: Praeger.

Millett, K. (1970). *Sexual politics.* London: Virago.

Minkler, M. (1991). Generational equity and the new victim blaming. In M. Minkler & C. Estes (Eds.), *Critical perspectives on aging* (pp. 67–79). Amityville, NY: Baywood.

Minkler, M., & Estes, C. (Eds.). (1991). *Critical perspectives on aging: The political and moral economy of growing old.* Amityville, NY: Baywood.

Minkler, M., Roe, K. M., & Price, M. (1993). The physical and emotional health of grandmothers raising grandchildren in the crack cocaine epidemic. *Gerontologist, 32,* 752–761.

Minkler, M., & Stone, R. (1985). The feminization of poverty and older women. *The Gerontologist, 25,* 351–357.

Mitchell, J. (1966). Women: the longest revolution. *New Left Review, 40,* 11–37.

Mokuau, N., & Browne, C. (1994). The life themes of Native Hawaiian aged women. *Social Work, 39,* 43–50.

Moody, H. R. (1988). *Abundance of life.* New York: Columbia University Press.

Moody, H. R. (1993). Overview: What is critical gerontology and why is it important? In T. Cole, W. A. A. Achenbaum, P. Jakobi, & R. Kastenbaum (Eds.), *Voices and visions of aging: Toward a critical gerontology.* New York: Springer Publishing Co.

Moody, H. R. (1994). *Aging: Concepts and controversies.* Thousand Oaks, CA: Pine Forge Press.

Moon, M. (1990). Public policies: Are they gender-neutral? *Generations, 14,* 59–63.

Moon, M., & Mulvey, J. (1996). *Entitlements and the elderly: Protecting promises and recognizing realities.* Washington, DC: The Urban Press.

Moraga, C. (1993). *The last generation.* Boston: South End Press.

Moraga, C., & Anzaldua, G. (Eds.). (1983). *This bridge called my back: Writings by radical women of color.* Watertown, MA: Persephone.

Morgan, R. (1970). *Sisterhood is powerful: An anthology of writings from the women's liberation movement.* New York: Vintage.

Morris, J. K. (1993). Interacting oppressions: Teaching social work content on women of color. *Journal of Social Work Education, 29,* 99–110.

Mui, A. C., & Burnette, D. (1995). Long-term care service use by frail elders: Is ethnicity a factor? *The Gerontologist, 34,* 190–198.

Mulrow, C. D., Chiodo, L. K., & Gerety, M. B. (1996). Function and medical comorbidity in South Texas nursing home residents: Variations by ethnic group. *Journal of the American Geriatrics Society, 44,* 279–284.

Mulroy, E. A. (1995). *The new uprooted: Single mothers in urban life.* Westport, CT: Auburn.

Murray, C. (1984). *Losing ground: American social policy, 1950–1980.* New York: Basic.

Murray, C. (1988). *In pursuit of happiness and good government.* New York: Simon and Schuster.

Nabulsi, A. A., Folsom, A. R., White, A., Patsch, W., Heiss, G., Wu, K., & Szklo, M. (1993). Association of hormone replacement therapy with various cardiovascular risk factors in postmenopausal women. *New England Journal of Medicine, 328,* 1070–1075.

Naples, N. A. (1991). A socialist-feminist analysis of the Family Support Act of 1988. *Affilia, 6,* 23–38.

National Academy on Aging. (1996, July). Facts on Medicare: Hospital insurance and supplementary medical insurance. *Gerontology News,* pp. 7–8.

National Center for Health Statistics. (1991). *Health Statistics United States, 1990.* Hyattsville, MD: Public Health Service.

National Center for Health Statistics. (1995, September). *Monitoring health care in America.* Hyattsville, MD: Public Health Service.

National Center for Health Statistics. (1990). Current estimates from the National Health Interview Survey: U.S. 1989–1990. *Vital and Health Statistics,* Series 10, 176.

Nechas, E., & Foley, D. (1994). *Unequal treatment: What you don't know about how women are mistreated by the medical community.* New York: Simon and Schuster.

Neugarten, B. L. (Ed.). (1968). *Middle age and aging: A reader in social psychology.* Chicago: University of Chicago Press.

Neugarten, B. L. (1975). Successful aging in 1970 and 1990. In E. Pfeiffer (Ed.), *Successful aging: A conference report.* Durham, NC: Duke University Press.

Neugarten, B. L., & Datan, N. (1974). The middle years. In S. Arieti (Ed.), *American handbook of psychiatry* (2nd ed., Vol. 2, pp. 592–608). New York: Basic.

Neugarten, B. L., Havighurst, R. J. L., & Tobin, S. S. (1968). Personality and patterns of aging. In B. L. Neugarten (Ed.), *Middle age and aging: A reader in social psychology.* Chicago: University of Chicago Press.

Neugarten, B. L., Wood, V., Kraines, R., & Loomis, B. (1968). Women's attitudes toward menopause. In B. L. Neugarten (Ed.), *Middle age and aging* (pp. 195–200). Chicago: University of Chicago Press.

Newschaffer, C. J., Penberthy, L., Desch, C. E., Retchin, S. M., & Whitttemore, M. (1986). The effect of age and comorbidity in the treatment of elderly women with nonmetastatic breast cancer. *Archives of Internal Medicine, 156,* 1, 85–90.

Noelker, L., & Bass, D. (1994). Relationships between the frail elderly's informal and informal caregivers. *Journal of Gerontology, 44*(2), S63-S70.

Northrup, C. (1995). *Women's bodies, women's wisdom: Creating physical and emotional health and healing.* New York: Bantam.

Notelovitz, M., & Tonnessen, D. (1996). *The essential heart book for women.* New York: St. Martins.

Newman, S. A., & Stuyk, R. (1990). Overwhelming odds: Caregiving and the risk of institutionalization. *Journal of Gerontology, 45*(5), S173–S183.

Oakar, M. (1990, May 22). *Women and retirement: Are they losing out* (101–763) [U.S. House Select Committee on Aging.] Washington, DC: U.S. Government Printing Office.

Odyssey Forum. (1996). Summary of meeting of Odyssey Forum participants, January 26–27, 1996. McLean, VA: Author. Contact: P.O. Box 21223, McLean, VA 22101-1223 or call (703) 734-3266.

O'Grady-LeShane, R. (1990). Older women and poverty. *Social Work, 35,* 422–424.

Older Women's League. (1986). *The road to poverty.* Washington, DC: Author.

Older Women's League. (1987). *The picture of health for midlife and older women.* Washington, DC: Author.

Older Women's League. (1990). *Heading for hardship: Retirement income for American women in the next century.* Washington, DC: Author.

Older Women's League. (1996). OWL pushes for changes, secure future. *The OWL Observer, 16,* 1, 5.

Olsen, F. (1991). The sex of law. In D. Kairys (Ed.), *The politics of law: A progressive critique* (rev. ed.) (pp. 453–467). New York: Pantheon.

Omnibus Budget Reconciliation Act of 1990. (1990). H.R. 5835, 106th Congress, Public Laws 101-403. Washington, DC: U.S. Government Printing Office.

O'Rand, A. (1983). Loss of work role and subjective health assessment in later life among men and unmarried women. In A. C. Kerchoff (Ed.), *Research in sociology of education and socialization* (Vol. 4, pp. 265–286). San Francisco: JAI.

O'Rand, A. (1996). The precious and the precocious: Understanding cumulative disadvantage and cumulative advantage over the life course. *Gerontologist, 36,* 230–238.

Ozawa, M. N. (1993). Solitude in old age: Effects of female headship on elderly women's lives. *Affilia, 8,* 136–156.

Ozawa, M. N. (1995). The economic status of vulnerable older women. *Social Work, 40,* 323–333.

Ozawa, M., & Kirk, S. A. (1996). Welfare reform. *Social Work, 20,* 194–195.

Paglia, C. (1991). *Sexual personae: Art and decadence from Nefertiti to Emily Dickinson..* New York: Vantage.

Pardeck, J. T., Murphy, J. W., & Choi, J. M. (1994). Some implications of postmodernism for social work practice. *Social Work, 39,* 343–346.

Parsons, R., & Cox, E. (1989). Family mediation in elder caregiving decisions: An empowerment intervention. *Social Work, 34,* 122–126.

Pearlin, L. (1992). The careers of caregivers. *Gerontologist, 32,* 647.

Pearlin, L., Mullan, J. T., Semple, S. J., & Skaff, M. M. (1990). Caregiving and the stress process: An overview of concepts and their measures. *Gerontologist, 30,* 583–594.

Perkins, K. (1992). Psychosocial implications of women and retirement. *Social Work, 37,* 526–532.

Perry, S., & O'Hanlan, K. (1992). *Natural menopause.* Reading, MA: Addison-Wesley.

Peterson, P., & Howe, N. (1988). *On borrowed time: How the growth of entitlements threatens American's future.* San Francisco: Institute for Contemporary Studies.

Pinderhughes, E. (1983). Empowerment for our clients and ourselves. *Social Casework, 31,* 214–219.

Pogrebin, L. C. (1996). *Getting over getting older: An intimate journey.* Boston: Little, Brown.

Price, K. (1988). Empowering preadolescent and adolescent leukemia patients. *Social Work, 33,* 275–276.

Quadagno, J. (1988). Women's access to pensions and the structure of eligibility rules and the systems of production and reproduction. *Sociological Quarterly, 29,* 541–558.

Quadagno, J. (1990). Generational equity and the politics of the welfare state. *International Journal of Health Services, 20,* 631–649.

Quadagno, J. (1996). Social security and the myth of the entitlement "crisis." *Gerontologist, 36,* 391–399.

Quadagno, J., & Meyer, M. H. (1990). Gender and public policy. *Generations, 14,* 64–66.

Quam, J. K., & Whitford, G. (1992). Adaptation and age-related expectations of older gay and lesbian adults. *The Gerontologist, 32,* 367–374.

Radner, D. B. (1993). *Studies in income distribution: An assessment of the economic status of the aged.* Washington, DC: U.S. Department of Health and Human Services.

Randall, M. (1986). From: The journals. In J. Alexander, D. Berrow, L. Domitorvich, M. Donnelly, & C. McLean (Eds.), *Women and aging: An anthology by women* (pp. 127–130). Corvallis, OR: Calyx Books.

Random House College Dictionary (rev. ed.). (1988). New York: Random House.

Ray, R. E. (1996). A postmodern perspective on feminist gerontology. *Gerontologist, 36,* 674–680.

Reagon, B. J. (1983). Coalition politics: Turning the century. In B. Smith (Ed.), *Home girls: A Black anthology* (pp. 356–368). New York: Kitchen Table Women of Color Press.

Reinhardt, J., & Fisher, C. (1989). Kinship versus friendship: Social adaptation in married widowed elderly women. In L. Grau (Ed.), *Women in the later years* (pp. 191–212). New York: Harrington.

Reinharz, S. (1986). Friends or foes: Gerontological and feminist theory. *Women's Studies International Forum, 9,* 503–514.

Reinharz, S. (1992). *Feminist methods in social research.* New York: Oxford Press.

Report of the Fourth World Conference on Women, Bejiing. (1995, September). Resolution 1, annexes I and II. Cited in *Bulletin on Ageing* (1995). United Nations, Nos. 2 & 3. New York: United Nations.

Ricci, I. (1985). Mediator's notebook: Reflections on promoting equal empowerment and entitlements for women. *Journal of Divorce, 8,* 3–4, 49–61.

Rich, A. (1976). *Of women born.* New York: W. W. Norton.

Rich, A. (1980a). Afterward in L. Lewderer (Ed.), *Take back the night: Women on pornography.* New York: William Morrow.

Rich, A. (1980b). Compulsory heterosexuality and the lesbian experience. *Signs, 5,* 631–660.

Riley, M. W. (1981). Health behaviors of older people: Toward a new paradigm. In D. L. Parron, F. Soloman, & J. Rodin (Eds.), *Health, behavior, and aging: Summary of a conference* (pp. 25–39). Washington, DC: National Academy Press.

Riley, M. W. (1985). Women, men and the lengthening lifecourse. In A. S. Rossi (Ed.), *Gender and the life course* (pp. 333–348). New York: Aldine.

Riley, M. W. (1996). Discussion: What does it all mean? *Gerontologist, 36,* 256–258.

Riley, M. W., & Riley, J. (1986). Longevity and social structure: The potential of the added years. In A. Pifer & L. Bronte (Eds.), *Our aging society: Paradox and promise.* New York: W. W. Norton.

Riley, M. W., & Riley, J. W. (1989). The lives of older people and changing social roles. *Annals of the American Academy of Political and Social Sciences: The quality of aging, 503,* 14–28.

Riley, M. W., & Waring, J. (1976). Age and aging. In R. K. Merton & R. A. Nisbet (Eds.), *Contemporary social problems.* New York: Harcourt, Brace, Jovanovich.

Rivlin, A. M., & Wiener, J. (1988). *Caring for the disabled elderly: Who will pay?* Washington, DC: The Brookings Institution.

Rix, S. (1984). *Older women: The economics of aging.* Washington, DC: Women's Research and Education Institute.

Rodeheaver, D. (1987). When old age became a social problem, women were left behind. *The Gerontologist, 27,* 741–746.

Roebuck, J. (1983). Grandma as revolutionary: Elderly women and some modern patterns of social change. *International Journal of Aging and Human Development, 17,* 249–266.

Rosenthal, E. (Ed.). (1990). *Women, aging, and ageism.* New York: Haworth.

Rountree, C. (1997). *Women turning 60.* New York: Harmony.

Russell, C. (1987). Ageing as a feminist issue. *Women's Studies International Forum, 10,* 125–132.

Sandell, S. H., & Iams, H. (1994). Caregiving and women's social security benefits: A comment on Kingson and O'Grady-LeShane. *The Gerontologist, 34,* 680–684.

Sands, R. G., & Nuccio, K. (1993). Postmodern feminist theory and social work. *Social Work, 37,* 489–494.

Sarton, M. (1984). *At seventy: A journal.* New York: Norton.

Sempos, C., Cooper, R., Kovar, M., & McMillen, M. (1988). Divergence of the recent trends in coronary mortality for the four major race-sex groups in the United States. *American Journal of Public Health, 78,* 1422–1426.

Settersten, R. A., & Hagestad, G. O. (1996). What's the latest? II. Cultural age deadlines for education and work transitions. *Gerontologist, 36,* 602–613.

Sharp, P. A. (1995). Older women and health services: Moving from ageism toward empowerment. *Women and Health, 22,* 9–23.

Sheafor, B., Horejsi, C., & Horejsi, G. (1988). *Techniques and guides for social work practice.* Boston: Allyn and Bacon.

Silverstone, B. (1996). Older people of tomorrow: A psychosocial profile. *The Gerontologist, 36,* 27–32.

Sixty-five plus in the United States. (1995). *Washington Social Legislation Bulletin, 34,* 38. Washington, DC: Social Legislation Information Service.

Skocpol, T. (1995). *Social policy in the United States: Future responsibilities in historical perspective.* Princeton, NJ: Princeton University Press.

Smith, B. (Ed.). (1983). *Home girls: A Black anthology.* New York: Kitchen Table Women of Color Press.

Soldo, B. J., & Manton, K. G. (1985). Health status and service needs of the oldest old: Current patterns and future trends. *Milbank Memorial Fund Quarterly, 63,* 286–319.

Solomon, B. (1976). *Black empowerment: Social work in oppressed communities.* New York: Columbia University Press.

Sommers, C. H. (1994). *Who stole feminism? How women have betrayed women.* New York: Touchstone.

Sommers, T. (1975, November–December). On growing old female: An interview with Tish Sommers. *Aging*, p. 11.

Sommers, T. (1993). Changing ourselves and society. In P. Doress-Worters & D. L. Siegal, *The new ourselves, growing older: Women aging with knowledge and power* (pp. 427–440). New York: Touchstone.

Sommers, T., & Shields, L. (1987). *Women take care: The consequences of caregiving in today's society*. Gainesville, FL: Triad.

Sontag, S. (1972). The double standard of aging. *Saturday Review, 55*, 29–38.

Spakes, P. (1989). A feminist case against the goals of family policy: A view to the future. *Policy Studies Review, 8*, 610–621.

Starr, B., & Weiner, M. (1981). *The Starr-Weiner report on sex and sexuality in the mature years*. New York: Stein & Day.

State of Hawaii, Executive Office on Aging. (1993). *Long-term care plan for the State of Hawaii*. Honolulu, HI: Author.

Stauffer, V. (1989). OWL co-founder Laurie Shields dies. *OWL Observer, 8*, 2, 1–6.

Steinem, G. (1992). *Revolution from within*. Boston: Little, Brown.

Steinem, G. (1994). *Moving beyond words*. New York: Simon and Schuster.

Stansell, C. (1992). White feminists and Black realities: The politics of authenticity. In T. Morrison (Ed.), *Racing justice, engendering power* (pp. 251–268). New York: Pantheon.

Stoller, E. P. (1993). Gender and the organization of lay health care: A socialist feminist perspective. *Journal of Aging Studies, 7*, 151–170.

Stoller, E. P., & Gibson, R. C. (Eds.). (1994). *Worlds of difference: Inequality in the aging experience*. Thousand Oaks, CA: Pine Forge Press.

Stone, R., Cafferata, G., & Sangl, S. (1986). *Caregivers of the frail: A national profile*. Washington, DC: Department of Labor.

Swigonski, M. E. (1993). Feminist standpoint theory and the question of social work research. *Affilia, 8*, 171–183.

Swigonski, M. E. (1994). The logic of feminist standpoint theory for social work research. *Social Work, 39*, 387–395.

Taeuber, C. (1993). *Sixty-five plus in America*. (U.S. Department of Commerce, Bureau of the Census, Current Population Reports, Special Studies, P23-178RV.) Washington, DC: U.S. Government Printing Office.

Taeuber, C., & Allen, J. (1993). Women in our aging society: The demographic outlook. In J. Allen & A. Pifer (Eds.), *Women on the front lines: Meeting the challenges of aging America* (pp. 11–45). Washington, DC: Urban Press.

Takamura, J., & Seely, M. (1994). Beyond mirrors and smoke: The challenge of longevity and long care. In B. Grossman & J. Shon (Eds.), *The unfinished health agenda: Lessons from Hawaii* (pp. 17–32). Honolulu, HI: Hawaii State Primary Care Association.

Tennstedt, S. L., Crawford, S. L., & McKinlay, J. B. (1993). Is family care on the decline? A longitudinal investigation of the substitution of formal long term care services for informal care. *Milbank Quarterly, 71,* 601–624.

Tennstedt, S. L., & Gonyea, J. (1994). An agenda for eldercare research. *Research on Aging, 16,* 85–108.

Thone, R. R. (1992). *Women and aging: Celebrating ourselves.* New York: Haworth.

Thurow, L. C. (1996, May 19). The birth of a revolutionary class. *New York Times Magazine,* pp. 46–47.

Torres-Gil, F. (1990, April/May). Diversity in aging: The challenge of pluralism. *Aging Connection,* p. 1.

Torres-Gil, F. (1992). *The new aging: Politics and change in America.* New York: Auburn.

Towns, K., & Gentzler, R. (1985). Empowering re-entry women: An organizational case study: The Study of PROBE. *Women and Therapy, 5,* 159–166.

Trask, H. K. (1993). *From a native daughter: Colonialism and sovereignty in Hawaii.* Monroe, ME: Common Courage Press.

Trask, H. K. (1996). Feminism and indigenous Hawaiian nationalism. *Signs, 21,* 906–916.

Treichler, P. A. (1986). Teaching feminist theory. In C. Nelson (Ed.), *Theory in the classroom* (pp. 57–128). Urbana-Champaign, IL: University of Illinois Press.

Trzcinski, R. (1994). Family and medical leave, contingent employment, and flexibility: A feminist critique of the U.S. approach to work and family policy. *The Journal of Applied Social Sciences, 18,* 71–88.

Turner, B. (1984). Health is the main thing: Sex differences, health, and psychological variables in later life. In B. Hess & E. Markson (Eds.), *Growing old in America* (pp. 171–180). New Brunswick, NJ: Transaction.

Turner, B. (1994). Introduction. In B. Turner & L. Troll (Eds.), *Women growing older: Psychological perspectives* (pp. 1–34). Thousand Oaks, CA: Sage.

Turner, B. F., & Troll, L. E. (1994). *Women growing older: Psychological perspectives.* Thousand Oaks, CA: Sage.

Uhlenberg, P. (1996). Mutual attraction: Demography and life-course analysis. *Gerontologist, 36,* 226–229.

United States Bureau of the Census. (1990a). *Money income and poverty status in the United States: 1989 Current Population Survey.* Washington, DC: U.S. Department of Commerce.

United States Bureau of the Census. (1990b). *Statistical abstract of the United States (110th ed.).* Washington, DC: U.S. Government Printing Office.

United States Bureau of the Census. (1991). *Poverty in the United States: 1990.* Current Population Reports, series P.60, no. 175, Washington, DC: U.S. Government Printing Office.

United States Bureau of the Census. (1992). *Statistical Abstract of the United States, 1992* (112th ed.). Washington, DC: U.S. Government Printing Office.

United States Bureau of the Census. (1993a). *Poverty in the United States, 1992. Current population reports* (Series P60-185). Washington, DC: U.S. Government Printing Office.

United States Bureau of the Census. (1993b). *We the American Asians*. Washington, DC: U.S. Government Printing Office.

United States Bureau of the Census. (1993c). *We, the American elderly*. Washington, DC: U.S. Government Printing Office.

United States Bureau of the Census. (1993d). *We the American Pacific Islanders*. Washington, DC: U.S. Government Printing Office.

United States Bureau of the Census. (1996). *Special Population Reports, Special Studies P-23-190*. Washington, DC: Government Printing Office.

United States Congressional Budget Office. (1988). *Changes in living arrangements of the elderly: 1960–2030*. Washington, DC: Government Printing Office.

United States Department of Health and Human Services Newsletter *News*. (1995, June). Washington, DC: U.S. Government Printing Office.

United States Department of Health and Human Services. (1991). *Vital statistics of the United States, 1988* (Vol. 2) (DHHS Pub. No. (PHS). 91-1104). Washington, DC: U.S. Government Printing Office.

United States Department of Labor. (1990). [Unpublished tabulations from the current population survey, 1989: *Annual Averaging*]. Washington, DC: Author.

United States Department of Labor. (1991a, June 24). BLS reports on its first survey of employee benefits in small private establishments. *News*, p. 1.

United States Department of Labor. (1991b, January). *Employment and earnings, 38, 1*. Washington, DC: U.S. Government Printing Office.

United States Department of Labor, Women's Bureau. (1993). *Midlife women speak out: Assessing job training and the status of working women: A statistical profile of midlife women aged 35–54*. Washington, DC: Author.

United States Department of Labor. (1994a, May). Report of employee benefits in medium and large firms, 1993 (Bulletin 2422). Washington, DC: U. S. Government Printing Office.

United States Department of Labor. (1994b). *Violence in the workforce comes under closer scrutiny: Issues in labor statistics*. Washington, DC: Author.

United States House Select Committee on Aging. (1980). *The status of mid-life women and options for their future*. (No. 96-215). Washington, DC: U.S. Government Printing Office.

United States House Select Committee on Aging. (1988). *Exploding the myths: Caregiving in America* (No. 99-611). Washington, DC: U.S. Government Printing Office.

United States House Select Committee on Aging. (1989). *The quality of life for older women: Older women living alone* (No. 100-693). Washington, DC: U.S. Government Printing Office.

United States House Select Committee on Aging. (1990a). Women and retirement: Are they losing out? (No. 101-763). Washington, DC: U.S. Government Printing Office.

United States House Select Committee on Aging. (1990b). *Women, caregiving, and poverty: Options to improve Social Security.* (No. 101-779). Washington, DC: U.S. Government Printing Office.

United States House Select Committee on Aging. (1990c). *Women health care consumers: Short-changed on medical research and treatment* (No. 102-794). Washington, DC: U.S. Government Printing Office.

United States House Select Committee on Aging. (1991). *Women at mid-life: Consumers of second-rate health care?* (No. 102-814). Washington, DC: U.S. Government Printing Office.

United States House Select Committee on Aging. (1992a, March 26). Subcommittee on retirement income and employment. *How will today's women fare in yesterday's traditional retirement system* (102-873). Washington, DC: U.S. Government Printing Office.

United States House Select Committee on Aging. (1992b). *How well do women fare under the nation's retirement policies?* (No. 102-879). Washington, DC: U.S. Government Printing Office.

United States House Select Committee on Aging. (1992c). *Congressional Symposium on Women and Retirement* (No. 102–897). Washington, DC: U.S. Government Printing Office.

United States House Committee on Ways and Means, Subcommittee on Social Security. (1985). *Report on earnings sharings implementation study.* Washington, DC: U.S. Government Printing Office.

United States Office of Social Security Administration. (1993). *Facts about Social Security.* Washington, DC: Author.

United States Senate Special Committee on Aging. (1988). *Aging America: Trends and projections, 1987–1988 edition.* [Department of Health and Human Services]. Washington, DC: U.S. Government Printing Office.

United States Special Committee on Aging. (1992). *Aging America: Trends and projections* (1991 ed.) [Department of Health and Human Services]. Washington, DC: U.S. Government Printing Office.

Van Den Bergh, N. (1995). *Feminist practice in the 21st century.* Washington, DC: NASW Press.

Van Den Bergh, N., & Cooper, L. (1986). *Feminist visions for social work.* Silver Spring, MD: NASW Press.

Vasil, L., & Wass, H. (1993). Portrayal of the elderly in the media: A literature review and implications for educational gerontologists. *Educational Gerontology, 19,* 71–85.

Vasudeva, A. (1993). To my grandmother. In Women of South Asian Descent Collective (Eds.), *Our feet walk the sky* (pp. 64–65). San Francisco: Aunt Lute Books.

Verbrugge, L. (1984). A health profile of older women with comparisons to older men. *Research on Aging, 6,* 291–322.

Verbrugge, L. (1989). Gender, aging, and health. In K. Markides (Ed.), *Aging and health* (pp. 23–78). Newbury Park, CA: Sage.

Waldron, I. (1976). Why do women live longer than men? *Social Science and Medicine, 10,* 340–362.

Walker, B. G. (1985). *The crone: Woman of age, wisdom, and power.* San Francisco: Harper.

Wallis, V. (1993). *Two old women.* Fairbanks, AK: Epicenter Press.

Waxman, B. F. (1990). *From the hearth to the open road: A feminist study of aging in contemporary literature.* Westport, CT: Greenwood Press.

Weaver, F. (1996). *The girls with the grandmother faces: A celebration of life's potential for those over 55.* New York: Hyperion.

Webb, C. (Ed.). (1986). *Feminist practice in women's health care.* Chichester, UK: John Wiley and Sons.

Weick, A. (1994). Overturning oppression: An analysis of emancipatory change. In L. V. Davis (Ed.), *Building on women's strengths: A social work agenda for the twenty-first century* (pp. 211– 228). Binghamton, NY: Haworth.

West, C. (1991). The dilemma of the Black intellectual. In b. hooks & C. West (Eds.), *Breaking bread* (pp. 136–146). Boston: South End Press.

West, C. (1992). Black leadership and the pitfalls of racial reasoning. In T. Morrison (Ed.), *Racing justice, engendering power* (pp. 390–401). New York: Pantheon.

West, G., & Blumberg, R. L. (1990a). Reconstructing social protest from a feminist perspective. In G. West & R. L. Blumberg (Eds.), *Women and social protest* (pp. 3–35). New York: Oxford University Press.

West, G., & Blumberg, R. L. (1990b). Women and grassroots protest for economic survival. In G. West & R. L. Blumberg (Eds.), *Women and social protest* (pp. 37–40). New York: Oxford University Press.

Wetzel, J. W. (1976). Interaction of feminism and social work in America. *Social Casework, 57,* 227–236.

Wetzel, J. W. (1986). A feminist world view conceptual framework. *Social Casework: The Journal of Contemporary Social Work, 4,* 166–175.

Williams, P. (1988). On being the objects of property. *Signs, 14,* 5–24.

Williams, W. (1993). Equality's riddle: Pregnancy and the equal treatment/special treatment debate. In D. K. Weisberg (Ed.), *Feminist legal theory: Foundations* (pp. 128–155). Philadelphia: Temple University Press.

Wingard, D. (1982). The sex differential in mortality rates: Demographic and behavioral factors. *American Journal of Epidemiology, 115,* 205–216.

Wolf, N. (1991). *The beauty myth.* New York: William Morris.

Wolf, N. (1994). *Fight fire with fire.* New York: Random House/Ballantine.

Women of South Asian Descent Collective. (Eds.). (1993). *Our feet walk the sky: Women of the South Asian diaspora.* San Francisco: Aunt Lute Books.

Woo, M. (1983). Letter to Ma. In C. Moraga & G. Anzaldua (Eds.), *This bridge called my back: Writings by radical women of color* (2nd ed., pp. 140–147). New York: Kitchen Table, Women of Color Press.

Woodward, K. (1991). *Aging and its discontents: Freud and other fictions.* Bloomington, IN: Indiana University Press.

Young, I. (1981). Beyond the unhappy marriage: A critique of the dual systems theory. In L. Sargent (Ed.), *Women and revolution: A discussion of the unhappy marriage of Marxism and feminism* (pp. 43–69). Boston: South End Press.

Zarit, S., Reever, K., & Bach-Peterson, J. (1980). Relatives of the impaired elderly: Correlates of feelings of burden. *Gerontologist, 20,* 649–655.

Zedlewski, S. R., & Meyer, J. A. (1987). *Toward ending poverty among the elderly and disabled: Policy and financing options.* Washington, DC: The Urban Institute.

Zinn, M. B. (1990). Family, feminism and race in America. *Gender and Society, 4,* 68–82.

Zones, J., Estes, C., & Binney, E. (1987). Gender, public policy, and the oldest old. *Ageing and Society, 7,* 275–302.

Index